TRANSLATOR'S NOTE

THIS translation has been made from Herr Heiden's two books, *Geschichte des Nationalsozialismus* (1932) and *Geburt des dritten Reiches* (1934). In making it, the Translator has been careful to avoid altering the sense of Herr Heiden's text. All that has been done is to omit portions, chiefly relating to the earlier history of the Nazi Movement, for the purpose of keeping the English translation within a reasonable compass. A "Final Chapter" has been added, to include events subsequent to the original publication of this work.

A HISTORY OF

NATIONAL SOCIALISM

A History of
NATIONAL SOCIALISM

by

KONRAD HEIDEN

TRANSLATED FROM THE GERMAN

METHUEN & CO LTD
11 NEW FETTER LANE LONDON E.C.4.

First published in 1934

This edition published 1971

Printed in the USA

ISBN 416 60760 8

CONTENTS

PRINCIPAL EVENTS

1889

April 20 — Adolf Hitler born at Braunau.

1912

Hitler takes up residence in Munich.

1914–18

European War. Hitler twice wounded and severely gassed. He wins Iron Cross, First Class.

1918

March 7 — Drexler founds his " Committee of Independent Workmen."

November 9 — Outbreak of Revolution in Germany. Hitler in hospital at Pasewalk.

1919

January 5 — Drexler founds German Workers Party.

June — Hitler hears Feder lecture and subsequently becomes an " education officer."

July — Hitler joins German Workers Party as its seventh member.

October — Hitler makes his first speech.

1920

April 1 — Hitler resigns from Reichswehr.

August 7–8 — Congress of German National Socialist Parties at Salzburg.

December 19 — Purchase of *Volkische Beobachter*.

1921

February 3 — Hitler's first mass meeting.

July — Hitler in Berlin.

1921 (*continued*)

July 29	Hitler elected president of the Party.
August 3	SA founded.

1922

October	Triumph of Fascism in Italy.

1923

January 11	Occupation of the Ruhr by French troops.
June–November	Fall of the Mark.
	Göring becomes SA leader.
November	Nazi Party membership numbers 15,000.
November 9	Hitler's Putsch defeated at Munich.

1924

Hitler's trial and imprisonment in Landsberg.

1925

February 27	Hitler reorganizes the Nazi Party.

1926

January	Organization of SS.

1926–27

Nazi Party membership increases from 17,000 to 40,000.

1928

Nazi Party sends 12 deputies to Reichstag.

1929

Hitler makes a pact with Dr. Hugenberg to organize protest against the Young Plan.

1930

January	Frick becomes Thuringian Minister of the Interior.
March	Party membership reaches 210,000.
May 21–22	Hitler's debate with Otto Strasser.
May	Brüning becomes Chancellor.
September 14	Reichstag Election. Nazis gain 107 seats and receive 6,400,000 votes.
October	Metal workers' strike in Berlin.

1931

January	Röhm becomes Chief of Staff of SA.
April	Osaf Stennes' revolt.

August 9	Stahlhelm plebiscite in Prussia.
October 11	Harzburg meeting.

1932

January	Hitler visits Brüning.
March 13	Presidential Election. Hitler receives 11,300,000 votes.
April 6	Severing's revelations.
April 10	Presidential Election: Second Poll: Hitler receives 13,-400,000 votes.
April 14	Suppression of SA and SS.
May 30	Brüning resigns.
	Franz von Papen becomes Chancellor.
July 30	Expulsion of Prussian Ministers.
July 31	Reichstag Election. Nazis win 230 seats.
August 9	Government decree against terrorization.
August 13	Hitler sees Papen and Hindenburg.
September 12	Dissolution of the Reichstag.
November 6	Reichstag Election. Nazis win 197 seats and receive 11,-730,000 votes.
November 17	Papen resigns.
	Hitler offered the Chancellorship. He refuses it. Schleicher becomes Chancellor.
December 8	Gregor Strasser's resignation.
December 11	Disarmament Conference recognizes German claim to equality.

1933

January	Hitler meets Papen.
January 28	Hindenburg refuses to dissolve Reichstag.
January 30	Formation of a Government of National Concentration under Hitler.
	Nazi Triumphal March-Past Hitler and Hindenburg.
February 4	Decree "For the Defence of the German Nation."
February 17	Göring order to shoot.
February 22	Hitler appeals to the Party to maintain discipline.
	Göring organizes special constables.
February 24	Police raid Karl Liebknecht House.
February 25	Fire in Palace in Berlin.
February 27	Burning of the Reichstag.
February 28	Decree "In defence of the Nation and State."
	Communist Party declared illegal.
March 5	Reichstag Election. Nazis gain 17,200,000 votes.

1933 (*continued*)

	Prussian Diet Election. Nazis win 211 seats.
March 9	Nazi Governor appointed for Bavaria.
March 14	Goebbels becomes Minister for National Enlightenment and Propaganda.
March 16	Resignation of Bavarian Government.
	Schacht becomes President of the Reichsbank.
March 21	Opening of the Reichstag.
March 23	Act of Authorization.
March 31	Law for Co-ordination in the States.
April 1	Boycott of Jews.
April 7	Law to ordinate the States with the Reich. Civil Service Law.
April 11	Göring becomes Prussian Prime Minister.
May 2	Trades Unions suppressed.
May 3	Decree for compulsory labour service.
May 17	Hitler's speech to Reichstag.
June 22	Social Democrat Party suppressed.
June 27	Hugenberg resigns.
June 28	Dissolution of German Nationalist Front.
July 5	Dissolution of Centre Party.
July 8	Göring establishes State Council for Prussia.
	Concordat signed between the Reich Government and the Vatican.
July 14	Law against formation of new Parties.
July 15	Signature of the Pact of Rome.
September 21	Trial of the Reichstag fire case begins.
October 21	Germany leaves the League of Nations.
November 12	Plebiscite, and election of new Reichstag. Nazi list approved by 39,650,000 voters.
December 23	Trial of the Reichstag fire case ends. Van der Lubbe found guilty of high treason. Torgler, Dmitroff, Popoff, and Taneff acquitted.

1934

January 10	Van der Lubbe executed.
January 26	Pact of friendship and non-aggression with Poland.
January 30	State frontiers abolished within Germany.
May 1	Law to regulate National Labour promulgated.
June	Negotiations between Nazi Government and the Curia.
June 14	Germany refuses to pay Government guaranteed loans.
June 17	Papen's speech at Marburg.

June 30	"Purging" of the SA. Murder of Röhm, Heines, Ernst, Schleicher, Klausener, Strasser, etc.
July 13	Hitler's speech to the Reichstag.
July 25	Assassination of Dollfuss.
August 1	Death of Hindenburg. Hitler assumes the Presidency.
August 2	Schacht made Reich Minister of Economics.
August 19	Plebiscite. Hitler endorsed by 38,360,000 voters.

INTRODUCTION

NATIONAL SOCIALISM as an intellectual movement emanated in the years 1926–28 from the brains of a few — chiefly north — German thinkers. As a political force it sprang from the mass-membership of the great Fatherland Party and the Pan-German Association. In a word — it was born of the annexationist militarism of 1917. In 1919 it became an independent political movement. Out of its raw material the Reichswehr in Munich forged a political weapon. This weapon was given shape in 1921 by Captain Ernst Röhm, and by a man of outstanding intellect but unstable character — Adolf Hitler. The movement derived its title from Hitler's native Austria. It was adopted against the wishes of the present leaders and does not represent their political ideas. Those members of the National Socialist Workers Party who subsequently sought to give a literal interpretation to its title found themselves compelled by force of logic to leave its ranks.

The swift growth of the Party prevented the maintenance of a harmonious balance between its principles and its actions. A Party whose guiding principle has been pure expediency could not have any definite and rigid programme. Its lack of a programme — the well-known Twenty-Five Points are not a definite programme — is in truth more than a successful trick played upon a generation too lazy to think for itself. It is a recognition of the fact that a movement depends for its success upon causes rather than aims, and that mankind values leadership above moral codes. In their interpretation of history as in other matters the Nazis have shown themselves apt pupils of Karl Marx. The Communists indeed sought to take politics out of the sphere of emotions and elevate them to the dignity of an abstract science. In refusing to do this the Nazis have shown themselves possessed of greater knowledge of the world. Indeed, they have remained faithful to their conception of an ordering of society in which the masses have only to concern themselves with the cares of daily life, whilst the task of government is left to an élite of inspired leaders. Individual opinion is certainly given free play within National Socialism. Organization — the tactics peculiar to National Socialism — is regarded as a secret craft known only to the leaders. Every kind of political theory, from the most reactionary monarchism to pure anarchy, from unrestricted individualism to the most impersonal and rigid Socialism, finds representation within the Nazi Party. The Party has a welcome for each and every form of political theory. Each Nazi is left under the illusion that the Party's only aim is to realize his own pet theory. Hitler makes a single categorical demand of his followers in return for this liberty — unconditional submission to his personal leadership. It has thus become possible for every German — time-server and idealist alike — to see in the Nazi Party *the* Party specially created for his purpose, and in Hitler *the* leader specially summoned to realize his own particular theory. The Nazi Party resembles a vast army of individualists on the march, each of whom believes that the army is moving towards his own objective. What will happen when one day the march comes to an end and the marchers realize that not a single one of them has attained his aim?

A HISTORY OF

NATIONAL SOCIALISM

CHAPTER I

THE ORIGINS OF NATIONAL SOCIALISM

ON March 7, 1918, Anton Drexler set up a " Committee of Independent Workmen " in Munich for the purpose of advocating the conclusion of peace on terms that would be compatible with Germany's honour and glory. Out of this small group of forty men gathered round a table in a Munich *Bierhaus* sprang the great National Socialist German Workers Party.

A FORGOTTEN FOUNDER

Anton Drexler was a locksmith by trade. He was a quiet manual labourer rather than a gifted man precluded from achieving fame by a lack of education. Thought and speech alike were difficult for him. Ideas that are hardly won are apt to seize fast hold upon the mind. This narrow-chested and bespectacled man, unfit for military service, believed with fanatical seriousness in the fruits of his reading. He mistook them for fruits of the Tree of Knowledge. His faith in his own knowledge was mercifully accompanied by a complete blindness to the hardness of his self-appointed task. Adolf Hitler inherited from Drexler both his naïve self-confidence and his burning faith. If he made more of his inheritance than its donor would have believed possible, Hitler at least owes more to his humble comrade of former days than he is now prepared to admit. Drexler was subsequently to part company with Hitler, whose rapid success he held to be a misfortune for the Party. It still remains to be seen whether Drexler was not right.

It is remarkable how similar in many respects were the careers of Drexler and Hitler. As a youthful workman, Drexler, like Hitler, found himself in conflict with the independent trade unions. Afterwards he complained that their terroristic methods drove him out of employment and forced him to earn his living by playing a zither in cafés. His hatred of Marxism took root and grew. Nevertheless his chief interest — as also Hitler's — was in foreign policy. This " enlightened workman " spared no pains to assess for himself Germany's responsibility for the World War. As a member of a travelling company of singers, Drexler had sung a chorus in Zürich in 1914 that ran:

> " With lances at rest,
> With reins held loose,
> To the fight, to the fight!
> Let us hasten."

And it was no mere quixotry but a fine sensitiveness to popular feeling that caused Drexler to reproach himself for having sung that chorus with his comrades. He perceived that the fate of Germany depended less upon lances than upon the national character. " The German Socialist spirit will put the world to rights." The salvation of Germany from international capitalism — " the parasite upon the German body " — was to be found in Socialism. In reality there was little difference between the theory of a German Socialism that should confer benefits upon the world and the practice of an International in which German Social Democracy formed the most powerful party. Drexler quotes Scheidemann's words with approval: The War is not being fought to benefit solely the great industrialists and large farmers, but also for the sake of the workers in factories and workshops, mines, and fields. Majority Socialism — Left Wing Socialists called its adherents the " Kaiser's Socialists " — would have been acceptable to many present-day Nazis.

The Peace Resolution passed by the Reichstag in 1917 cost the Pan-Germans many a night's sleep. Drexler joined the Munich branch of the Fatherland Party and was speedily disillusioned by the blindness to the spirit of the people displayed by the lawyers, scholars, artists, &c., who were his fellow-members. Although Drexler advocated in his speeches the prosecution of the War and denounced the munition workers' strike, he failed to understand why the Government acquiesced in the rise in food-prices and treated the smaller producers so harshly. In this can be seen the beginnings of that dislike entertained by city-dwellers for the farming class that to-day inspires, and for years to come will continue to inspire, the Nazi Party notwithstanding its present agrarian sympathies.

Early in 1918 an Association for the Promotion of Peace along Working-class Lines was founded in Bremen that reputedly counted some hundreds of thousands of members. Drexler established a branch of this association in Munich with a membership of forty. This branch was founded on March 7, 1918, and was the above-mentioned " Committee of Independent Workmen." Almost unconsciously Drexler thus arrived at the conception of a militarist Labour Party: a disciplined Party whose aim should not only be national victory in the War, but also unquestioning obedience to the national leaders. Drexler declared in 1918 that the task of peace-making might safely be left to the Supreme Command who were deserving of the entire confidence of the nation. In Drexler's mouth this pronouncement probably did not amount to more than the modesty of an uneducated man who is forced at a public meeting to ask to have the words ' Anti-Semitism ' explained to him. The romantic notion of a nation of producers was born of the endeavour to identify labour interests with national interests. The creative German nation was the victim of the bellicose Western Powers. " Citizens and workmen! Unite! " Drexler cried to a meeting that he had summoned with the aid of the Fatherland Party. All classes were to unite in a " National Union of Citizens." His listeners replied with uproar and abuse to his summons. The moment was certainly not propitious for uttering the warning that Germany — a nation of producers — was about to be brought under the sway of Mammon.

Drexler found it impossible to divest himself of his class-feelings. He rejoined the Independent Union of Railwaymen in 1918, and soon revealed himself to be inspired by singular ideas. In publicly denouncing " the systematic strangulation of the manual worker by the railways," the proud craftsman was declaring war upon the class-conscious proletariat. This singular proletarian saw in the wages policy of the trade unions "the destruction by the working class of the middle class, the independent worker, and the national culture." The writer of these words dreamt of raising the working man to be a lower or even upper middle-class citizen, and wished to substitute a crowd of hard-working and self-made men for a united working class.

Who gave its first lessons in politics to this slow-moving intellect? A most unlikely teacher — Walter Rathenau. Here was an enemy from whom the Nazis had much to learn. His polished sentences became a deadly weapon in the hand of the Nazi railway mechanic. "The World Revolution began with the outbreak of the World War. Its unconscious but real and practical object was the substitution of a capitalist middle class for the feudal nobility as rulers in a plutocratic State governed on constitutional lines." Thus Rathenau in a mood of mingled cynicism and sadness. On Drexler's lips these words became lambent with hatred. Rathenau spoke once of the three hundred men in whose hands lay the economic and financial destinies of the world. This aphorism appeared for a decade as a Nazi battlecry on placards and newspaper headlines. The most skilful propagandist could not have thought of anything more effective. The same fate overtook Disraeli's saying that racial problems are the key to world history. It is true that Drexler was not prepared offhand to declare that Trotsky was in capitalist pay. Many years later Goebbels and Rosenberg were to quarrel seriously over this very question. For Drexler it was impossible for *Vorwärts* and the *Frankfurter Zeitung* to hold the same opinion in any question if *Vorwärts* truly represented Socialist opinions. Prejudice? The day was not far off in which it was to become more important to be a good hater than a sane thinker.

Drexler was not prevented by his narrow-mindedness from retaining his intellectual independence. Although he accused Marxism of having turned the revolution into a wages issue, and of having thereby rendered it impossible for Germany to compete in the world market, Drexler demanded that employers should display more sympathy with their employees' demands. In other words — the old trade unionist policy of avoiding economic warfare. But Drexler lent his approval to belligerent trade unionism, and only denounced its "abuse" by political parties. The future of Germany depended upon whether the intellectual and economic leaders possessed sufficient social feeling to regain the trust of the masses that had been led astray. That is the raw material of the Nazi doctrine expressed in its simplest form. Moreover, Drexler himself was both as a man and a politician the raw material from which Hitler modelled his Party in outline. Under Drexler's leadership the "German Workers Party" would have remained a debating society. Without Drexler neither the debating society nor even the Party itself would have been founded. Hitler would then have been forced to seek elsewhere for his inspiration. For Hitler is a genius in adopting and developing the ideas of others.

The fate of all discoverers overtook Drexler. As soon as he gained control over the Party funds in 1921, Hitler swept him aside. Drexler remained as honorary president of the now more imposing Party until some of his more embittered comrades in the railway shops beat the reactionary with iron rails in the spring of 1923 and drove him from his employment. At the time of the November Putsch in 1923, Drexler was ignored by Hitler and parted company with him. He continued to be a member of the Bavarian Parliament until 1928, when he disappeared from politics.

A DEBATING SOCIETY AND ITS BENEFACTORS

The Revolution in Germany deprived the Association for Promoting Peace on Working-class Lines of its task. On January 5, 1919, Drexler reconstituted this organization under the title of the German Workers Party. A journalist named Karl Harrer was its first chairman. This "Party" of forty members nevertheless felt itself large enough to set up in its midst an inner circle of six members composed of politically-minded working men.

The events of May 1, 1919, gave a certain — if very small — political significance to the new Party. The Munich Soviet Republic collapsed; a Social Democrat and middle-class Coalition Government took its place; power in reality rested in the hands of the military authorities. These officers were filled with pride in the unbroken resistance offered by the German army to its enemies through four years of warfare. They were also inspired by hatred for the "betrayal" of that army, and by a blind anger against Fate for having given its decision in the enemies' favour. The middle-class political parties were too tired and too dispirited for any such emotions. The vast Fatherland Party had resignedly acquiesced in the Armistice and disappeared from the political scene. The other great political parties saw in the Armistice an end to the War. At this moment the tiny group whose primary object had been the achievement of a " good " peace raised their heads. The soldiers and the " German Workers Party " were alone in refusing to recognize that the War had come to an end. This common feeling brought them together, and out of their union sprang the Nazi movement.

In those days Germany was dotted over with the camps of innumerable volunteer corps. There were Ehrhardt's Brigade, the Baltic Landwehr, von Heydebreck's Huntsmen's Corps and the Pfeffer, Rossbach, Loewenfeld, Lützow, Lichtschlag, Chiemgau, Oberland, and Epp Corps. The largest of these armed companies — the Bavarian *Einwohnerwehr* — was not established until later, and out of it arose the organization known as Escherich (Orgesch), which was spread over the entire extent of Germany. It was these armed companies that in the following years supplied the first members of the Nazi Party.

In 1919 the " German Workers Party " gained a new member from among Epp's followers — Captain Ernst Röhm. His membership of the Party was destined to be of decisive importance for its future. A brave soldier, but no more than a soldier, battle-scarred and patched-up, the living personification of war itself, Röhm was inspired after the Revolution with but a single sentiment: " I declare expressly that I am no longer a member of this nation. I can only remember that at one time I served in the German Army." Although Röhm put the words into the mouth of one of his comrades, they express his own feelings with great exactitude. This rough son of a Bavarian official was inspired with feelings of hatred for a great number of the German officers. His stories of their conduct during the War would justify a dozen mutinies. He himself is a brilliant leader of men. His talent for organization revealed itself in the years 1920–23 in the creation of an illegal military organization in Bavaria. He is a passionate politician who as passionately fails to understand politics. " I look upon the world from the soldier's standpoint. I know I am one-sided." Röhm was about the sixtieth member of the German Workers Party. He gradually brought into its ranks many of his friends — officers and privates alike — in the Reichswehr. In those days this was a perfectly natural proceeding. The backbone of the Nazi movement was composed up till 1923 of members of the Reichswehr and the police.

The German Workers Party already possessed two influential supporters in the writer, Dietrich Eckart, and the civil engineer, Gottfried Feder. Eckart was a Suabian who appreciated good living and had written a couple of plays on historical subjects whilst serving on the staff of Scherl's *Lokalanzeiger*. He had also translated *Peer Gynt* into German. It was this that drew his attention to Nordic folklore. The Revolution awoke his political instincts. His satiric talent found ample scope in castigating in his paper, *Auf gut Deutsch,* the weaknesses of the Revolution and more especially of the Bavarian Communist Republic. At first Eckart was no more than a well-wisher of the German Workers Party. His real interests were in the " Union of German Citizens " which he tried to establish in May 1919, with a proclamation that ran: " Is the factory-hand not a citizen? Is every propertied person a good-for-nothing, a capitalist? Down with envy! Down with pomp and false appearances! Our aim is to regain simplicity and to be once more German. Our demand is true Socialism. Power should only be given to him who has German blood alone in his veins! " This is the oratory of a Bohemian who would like to be a householder earning a comfortable living with his pen and looked up to by his doorkeeper as an honest employer. Some time had still to pass before Eckart discovered that his " Union of Citizens " already existed in the German Workers Party.

Feder indoctrinated the German Workers Party with scientific notions. He was a constructional engineer who had worked abroad and also as an independent contractor. At the age of thirty-five in 1918 Feder suddenly thought of a plan for the abolition of interest. He spent a whole night in drafting a memorandum which he subsequently handed to the Bavarian Government only to receive the customary polite acknowledgement. He thus became a disappointed doctrinaire fighting for the public recognition of his favourite theories. Gottfried Feder gave the Nazi Party an ideology. Its essential points were paramount State ownership of land and the prohibition of private sales of land, the substitution of German for Roman law, nationalization of the banks and the abolition of interest by an amortization service. It was he, too, who inspired the Party with its doctrine of the distinction between productive and non-productive capital and of the necessity for destroying the " slavery of profits." On the subject of the Jews, Feder displayed comparative tolerance. He proposed to exclude them from all legal and educational posts and to declare them unfitted to be leaders of the German nation. Nevertheless they were to be permitted to send representatives to the Reichstag in proportion to their numbers. As for all other projects for the future, " these need not be mentioned here since they are to be found in the demands put forward by other Left Parties." Thus Feder in the *Völkischer Beobachter* (then the *Münchener Beobachter*) of May 31, 1919. (In those days the Nazi Party was still a Party of the Left.) Moreover, Feder gave Hitler many of his ideas. History knows such Archimedean natures who can only accomplish great achievements after another has given them an idea or what passes for an idea.

It was nevertheless Captain Röhm who exercised the greatest influence over the destiny of the new German Workers Party. He built up within it a political organization to give support to the counter-revolutionary policy of the Reichswehr and Free Corps. The German Workers Party became, as it were, the carriage bearing the big gun that was to be fired off by the officer-politicians in Munich. Röhm was also indefatigable in organizing the numerous defence corps, volunteer corps, and other associations seeking a centre in Munich for their fight against the " Marxist " Republic and its Government in Berlin. It was nevertheless the Reichswehr which sent Corporal Adolf Hitler as a political liaison officer into the German Workers Party.

SOLDIERS IN SEARCH OF A PARTY

Hitler had spent the winter months of 1918–19 with a reserve battalion of his regiment at Traunstein, in Upper Bavaria. At the time when the Soviet Republic was set up, he was again serving with his regiment in Munich. People who knew him at this time have stated that he professed himself a Majority Socialist, and that he even declared his intention of joining that Party. If this is true, then it was certainly as a matter of tactics and not of principle. The Majority Socialist Party was at that time regarded by many as a Party of the Right because it had lost its pre-War programme and not yet found a new one. After the capture of Munich by the Reichswehr and the Volunteer Corps, Hitler was attached to the Second Infantry Regiment for duty that would certainly not have been to every one's taste. He joined the staff of the commission that had been established to investigate the events of the Bolshevist revolution in Munich and drew up indictments against persons suspected of complicity in the revolution.

In attending a course of lectures on politics delivered to soldiers of the Reichswehr, Hitler took a step of decisive importance for his future career. In June 1919 he was filled with enthusiasm by hearing Gottfried Feder lecture for the first time. The soldiers of the Counter-Revolution were desirous of being more than soldiers. They wanted to found a Party and become politicians. Hitler became their spokesman by championing Feder's theories. His distinction between productive and unproductive capital was, moreover, heartily supported by Hitler's commanding officer, Major Giehrl.

An anti-Semitic debate at which Hitler spoke caused his commander to regard him as suitable to be an " education officer " in a Munich regiment. It was an education officer's duty to give political lectures; the troops were to be taught to " think and feel nationally and patriotically " again. Hitler took the opportunity of practising oratory, and especially of training his voice, which had suffered from his being gassed. Among his audience were many who later became members of the Nazi Party.

Moreover, his new friend Feder was favourably inclined to the " German Workers Party " of Drexler and Harrer. Thus the opportunity was given for linking up the officer-politicians with a Party. In addition, Hitler was officially commissioned to investigate this Party. The Reichswehr, which was then developing out of the Volunteer Corps, was permeated with the spirit of politics. It sought a Party whose policy should be identical with its own — or rather, one which it might use as an instrument of its own policy. It is Hitler's achievement to have found this Party for the Reichswehr officers in Munich, and to have made it ready for their use with the assistance of his friends.

At his first visit to a meeting in the private bar of a public-house, he allowed his emotions to run away with him and completely flattened out a separatist debater. As a result, Drexler asked him to join his Party. He accepted the offer and became No. 7 in the inner political "cell" of the Party but not in the Party itself, which was already somewhat larger. That was in July 1919. For another nine months until April 1, 1920, Hitler remained with his regiment. While the Reichswehr was still providing for his material existence, he was already a well-known speaker, an agitator, a mob-orator.

The members of this political "cell" in the German Workers Party were of the type to whom it is more important that seven members should agree upon every single point than that many thousands should agree upon a few essentials. As a result of their pedantry, Hitler was driven to seek to attain dictatorial control over the "cell." At first he sought to make himself master of some one of its activities. He had himself made responsible for its propaganda and allowed no one to interfere with him in this work. Was a mass-meeting to be called, on what subject were the speeches to be made, where was it to be held — that was his affair entirely. On the other hand, he did not concern himself with the important question whether the stamp of the Party should be round or square.

This division of power was not immediately successful. The year 1919 passed amid the most absurd and violent dissensions within the membership. In particular, the "national chairman" Harrer did not wish to bring forward No. 7 as speaker. He thought fairly highly of him, but simply did not consider that Hitler was an orator; and even his first successes did not change Harrer's opinion. When in October 1919 Hitler spoke for the first time in the comparative publicity of an audience of something over a hundred people, Harrer at the conclusion stepped on to the platform and uttered a warning against noisy anti-Semitism. For at this period the youthful Party still felt itself to be a Party of the Left.

The subject of Hitler's first public speech was " Brest-Litovsk and Versailles." It was a subject beloved of the Reichswehr, just as the treaty of Brest-Litovsk had been a peace according to Reichswehr ideas. It was Hitler's desire, if not his duty, to destroy the idea that the Peace of Versailles was a just punishment for the hard conditions of the dictated peace of Brest-Litovsk. Thus the first proclamations of the Party were connected with foreign policy. Personally, Hitler was trying to work out some plan for breaking the " slavery of profits " and for dealing with Judaism. The Party as such, however, was intended to become an instrument for foreign policy.

This had also been the idea of Drexler, who was prepared to leave everything in the hands of the Supreme Military Command. The Great General Staff no longer existed, but the character of the new Party as an instrument of policy remained unchanged. The Labour movement was not intended to benefit the workers but " the nation." This " nation," however, consisted of the Reichswehr officers, of men like Epp and Röhm, who now saw their pupil Hitler working as a sapper in the political terrain.

THE TWENTY-FIVE POINTS

Hitler provided the youthful Party with something that no other Party at that date possessed in anything like so developed a form, namely, systematic propaganda. He himself defines it as " to influence large masses of people, to concentrate on a few essential points, never to allow these to be lost sight of, to enunciate principles in the form of a categorical statement, to exercise the greatest possible patience in disseminating ideas, and to be infinitely patient in awaiting results."

It was very well expressed, but did not immediately convince the other members. There was much discussion, which culminated in January 1920 in the retirement of Harrer.

Meanwhile a new supporter had approached the Party — a Doctor Johannes Dingfelder. He contributed to popular journals under the pseudonym of " Germanus Agricola "; his contributions can most accurately be described as popular mystical economics. Feder's agitation against the slavery of profits turned in his hands to a fight against the "pride of wealth." He visualized the approaching downfall of humanity owing to a cessation of production in every sphere — so strongly did the lack of food in Germany, due to the after-effects of the English blockade, influence men's minds. He foresaw "nature beginning to strike, her goods involuntarily growing less, and the remainder devoured by vermin." Dingfelder, not Hitler, was the chief speaker at the meeting about which so many legends have gathered and which took place on February 24, 1920, in the Hofbräuhaus at Munich, with the object of deciding on a programme.

Hitler's description of this meeting in his book is very one-sided. The most important event was Dingfelder's speech, which was listened to in silence. Hitler, in conjunction with Feder and Drexler, had worked out the well-known twenty-five point programme and read it to the meeting to the accompaniment of great disorder on the part of the opposition. The twenty-five points were thereby made public, but nobody took any further notice of them. The *Völkischer Beobachter* said not a word about them. And the meeting itself culminated in a resolution protesting against the allotment of flour to the Jewish community for baking mazzes.

Little attention has been paid to the fact that there is no programme of the German National Socialist Workers Party but only one of the German Workers Party. This was still the name of the Party at the time of its first public appearance. Hitler himself would have preferred to call it the "Social Revolutionary Party."

The twenty-five points of the Nazi Party are not to be taken as a definite programme, nor did they have the success as a means of propaganda that Feder and Drexler expected. At the same time they contain so much of the spirit of the Party that they cannot be passed over. They are as follows:

"The programme of the German Workers Party is an epochal programme. The leaders refuse to set up new aims after those mentioned in the programme have been achieved merely in order to make possible the further existence of the Party by artificially induced discontent among the masses.

" *1.* We demand the union of all Germans in a Pan German state (*gross Deutschland*) in accordance with the right of all peoples to self-determination.

" *2.* We demand that the German people shall have equal rights with those of other nations; and that the Treaties of Versailles and St. Germain shall be abrogated.

" *3.* We demand space (colonies) for the maintenance of our people and the settlement of our surplus population.

" *4.* Only those who are our countrymen shall be citizens of our State. Only those who are of German blood can be considered as our countrymen regardless of creed. Hence no Jew can be regarded as a fellow-countryman.

" *5.* Those who are not citizens of the State must live in Germany as foreigners and must be subject to the law of aliens.

" *6.* The right to choose the government and determine the laws of the State shall be the privilege only of the citizens. We therefore demand that no public office, of whatever nature, whether central, local or municipal, shall be held by any but a citizen of the State.

" We actively combat the demoralizing parliamentary administration whereby posts go by Party favour without regard to character and capability.

" *7.* We demand that the State shall undertake to ensure that every citizen has a fair chance of living decently and of earning his livelihood. If it proves impossible to provide food for the whole population, then aliens (non-citizens) must be expelled from the State.

" *8.* Any further immigration of non-Germans must be prevented. We demand that all non-Germans who have come into Germany since August 2, 1914, shall be forced to leave the realm immediately.

" *9.* The rights and duties of all citizens shall be the same.

" *10.* The first duty of every citizen shall be to work mentally or physically. No individual shall carry on any work that is deleterious to the community, but shall contribute to the benefit of all.

" Hence we demand:

" *11.* That all unearned incomes shall be abolished,

BREAKING THE BONDAGE OF INTEREST

"*12.* In consideration of the tremendous sacrifices of property and life which every war imposes upon the people, all personal gains resulting from war must be regarded as treason to the nation. We therefore demand that the returns from all war-profiteering shall be forfeited down to the last farthing.

"*13.* We demand that the State shall take over all trusts.

"*14.* We demand that the State shall share in the profits of large industries.

"*15.* We demand that provision for the aged shall be made on a very greatly increased scale.

"*16.* We demand the creation and maintenance of a sound middle class; that the large stores shall be immediately communalized and rented cheaply to small tradespeople; that for all public supplies, whether national or local, preference shall be given to small traders.

"*17.* We demand an agrarian reform suitable to our national requirements; the enactment of a law to expropriate without compensation the owners of any land that may be needed for national purposes; the abolition of ground rents; and the prohibition of all speculation in land.

"*18.* We demand that relentless measures shall be taken against any who work to the detriment of the public weal. Traitors, usurers, profiteers, &c., are to be punished with death, regardless of race or creed.

"*19.* We demand that the Roman law which serves a materialist ordering of the world shall be replaced by German Common Law.

"*20.* In order to make it possible for every capable and industrious German to obtain higher education and thus the chance of rising to important posts, the State shall organize thoroughly the whole cultural system of the nation. The curricula of all educational establishments shall be arranged according to the requirements of practical life. The conception of the State Idea (the science of citizenship) shall be taught in the schools from the very beginning. We demand that specially talented children of poor parents, no matter what their station or occupation, shall be educated at the cost of the State.

"*21.* It is the duty of the State to help raise the standard of the nation's health by providing maternity welfare centres, by prohibiting juvenile labour, by increasing physical fitness through the introduction of compulsory games and gymnastics, and by the greatest possible encouragement of all associations concerned with the physical education of the young.

" *22.* We demand the abolition of the professional army and the formation of a national army.

" *23.* We demand that legal action be taken against those who propagate what they know to be political lies and disseminate them by means of the Press. In order to make possible the creation of a German Press, we demand that:

" (*a*) All editors and their assistants on newspapers published in the German language shall be German citizens.

" (*b*) Non-German newspapers shall require the express assent of the State to publication. They must not be published in the German language.

" (*c*) Non-Germans shall be forbidden by law to have any financial interest in or in any way to influence German newspapers. The punishment for transgression of this law to be the immediate suppression of the newspaper in question and the deportation of the offending aliens.

" Journals transgressing against the common weal shall be suppressed. We demand that legal action be taken against any tendency in art or literature having a disruptive effect upon the life of the people, and that any organizations which offend against the foregoing requirements shall be dissolved.

" *24.* We demand freedom for all religious creeds in the State, in so far as they do not endanger its existence or offend against the moral or ethical sense of the Germanic race.

" The Party as such represents the standpoint of positive Christianity without binding itself to any one particular confession. It opposes the Jewish materialist spirit within and without, and is convinced that a lasting recovery of the nation can only be achieved from within on the principle,

THE GOOD OF THE STATE BEFORE THE GOOD OF THE INDIVIDUAL

"*25.* In order that all this may be carried out, we demand the creation of a strong central authority in the State; the unconditional control by the political central parliament of the whole State and all its organizations. The formation of professional committees, and committees representative of the several estates of the realm, to ensure the laws promulgated by the central authorities being carried out in the individual States in the union.

"The leaders of the Party undertake to promote the execution of the foregoing points at all costs, if necessary at the sacrifice of their own lives.

"MUNICH, *February* 24, 1920."

The key to this programme (which is obviously drafted in awkward phraseology) lies in the date. The compiler called it an epochal programme. And, in fact, it is a programme in which time not only plays a part, but which is of a time and for a time that is long past. Struggles for power within the Party itself forced Hitler in 1926 to declare the programme to be unalterable, although he himself was doubtful about many of its statements, and has expressed these doubts openly in his book. For in 1926 a new National Socialist movement was inaugurated, which has little connexion with the old lower middle-class programme.

This had been a Pan-German programme transmuted into a lower middle-class programme, and blended with ideas culled from the revolution and counter-revolution of 1918–19. It came into being before National Socialism began its civil war against the physical majority of the "far too many-headed" as an internal imperialist minority; and especially before it pledged itself to win over and change the minds of the majority. The programme states definite pretensions but only makes demands of the State. Instead of the proud "We shall," the points begin with the demagogic "We demand."

The future leader of the Party gave the Pan-German demand first place in his programme. The predominant part played by foreign policy in the councils of the Party is proved by this and the second Point. The third Point has long ago been rejected in its literal sense;

the Party renounces the idea of overseas colonies and demands instead expansion towards the East.

The anti-Semitic Points 4 to 8 and 23 and 24 witness to Hitler's victory over Harrer, although temporarily only a victory of compromise. It is an artificial and theoretical anti-Semitism put forward as a racial ideal, and is very far removed from any advocacy of actual physical ill-treatment of Jews. The points, however, and this has seldom been observed, are not exclusive. In case of need they admit of being widened, and in his speeches during the next few years Hitler greatly augmented and expanded certain parts. Much later, in 1928, he returned to the milder interpretation: that Jews might be allowed to remain in Germany as long as they behaved themselves; but, of course, still without being admitted as citizens.

Point 9, with its " equal rights and duties," is obviously a concession to modern views. The State which the Nazi Party began to build up within the State in 1930 is founded simply upon inequality of duties as of performance, as also is the future State which the leaders began to foreshadow in their speeches.

Points 10 to 14 and Point 17 are the Socialistic portions of the programme. Later they were in part publicly ignored and privately renounced. In 1928 Point 17 was simply dropped. On the other hand, Point 11, the most equivocal and disputed, which has been rejected by large sections of the Party, the famous " breaking of the bondage of interest," achieved a significance which was undreamt of by the compilers of the programme and not recognized until much later. In conjunction with the rejected Point 17, it has since 1929 won for the Party the hearts of the debt-burdened landowners.

Point 15 is the " social " part, Point 16 possibly the real kernel of the programme, namely, the section dealing with the middle classes. Without inquiring whether anything was to be said for the owners of and assistants in large shops, the National Socialist German Workers Party decided in favour of the small shopkeepers.

As a tactical manœuvre, Point 24 is excellent. It emphasizes the non-sectarian character of the Party and combines it with its economic morality. Point 23 might be called a cultural scheme, which with a sharp eye to the main chance is concerned with the *means* of culture, but on the other hand leaves the cultural *substance* to develop along its own lines. Here Hitler, the propagandist, assured to the National Socialist State all the instruments for cultural propaganda, and left himself with a free hand as regards their employment. The programme at this point even indulges in a joke, for — as will be shown later — section (*b*) means that the *Berliner Tageblatt,* for example, may indeed be published, but only in Hebrew.

Point 25 — the strong central authority — is Hitler's spiritual child. It is true that in the next few years he modified to some extent his desire for centralization. It is on this very point that he has exemplified the power of his art of ambiguous expression; and indeed he has shown altogether how he can gild the iron letters of his principles with rhetorical decoration so that they glitter vaguely and delusively. One thing, however, was clear to him — he might during the struggles in the next few years turn Bavarian national feeling to full account, but at the same time organized Bavarian federalist opinion was to be his fiercest competitor. Point 25 says: Observe, this is no Bavarian, no anti-Prussian programme. The State rests upon power, not upon treaties; the country is not a confederacy but an articulated unity; Germans do not live together but are ruled. The Reich was to move forward openly on the steel rails of national unity and not to be hindered in its progress by an opposition concealed beneath the sheepskin coat of a Bavarian cattle-herd.

All other demands made in the programme have been more or less dissipated by the growth of the Party. The Party itself remained, and it was within the Party that the Nazis made their first essays in the art of government.

TWO MEN ATTACK A CITY

So on the eve of the year 1920 Hitler faced the future almost alone with his uncertain programme. The Party contained few besides himself. Dietrich Eckart's brain held a bourgeois miscellany of ideas under the swastika. Feder was probably pleased to see that the programme embodied so many of his ideas, but the militant association that he founded in May 1920 to break the slavery of interest was more important in his eyes, and had little in common with Hitler and his rough warriors. Feder's association " regarded the poisoning of public life by the spitefulness of indefinite, one-sided, and lying leadership as due solely to the delusions of money, to blind greed for money, and the unlimited power of money." This was actually the programme of the quill-driving Nazi economic theorist at one time. A poor ally for a Hitler who preached " fanaticism, indeed intolerance " as an indispensable preliminary to victory. Whose cry was: " The hatred of the enemies of our people and of our views is something that you should strive for rather than avoid! "

One comrade, however, Hitler did acquire early in 1920 who was more than a cipher. This was the journalist Hermann Esser, then a very young man. Hitler had got to know him as a press reporter at the divisional headquarters of the Reichswehr. He was no honest plodder, no quiet worker, but an agitator, and one who understood the art of mass-excitation almost better than Hitler himself. Hitler spoke on the " Jewish question " picturesquely and often with a certain popular jocoseness; but Esser would discover that a Jewish shoemaker had illegally obtained a seven-roomed house in Munich. By describing the wretched man's luxurious mode of living, he roused his ill-clad audience, many of whom were still living on their food-cards, to fury. He was the archetype of the " spit-fire " orator. The inhibitions which Hitler still had were lacking in the downy-chinned youth who in November 1918 had founded a revolutionary soviet at his school in Kempten, had demanded that sundry bourgeois should be hanged by the Soldiers' Council, and in 1919 had worked as a volunteer on a Socialist newspaper. Not until he came in touch with the Reichswehr did he find his true political path. He is certainly not an ideal type; even Hitler has never allowed his oldest fellow-campaigner to come right to the fore. In the early days, however, he was irreplaceable, because unique.

These two unknown men, Hitler and Esser, did not at first succeed in taking the city of Munich by storm, nor did they achieve anything remarkable at their first meetings. Hitler's statements in his speeches and writings that the bourgeoisie at that time had held no great political meetings are false. On the contrary, the People's Offensive and Defensive Association (*Völkischer Schutz- und Trutzbund*) held enormous meetings at frequent intervals, during which the audience raged with excitement when such men as the anti-Semitic agitator Kerlen or the leader of the German minorities' movement, Dr. Rohmeder, spoke. At one time there were one hundred thousand members of the Offensive and Defensive Association in the country. At that time any one who spoke in Munich against the Jews was certain of applause from the outset, and as far as the public was concerned the National Socialist German Workers Party was at first no more than one of the many anti-Semitic societies. Nor was such an undertaking as dangerous to life and limb as Hitler would have us believe. Since the overthrow of the Soviet republic, the " red rabble," which by the way had previously listened quietly to antagonistic opinions at its own meetings, had been almost entirely suppressed. There were, of course, at times disturbances and contradiction, when the Socialist leaders were designated as a treasonous mob who had been bribed by the Jews. But it never went beyond the normal, and was very far from being a systematic terrorization of meetings.

THE RIVALS

Actually the worst enemy of the bourgeois agitation at that time was the National Socialist German Workers Party itself. As yet it did not break up bourgeois meetings, but it remorselessly bore down its weaker rivals. Dr. Gerlich, the bourgeois editor of the *Münchener Neueste Nachrichten,* now a determined antagonist of the Nazi Party, at that time invented the phrase that describes Marxism in its present polemical sense as the sum-total of Socialists combined under the International, whether Majority Social Democrats, Independents, or Communists. Gradually the Nazis adopted this splendid catchword, but then they directed it against almost every one else. Even its inventor was suspected of being an abettor of Marxism and the friend of Jews.

Rivalry which serves to keep up the first enthusiasm was soon to be found in plenty. There was, for instance, the German Socialist Party, which was larger and which celebrated a real Party Day at Hanover in April. Its programme contained many of Feder's principles, advocated sterner agrarian reform than the Nazis, and embodied some of the ideas of "Germanus Agricola." Its strongest agitator was Streicher, an elementary school teacher of Nuremberg. It even went so far as to put forward a candidate for the Reichstag elections in 1920 — which the Nazis omitted to do only for lack of funds — but did not get him elected.

More successful was a rival in North Germany — the German Social Party of Richard Kunze, who was nicknamed "Cudgel-Kunze," and has now become an unobtrusive member of the Hitler Party. Kunze had the courage to advocate one demand of Feder's which Hitler never dared to uphold — namely, State bankruptcy. Originally Feder wished to have all War Loan Certificates declared legal tender, apparently without troubling about what had then not yet occurred — inflation. He had now taken up the idea of the State's repudiating its debts as a deadly blow at loan capital — a programme that the inflation carried out very successfully later. At all events, Kunze soon got the reputation of being a dangerous agitator who seemed to have started a promising Party.

These were the competitors for the favour of the socially roused people. Anti-Semitism, however, apparently was solely in the hands of the purely democratic associations.

So it was to be war. In the first place, a new and more attractive name was opposed to the German Social Party and the German Socialist Party. Through the intermediary of Dr. Alexander Schillings the Party had come in contact with the National Socialists of the former Danubian monarchy. These were engaged at the time in disputing as to whether they should call themselves the National Socialist Workers Party; the word "Worker" was a cause of some offence among the Viennese. In Munich, again, the word "Socialist" was under dispute, but was eventually adopted, against the wish of Hitler. From April 1920 Anton Drexler's Party, which had hitherto been known as the German Workers Party, was called National Socialist German Workers Party.

Very soon the first clashes occurred with the bourgeois. Oskar Körner, one of the founders of the Party, rose as an avowed enemy at a meeting of the German People's Offensive and Defensive Association, and accused them sarcastically of having no idea of the real feeling of the people, of not having the people behind them. There was a period of considerable tension, and this eventually led to a change of editors and finally a change of ownership of the *Völkischer Beobachter*. Köhler, a sub-editor, who is now in the Press Department of the Brown House, used frequently to remark loftily that the democratic idea should never be held out before any single Party. Hitler therefore openly reproached him for want of courage, and Körner wrote furiously in the paper that he declined to permit any one to stamp him as a socialistic proletarian because he did not chance to look as if he had come out of a band-box.

Körner was one of the lesser and unknown members of the Party, but its whole spirit spoke through him — the hatred alike of the propertied middle class and of the proletariat.

The quarrel was of necessity made up again. The National Socialist German Workers Party was not yet strong enough to take up the fight against its opponents directly. More especially since Hitler had resigned from the Reichswehr on April 1, 1920. It was now necessary for him to try to earn at least a part of his living expenses; the rest was found for him by friends such as Dietrich Eckart. For a time Hitler became an itinerant speaker for the German People's Offensive and Defensive Association, and expounded his theme, "Brest-Litovsk and Versailles." He refused to take fees for Nazi meetings, but for others he accepted them.

Even at that time his hastily compiled programme caused trouble. Thus at a meeting at Munich in August 1920 he declared that it was a matter of course for the Nazis that industrial capital, being productive, would be left untouched, and that his enmity was only directed against the Jewish international loan capital. This meant that Point 13 was sacrificed. On the other hand, Point 15 was expanded vastly: "Every worker must be guaranteed a minimum living wage by the State" — a vision of the State as a charitable institution, which far exceeds anything that has been achieved along these lines in the past years.

Meanwhile politics had gone ahead of the little Party. It was not yet able to speak authoritatively. The Kapp-Putsch failed in Berlin; at Munich, on the other hand, the Socialist-bourgeois government under Hoffmann was overthrown by the Reichswehr and the short term volunteers and replaced by the Kahr government. Röhm, too, had his part in this affair, but not Hitler. He had at that time been introduced into the circle of officers surrounding Röhm as a visitor and a valuable political liaison-officer. Apart from this, Hitler devoted his energies to holding meetings and furnishing the " business premises " of the Party — a shabby room in an inn in the old part of Munich — with a few shelves and cupboards.

The change of government had important effects upon the fate of the Party. It became the official favourite, was praised by the new Prime Minister in the local parliament, and was supported by the police. Kahr himself was more in the nature of an umbrella which is useful by its very existence; but Pöhner, the chief of the police, and his assistant, Dr. Frick, the leader of the political department, were most active.

Pöhner was a hard-headed official and a gifted man, whose Bavarian royalism was unrelieved by the usual good humour of his province and was much more akin to Prussianism. Every conception — even inimical — of the tendencies of the day was lacking in him. He did not reject them, he simply did not understand them in the very least. The devil who undoubtedly possessed Pöhner was a cold devil.

After the revolution, as he later declared nonchalantly in the law courts, he carried on treasonable practices as though they were a sacred duty for five solid years.

Dr. Frick had most of the qualities necessary for a good substitute for his interesting Chief, apart from his somewhat gloomy and dissatisfied outlook. He was also to be useful to Hitler in this capacity later on. It is true that he had no feeling for fine distinctions; he proved this later when he suggested that Hitler should be appointed to the police at Hildburghausen. Both men showed the Nazis every consideration that the police could show. To the remark of an initiate: " It is a fact that there are political murder organizations, sir! " Pöhner once replied: " Oh, really? But there aren't enough of them! " The small Workers Party was, it is true, at the beginning rather carried away in the general enthusiasm for everything " national." Until the beginning of 1923 other groups were more important politically. But since the Nazis always showed the greatest effrontery, they were obviously obliged to make greater demands upon the goodwill of the police than their rivals.

Disturbances, fisticuffs in halls and in the streets, earned for the Party a greater popularity than that enjoyed by the German Socialist and People's Parties. It achieved a very dubious reputation, but that was better than having no reputation at all, like its rivals. Chance favoured it further. A Munich rabbi tried to refute an anti-Semitic speech at a Nazi meeting. Of course, there was a great commotion in the hall. The result was that in future every Nazi announcement bore the warning: " No admittance for Jews." That was even more effective than the most biting abuse of the Republic, which every lounger at street corners indulged in in Munich at that time. It proved that the Nazis were in grim earnest about their anti-Semitism; it proved that their hatred was sincere, and this sincerity attracted the masses, who had for two years been dulled by political catchwords.

Nazi propaganda, a system of brutal words and savage deeds, took shape and form. But before its further development could be forecasted, the movement underwent a spiritual rebirth — its union with Austrian National Socialism at the Party meeting in Salzburg.

AUSTRIA AND NATIONAL SOCIALISM

In Austria National Socialism already existed both as a name and an idea in pre-War days. Two bookbinders, Ludwig Vogel and Ferdinand Buschofsky, founded a German National Labour Union among the German Bohemians, in opposition both to the Czech *entrepreneurs* and the German Social Democrats. Thus the first feeble resistance on the part of the workers against " the enemies of the people and against Marxists " emerged as a result of the struggle of the nationalities within the Danubian monarchy. The Union soon came in contact with George von Schönerer's anti-Semitic Pan-German Party and fell with it when the Pan-German Party collapsed as a result of the quarrel between its leaders Schönerer and Wolf. In 1904 another small " German Labour Party " arose in Moravia, which by 1911 was sending several representatives to the Moravian Diet as well as to the Reichsrat in Vienna, among them the present-day leaders

Jung and Knirsch. The party congress at Iglau in 1913 was already discussing agrarian reform and the struggle against interest and ground rents. Thus Feder's doctrine was not original even in his own movement. On May 5, 1918, at its Vienna meeting, the Party adopted the name " German National Socialist Party of Austria " which had been put forward as early as 1913.

Nevertheless, in spite of name and programme, there was no uniformity as regards the most important principles. The Bohemian Germans under the spiritual leadership of Rudolf Jung wished the Party to be a Labour — indeed a class — Party. The Viennese, a practically negligible group under Dr. Walter Riehl, were violently opposed to this. A Party meeting was expected to resolve the dissonance, and was to take place on August 7 and 8, 1920, in Salzburg. The Munich Nazis, led by Drexler and Hitler, were to take part in it. The " German Socialists," whose headquarters were in Düsseldorf, also appeared, but even numerically they could not compete with the strong delegation from Munich.

After hearing a report from Jung certain basic principles were adopted, amongst them that the worker might only maintain his rights within the limits of his nationality. It was expressly required that there should be " no revolution or class-warfare, but definite creative reforms," which in certain circumstances might lead to nationalization of industries. And the programme continued categorically: " Private property is not in itself harmful so long as it is the result of honest personal endeavour, and is so used as not to be deleterious to the general good " — a statement that only serves to reveal its perpetrator's incapacity for thought. However, statements such as this, that something harmless is not harmful, will always find champions at a time when it is more important to be a good hater than a clear thinker.

A year later Jung forced through the change that made the Party into a class Party at the meeting of the inter-State representatives at Linz. Refusal to admit class-warfare was definitely crossed off the programme, and the following remarkable clause was put in: " The German National Socialist Workers Party is the class Party of productive Labour." Jung argued on virtually Marxist lines. There were only two groups in economic life — he affirmed — and these were in opposition to one another. The one did productive work and the others were in receipt of unearned income. Thus the Nazis were a class Party, only the idea of the worker class was not confined within narrow limits, but embraced all who lived on the results of their mental or physical labour, that is to say, all those who are economically weak. Further, he asserted, that in this sense the Party also advocated class-warfare, not in the way of economic revolution but of reform.

These are statements that might have appeared in the Heidelberg Programme of the German Social Democrats. They were not likely to be agreed to either by the little Viennese group or by the Munich movement that was already assuming important proportions. Here it was not admitted that there were two groups in the nation which were in natural opposition to one another. In fact, just before the Salzburg meeting Hitler announced: " There is no room for the class-conscious worker in the National Socialist German Workers Party, any more than for a class-conscious bourgeois." Thus Hitler. But what were the thoughts of his fellow-member Körner, who was a class-conscious bourgeois and refused to be called a proletarian? And Körner, after all, was the stuff of which the Party was made. There is in Hitler a great power of dismissing realities with impressive words or, as Feder once expessed it: " not to make our programme agree with facts but to make facts agree with our programme."

In the summer of 1920, however, Jung had not yet got so far. He was still sufficiently in sympathy with the Munich members to influence them. Hitler did not make his influence felt at the Salzburg meeting where the Munich representative on the Committee was Drexler. The Munich Party became a member of the inter-State bureau of the National Socialist Party of the German People, an institution which was never practically effective. The spiritual effects of the Salzburg meeting were, on the contrary, very important.

NATIONAL SOCIALISM IN BOHEMIA

It started with Rudolf Jung. He had already formed a very clear idea as to the pernicious significance of world-democracy, of the connexion between the international cult of Mammon and the State institutions all over the liberal world, of the anti-German character of

Occidental democracy. Fluid ideas of this description were still lacking to the Munich members. They were too rarefied for Drexler. Feder did not care to mix up his economic theories with high politics; Eckart's æsthetic political meanderings had no need of such fixed theories; and Hitler could do nothing with an idea until it had achieved expressible form. He now learnt from Jung that it was a peculiarity of the Jewish people always to Judaize other peoples more and more; that Luther's reformation was only superficial, because it did not separate Christianity from the Old Testament; that the Western cult of Mammon and Eastern Bolshevism were only apparent opposites, but were in reality allies for setting up a Jewish World Empire. He learnt furthermore that international democracy was nothing more nor less than the political outcome of the Jewish spirit, and hence it was necessary to destroy parliamentarianism and replace it by a constitution representative of the several corporations (professions or vocations) in the realm. Jung also indicated who were the two destroyers of the State. Germany had both the strongest social democratic Party and the strongest clerical Party, and, in addition, Jewish radicalism played a great part in German political life. The ideas that had dimly entered Drexler's mind and come stumblingly from his tongue came trippingly from Jung's mouth. During the World War, which was a political change comparable to the migration of the peoples, individualism stood on the side of the Entente, and Socialism — of which Marxism is only a caricature — on the side of the Germans: " Socialism means communal work and will, is the German nature, is, in short, the German spirit. It is founded upon the conception of work as a moral duty." So German was Socialism that even the German Empire under William II " was the only country in which Socialism was directly propagated by the State."

No single one of these theories is new. Lagarde, Houston Stewart Chamberlain, Spengler (who is usually treated with some mistrust in this company), and Russian emigrants had added their quota. But it was the union of them all which resulted in what may be called the Nazi outlook on life. Jung was probably the first to use the expression " outlook on life " for National Socialism many years before Hitler raised his political doctrine to so high an intellectual level. It might more accurately be called German Socialism; for this doctrine is carefully distinguished from "international" National Socialism as later propagated by Rosenberg, and which Moeller van den Bruck explained by saying that every nation has its own form of Socialism. Hitler attached no value to such distinctions.

Thus a doctrine arose rich in phrases and interpretations, which was at one and the same time able to assent to Socialist reform and the German Empire under William II. It met the spiritual needs of honest patriots who were anxious to have a revolution and yet not to disown the past. National Socialism as it developed in the years 1926–28 was to make a thorough clearance of this mass of incompatible ideas, but for that very reason was not able to maintain its connexion with the Party.

Moreover, Jung for the first time — and this was perhaps the most important fact of all — obtained a clear conception of his enemy. Things which did not belong together were forced into union simply because they were being jointly combated. The picture of the enemy, artificially made up of many enemies, was many years later to be called "The System."

FOR WHOM WAS HITLER FIGHTING?

In this case, as in so many others, it may be presumed that enmity existed before the enemy was known.

The end of the War had not been the most dignified for Germany. It had neither won a war against superior odds, as had once the Dutch, nor had it perished on a funeral pyre, as Carthage or Mexico in their day. On the contrary, its Commander-in-Chief had lost his nerve, its Emperor had taken to flight, and its people had not had the power to resist revolution. It is true that the people can no more be condemned for this than could the Parisians in 1871, who also capitulated to starvation. Nevertheless the nation was to be blamed for its hysterical misunderstanding of events, for hailing the collapse as the victory of a revolution which never occurred. The unfurling of the red flag was neither a great act not a great crime. But the fact that nothing was done in its name but to implore those who had been overthrown not to refuse co-operation, and that in exchange for their co-operation the flag was quietly refurled — that was the sin committed by the Revolution. The Revolution was first compromised because nobody had the courage to rule in the name of the Revolution. Those least guilty were the representatives of the people, who accidentally found a place in history as Jacobins. A government which had an aim instead of referring to aimless electors, which had laid a plan before the nation instead of letting it be worked out for them by Liberal professors, which promised reformation instead of setting up Law and Order as the highest ideal, such a government might even have signed the Treaty of Versailles and it would still have been a revolutionary act. As things were, it was only a business deal on behalf of the imperial Government, which did not care to soil its fingers with the fatal penholder.

Any one who knows the conditions at the time must realize that anything of that sort was difficult; any one who knows the protagonists must admit that it was impossible. The Spartacus group tried to negotiate, and the Independent Socialist Party vaguely thought of negotiation. Some of these politicians, moreover, harboured bourgeois opinions without realizing the fact. For the German bourgeoisie was at first not at all opposed to revolution. The transition to revolution was by no means entirely an act of cowardice; it was inspired by a certain covert sympathy, a readiness to accept great events. Naturally, when no great events emerged from the Revolution, the bourgeoisie began to act again, and it acted consistently with its nature — that is, in an anti-revolutionary manner.

Nevertheless, the remembrance of its sympathy remained. Josef Hofmiller, an excellent writer and an acute observer, recently published extracts from his diary, descriptive of the Revolution in Munich. Even in these reticent pages there is hardly a word of criticism of the events. So deep lay the feeling that the new system must be given a chance. Journalists with royalist leanings wrote hymns to the political rebirth. When the revolutionaries disappointed expectations, the bourgeoisie felt as though it had itself made a false decision. It now acted in perfect accord with the character given to the Germans by Bogumil Goltz: "We are a people whose character is temperate but whose spirit tends to extravagance; who are easily moved to enthusiasm and as easily go to the other extreme; and who in the end are racked by remorse and qualms of conscience."

National Socialism became the sin on the conscience of the German bourgeoisie.

There were special reasons for bad consciences in Munich. Here Kurt Eisner, a man who was purely and sincerely an idealist, the archetype of the radical Liberal, had been leader of the Revolution. He was an author, something of a Bohemian, and a North German Jew who nevertheless adored the Bavarian spirit as do most of those who have lived in close contact with it. Unlike most of his political friends, Eisner was a federalist who by temperamental attacks on Berlin enlisted Bavarian pride of race and State in the cause of revolution. In company with war-weary peasants who hated Prussia, he had overthrown the unpopular king, and for a few weeks had been a popular hero. After his murder hundreds of thousands followed his coffin with genuine grief.

Thus even Bavarian federalism had compromised itself with the Revolution. The population here was politically more united than in the north; the class distinctions were less sharp. Its political temperament was normally static; but if once the political basis was tilted, then the whole mass of practically united opinion flowed over to one side, and when the reaction came it flowed in just the same manner over in the opposite direction. Thus the character of the people logically prepared its own fate. It went furthest in the Revolution, as far as becoming a Soviet Republic; and it also swung back furthest in the Counter-Revolution, namely, as far as the Hitler Putsch.

CHAPTER II

HITLER'S FIGHT FOR THE PARTY LEADERSHIP

In 1920 the thirty-one-year-old Hitler went through a process of self-education. He learnt from the now moving masses of the people what they themselves were learning — to view new political conditions from a new standpoint. Whatever opinion may be held as to his process and its results, Hitler's personal achievement, his complete success, can only be regarded with admiration.

In the Bavarian capital the tide of anti-Semitism still ran high and must be made the most of. Meetings of the Offensive and Defensive Association, or of any that took the trouble to hire a hall and design posters, were still crowded out. The popular cause had plenty of clever propagandists. For months a notice was inserted in anti-Semitic papers: " Put the Jews into protective detention camps, and there will be peace in the land." Hitler himself could not put it any better.

A good idea is not everything, nor even months of steady payment for a notice in the papers. The out-of-work Hitler excelled all his rivals in assiduity. During the second half of the year 1920 the popular associations began to get tired of the success of their meetings. " We do not want agitatist meetings; to flatter the instincts of the mob is unworthy of us," wrote a genteel person in the *Völkischer Beobachter*. It was all very well to have a full house every week; but what results were achieved? Would that achieve the abrogation of the Treaty of Versailles? Would it drive out the Marxists from Berlin? Would it make those who got up the meetings masters of the house again? The government of Bavaria was national as it was.

It took a Hitler to show these weary souls that a man who hopes to win real power must not get tired of the success of his agitatorial efforts for thirteen years. But then Hitler came from below. To most people the acclamation of the masses is sweet; to Hitler, who had hitherto failed to receive other middle-class recognition, it was infinitely sweeter than to well-off, well-connected gentlemen from the popular associations, from the conservative Party (*Ordnungsblock*), from the Citizens' Council, and from the local volunteer Defence Corps (*Einwohnerwehr*). To them the cheering multitude was a somewhat questionable political expedient. To him it was an end in itself.

Thus as early as the summer of 1920 he was designated as the " wiliest agitator " in Munich by an opposition paper. That was a mistake. He was only the most diligent. And, moreover, he had no mistaken inclination to refinement.

His method of propaganda was developed by practice, and he gave a masterly description of it later. Practical experiment made of him a past master of political agitation, the greatest that Germany possesses on the last decade. The posters advertising his meetings were of a size never before seen. They were bright red and covered with long leading articles. Long? At all events they could be read in three minutes and the print would not hurt the eyes. The style was still that of the commercial college; the sentences were often long and involved, but large and spaced types broke up the wilderness of words. The slogans were easy to remember: Jewish stock exchange and profiteer republics, November criminals, Marxism, Germany's gravedigger. The intelligentsia shuddered, but it remembered the slogans.

Twice a week at least these posters appeared on the hoardings, and people crowded to read them. Twice a week at least the same words were repeated to two thousand people in one of the many public-houses. By the third time, the audience began to think that these were its own ideas, and was delighted at hearing the speaker express its own opinion. By a few months' work on these lines some thousands of adherents were won for the cause, people to whom it was already a necessity to listen to the expression of their innermost opinion. The audience was no longer composed merely of people listening to a speaker, but of enthusiastic collaborators, who carried along the newcomers in their exaltation.

WHO BEGAN THE TERROR?

One side of the propaganda was persistent. But another was even more important, and that was energy. This must not be understood to mean powerful speeches. Energy meant this sort of thing: small bodies of National Socialists, euphemistically called defenders of order, roamed through the streets at night. If they saw a nose they did not like the look of, its unlucky owner was hustled into a corner, somebody stamped on his toe, he resented it, provocation had been given, and legal brawling could begin, in the course of which it is seen that God and the police are with the stronger battalions. Grotesque cases occurred. Men upon whom suspicion had fallen, and who denied being Jews, were subjected to a physical examination, as actually happened to the aquiline-nosed representative of a Latin-American Republic. That such excesses were not merely individual extravagances but were a definite part of the Party system was shown by a retrospect of the year 1921 that was given by the Party leaders in the *Völkischer Beobachter*. The hope is there expressed that " all members of the Party who were engaged in the movement would in the new year be once again imbued with a spirit of ruthless energy " (*Draufgehen*).

The defensive troops of the National Socialists had been organized in the summer of 1920. Their commander was an ex-convict and clockmaker called Emil Maurice. In common with that part of the National Socialist historical legend which has been founded on his own representation, Hitler asserts that the defensive troops only defended their own meetings from people who tried to break them up. That is not true. As early as the summer of 1920 one of their more harmless activities consisted in howling down any who wished to start a discussion. The old Liberal habit of free discussion which had been characteristic of the excited revolutionary meetings was everywhere still current. Very soon the National Socialists substituted for this older style of meeting the new idea of " proclamation," at which no opponent might disturb the expression of the Party will. Until they had reached that stage, those who tried to argue or to talk on equal terms with the chief speaker were simply prevented from speaking at all. The *Völkischer Beobachter* indeed complained on June 20, 1920, that certain persons " rather spoil some of our meetings by howling down the opposition." Since then that paper has learnt to regard worse things as harmless.

It was already dangerous for people who went to the meetings and tried to make use of the good parlimentary custom of questioning the speaker. A man whom Hitler particularly disliked, for instance, an engineer called Ballerstedt, the leader of the federalist " Bavarian Association," had a particularly bad time. According to the *Völkischer Beobachter,* he was " removed from the hall by the indignant audience and not before he had been given something to remind him of the occasion." As time went on it became the custom to throw interrupters out of the meetings " gently but firmly," as the National Socialist paper put it.

The Nazis, however, were not content with these " defensive " measures. During the years 1920 and 1921 they broke up several opposition meetings. In September 1921, for instance, Hitler appeared personally with his followers at a meeting of Ballerstedt's and stormed the platform. There was a nasty brawl, and Ballerstedt again came off badly. In reply to the police commission which inquired into the incident, Hitler said coolly: " It's all right. We got what we wanted. Ballerstedt did not speak." In February 1921 the Nazis even broke up a charitable entertainment in Munich organized by the Press.

That these were not merely sporadic manifestations is shown by the report in the *Völkischer Beobachter* of Hitler's speech on January 4, 1921, to an audience at the Kindl Keller in Munich, in which he said ". . . that the National Socialist movement in Munich will in future ruthlessly prevent — if necessary by force — all meetings or lectures that are likely to distract the minds of our fellow-nationals, which are in any case liable to waver."

In the summer of 1922, at the Munich Trade Exhibition in Peter Behrens' Dombauhütte, a somewhat expressionistic image of Christ by Gies displeased the conservative taste of the inhabitants of Munich. Hitler threatened that unless the image were removed he would bring in some of his followers and smash it. The image was removed.

Hitler does not seem to have observed that the Christ was conceived nordically.

None of these things, of course, appear in *Mein Kampf* (My Struggle). Any historian of the National Socialist movement must admit that its excesses show an audacity and a restless activity that contained many of the seeds of success. But the outcries about " Marxist Terrorism " do not go well with it, and are inconsistent with the official Party commands to " ruthlessness " in addition to being undignified and bearing the mark of insincerity. It must be emphasized that at this time Nazi activities did not yet lead to bloodshed, for the simple reason that their opponents were not accustomed to this form of procedure and took some little time to put themselves into a state of defence.

It cannot be denied to National Socialism that it introduced into the political struggle new methods which had not until then been known in Germany, and which were no doubt in part copied from the Italian Fascisti but also from the Russian " Black Hundred." Of course, as soon as any opposition was organized, there was bound to be bloodshed — and there has certainly been plenty of it in the years that have passed since then. The responsibility for the terrorization which has since taken place all over Germany rests primarily upon National Socialism and upon Hitler. A regard for historical truth demands that these facts should be clearly stated inasmuch as they are demonstrable from actual Nazi sources. For the above statements are mainly derived from the *Völkischer Beobachter*. Moreover, the part played by Hitler personally in the terror is a matter of legal fact. In January 1922 he was condemned to three months' imprisonment for breaking up the Ballerstedt meeting, though it is true that he was not required to serve two of them.

It would be an insult to assume that a man as clever as Hitler undoubtedly is had not foreseen the consequences of his actions. But he regarded the gains to his Party as more important than the damage to the community at large; he put the precepts of law and order, of neighbourly love and of the criminal code, under the law of his movement, in which he already saw the future break-up of the nation. His policy of the unceasing offensive gained respect for his cause and broke through the conspiracy of dangerous silence. Hitler was overjoyed when at last the enemy proceeded to counter-attack and attempted to break up one of his meetings at the end of 1921, which lives on in Party legend as "The Battle in the Hofbrauhaus." For as long as this counter-offensive did not happen, Hitler had to stir up his own battles.

HITLER'S FIRST NEWSPAPER

The Party's most successful financial collector at that time was Dietrich Eckart. Hitler personally owes much to Eckart. His most brilliant service, however, was rendered in December 1920.

The *Völkischer Beobachter* was for sale; it was overburdened with debt. Dietrich Eckart and Feder were anxious to do what they could for the paper. But Eckart was himself in a tight place. His weekly paper, *Auf gut Deutsch* (In Plain German), had also come out with a balance on the wrong side and was about to go into liquidation. Then the Reichswehr sprang into the breach. Eckart obtained the necessary money through General von Epp. He and Röhm had brought together a number of people in order systematically to influence the Press in a nationalist sense. Ostensibly the sixty thousand Marks that he provided were to liquidate *Auf gut Deutsch*. Actually Eckart was put in a position to buy the *Völkischer Beobachter*. In view of the involved state of the paper's finances this step incurred grave risks. But the National Socialist German Workers Party decided to make itself responsible for the venture.

What a change had taken place in only fifteen months! The unknown corporal, the Party orator with thirty followers and a typewriter, had become owner of a newspaper. True it was only a weekly paper, but none the less it was the same organ in which a year and a quarter earlier Hitler had tentatively inserted a notice; the same paper that had given twenty lines to his speeches, and had often enough twitted him enviously, was now his property. On December 19, 1920, the *Völkischer Beobachter* came into the possession of the Nazi Party, and Hitler had the means for publicity.

Let the German Socialists, the German Nationalists, and all the rest of them put that in their pipes and smoke it! But then they never spurned Jews or broke up meetings, they did not make a noise or extort things forcibly. And, of course, they had no Reichswehr and no Röhm to back them.

THREE THOUSAND MEMBERS

Hitler had every reason to be satisfied with the past year. His friend Esser was already describing Hitler's brilliant oratory and power over his audience in the reports of the meetings that he sent to the *Beobachter*. He expressed the view that Hitler should speak in every city in Germany. This was the beginning of that personal glorification which was later to be so important a factor in creating the desired atmosphere.

The past year had seen forty-six Nazi meetings in Munich, that is to say, practically one a week. It is curious that others did not realize the open secret of their success — the stubborn pursuit of an aim, for which even Horace had promised the help of the gods. All over the country there had been as many as thirty-two recruiting meetings in spite of the fact that sometimes it was a problem how to raise the travelling expenses of the speaker. Local branches had been established at Rosenheim and Landshut, and even in Frankfurt-am-Main there was a Nazi club. And at Pforzheim in Baden a real, obedient, local branch of the National Socialist German Workers Party had been formed under a foreman named Wittmann, while a certain Ulshöfer was leader of a Nazi Association in Stuttgart.

It was, taken all in all, a good year. The Party had begun it with a membership of sixty-four, which had now grown to three thousand; that is to say, it had increased fiftyfold. Such a success is not to be explained even by the oratorical gifts of a Hitler. But Hitler was merely the name for an only partly visible group of which, above all, Röhm was a member. And though Röhm was not the secret master, he was the virtually all-powerful liaison man between the Volunteer Corps and the Defence Associations from which the Reichswehr gradually developed. He drove men and officers into Hitler's camp, pushed all available Activists into the Nazi Party. Another source of men and munitions was the Bavarian Conservatives (*Ordnungsblock*), an influential semi-political association of Right Wing organizations. All help, however, is vain unless there is some one who is determined to make the fullest use of it. In public, and especially in the matter of propaganda, it happened to be Hitler who never grew tired of repeating to the masses four, five, or a dozen times what others would at the outside say three times. It was he who was not above any kind of baseness of assertion, so long as there was some prospect of its sticking in people's heads. Baseness? He did not stick at worse things. It was he who went out into the highways and organized free fights in lecture halls and broke up opposition meetings. He dared to use what others did not dare — terrorization. He assumed responsibility for moral wrong, because he knew that power is not to be won without inflicting injury. Others shrank back and were obliterated. Hitler bore the responsibility before History and the three thousand Party members.

NAZI FOREIGN POLICY

In January 1921 it became known that Arnold Rechberg, a man engaged in the potash trade and a keen student of foreign policy, had addressed a memorandum to leading personages in the Entente, in which he advocated armed intervention in Soviet Russia. In earlier times Rechberg had written anti-Bolshevik articles for the *Völkischer Beobachter*. His memorandum had been compiled at the instigation of General Ludendorff, who had recently taken up his abode in Munich.

This was the time when National Socialism adopted a definite attitude in the question of foreign policy — no longer a mere system of gestures and protests, but of tactical calculations. In the New Year number of the *Völkischer Beobachter*, which had by this time been the property of the National Socialist Party for ten days, appeared an anonymous article, the cunningly woven phrases of which have in one way and another constituted the programme of the Party's foreign policy ever since. Although Russia had just lost the war with Poland, the writer prophesied that Poland would within measurable time be overrun by the Soviet Power, and said:

" And when the time comes and the storm is brewing over the eastern marches of Germany, it will be a case of collecting a hundred thousand men who are prepared to sacrifice their lives there. If, at the instigation of Messrs. Cohen and Levi, the German railwaymen should strike, then the men must go there on foot, and must go quickly. A temporary local Soviet rule must be reckoned with — 'what care I for wife or child.' Those who are determined to dare all must also be prepared for the attitude of the Western Jews, who are lurking beyond the Rhine with French tanks and artillery, and who will raise woeful voices when the Eastern Jews are attacked. Even if Lenin occupies Poland, there will still be time to liberate Poland. Poland is like a hysterical female who has to be hit hard over the head before she will let her rescuer pull her out of the water. What is certain is that the Russian army will be driven back across its frontiers after a second Tannenberg. That is a purely German affair, and the real beginning of our reconstruction. An army in flight will be the bitterest enemy of the Soviet Government."

Thus the "great foreign policy" of National Socialism began with a plan for a German crusade to Russia; for the author of this article was the new political theorist of the Party, the German-Russian, Alfred Rosenberg.

German by descent but Russian in mentality, he was born at Reval in 1893. He spent the War years as a student in Russia; and when the Germans came he offered himself as a volunteer, but was not accepted. Like many other Russian refugees he fled to Munich in 1919, and came in contact with the Nazi movement through Dietrich Eckart. He was educated to be an architect — which, of course, gives him a point of contact with Hitler, who is impressed by a man who has the gift of erecting systems of ideas on a truly noble scale from the most improbable premises. There are probably few people in Germany to-day who systematize and dogmatize in politics as inexorably as Rosenberg, or who are so capable in an ungovernable fury of construction of basing a detailed fabric of conclusions upon nothing at all. Rosenberg's schemes for foreign policy consist of tremendous compendiums for the archives, and of plans that are not carried out.

RUSSIAN INFLUENCES

What Rosenberg now brought to National Socialism was not German but White Russian foreign policy. Munich was the Coblenz of these emigrants, who would have liked to have incited Germany to a Valmy campaign against the " Jew " Lenin. This policy is only to be understood from the key position that it accords to the Jewish question.

It would be too much to call the Nazi foreign policy that was now inaugurated a Tsarist policy. None the less, its spiritual sources were actually in the Russia of the Tsars, in the world of the Black Hundred and of the true Russian people. These Russian *émigrés,* when obliged to leave their native soil and become nomadic and homeless, brought their ideas, their hopes, and their hatred to Central and Western Europe. The gloomy, bloodthirsty Russian anti-Semitism infected the quieter German type. Merejkowski preached horror of the Bolshevist Antichrist; the protocols of the Wise Men of Zion were eagerly read in Germany. The old Russian anti-Semitism was the obvious instrument for the anti-Bolshevism of the White Russian *émigrés.* Now, in an altogether false connexion, it became the vehicle for the ideas on foreign policy of the German National Socialists. Regarded from the German point of view, the Jewish question is the same as it always was — the anti-Semitism of Hitler and his Baltic friends is not German. It is the companion piece to Ahasuerus — the eternal anti-Semite roaming the earth in pursuit of the Wandering Jew.

At the end of May 1921 the Russian Monarchists held a congress at Bad Reichenhall, in Upper Bavaria. The Hetman Skoropadski, who had been made governor of the Ukraine in 1918 by the German General Staff, played an important part in it. For some years his party had preserved a connexion with the National Socialists until Skoropadski was suspected of French leanings. Russian emigrants, such as Dr. Nemirovitch-Dantchenko, the chief director of Skoropadski's Press, wrote in the *Völkischer Beobachter* and spoke at Nazi meetings.

Rosenberg having had uncomfortable experience of men like Trotsky, Zinovieff, and Kameneff as representatives of Jewry, he decided that: " At bottom practically every Jew is a Bolshevist " — and it has been shown that he was firmly convinced that the Jewish financiers in France were confederates of the Bolshevists. Hitler very soon learnt these facts. In the same New Year's number of the *Völkischer Beobachter* he announced his conviction that the Jews think of one thing only, namely, to make revolutions and to sully the blood of other races, and — fiends that they are — that " every single Jew is active, politically active, at his post in the endeavor to achieve this last great aim."

"FRANCE! AWAKE!"

National Socialist foreign policy was at that time both anti-Semitic and anti-British far more than anti-French. A French Cabinet was described as consisting of " agents of the International Anglo-Saxon Firm," which sounds rather compassionate than malevolent. At the same time a " European Springtime " is promised in the *Völkischer Beobachter,* " as soon as the French nation, whose noble heart we recognize without thought of malice, comes to a realization. . . ." (of what?) " In France as in other parts of the world one can even now see the tendencies which will bring to life the National Socialist of the future." All that France had to do was to shut up its Jewish rabble in the ghettos again. The National Socialist World Revolution was on the way, and its battlecry was: " Anti-Semites of all nations, unite! "

At the same time Hitler, at his first mass meeting at the Zirkus Krone,[1] in February 1921, fulminated against " this England that by systematic devilry harries the people of Ireland to death, and has tricked and deceived the Indians out of their ancient civilized land. Who now believes that England ever cared about the freedom of small nations, since it is trying to rob one of the greatest of civilized peoples on earth of the last shred of liberty? "

At that time Hitler regarded the material goods of a nation as more important even than its military honour. If reparations were abolished, Hitler was prepared to agree to the complete disarmament of Germany.

" Settle the question of indemnities " (they were not yet called tribute), he admonished the German Foreign Minister Simons in the *Völkischer Beobachter* on February 13, 1921, " abolish the twelve per cent. export duty, prevent any possibility of further humiliating supervision by this robber band (i.e. the Allies), give us thereby the means to subsist and free us from the ever-present danger of civil war in Germany, and then we are prepared to free the rest of the world from the terrible danger of the Bavarian Citizens Defence Corps. *Then we will disarm.*" That was a form of foreign policy which Hitler

[1] A place like Olympia in London.

would in later years call bourgeois, a foreign policy that would barter its right to arms and self-defence for the cancellation of a debt.

This was at the time of the London Agreement, which fixed German reparations at one hundred and thirty-two milliards of Marks. Hitler and Rosenberg preached resistance. But not at random. As men who took their politics in a cynical spirit, they had made sure of a strong ally in the East: " Never again will we sign anything a few minutes too soon! All Russia is now in revolt against the Jewish terror." (Rosenberg.) And: " The Bolshevist régime is beginning to totter, the Russian worker is waging desperate war on the Jewish bloodhounds." (Hitler.)

This foreign policy of the year 1921, urged on by General Ludendorff, General Hoffmann, and Rechberg, written out fair by Rosenberg, and presented to the people by Hitler in serial form, aimed at an anti-Semitic, anti-Bolshevist, anti-British Europe. Its backbone was to be an alliance between an enlightened Germany and an enlightened France.

THE FIRST MASS MEETING

Whether danger was to be apprehended from this foreign policy or not, it gave Hitler more elbow-room. He came to know Ludendorff personally. The two men had a bond of sympathy over a matter of domestic policy, namely, the fight against South German Federalism. Later on their paths diverged, and they did not come together again until the summer of 1923.

Hitler's following increased. True, he had not " got " the masses yet. Shortly before the London Agreement the " patriotic " opposition arranged a mass meeting of more than twenty thousand people on the Odeon Square. Hitler was anxious to speak, but at that moment the band struck up a lively tune and the voice of Munich's most fiery speaker was drowned in the noise. At all events he had seen what crowds could be brought together by the desire to protest against the London Agreement. One hundred and thirty-two milliards of Marks would be at the disposal of any one who could stage a protest demonstration. For the first time Hitler ventured to take Munich's largest hall, the Zirkus Krone, on February 3, 1921. The hall holds a maximum of eight thousand people; four thousand came. The audience was carefully spaced out, and the place looked reasonably full. And although this might be regarded as a partial failure, Hitler now showed the rest of the world what fighting meant. His rivals went proudly home congratulating themselves on their twenty thousand. Hitler indefatigably drummed his people into the Zirkus Krone again the following week, because he knew that at a time when the whole atmosphere is electric the masses too are tireless. And so gradually he got his eight thousand together. In days to come he was to bring up the numbers far beyond the twenty thousand with which his rivals had been satisfied.

The movement grew. The little association of butchers and bakers and candlestickmakers gradually faded into obscurity. A new coterie gathered about Hitler, of a different, but remarkably lower, middle-class type. Excitable, reckless, even dubious characters, but at all events interesting, like Hitler himself. Most of them were more worldly-wise than he, but none of them was able to rise to his heights of nervous fury at decisive moments. Hitherto the only " gentleman " of the Party, Dietrich Eckart was now joined by Rosenberg and the young overseas German student, Rudolf Hess, who was to become Hitler's best friend, his private secretary, and constant companion. These were the men who — selflessly or otherwise — believed in him.

THE "LEADER"

Once again the old saying proved true that if three persons make up their minds to work for anything, they will get it, even if it be the conquest of the world. For the first time Hermann Esser hailed Hitler as " the Leader " after the meeting in the Zirkus Krone, and thus brought the " Round Table " company of National Socialist leaders into being, a group of men whose constant tenet is the despotic authority of Hitler over the common herd of Party members.

From outside, too, " smart people " with famous names began to display an interest in the movement. Helmuth von Mücke, the commander of the *Ayesha* and a national hero, joined the Party. He was a man who took social service very seriously, and he interpreted the name of the National Socialist Party more literally than did the Leader himself. Already, however, dissensions were beginning to appear among the leaders. Esser conceived a violent hatred against

Rosenberg, which in moments of aberration he also directed against Hitler.

Hitler began to believe in himself. For some time to come he was still to remain the humble " corporal " beside other more influential, better educated, quicker-witted men. He might even realize this for a moment when he faced Ludendorff or Pöhner. But when he was alone, when words streamed from his lips or his pen, then he was already dreaming of " a day when some iron-willed man shall appear, possibly with dirty boots but with a pure soul and a mailed fist, who will put an end to the words of drawing-room heroes, and give the nation deeds."

The man with the iron will! It was a fair assumption that this was intended for none other than the gifted orator who addressed four thousand people and probably thought there were eight thousand in the heat of the moment. He himself wore " dirty boots," since he had failed in his examinations, and regarded it as a mark of distinction to be only a " simple corporal " among his companions the Lieutenant and the General. Surely he was the man who, in spite of dirty boots, surpassed all the rest in intelligence, in rapid adjustment to unusual situations; who not only understood Fascism which was then arising in Italy, but also the methods of his spiritual brother, Mussolini, who had also come out of the trenches with dirty boots — he would " give the nations deeds."

An Italian Fascist was later to dub this quasi-Roman a " Julius Caesar in a Tyrolese hat." As yet, however, the Viennese bricklayer's labourer was more to the fore. Scoffing at the new German eagle, he declared in the *Völkischer Beobachter*: " The majority of the populace are much more interested in barndoor fowls, the sound common sense of the people laughs at the flaunting creature." But then comes the deeper note: " The overwhelming majority of the people does not regard the new *Reich* symbol as the mark of free and honourable men, but as the brand of Cain and of the vilest treason." In this mosaic of styles the popular note rings true and the Caesarean note forced. His aim, meanwhile, was to become a Caesar of propaganda, to whom the imperial tone is natural but who can descend to the level of the people if necessary. A few years later he was to exclaim without a blush at the end of a New Year speech: " The Brown Guard greets Destiny." And when, finally, in 1932 the SA was for a short time prohibited, Hitler echoed the words of the Duce: " So long as they have hearts they will be devoted to me."

THE CALL TO THE GALLOWS

At the time of his first great successes a dangerous tendency to sarcasm threatened to ruin his effectiveness. His speech was at times reminiscent of the Jewish jargon. That was nature's punishment for his giving too close an imitation of the manner and way of thought of the " chosen people " to his audiences. When he refers to the " gabbling of hysterical revolutionary geese, beginning with the old Jewish slut Rosa (Luxemburg) and going on to this old Jewish bastard, this Solomon, our beloved Kurt Eisner," then his invective is no longer telling. He has overstepped the mark. It is much more effective when he cries: " Our suggestion is that Viktor Kopp shall be hanged before the windows of the Russian — that is, nowadays, the Jewish — Embassy. Severing and Hörsing should be given not less than twenty years' hard labour. . . ."

Here are the first definitely formulated threats of revenge. For the first time he openly mooted the idea of " heads rolling." The Programme announced the death penalty only for usurers and profiteers. But on April 28, 1920, Hitler declared: " We demand that all the traitors to the nation from Erzberger to Simons (afterwards President of the Supreme Court), including all the parliamentary rabble that has participated in their crimes, shall be brought before a Supreme Court of Justice. We categorically insist, moreover, that these criminals shall not die by an honourable bullet but by the rope. We venture even now to draw the attention of a future Supreme Tribunal of the Nation to the fact that as a result of economy in lighting, a great number of our lamp-posts are unused."

The *Völkischer Beobachter* published that word for word. In spite of its bombast it was in those days an excellent paper for its purpose, much better than it ever was afterwards. This was due to the successful efforts of the young leader-writer Esser in unearthing the secrets of Jewish homes. He had far more journalistic talent than Hitler.

Hitler understood how to appeal to the masses, but not to the individualist—the reader. The crowd is credulous, the reader critical; he must be approached concretely, which Hitler never could do. In this respect the more robust, more daring, and more unscrupulous Esser was superior to Hitler. The nursery of this National Socialist journalism was the *Miesbacher Anzeiger*, a tiny local paper that became almost world-famous for a few years on account of its hatred of the Republic. The *Völkischer Beobachter* soon adopted its tone, and it had this advantage over the *Miesbacher* that it had a private political aim.

PALACE REVOLUTION

Hitler's name became known beyond Munich. In the early summer of 1921 he spent a few weeks in Berlin and got in touch with North German Right Wing circles, and spoke at the National Club. His aim was to carry the movement across the borders of Bavaria, and he negotiated amongst others with the Conservative leaders of the former Prussian House of Lords, Count Yorck von Wartenburg and Count Behr. Then, while his back was turned, an episode occurred that forced him to a speedy return. The founders of the Party wanted to overthrow Hitler, who had grown too popular for them.

The impetus was given by the premature extension of the movement beyond the gates of Munich. Outside groups, outside leaders, had been swallowed and not digested. In Nuremberg Julius Streicher, a member of the German Socialist Party, had been working since 1920. By profession he was a schoolmaster, by conviction anti-Semitic and contemptuous of " grand people," by the grace of God an agitator who could compete with Hitler in local effectiveness. He had an inferior intellect to Hitler, his philosophy was more primitive, his speech clumsier, weaker, and more confused. But he surpassed Hitler in moral courage and unscrupulousness. Any mud he threw he picked up himself, and provided at short intervals a grand scandal for the people of Nuremberg, who, like all inhabitants of great cities, enjoyed a sensation. If ever he attacked an opponent — and it was generally a Jew — for any kind of misbehaviour, he was always right up to a point despite exaggerations and generalizations. In short, Streicher, like Esser, surpassed Hitler in concreteness, and thereby made up for his lack of political far-sightedness as well as for his want of good taste and good manners.

Streicher was Hitler's deadly enemy. There had up to the present been no reason why he should submit to him, but he wanted even more — he wanted to conquer him, to take from him the leadership of the Munich Party. Very soon he found an ally in an educationalist, Dr. Dickel, who was head of a Workers' Association in Augsburg, which had been in existence from time immemorial and which was despised by the Trades Unions as a "Yellow Society." He saw something akin to his own views in those of the German Workers Party. At the same time he held extreme views on many points. At the invitation of the Munich Party Dickel made a violent speech in July 1921 against the ownership of large estates, which he regarded as being as dangerous as Judaism — about the only attack that National Socialism ever made on landowners in such a prominent place.

DREXLER AND STREICHER AGAINST HITLER

Dickel's appearance was the signal for revolt. Hitler was in Berlin and was not one of the "Party authorities" who had invited Dickel to speak. These were the old Party Committee, the founders, who had once upon a time brought the German Workers Party into existence with thirty members at the *Café Deutsches Reich,* and who were now forced to watch it slipping more and more out of their control into Hitler's hands.

The founders were not workers, as they believed, nor were they Socialists, as they allowed other people to persuade them. But they were, consciously and with a kind of class-pride, poor people. They regarded the want of creases down their trousers as a sign of higher morality, as something that differentiated them from "profiteers." A sort of ethics of middle-class poverty came into being, the surest sign of a new class. Trousers that needed pressing came to be the pride of the proletarianized middle class as once calloused hands had been of the real proletarians. These people made Anton Drexler the first president of the Society; the Party leadership was put into the hands of a committee of which Hitler was only one member among a number — nevertheless the rest had no influence.

Member No. 7 had managed to make his department — propaganda — into almost the only activity that the Party took seriously. President, committee, members, were nothing but the appendages of this inflated section. Propaganda and the propagandist were externally obvious; the nominal leader might air his meagre powers of oratory in the country. Possibly it is partly due to this division of functions in the old National Socialist Party structure that Hitler turned into a one-sided propagandist who for years regarded political action, the plucking of the fruit, as a subsidiary matter.

The whole shifting of the balance of power was due to the fact that a few hypercritical members whose views were formed slowly and with difficulty, and whose temperaments were unstable, suggestible, but always explosive, had collected themselves into a group against whom nothing could be done. And this temperament had attracted fresh people from more self-confident classes, students and soldiers, who, although they as yet held no Party office, wrote for the *Völkischer Beobachter*, spoke at meetings, covered all their actions with the authority of the propaganda leader, Hitler, and did not care in the least who was the real authority in the Party.

It now became essential to decide who was the real leader. The opportunity arose while Hitler was away. A certain interest had been shown in the National Socialist Party in Berlin. Might not Hitler's interest be weakened by shifting him to Berlin? Would not this be the favourable moment for uniting with Brunner's and Streicher's German Socialist Party? Dickel encouraged Drexler, and Streicher supported the idea. A union with other groups on a basis of equality would have limited Hitler's authority for a long time, especially if he had had to deal with men made of sterner stuff than were the Bavarians.

Hitler returned the attack with the utmost violence. He went straight back to Munich and declared that he would resign from the Party. His opponents, especially Drexler, unprepared for this, tried to reason with him. Compliments like "weak fool" and "low hound" were all that Hitler vouchsafed by way of answer, and he furiously offered to fight out the matter before the whole Party. The Party leaders were not ready to agree to this course. Confronted with the choice between losing Hitler altogether or submitting to him, they preferred the latter alternative. The influences that led them to make the decision will be obvious when it is remembered that Hitler controlled the material weapons of the Party, and, above all, the *Völkischer Beobachter*. For Feder was on his side, and Eckart, who had General von Epp's money, also Rosenberg and Hess — all the " best people," in fact. Esser, too, supported him, and he was, next to Hitler, the most powerful speaker in the Party. The Party could not afford to lose its best men as well as its chief financial resources.

"WHAT DOES HE REALLY LIVE ON?"

Hitler's victory seemed assured when he wrote a letter in the form of an ultimatum to the Party authorities and demanded dictatorial powers. The opposition, however, returned to the fight again. A leaflet was circulated among the members in which serious, and to some extent justifiable, allegations were made against Hitler. Part of it ran as follows:

" A lust for power and personal ambition have caused Herr Adolf Hitler to return to his post after his six weeks' stay in Berlin of which the purpose has not yet been disclosed. He regards the time as ripe for bringing disunion and schism into our ranks by means of shadowy people behind him, and thus to further the interests of the Jews and their friends. It grows more and more clear that his purpose is simply to use the National Socialist Party as a springboard for his own immoral purposes, and to seize the leadership in order to force the Party on to a different track at the psychological moment. This is most clearly shown by an ultimatum which he sent to the Party leaders a few days ago, in which he demands amongst other things that he shall have a sole and absolute dictatorship of the Party, and that the Committee, including the locksmith Anton Drexler, the founder and leader of the Party, should retire. This is what he requires for himself. Further, he demands that no negotiations for union with the other National Socialists and the German Socialists shall be entered into within the next six years. These demands mean nothing more than that the Party is to be kept small and to be made incapable of extension. . . .

" A further point is the question of his occupation and finances.

If ever individual members inquire what he actually lives on and what his previous occupation has been, he always gets excited and loses his temper. . . .

" And how does he carry on his campaign? Like a Jew. He twists every fact and makes out that Drexler is not sufficiently revolutionary and that he wants to return to the parliamentary system. What are the real facts? Drexler has never budged an inch from the standpoint that he occupied when he first founded the Party. It is true that Drexler, in addition to his revolutionary activities, is anxious to show the German workman the path he must follow in order to reach his goal. That is to say, in addition to a biting criticism of the present unacceptable conditions, to encourage sound ideas of political economy.

" Hitler has found a confederate in his intrigues — Hermann Esser. This man whom Hitler himself has repeatedly designated as a baneful influence in the movement, who has repeatedly demanded Hitler's overthrow of Drexler, this man has now suddenly been chosen by Hitler to help him carry out his nefarious intentions. The most curious circumstance of all is that Hitler himself has often said — and there are many witnesses to it: ' I know Esser is a scoundrel, but I shall hold on to him as long as he can be of use to me! ' National Socialists! Make up your own minds about such characters! Make no mistake. Hitler is a demagogue and relies solely on his talents as a speaker. He believes himself capable of leading the German people astray, and especially of filling you up with all kinds of tales that are anything but the truth. Protest against that being done to the honest founders of the National Socialist Party which has been done with those of other Parties! . . ."

HITLER CONQUERS THE PARTY

The leaflet was a bad tactical error. It was undoubtedly right on many points. Hitler really had usurped the Party and diverted it from its original aims — into what direction perhaps he hardly knew himself at that time. He also had men behind him who were shadowy, and who must at all costs remain shadowy, for they belonged to the Reichswehr.

Since, however, the critics had nothing but their suspicions, no proofs and no witnesses, their attack presented no difficulties to the victim. Drexler himself and Körner, his second in command, were obliged to repudiate the leaflet in a public announcement. Hitler confirmed his victory in two extraordinary meetings on July 26 and 29, and dictated the peace terms. The statutes were altered to give the president unlimited authority, and Hitler himself was made president on July 29, with Körner as vice-president. After a laudable submission Drexler was fobbed off with the post of honorary president. He was first defeated and was then put under restraint. The more independent members of the committee left the Party. A certain number of them found their way back again a few months later. In order that there might be no doubt as to who was now master in the Party, Hitler appointed his friend Max Amann as its business manager.

It was the victory of the Cavaliers over the Roundheads in the Party. Its revolutionary temper now acquired a different tone. The influence of the theorist Rosenberg, which was inimical to all forms of Socialism, increased, and the path was made clear for army officers like Röhm and Göring. The money placed in Dietrich Eckart's hand six months earlier by the Reichswehr General von Epp was already paying a dividend. The men now at the head of the Party were on the whole not wealthy people. Behind them, however, stood a financial power. As yet a modest power. Hitler's victory of 1921 was the victory of the financially stronger. It will be seen how later a number of other leaders " bought their way " into the movement.

Instead of the old Party founders who were quietly pushed aside, Hitler now had to deal with more adroit people. He did not in any way become their creature, but he had to learn to play the diplomatic game, to put a counterpoise to any weight that might be growing too heavy. Until 1926 he managed to do this through rise and fall, decay and resurrection. Then began a new and more difficult period that saw the field cleared for a greater game that is still not played out.

CHAPTER III

THE LEADER: A PORTRAIT

THE TIME has now come to study more closely the personality of the man who is regarded by his followers as synonymous with his Party, and who at their desire is to become identified with the fate of Germany. The German nation might surely demand of a politician who exacts such absolute trust from it as Hitler does that he should tell them more about himself than he has hitherto done. The secrecy surrounding the movement and its leader has from the very beginning greatly increased its attractive power, but has caused uneasiness even to some of the most enthusiastic adherents.

HITLER'S PAST

Adolf Hitler was born on April 20, 1889, in Braunau, on the Inn, where his father was an Austrian Customs official. The only sources of information available for his early life are the statements contained in his own autobiography *My Struggle* (*Mein Kampf*), a book lacking in autobiographical talent, very incomplete, and rendered still more unintelligible by much retrospection. All that is known of Hitler's forbears is that they were small farmers in Upper Austria. The so-called *Waldviertel* (Forest Province) where Hitler's ancestors seem to have lived is a poor district remote from the great world, that has in centuries past been the scene of peasant revolts and religious dissensions. For many decades, however, it has been rigidly Catholic. Alois Hitler, Adolf Hitler's father, began life as a cobbler, and after years of hard struggle achieved his dearest wish of becoming a Government official. His tenacity has been transmitted to his celebrated son. The name Hitler — exceedingly rare in that form — was originally spelt Hiedler (or possibly Hüttler) and appears to be derived from *Hütte*, a hut. Adolf Hitler's paternal grandfather was named Johann Georg Hiedler; his paternal grandmother's maiden name was Schicklgruber. At first Alois Hitler — Adolf's father — bore his mother's name. It was only in later life that his father legitimized him. This is a common occurrence in those parts and is not looked upon as in any way remarkable. It is worthy of note that many of the Hitler family have been very long-lived. Alois Hitler's mother was forty-two when he was born. Adolf Hitler himself is the child of a third marriage. His father was fifty-two at the time of his birth. These facts go to prove the existence of a strong peasant vitality in the family.

Adolf Hitler spent his early childhood in Passau, on the Bavarian-Austrian frontier. The family later moved to Linz, on the Danube. There Hitler was taught history by a teacher whose Pan-German views were regarded as revolutionary in the Austria of Francis Joseph. As a teacher his greatest fault was his distortion of world history into a Teutonic heroic epic. To this day Hitler has never recovered from the after-effects of this partisan and megalomaniac mental diet, and the favourite hero of the Austrian Hitler is the Prussian Frederick the Great. Moreover, Hitler had no check put upon his childlike credulousness and his tendency to see everything in broad and far too simple outlines. By the age of sixteen Hitler had already lost both his parents and had recovered from a severe pulmonary illness. He himself declares that in the eyes of his dying father he appeared as a misbegotten son destined to be a failure in life. He was no good at school and spent the last two years of his mother's life in idleness at home. These unpromising traits are touched upon lightly, but sufficiently clearly, in his own autobiography. He excuses his failure at school by saying that his " ideal " was to become a painter. The Principal of the Academy of Fine Arts in Vienna subsequently told Hitler dryly that he was wholly devoid of artistic talent. Nevertheless, Hitler certainly possessed an aptitude for drawing. At the same time his lack of a proper elementary education as well as his not having passed the customary examinations made it impossible for him to study at the Viennese School of Architecture.

The youthful Hitler began his career by reproaching himself for having wasted his talents rather than for being undisciplined. He refused to avail himself of the free education which he might have enjoyed in common with his fellow-citizens. Of private study there is no suggestion. It is true that Hitler was a voracious reader and a passionate theatre-goer. Wagner was the greatest star in his musical firmament. All that is known of this period in Hitler's life would seem to indicate that he was then well on the way to being a wastrel. Then, suddenly, Fortune smiled upon him. His monetary resources gave out. Hitler found himself compelled to abandon his pretence of study and to accept any work that came his way. Unfortunately he was not trained for anything, and was therefore obliged to become a casual bricklayer's labourer. He had fallen from his high estate as student, artist, genius; he had become a hod-carrier. His father had handed on to him his feeling for class distinctions. If he were to keep faith with that belief Hitler would have to show himself a strong character indeed. Otherwise misfortune would prove his moral undoing. As it turned out, Hitler had sufficient strength of will to carry out his determination never to become a "proletarian." In theory he was disposed to hold Socialist views. In practice, however, Hitler still had much to learn. One of his earliest discoveries in this field was the solidarity of the working class. His fellow-workers tried to force him to become a member of their trade union. What? He — an artist? In that instant the Hitler who had temporarily fallen from his high estate resolved to break for ever with the proletariat. "My clothes were still comparatively tidy, I was careful in my speech, and reserved in manner. I only wanted work so as not to starve, so as to give myself the means of furthering — however slowly — my education. I should probably not have troubled about those around me if. . . ." If those surrounding him had not troubled about him and demanded that he should join the organization that defends the workers' modest rights.

Hitler absolutely refused to join the Union. He neither could nor would become the comrade of people who "deny everything," who dub the nation an invention of the capitalists, the country the instrument of the middle class for the exploitation of the workers, the Law a means of oppressing the proletariat, schools an institution for breeding slaves, morality the sign of meek and foolish patience.

The immediate consequence was that his companions forced him to give up his job; and by so doing sowed the seed of anti-Marxism in him.

At the age of about twenty, Hitler changed his occupation and began to learn architectural drawing. Politically he remained an observer, and probably at that time politics were not his chief interest. A belief in Pan-Germanism and a hatred of the Danubian monarchy were relics of his schooldays at Linz. This faith and this hatred had animated German Austria from 1897 onwards, since Badeni's Czechophil language regulations, and since the rise of the German Nationalist movement under the leadership of Wolf and Schönerer in the 'eighties.

The racial question was bound to arise in a town like Vienna, that was inhabited by Germans and Slavs, by Magyars, Italians, and Rumanians. Its special characteristic, anti-Semitism, was of a particular national type there, owing to Vienna's harbouring so many Eastern Jews. Dr. Karl Lueger, the burgomaster of Vienna, was the leader of the Christian Socialists and a champion of the anti-Semitic movement. This distinguished man made a great impression upon Hitler, and certainly a much stronger one than did the then existing Austrian National Socialists, with whom he had no dealings. Lueger's anti-Semitism, however, was directed towards suppressing Jewry by baptism. Hitler, on the other hand, developed a biological anti-Semitism, regarding heritage as all-important and opinion not at all. According to his own account all this must have been germinating in his mind during the years he spent in Vienna. It is possible that he left Vienna a confirmed anti-Semite; but it may be doubted whether he was then already a fully fledged anti-Marxist.

In 1912, ostensibly as an architectural designer, actually as a house painter, he removed to Munich, where he felt much more at home than he did in Vienna. It is not known why he disliked living in Vienna. Munich became the city of his choice. He had been exempt from Austrian military service on account of physical unfitness. In the middle of August 1914 he volunteered like others of his age. He was drafted to the sixteenth Bavarian Infantry Reserve Regiment. This regiment suffered tremendous losses. As regards Hitler's military exploits it may suffice to say that he won the Iron Cross, First Class, a decoration rarely bestowed upon a corporal. He was twice wounded. It may seem curious that he was never promoted to the rank of sergeant; that a man with a gift for leadership should not have made himself felt in circumstances in which a clever man could so easily come to the fore. In 1916 he refused a summons to transfer to the Austrian army. Towards the end of the War he was severely gassed and almost blinded. For a second time he went through a period of serious physical disturbance, which showed itself mentally in hysterical outbursts.

At the time of the German Revolution, Hitler was in hospital at Pasewalk. He was now twenty-nine years old and a man of many talents and many shortcomings. He paid a great price for his advantages; he was less mature than the average man of his age; and while he had perhaps read and pondered more deeply than many, he was seriously lacking in ordinary common sense and in an understanding of and sympathy for other people's points of view. His regimental comrades looked on him as not quite normal, and he had no friends. There are advantages to this isolation. He had no ordinary sound common sense to teach him respect for others, and he cared nothing for public opinion. His outbursts of childishness have become his strength as a propagandist. He can sway assemblies of people just as a hysterical child will tyrannize over its family.

Hitler's life from the time he left the army until the time he became a politician is well known and has already been described. Most professional politicians are anxious to preserve existing authority and only want to make their own share in it as great as possible. That is not Hitler's way. His attitude to the pre-War Powers remains conservative, but he never dreamt of trying to preserve their existence. It was enough for him that they did exist; he himself wanted to be a painter or an architect. He believed in the aristocracy. An aristocracy needs vassals and he was by nature quite ready to be a vassal. He was one of those who was introduced to politics by the War, that is, by a national experience. People who are driven into politics not by a native urge but by the chances of life do not always prove to be the most politically gifted. Hitler, however, is certainly not one of the least gifted among them.

He was an admirer of Bismarck and of Frederick the Great, and while he observed certain excrescences in the Empire of William II that might well be pruned away, he relied in the main upon the recuperative power of the nation, and his conservatism was on the whole content to leave things as they were. Then all at once the Revolution seized upon his imagination and forced him to protest. He had enough temperament to carry his protest as far as counter-revolution, but anything revolutionary was utterly antagonistic to his disposition. It may be said of him that a man who advocates the principle of leadership, of the authoritarian State, and who admires Bismarck, has for fourteen years been a revolutionary despite himself. At the beginning he was still the indignant, loyal subject who had been robbed of his king. It was the well-planned policy of his fellow-workers, possibly also the example of Mussolini, that turned him into the "Leader," and at first it was a leader in indignation, who regarded his task to be the crushing of the Marxists. It was in October 1923 that he declared that his work would be completed when he had raised up the German people.

The length of the work and the shortness of life gradually turned his conception of himself as the leader of a revolution into that of himself as a ruler. Early tendencies to an exaggerated self-esteem alternated with an interesting, if somewhat turgid, habit of thought. In April 1922, not long before he was given a month's imprisonment for breaking up a meeting, he said that two thousand years ago another man had been dragged away to prison, and that it had been done by the same race that wanted to put him there now. A year later in a private conversation he said: "We are only forerunners; I am waiting for the Redeemer." That is no small personal tragedy. One who is waiting for the Messiah, who yearns to be ruled, will in the end take authority unto himself, because no other is found to do it. His character cannot bear the strain. Hence his governance will always remain a symbol and a promise, and will never be a fact.

AN EDUCATIONAL TRAGEDY

Across this sense of personal failure runs a more personal one. Opponents and certain disrespectful members of his Party have sneered at Hitler as a half-educated man. This is the cheapest of all insults and is in this case only partly true. If it is a question of a mere accumulation of knowledge, Hitler certainly surpasses the average university man. An amazing memory has stored in his brain a mass of facts culled from his reading, and they are by no means undigested facts. The form in which he passes on his information to his audiences proves the opposite, even though the speaker's own inferences are at times surprising. It is also false to say that he is lacking in specialized knowledge. He was probably a fair architectural draughtsman. His ideas on foreign policy, which have become more mature as time has gone on, show evidence of serious mental effort.

The absurdities of his oratorical style are well known. It is painful to hear him raving over and over again about the great and unexampled genius of those who have made world history — then he is really reminiscent of the Lower Fourth Form. Then he speaks like an ignorant, rapturous hobbledehoy from Linz repeating a poem on the history of the world at the school speech-day, and who moreover finds it difficult not to talk in dialect: "How are Nations founded? By glorious leaders and by a people that deserves to have a crown of laurels bound about its brows."

That is at all events a passionate call to arms. But it is terrible when it is to be written with a "brazen stylus," like his rejection in 1928 of the Stahlhelm demand for the extension of the President's powers: "Only the determination to do battle of a man who is fighting for his life leads to effective freedom of action in regard to the lives of others. . . . Advocating the opinion that men can be rendered capable of reconstituting the fate of nations by means of the concession of greater constitutional rights achieved along the lines of democratic sanction, only shows how one is oneself — even though quite unconsciously — infected with the virus of Democracy, and for fear of the power of a personality prefers to increase the importance of the office."

It sounds like an office-boy let loose on the dictionary. The idea is excellent. What it really comes down to is that Hitler wants to say: "Why put Hindenburg on the throne when you've got somebody like me?" Obviously his inferior command of language is not due to his never learning to write essays in the Sixth Form. Faults of style imply faults of character.

The tragedy of his education is a tragedy of character. He is an unsuccessful pupil who has failed in his examinations. It was not simply bad luck, it was his own fault; and he will always be haunted by the remembrance. Any one who has had dealings with him has remarked his awkwardness when confronted with men who are secure in position and reputation, who possess degrees and diplomas. It shows itself either in shyness or in an exaggerated brusqueness. Before the law courts, for instance — how undignified is the alternation between shouting and uncertain, positively fawning, subservience to the Judge. Not, of course, during the last few years when he has only appeared for a brief examination as a witness, but at earlier trials when he was still a member of the Party and not a famous man.

It seems hardly credible that a man of Hitler's repute should be embarrassed by the mere social position of others. Probably men of rank and dignity seem to him examples of what he might have become if he had not wasted opportunities in his youth. Even his fantastic fame cannot be a satisfactory substitute for the good conscience that he might have enjoyed. Over-compensation is one of the traits of this man whose talents are so one-sided.

THE LEGEND OF THE "INSTINCT-MAN"

What natural gifts determined Hitler's fate?

Early pulmonary trouble, and being so severely gassed during the War that he nearly lost his sight and his mental stability, have given him that physical delicacy that often liberates the mind and sometimes strengthens moral fibres. From the very beginning of his political career Hitler — an ex-soldier — was markedly civilian in outlook. During the inflation years, when almost every young German wore puttees, he invariably wore slacks. He was very careful at that time always to deal with the SA and its officers in the character of people's commissioner. He describes a high value to force in politics; according to the views of the Left, too high a value. But within the Right he has always been the most pronounced anti-militarist — in so far as militarism is taken to mean the conduct of political affairs by the army. Arms are in his opinion the most important political tool — but only a tool; neither hand nor head. It was over this point that the gulf yawned between him and Röhm (later SA leader), which was bridged by the latter's honest and straightforward nature.

Hitler is not a strong man. Abundant testimony on the part of his staff, of his political followers, witnesses to his lack of self-control, to his hysterical outbursts even in private conversation, and to their sudden dying away to stuttering as soon as any one else speaks, asks questions, or insists upon a reasonable discussion. There is nothing stable in this effervescent character. He has powers, but the decisive test of power — self-mastery — is not found in him. A gloomy, indeed brutal, sternness at certain times replaces his lack of that natural dignity which can only come as a result of self-control. An exact analysis of his great apparent success even during recent years would make it plain how nervously he avoids any really big decision. He has not achieved greatness so much as had greatness thrust upon him.

He is not a will-man but a brain-man, and, it must be admitted, a notable one. The planning of his campaign for power is an intellectual achievement of a high order.

He is the worst kind of player, the man who cannot bear to lose, who sees defeat approaching in the innocent guise of an awkward question; he is like one possessed, raging through his offices on the least provocation; threatening to box the ears of his oldest fellow-workers because the manuscript of his latest speech has been lost — the latest is always the most important. He is easily impressionable, and his calmer friends — and which of them is not calmer? — often shamelessly abuse their influence over him. Nevertheless, in spite of all, he manages to assert his convulsive will. And it is all due to his brains.

Those of his opponents who underrate him — and most of them do — regard him as an instinct-man, who as a result of his clairvoyant understanding of the spirit of the masses always knows how to say what is the right thing at any given time without regard for objective truth. A character that can after all be freely tested could hardly be judged more superficially. In the early days Hitler not seldom failed as a popular speaker in spite of all his cleverness; he himself admits this in his book. Like all speakers, he had to learn. His excellent brains helped him to learn quickly and to acquire all the routine tricks that any orator could possibly possess. But instinct —— ?

Instinct-men are usually cool and collected, for instinct is a still, small voice. Hitler, on the other hand, who on the smallest provocation shouts himself and his inhibitions down, who always chooses wrong when he has to make a quick decision, who is never master of an unexpected situation — this Hitler is not the man to obey the directions of an inner voice. Any one who studies his speeches, not in an abridged form in the newspapers, but at the meetings themselves or in the practically verbatim reports of the *Völkischer Beobachter*, will find them distinguished by quite a different characteristic than a demagogic sureness of aim — namely, logic.

NO WILL BUT A BRAIN

His utterly logical way of thought is Hitler's strength. There seems to be no other German politician of the present day who has the moral courage that he possesses to draw the inevitable conclusions from any given situation, to announce them despite the mockery of those who think they know better, and, above all, to act on them. It is this gift of logic which makes Hitler's speeches so convincing. When in 1923 the Reichswehr General von Lossow allowed himself to be forced by the Bavarian Government into requiring the VIIth Division of the Reichswehr to take an oath of loyalty to the Bavarian State, and when Lossow then sought some means to retreat and to make his peace with the Reich authorities, Hitler said to him: " It is impossible from a military point of view that there should be forgiveness or reconciliation. A military commander of your standing who rebels against his chief, must have made up his mind beforehand to go on to the bitter end; otherwise he is an ordinary mutineer and must fall."

It reads very simply, and the course of events proved to be as he said. But Lossow refused to admit it or, which was more important, to act on it. Five months later he did in fact fall, although he had in the meantime acquired merit for his conduct during the suppression of Hitler's attempted *coup*. Hitler had seen what was historically obvious five months sooner than other people because, as he said, the old saw was always true that if a man was " in for a penny " he was always also " in for a pound! " It was only logical.

Any one who refuses to realize the Nazi Leader's gift of logic will probably also think that there is nothing much in his book *My Struggle*.

At the risk of contradiction not only from his opponents but also from those of his followers who are critically inclined, the present writer maintains that it is an excellent book, full of keen criticism often excellently expressed. True, it is also an ill-constructed book, full of repetitions, and therefore on the whole dull. Nevertheless, it contains a number of excellent points. It is, of course, the work of an international anti-Semite, whose premises must for the time being be admitted.

A BAD PROPHET

The good qualities of this man's intellect here come to an end. Clever though his conclusions are, his discernment shows to the same degree unreliability, carelessness and ignorance. At deduction from a given fact he is unrivalled; at establishing the fact he is often seriously at fault, because instead of investigating the truth or otherwise of facts for himself, he is fettered by previous opinions. Thus in the year 1921 he definitely prophesied that the Soviet power would very soon fall. In the autumn of 1923 he exclaimed indignantly that surely the hypocrite Stresemann must know very well that the French would never clear out of the Ruhr again. During his imprisonment at Landsberg he announced solemnly to his fellow-prisoners that the swastika flag would float from the Palace in Berlin in the year 1928, and in the autumn of 1931 he assured his Harzburg followers that he would be in power in three months at the latest.

One of the most noteworthy achievements of his syllogistic thought is the theory about expansion towards the East. Starting from the assumption that the German nation will increase during the next hundred years, he quite logically realizes that any plans of internal settlement must be inadequate, and demands extension towards the East by the use of military force. He would be perfectly right if the population of Germany were really still on the increase; but this is just where Hitler is wrong. The population is on the decrease and a realization of this necessitates statistical inquiry.

It is of course true that other politicians have also been known to make mistakes. But Hitler claims infallibility: "I have never told you," he cried in 1922 after the Rathenau murder, "that such and such things *may* come, but always that they *will* come, because they must come and it cannot be otherwise. And what we foresaw has now come to pass." He was talking at that time of the " prophecy " that the efforts of the Reich Government towards centralization and Bavarian Federalism would lead to conflict — which it hardly needed clairvoyance to realize.

It will be objected that logic that begins with false premises and leads to false conclusions cannot have much value. It must be admitted, however, that Hitler knows one thing very well indeed — he knows his own people. The systematization of error is the stuff of many of his theories. To err is human, and is international in politics; but systematization is German. And this is the germ of truth in his politics. He saw and prophesied most definitely how the Germans would react to certain political facts. He was right where all wisdom failed and all European conventions were outraged.

HOW HE CARRIES AN AUDIENCE WITH HIM

The following passage from a speech delivered in April 1922 gives an epitome of the whole man:

" The Jews have shown real genius in profiting by politics. This capitalistic people, which was brought into existence by the unscrupulous exploitation of men, has understood how to get the leadership of the Fourth Estate into its own hands; and by acting both on the Right and on the Left it has its apostles in both camps. On the Right the Jew does his best to encourage all the evils there are to such an extent that the man of the people, poor devil, will be exasperated as much as possible — greed of money, unscrupulousness, hard-heartedness, abominable snobbishness. More and more Jews have wormed their way into our upper-class families; and the consequence has been that the ruling class has been alienated from its own people.

" That was also the first step towards their work on the Left. For he was there on the Left too, the low demagogue. Men of intelligence and of our own people who were leaders among the working people were forced through sheer disgust to leave their posts, firstly owing to the international views that were propagated, and secondly owing to the Marxist theory that all private ownership was theft. That was too much for our national economic intelligence. And so the Jews succeeded in isolating the movement from all national elements. And furthermore, by cleverly exploiting the Press, they succeeded in influencing the masses to such an extent that the Right looked upon the faults of the Left as the faults of the working men, and the faults of the Right seemed to the German worker to be the faults of the so-called bourgeoisie. And neither realized that the faults on both sides were the intended outcome of these fiendish alien influences. And so the grimmest jest in history was brought about — that stock-exchange Jews became the leaders of the German Labour movement. While Moses Cohen, the chairman, stiffens the board of his Company so that they shall be as inflexible, that is to say, as unreasonable, as possible concerning the demands of their workpeople, his brother, the Labour leader Isaac Cohen, is in the factory yard egging on the masses: 'Look at them! They only want to oppress you! Throw off your chains!' And upstairs his brother is helping to forge those chains. The people is to destroy the backbone of its independence, its own trade, so as all the more surely to be fettered in the Jews' golden bonds of eternal slavery to money."

This must be imagined as being spoken in a hoarse voice rising from deepest bass to a shrill trumpet blast — no human crowd could listen and not rage. It is a brilliant elaboration and dramatization of the "Wise Men of Zion."

THE RABBINICAL CONSPIRACY

The whole is based upon a large number of demonstrable errors. That prototype of all Jewish Labour leaders, Lassalle, far from rejecting the non-Jewish intellectuals, encouraged them, and indeed warned his comrades against Jewish leaders. The Jewish Socialists may be shown frequently to be renegades from their *milieu* and the enemy rather than the friend of their brother Jews. Finally, the scene in which Isaac Cohen is supposed to be inciting the workers in the factory yard is altogether contrary to the usual assertions that the Jew is much too cowardly and indolent to mix with the workers. Nevertheless upon all these errors a great and forcefully expressed argument is finally based.

The proposition to be proved is the existence of a plot. By an ancient trick of sophistry, this turns in the course of the argument imperceptibly into a proved assumption. From this antecedent follow most conclusively the individual theorems and practical applications, which should really be themselves proved before being used as evidence: the conspiracy exists, for the Socialist-revolutionary activities of the Jews are only directed towards the destruction of national prosperity; they are only directed towards the destruction of national prosperity because they are the outcome of a Jewish plot; but the plot exists because —— And such chains of reasoning are impossible to attack at any one point because they are fallacious all round. Even if it were ever possible to force a discussion down to first principles, and to ask for the proof of the conspiracy, then the answer would be something of this sort: the conspiracy can only be recognized by its effects; if its origin were known it would have been destroyed long ago. In any case, people would always rather believe in a disclosure that is ninety per cent. not proved, than in a hundred per cent. denial.

Especially was that true of the people of the first post-War years who were unwilling to acquiesce in the issue of the War. It seemed to them no longer true to say that Germany had put up a magnificent defence in the great struggle, unless the unfortunate outcome might be to some extent explained by the black art. Siegfried died because of the leaf of a lime-tree, Balder by the magic wood of the parasite mistletoe. All the legends of kindly giants and malevolent dwarfs seemed to be symbolic of the fate of Germany, of the fall of this World Power because of something small, insignificant, despised, unnoticed — because of the Talmudist Congress at Bâle. That a great struggle had been greatly lost nobody was willing to admit; it seemed more honourable to have succumbed to vermin than to the sword. " It is the fault of the Jews " was the best comfort bad losers could give themselves. This, be it noted, was the popular anti-Semitism of the first post-War years. The deeper conception of the problem, which was always coexistent with it, was later cultivated especially by the Berlin Nazis with Otto Strasser at their head. Rosenberg, on the other hand, always clung literally and credulously to the orthodox views concerning the " Wise Men of Zion."

THE ORATOR

The speech quoted above makes it possible to look deep into the soul of the alleged " instinct-man," Hitler. No instinct could be more seriously at fault. His object was to open the eyes of the deluded working classes. How was it to be done? Hitler told them that they had been allowing themselves to be deluded by the Jews for the past fifty years. He told it them most emphatically. But he might have said it even more emphatically, and it would only have welded more closely the workers and their leaders. It is hopeless to expect to detach a man from his Party, his convictions, or his fellows, by telling him that the bonds have been forged with lies from the very beginning. That will only bring indignant denial. The people should be told that what they wanted, what they believed, is as right as it always was; but that traitors have lately come into the camp and have undermined everything. That is what the brothers Strasser did later, and they had at least a partial success. Hitler, on the other hand, having no understanding of the working man's mind, did not realize that he had insulted his audience — when he had one to insult. Actually the people did not come. The *Völkischer Beobachter* once complained that the Marxist Party successfully kept away the workers from National Socialist meetings.

Hitler's words to the workers came from the hearts of quite a different class. But that is for a later chapter.

Any one who really wants to study the art of his oratory will find all the elements in this speech. First of all, the fable of a world conspiracy. This alone has gone half-way towards giving him the victory. The idea of a conspiracy is arresting, firstly, because of its object which is the audience itself; secondly, because of the ingenuity of its methods. Those who are involved in it are people who have always been vaguely suspected of such ingenuity, namely, Jews. Its effects come to light in the most diverse places — it is a " world-wide " affair. They appear, moreover, in places where they would hardly be expected — among one's own surroundings. Having explained this in two or three different ways, Hitler uses it as a background for the picture he sketches in a few masterly strokes which now fits to a nicety into its place — that of the two brothers Moses and Isaac Cohen. An individual, a man reading this for himself, may by applying a little logic see the shallowness of the arguments. But a crowd, addressed forcefully as a whole, will be carried along without a protest.

Hitler's masterpiece is the brilliant finale. He says, in effect: "Who and what is international? Obviously, the German worker is the international brother of the Chinese coolie, of the Malay stoker, of the illiterate Russian lumberman. All these people are, of course, much nearer to him than his German employer. My dear friend, do not contradict, you have been told that for decades and you have believed it. But actually there is only one International, and it is able to exist because it rests upon a national basis — that is, the International of the Jewish Stock-Exchange dictatorship. That is a system controlled by a single people, who have a common origin, a common religion, and a common language — in fact, by . . ." The voice of the speaker is drowned in vociferous applause.

THE WANDERING JEW

Hitler has developed a good deal since he first came into the public eye — the question is whether he has developed for the better. Those of his own Party who criticize him have sought to transform his somewhat naïve ideas into more truly "intellectual" concepts, and to find an outlet for his bourgeois feelings in setting before him a programme to be realized. Is that for the better? A form of anti-Semitism that attacks not merely the world-conspiracy of a few dozen Rabbis but the destruction of civilization and prosperity by the "Jewish spirit," will naturally meet with more sympathy from better intellects and even possibly from opponents. But it is out of touch with the political spirit which needs a concrete enemy — just as Socialism is paralysed by attacking capitalism instead of the capitalist exploiters. There is reason to believe that Hitler — a great orator now and Chancellor — has not really given up his belief in Judaism as the personification of evil. As late as 1925 he averred without the quiver of an eyelash: "The *Frankfurter Zeitung* spends its time bellowing to the world at large that the Protocols of the Wise Men of Zion are based on a forgery — the best proof that they are genuine!" Such a simple belief in a Rabbinical conspiracy is hard to destroy by merely growing older and more experienced.

This picture may nevertheless be as nearly related to the world of realities as all the rest — it is in itself so complete, so perfect in the congruence of details as none other of its kind. Individual details come from other palettes; their union is the work of a strong head which is not interested in truth, but has evolved a design for a new world. The mind that constructed this system has been victorious with it over facts.

THE MASTERLY NEURASTHENIC

He uses the same means to get the better of his own weaknesses. Unstable though he is, irresolute, suggestible, and easily cowed by a stronger personality — his brain restrains everything and enforces self-control. Although he is diffidently expansive in his leisure hours, makes no attempt at a heroic pose before unimportant visitors, lets his ebullitions of feeling have free play unrestrained by personal pride, leaves his affairs to get into a muddle, puts off for months taking a minor decision, and delegates important parts of his work out of sheer indolence, this man at really critical times surpasses all his associates as a driving force. He will work out the tactics of his behaviour for days, indeed weeks, beforehand, planning attack and counter-attack, advance and retreat, step by step. He will weld together his band of sympathizers, neutralize opposition by counter-opposition, prepare arguments, charge himself with tense excitement — and before the discussion begins the decision has fallen. Then he can calmly steer his uncontrolled nature towards the required effect, give rein to his neurasthenia as well as to his wrong ideas at exactly the right moment, and when he lets himself go, no wise man will contradict him.

And that is exactly what he is aiming at. Colder intellects may persuade and influence him in his quiet moments; but they must have his agreement, otherwise they labour in vain. Admiring fellow-workers like young Esser sometimes boast of the quickness of his decisions. But they are people who cannot imagine any one's lying awake all night in order to spring a decision upon a committee in the morning.

Dissatisfied men, again, have complained of the opposite. They say that it is a work of art to make him give a definite opinion; that District Leaders, the highest Party officials in fact, have sometimes to wait for months to get one. That may not be the ideal behaviour for a leader. But it is a virtue in a ruler. Thus and no otherwise did Tiberius treat his favourites, Frederick the Great his landowners, Napoleon his marshals. Such dilatoriness certainly does not fit in with the modern machinery of State, which, according to Bismarck, does not expect to be controlled but attended. The National Socialist political system, however, has not got beyond its feudal period yet; at most it might be called a Sultanate with semi-independent Viziers. How can critics imagine that this bundle of unrest is directed by touching a button? Procrastination is not a personal weakness, but is practical political wisdom in face of the Hassans and Mahomet Alis of the National Socialist Party, who seldom wish the leader well, and looked at from the most favourable aspect can be regarded as one-third ambitious servants, and two-thirds ambitious vassals.

Whether the shrewd ruler of the National Socialist Party will also be able to rule a highly organized modern State is at least questionable when his achievements as a Party leader are called to mind.

This man, who changes his moods with such rapidity, clings to his opinions with an obstinacy that wearies political dilettantes — not, indeed, the masses; but then they are not political dilettantes. The brain that is enthroned above this wayward nervous system always guides it back again into the path that it has recognized as the right one. All his vacillations finally lead him back to the rules which he followed at the beginning. He is as true to himself as the magnetic needle that always returns to the North however much it may oscillate.

Opponents have frequently and with great satisfaction quoted the words of General von Lossow, who came to know Hitler thoroughly: "Hitler's moving and suggestive eloquence at first made a great impression on me too. But the more often I heard him, the more did the first impression wear off. I observed that his long speeches practically always contained the same thing. . . ." Most annoying of a politician always to be asking the same thing of an authority that is determined not to do this same thing at all! General von Lossow would probably have been much more pleased if Hitler had told him a different story at times. But then Hitler would have been a story-teller and not a politician.

THE DIPLOMACY OF STRONG WORDS

What was originally a talent for diplomacy is robbed of its efficacy by a lack of self-control. The scene when Lossow spent hours listening to Hitler's dissertations upon his march on Berlin must have been very funny. Lossow had allowed himself to be persuaded by Hitler and Kahr into a " mutiny " against the Reich Government in Berlin, and he was not feeling comfortable. " General von Lossow sat there absolutely broken down," said Hitler during the subsequent trial for high treason. " That may well have been," answered Lossow, as a witness, grinning, " I really was utterly broken down by Herr Hitler's interminable speeches." Lossow had tried to show the People's Tribune by a politely uninterested attitude that he could dispense with his presence. But Hugenberg, Brüning, and Hindenburg can bear witness that when Hitler is seized with the spirit of oratory he is deaf and blind, and gentle hints will not have the smallest effect upon him.

On the other hand, when Hitler has had time to reflect, he can also use his gifts diplomatically. For example, if he is no longer able to avoid a question as to his sources of financial supply: " The Party of Barmat and Kutisker," he shrieks, and his eyes blaze, " the Party of Parvus, Sklarz, and Jacob Goldschmidt, the Party of the Jewish millionaire Rosenfeld think they can sully an idea whose adherents day after day make clear to the German nation by hazarding life and limb how we have grown great — by the heroic devotion of thousands and tens of thousands of German men and youths, who, deterred by no fear of sacrifice, have attacked the enemy and will continue to do so until he finally lies dead on the ground. . . ." From this point on, the reporter need not trouble to continue taking notes. The excited meeting now saves the speaker the trouble of making further explanation as to where the money really does come from.

If he is questioned concerning his attitude to South Tyrol, which, at all events before an audience that tends to the Right, is uncomfortable, he has his answer ready: " Not we have betrayed South Tyrol, but the cowards who stabbed the German army in the back in 1918."

And if a disappointed former fellow-worker like Herr von Graefe asks whether Hitler is still the humble drummer of yesterday or the Caesar of to-morrow he answers: " Do not remind me of the drummer of yesterday, Herr von Graefe. I am and shall always be the drummer of national resurrection, but not for you and your like! "

This shows no small skill — it is tacking with all sails set. Hitler knows how to avoid, to suppress, and to obscure things, in such a manner that his listeners get the impression of temperamental frankness. He makes the most anxious, awkward evasions seem like blows with a battleaxe, and even on his bypaths he travels at ninety miles an hour.

WORDS OF HONOUR

One of the least pleasing aspects of his tactics is the story of his promises and words of honour. Any one who comes to any arrangement with him must be prepared subsequently to be told that his promise was something quite different from what he understood. So it happened in the case of Seisser, the chief of the Bavarian police, who believed himself to have Hitler's promise not to attempt a *coup.* Nonsense, said the Leader, on the contrary! Until a particular date he would cause no disturbances; but from that time on he, Hitler, would regard himself as free of all promises and assurances. How extraordinary that Colonel Seisser should have misunderstood Herr Hitler. But General von Lossow averred that he had received the same promise from Hitler — and, strange to say, the General had also misunderstood the great orator! And so it goes on through the years. Hugenberg and Brüning also lived to discover that it is impossible to understand anything Hitler says aright. In 1932 President von Hindenburg had Hitler's promise to tolerate the Papen Cabinet; and this time the old Field-Marshal was the one to misunderstand Hitler. And later on when Hitler told him that he claimed the whole Government authority, the President misunderstood him again! Dr. Schweyer, the Bavarian Minister of the Interior, to whom Hitler declared unasked: " I give you my word of honour I shall never in this life attempt a *coup* " — he too found that a word of honour can be broken, even if the recipient challenges the giver to keep it three months later. And every time Hitler is morally indignant and insulted at being taken at his word. Since the alleged misunderstandings over Hitler's promises occur so frequently and in connexion with so many different people, it is justifiable to conclude in view of Hitler's uncontrolled character that he simply does not know what he is promising, and that his promises cannot be regarded as those of a person completely capable of conducting business. He will break them as soon as it suits him to do so, and he will still look upon himself as an honourable man.

Schott, who has written a biography of Hitler, calls this man who is sometimes overcome by his nervous fits, and sometimes uses them deliberately for his own ends, an " emotional man," a " dreamer." Schott, himself an emotional preacher, whose heart runs away with his head, has no more realized than have most of the others who have tried to solve the riddle of this greatest popular orator of our time, that a political speaker must have the gift of bringing out things that he has considered coolly as though they were the immediate issue of fiery enthusiasm. Hitler has in his book defended himself indignantly against the charge of being a clumsy retailer of popular *clichés,* or a pious babbler, but his enraptured followers as well as his opponents prefer the ordinary picture. One of his earliest admirers, Houston Stewart Chamberlain, perhaps the first member of the Nazi Party who enjoyed world-wide fame, came nearer to the truth. In 1923 he wrote to Hitler: " You are not in the least like the descriptions I have had of you as a fanatic. In fact, I should describe you as the exact contrary to a fanatic. A fanatic wants to talk people over — you want to convince them."

WHY HE LOOKS AS HE DOES

Hitler is extravagantly vain. So were Napoleon, Goethe, and Bismarck in a more or less subtle manner. Frederick the Great, Scharnhorst, and Lenin were not. Vanity in itself is neither a vice nor a virtue — it all depends on what a man is vain of. " What I say and do are a matter of History " — Hitler said once in the early days of his rise. It is nicely balanced between inspired self-confidence and silliness.

At the beginning his vanity took a negative form — he forbade the publication of any pictures of himself. Possibly an external circumstance was partly responsible in this case, for he had had the small pointed military beard that he had worn in the first post-War years shaved off, and he and his friends had first to grow accustomed to his new appearance. Still, even if it was only a lucky chance, he became the man whose face nobody knew, an exciting secret. The question, " What does Hitler really look like? " excited the population of Munich no less than the other, which was current for several years, " Who is this Hitler who is continually being forbidden by the Government to speak? " The secrecy about his person is, however, not only a propagandist trick. The man is by nature secretive, his life does not lie open to his friends. Questions regarding his private affairs offend him. And although his friend Hess, being ostensibly better informed, may assure them: " I know that this page is clean too " — people do not believe him. It is possible that there really is nothing to hide. All the signs point to Hitler's being a nature incapable of frankness. Any one who trusts him must believe without knowing. His very secrecy gives peculiar emotional power to the attitude of his followers towards him — an old trick of the trade!

His ordinary civilian clothes, to this very day purposely obtained from no sartorial artist of repute, set him apart during the first few years from the fancy grey uniforms of the then leaders of the Right. Since then he has more usually worn the SA uniform, so that his soldiers should not forget their supreme War Lord. " Properly " dressed, however, he is not until after two hours' ardent oration, when his collar is curled like a damp string round his neck, his hair is plastered to his brows, his sleeves are twisted, and buttons torn off.

For public appearances in a " statesmanlike " attitude, he has excogitated a pose that is obviously intended to be reminiscent of Napoleon's folded arms. He lays the lower arms at right angles to the upper arms, straight across the body, cupping one elbow in the opposite hand. It looks very controlled.

His face is a source of embarrassment to his followers and of malicious joy to his opponents. No euphemism will make it anything but an expressionless face. The Munich anthropologist von Gruber has declared it to be racially inferior, and has given abundant reasons. The mouse-coloured strand of hair and the little toothbrush moustache are as ordinary as they can be. Possibly there is a glimmer of something in the eyes. When he is in an excited state, he seems suddenly to be a symbol, the unknown soldier uttering the thoughts of millions of nameless men. Thoughts that three years earlier had made his nameless fellows in the trenches laugh at him for a "lunatic." Possibly this may be the key to his whole personality — the absolute quintessence of mediocrity.

But do great men always look impressive? One is apt to feel distrustful of people who have Goethesque or Napoleonic heads; and it is a well-known fact that great men have generally looked very different from the portraits made of them by the popular imagination. The æstheticism of many epochs and notably of the nineteenth century was apt to bury under god-like traits the abnormality, lack of balance, and morbidity that is frequently the physical expression of greatness. It is only necessary to compare the real head of a man who has himself succumbed to this habit — Mussolini — with those of his photographs which have been got up to make him look like a pseudo-Napoleon. How human and ordinary this stout dictator is in real life. The fact that Hitler does not look like a great man is no proof that he does not possess greatness. What tells more heavily against him is the fact that he talks as great men do in school-readers.

His countenance has altered several times in the last few years. First of all, it gained character — Fate seemed to have turned a piece of raw material into a man. Still more recently there have begun to be signs of an early approach of age and a consequent loss of mental grasp.

How far Hitler's mind is a pathological problem remains for the present a secret among his doctors. No one who sees him frequently, however, could avoid recognizing the pathological features. Some of the symptoms are attacks of morbid shyness, flight into solitude, and at times irresponsible speech.

A LIKENESS

A curious description from an intimate source is extant:

"He has a quick, lively, resourceful mind. The proclamations he issues show stylistic originality and power in spite of a certain coarseness. Finally, most important of all, he has a great and striking gift of natural eloquence.

" Once during a conference the following incident occurred. The Social Democrats had published a leaflet in which he was rudely referred to as a foolish figure of an insolent demagogue. Some one brought this leaflet to the meeting. He read it and suddenly changed. He seemed to grow, and his eyes blazed. He crashed his fist on to the table and began to speak. He spoke words that were not only without significance but that had not even much sense. He threatened ' to wipe the Social Democrats off the face of the earth,' after having demonstrated ' their hypocrisy and shamelessness to all the workers.' Other wild statements followed. But it was not what he said that impressed one. I have often heard Bebel and Tauris. I never saw either of them draw his audience so completely under his spell as this man; and that not in a mass-meeting where it is much easier, but in a small room where a few men were met in committee, while he made a speech consisting almost entirely of threats. He had a real gift for oratory, and as I listened to his furious words I understood how it was that this man conquered the masses and yet was himself in subjection. When I looked at him more closely I found no great ardent love for revolution in him."

The man here described is the Russian priest Gapon, the leader on the famous " Black Sunday," January 9, 1905. The description is written by the terrorist Boris Savinkoff. Every word fits Hitler. Even their political rôles are not unlike. Gapon was also no real revolutionary. He was something more like " His Majesty's most faithful rebel." Hence it was his fate to be reckoned a spy, which he probably was not at first, though he became one later. Angry comrades " executed " him for it in a lonely house.

It would be obviously impossible to regard Hitler as a spy. But as he has grown greater he seems to have become a not altogether sincere representative of his followers' ideas, and very early justified the distrust that the proletarian founders of the Party entertained for him. Gapon, too, according to Savinkoff, possessed a gift that is not wanting in Hitler — when he liked he could be all things to all men. The same obscurity veiled Gapon's origin and early political life;

there is the same aloofness from their comrades, the same veil over their private lives.

HIS STYLE

His chief intellectual interest was for history, his second for art. Most German schoolboys in pre-War days had these interests, and the educational system took care to inculcate them into the pupils. Hitler had kept both these traditional tastes. The symbols, spectacular demonstrations, parades, and buildings of his Party have for the most part been designed by him. This is not only due to a childish love of display. The recruiting value of an SA standard or a placard for a special meeting proves that the results repay Hitler's spending several days in designing them. Crowds are attracted by flags and not by conferences. Hence the Leader can with a clear conscience devote part of his time to designing flags. As artistic efforts they are somewhat barbaric. The prototypes may be sought partly in Napoleonic standards and partly in the Lohengrin legends. Hitler has no feeling at all for the Gothic. His artistic theories are a mixture of schoolboy æsthetics and racial sociology. According to him all great art is both Nordic and "beautiful." He condemns all expressionism as Jewish and Bolshevist, and sees no connexion between expressionist War and post-War conceptions and the Gothic: a fact which raises a doubt as to the depth of his artistic and racial feelings.

The most important of his personal qualities still remains — his great gift of eloquence. A man already possesses the first essential for a good speaker if he does not worry about the lost thread of a sentence, does not hold fast to syntax, has no fear of drawn-out phrases — so long as they are drawn through the fire of his eloquence.

An even greater orator is he who is not bound by the sense of what he says, any more than by grammatical form. A speaker gets lost in the mazes of thought more often than an audience realizes. The great thing is that he should not obviously be bewildered, but should find his way back to a more ordered train of thought.

Greatest of all, however, is he who does not coldly become victor over unavoidable difficulties, but who lets the audience see and hear the drama of his victorious struggle with them. There are speakers who have impediments in their speech and who are so enraged by them that their audiences are not conscious of the defect, but only of its victorious overcomer, and applaud him.

Of all the speakers who have recently appeared before German crowds, Hitler is probably the most indomitable fighter. For an hour, two hours, he will stand on the platform, an inspired preacher, occasionally enlivening his arguments with witty remarks; a man with ideas, who is easy to listen to, but — it must be confessed — who is also at times apt to act as a soporific. But then he becomes inspired again. His figure shoots up and down on the platform; his arms saw the air in gestures that, though they are poor miming and do not illustrate what is said, do excellently convey the speaker's emotions, and infect the listeners with them. When during a recriminatory speech Hitler pecks at the audience with his forefinger like a bird of prey, each and every member of it feels personally responsible for the sins of the German nation.

The result is that the man on the platform no longer discusses anything, but gives battle. The masses do not see the enemy; they do not realize that the fighter has the enemy within himself. He is fighting against the disintegration of the nation, against the political indolence of the masses, against the culpable negligences of men who have been set in authority — and in reality he is fighting against the Marxist that was once himself, against the lazy schoolboy, against the irresolute man who missed his opportunity in 1922, was twice defeated in 1923, did not take power when he had the chance in 1930, and missed it in 1932. He is fighting against his own fear, against his private devil like an anchorite of old. He is no longer an agitator, nor is he indulging in oratorical exercises; this is exorcism. Hence he can say what he likes — even if it were that the moon is made of green cheese — and the audience will applaud. When bombs are falling, nobody troubles to see whether they are painted grey or green.

In 1923, convinced in his inmost heart of the impossibility of a war of *revanche*, he exclaimed: "If sixty millions had only the will to be fanatically nationalist — weapons would leap to their hands. . . ."

In 1932, as candidate for the presidency, knowing the hopelessness of his attempt, he thundered at his opponents: " And though you say a hundred times that you will remain in office at all costs — we answer that we shall overthrow you whatever happens. . . ."

And the walls rocked with the applause of the stronger battalions; millions trembled who read it on the following day; the State itself shook.

CRITICISM

Is Hitler, as his follower, disciple, and one-time rival, Dr. Goebbels, says, " a man built on an exceptional scale "?

As a mob-leader Hitler is certainly unrivalled to-day and almost unequalled in history. A comparison with Cleon, Wat Tyler, or Rienzi would be too inadequate. If only the number of men who are set in motion by his oratory is considered, he surpasses Peter the Hermit and Mahomet. Nothing like him has been seen in modern Europe.

Enthusiasts have likened him to Luther. He certainly shows traces of Luther's worldly wisdom. But on the occasions when he appears clever he is lacking in the touch of greatness that makes his enthusiasm so impressive. Those parts of his speeches and writings that give the impression of being well thought out, logical, and true are generally very mediocre in their content. Above all, they are unoriginal, copied from others. The politician has the right to be banal. Any one who only realizes the platitudes in Hitler's utterances misses the cleverness with which he is combining other people's ideas for a political purpose.

Historical " greatness " is not due to talent or character, but is a gift of fate. It has often been denied to the greatest natures and granted to the mediocre. It is not always men who make History; often History makes men and makes chance circumstances become a focus of action big with great decisions. Those who cause great changes seldom bring happiness to those of their fellow-men who are their raw material. Possibly posterity, feeling itself to be their creation, may value them.

Hitler is certainly a great agitator. Is he also a great creative genius? The structure of the National Socialist movement is only partly his work. His own peculiar achievement is an outstandingly clever political leadership. The most singular characteristic of this leadership is the fact that it deliberately chose the longest and most difficult road to power. It was also, however, the road which was most easily surveyed, on which nothing could appear unexpectedly, and on which everything could be prepared for in advance.

This was the path of the National Socialist Party through Germany. Can a similar road on which the objectives and obstacles are clearly to be descried be found between Germany and the other nations?

CHAPTER IV

THE TROUBLES OF A LEADER

No sooner had Hitler gained ascendancy over the National Socialist German Workers Party than he set to work to convert it into a political power. Hitherto he had possessed little more than the right to place his signature beneath its proclamations. Now he hastened to weld his old and new supporters into an instrument which would secure his control of the Party — the SA.

THE ORGANIZATION OF THE SA

Ever since 1920 Defence Sections of the Party had been in existence. At the commencement of 1921 these Sections had been organized into companies of a hundred men. Hitler now reorganized these companies, and in so doing introduced a new element into German political life. The SA was founded on August 3, 1921, and the proclamation announcing its foundation ran as follows:

" The National Socialist German Workers Party has set up within its organization a special Section for gymnastics and sport. It is intended to serve as a means for bringing our youthful members together in a powerful organization for the purpose of utilizing their strength as an offensive force at the disposal of the movement. It is for them to show themselves worthy representatives of a free people's desire for defence against its enemies, and to provide a protection for the work of enlightenment about to be accomplished by the leaders. This organization is intended above all else to implant an unrestricted will to action in the hearts of our young followers and to hammer and burn it into their minds that it is not History which makes men but men who make History, and that the man who defencelessly submits himself to slavery deserves to be a slave. Moreover, they are to be taught loyalty among themselves and joyful obedience to their leaders. . . . The leaders of the Party expect you all to join. Your services will be needed in the future."

This proclamation shows that something more was intended than was revealed by the name given to the new organization. For it was obvious that the name " Gymnastic and Sport Section " was only an ill-chosen cloak for the organization's true activities. Its permanent name speedily came into existence as the result of its purpose and its achievements. The proclamation declared the object of this organization to be the cultivation in its members of the idea of defence, of acting as a guard for the Party leaders, and of training for some unknown and unnamed action. This may be translated to mean the beating of opponents, the holding of military manœuvres, the expulsion of hecklers from Party meetings and in general preparation for a *coup d'état*. In the short space of two months this "Gymnastic and Sport Section " had been converted into a body of storm troops. The *Völkischer Beobachter* now openly published " Storm Section Notes " and shortly afterwards the abbreviation SA (*Sturmabteilung*) came into use. In the first regulations issued to these troops Hitler defined their purpose as follows:

" The SA is not only intended to be a means of defence for the movement, but above all a training school for the coming struggle for liberty."

A later circular of September 1922 declared that the SA were troops that were entrusted not only with the duty of defending " the meetings of the Party from all inimical attacks, but also of enabling the movement itself to take the offensive at any given moment."

The SA was composed very largely of former members of the Volunteer Corps and especially of those men who had served in Ehrhardt's Brigade. After Erzberger's murder their numbers increased owing to the break-up of the so-called " Organization Consul " in which were many of Ehrhardt's men. Old soldiers with " the swastika on their tin-hats " were forced to find a new outlet for their pugnacity. Captain Röhm enlisted them in the new SA. Ehrhardt saw himself forced to make the best of an awkward situation by offering Hitler his former officers as instructors. Thus the first SA leader, Johann Ulrich Klintzsch, was formerly one of Ehrhardt's lieutenants. The incorporation of the former " Organization Consul " in the SA enabled Röhm to fulfil his dearest wish of militarizing the Nazi Party. This brought him into conflict with no less a person than Hitler. Hitler wanted troops for political purposes. He wanted storm troops to form the backbone of his Party, to keep order in the streets, and to serve as propaganda by their parades and route-marches. "Toy soldiers " — the SA leaders exclaimed in fury. Röhm, on the contrary, wanted to organize a secret army as a replacement for the forbidden conscription. "Impossible! " cried Hitler. As an old soldier — he said — he knew that an army to be efficient required two years of training. Moreover, troops upon whom no penalty can be imposed for insubordination are no troops at all. The SA would never be the equal of professional soldiers until their officers could punish them by court-martial. Röhm was more moderate in his demands. He was content to make the best of existing conditions. Thus there arose between these two men, who were also intimate friends, a difference of opinion that continued — sometimes in tragic intensity — to influence the entire history of the Nazi Party. It is the age-long conflict between the soldier and the politician.

THE ÉLITE

In Hitler's eyes the most important task of the new SA was to gain control of the Party itself. For this purpose recruits were sought whose intellectual capabilities fitted them for the task. These recruits were young men whose very youth rendered them easy to discipline — students with a feeling for class-distinctions and rank, ambitious to lead themselves yet willing to submit their own individual wills to the dictation of an overriding will. In these days the middle class was beginning to take a sentimental interest in the labouring class. Pre-War class distinctions were beginning to disappear; and the Nazi movement was a symptom of this process. A conviction made itself felt that the parties of the Right should oppose at least an appearance of democracy to the popular parties of the Left.

It was for this public that Hitler made his discovery of the poisoning of the working man's soul by Jewish Marxism. These shopkeepers and students — not the working man — were stricken to the heart at the thought of Moses and Isaac Cohen. The workmen were more impressed by that part of Hitler's address which was apparently directed to the middle classes — the admonition to humanitarianism. Although they remained mistrustful, the labouring class could at least agree in principle to these sentiments.

The students, barristers, and ex-officers now clad in the SA field-grey would in the normal course of events have become professional soldiers or officers on the reserve. Now they were forced through the lack of normal employment to become mercenaries — a ruined generation with no future and penniless, hating the man in the street and at the same time filled with the desire to convert him, steering their vessel towards an unrecognized and unknown proletariat with the skull and cross-bones at the masthead and the proselytizing bible containing the Twenty-Five Points in the cabin locker.

WHAT IS SOCIALISM?

The Nazi Party had been too hasty in incorporating the word " Socialist " in its title. Hitler indeed wished it to be " Social Revolutionary," which may be taken to mean the maintenance of the existing economic system subject to certain practical alterations and the introduction of a system of social ethics that is militarist rather than humanitarian. But the name of the Party was already " National Socialist," and therefore Hitler found himself compelled to give a new meaning to the word " Socialism " which had hitherto — and notwithstanding all controversies — been customarily understood to mean the nationalization of the means of production. His definition runs:

" Whoever is prepared to make the national cause his own to such an extent that he knows no higher ideal than the welfare of his nation, whoever in addition has understood our great national anthem, ' Deutschland, Deutschland über alles,' to mean that nothing in the wide world surpasses in his eyes this Germany, people and land, land and people — that man is a Socialist." That speech was delivered on

June 28, 1922. The old conception of Socialism had already disappeared and the word itself was to follow suit: " National and Social are two identical concepts. ' Social ' means the building-up of the State and the community in such a manner that each individual works for the community and therefore must be convinced of the essential excellence and honourable uprightness of the community in order to be able to lay down his life for it." This speech is of importance chiefly because Hitler in explaining the title of his Party abandoned the word " Socialist " and introduced the new term " Social."

At the beginning of 1923 this new " Socialism " received more final definition. In delivering a speech of welcome to a National Socialist Party Congress on January 27, 1923, Hitler said: " Marxism propounds three horrific theories. First, denial of the value of personality; second, denial of the right to private property; third, destruction of all human culture and of every higher form of economy (since this must always presuppose private possession)." Here is a Socialist who finds the denial of the right to private property horrific! The Socialist group centred round Otto Strasser discovered in 1930 that Hitler had abandoned Socialism — a fact which shows how little trouble these sincere Socialists gave themselves to learn the opinions of the Leader.

HITLER'S CLASS STATE

Hitler changed his attitude towards those classes in the community for whom the " Socialist " had been placed in the Party title concomitantly with his changed attitude towards Socialism itself. In Drexler's eyes the workmen were citizens and the citizens workmen. At first Hitler himself wanted to throw out of the Party all class-conscious citizens as well as class-conscious workmen. In April 1922 he had changed his mind. " It is true," he said, " that we recognize that there must and will be classes; for example, those of the clock-makers and workers in heavy industry or those of the technicians, engineers, civil servants, &c. Yes. Classes can exist. But the economic struggle between these classes must never become so great that it bursts the bonds of race." Class distinctions are only possible between different races. The difference between workers and non-workers is in the main the difference between the Aryan who looks upon work as " the support of the community " and the Jew who only sees in it a " means to plunder other peoples." Thus Hitler quickly sought to conceal the existence of class warfare that he had admitted only a few sentences previously beneath a cloak of anti-Semitism. Although he called class warfare a struggle between professional or occupational corporations, the class character of his so-called corporations (*Stände*) is clearly revealed by the fact that they struggle among themselves for their own interests in the possession of private property. In Hitler's ideal State " only the pick of the best and most capable can attain to power just as in the animal world." The pick of the best and most capable in an economic system based on the right to private property and divided into " corporations " (*Stände*) — if that is not a State where class distinctions exist, then words have lost their meaning. As a matter of fact, Hitler turns to that one of all modern States in which class distinctions are most firmly rooted — almost the only State in which these distinctions are still sacrosanct — in saying: " We see this (the principle that only the best and most capable shall rule) in practice in the most powerful nations of to-day. For example — Great Britain is not the creation of traitors! "

The best and the most capable citizens have naturally as much right as the " clockmaker " to erect themselves into a corporation. Thus the " corporation " of managing directors will struggle with that of the factory-workers to achieve a " compromise in labour problems." The State itself is only concerned to see that the bonds of race are not broken — a danger that is not very imminent or probable in a non-Jewish community. There is nowhere to be found any indication that the best and most capable will find compensation in a comfortable feeling of the possession of a higher sense of duty or even in their ability to cast a proud glance around them from their lofty position. On the contrary, the noblest are those " who love the Fatherland more than all else. For this reason the Fatherland must love them more than others." In the conflicts that filled the year 1923 the Fatherland showed its affection by giving the noblest among its sons freedom of action. What would the National Socialist State have done? A few years later Rosenberg openly declared in his essay on "Houston Stewart Chamberlain as Forerunner and Founder of a German Future" (*H. St. Chamberlain als Verkünder und Begründer einer deutschen Zukunft*): "If Germany remains a republic, it is obvious that it must be a republic with a stronger and more purposeful leadership and an aristocracy of ability. That means however, that this republic will have recognized the monarchical principle as the sole upholder of the State and the inequality of corporations as a necessary encumbrance. Every miller knows that it is the difference in the height of the water that causes the wheel to turn." The aim was therefore to establish in Germany conditions similar to those obtaining in England.

Perhaps also similar to those in Russia? In July 1922 Hitler put forward Russia after Imperial Germany as a political pattern to be copied. In England — that England which only shortly before had been so praised — the Jew was already the master, and still more so in France. What, then, was the difference between Western Europe on one hand and Eastern and Central Europe on the other? "The Jew was forced to recognize that in these countries the revival of enlightened despotism was not impossible. The State had ready to hand three great instruments of power: the army with an immense and admirably trained corps of officers; a civil service composed of officials filled with a sense of duty; and, finally, a vast mass of the populace still free from all internal poison." Hitler did not value the Russian highly as a race; but he naturally placed the old Imperial Russia in its character as an anti-Semitic racial State high above the Republic while he valued benevolent despotism as a weapon for use against Jewry.

ÉLITE AGAINST MASS

The growth of an aristocratic consciousness in Hitler caused his feelings for the working class to change from a benevolent "winning (them) over to the national ideal" to public outbursts of hatred. "Marxism must of necessity become a movement of people who are only manual workers and who either are not capable of clear thinking or are disinclined for it in their leisure hours. A mass organization of working animals lacking leadership." Thus Hitler in the *Völkischer Beobachter* on January 27, 1923. Two weeks later the same newspaper published the following poem by Bogislaw von Selchow:

" Ich hasse
die Masse,
die kleine,
gemeine,
den Nacken gebeugt,
die isst und schläft und Kinder zeugt.

Ich hasse
die Masse,
die lahme,
die zahme,
die heut an mich glaubt
und die mir Morgen mein Herzblut raubt."

" *I disdain*
The profane,
Plebeian,
And mean,
Servile of gait,
That eat and sleep and procreate.

I disdain
The profane,
The weak,
The meek,
That are loyal to-day
And to-morrow will swear my life away."

" That are loyal to-day . . ." — did the audiences at his great mass meetings suspect that such ideas were passing through the mind of their beloved Leader?

Without realizing it, Hitler had contradicted himself. On the one hand, he sought to prove that it was the Jews who first of all introduced class distinctions among the masses, infected them with class hatreds, and reduced them to something less than men. On the other hand, he still believed in the natural inequality of mankind and in a biological aristocracy that certainly had some connexion with the aristocratic class in society. In one sense the degradation of the masses is solely due to Isaac and Moses Cohen; to foreigners who "bastardize and poison, who continually widen the gulf (between the classes), who regard fratricidal strife as something noble, who organize civil warfare and in this way perpetuate our state of internal revolution. . . ." It is due to foreigners for whom "the Jewish democracy of majority rule always and at all times serves as a means for the destruction of the real Aryan leadership." It is due to those foreigners of whom Hitler says: "The Jew knows not love but only the body. He seeks to soil and destroy our German race. Therefore he brings negroes into the Rhineland to set them amidst German women." Thus far his arguments are sound and logical anti-Semitism, and reveal sincere sympathy with his misled brothers. Indeed his pity for them goes so deep that in a speech in 1921, on the anniversary of the foundation of the German Empire, Hitler angrily asked: "Why is universal suffrage withheld from the people in Prussia?" But then comes the contradiction — his brother in distress is in himself inferior: "The idea of authority is overthrown; freedom of action and opportunity for creative work are forbidden to the individual; the capacity for leadership is bound in chains that paralyse all free development. And in their place (literally!) there has been set up that democratic principle of majority rule which only signifies the victory of the commoner, weaker, and, above all, more cowardly elements in those lacking in all sense of responsibility. Individuality is destroyed by the mass." It was no longer of any importance in Hitler's eyes, in January 1921, whether the masses were Aryan or not.

The insincere tone of the lamentation over the denial of universal suffrage coupled with the condemnation of democracy as the victory of the baser elements in national life — all that is only a small *lapsus* in comparison with the mingled stream of praise and vilification that is poured out upon the masses. Praise and vilification do in fact constitute two stages in the progress of the Nazi movement. The masses who have merely been led astray by the Jews — that is the view of the political world formed by the old German Workers Party, by Drexler, Harrer, and Körner, the view of the masses as not being innately "common" but as being capable of "redemption" by sermons delivered from the pulpit that was intended to be the Party itself. Now, however, the Party is no longer a pulpit. The grumblers and would-be enlighteners of the masses have either left it in anger or been pushed to one side. Their place has been taken by a cohort of silent warriors. The Party ideal is now embodied in the SA. "We do not want to be millions of indifferent people, but a hundred thousand men — resolute men," Hitler cried to his followers. And again: "Energy lies dormant like all great things only in minorities. World history has always been made by minorities." The masses have now become once more the herd to be led by an élite of leaders. "Our struggle will not be carried on by means of majorities composed of parliamentary groups but through the supremacy ("*Majorität*") of strength and will-power regardless of dead numbers." Hence "there is one thing this movement must not do: it must not see its work in winning more or less seats in the provincial parliaments or the Reichstag, and in thus increasing the mob of representatives of the people hungry for their parliamentary allowances." On the contrary, the task of National Socialism was "to spread enlightenment amongst the various classes in the nation, and to organize them as a mighty defensive weapon against the attempt to destroy our last common culture and to bring to nought our common destiny!" The nation as a weapon. Once more there appears at the beginning of 1923 the old democratic Party ideal of the people as an instrument of policy.

Whether the SA was regarded as the right hand of the nation, or the masses as its instrument, amounted in fact to no more than two ways of looking at the same method. The brilliant psychological achievement of this agitation was its success in inspiring enthusiasm in the masses for their own lack of volition. It was in reality an artificial cleavage. When Hitler spoke of the élite, each individual felt that it was he who was praised and his neighbour who was reproached. Every particle from the masses that allowed itself to be attracted by this agitation felt itself to be thus lifted out of the mass, individualized, and raised up above all others. This was subsequently elevated to the dignity of a system in the political organization of the Party, and still more of the SA with its many grades of rank, and thus constitutes an interesting counterpart to the sociological achievements of the Trade Unions. The Trade Union affords the working-man who is interested in politics virtually the only material possibility of advancement open to him to-day. At the beginning National Socialism was unable to give its followers this material opening. Instead it created an ideal advancement by giving its supporters a diploma to certify that they no longer formed part of the masses. Hitler's words on February 24, 1922, expressed the underlying principle guiding his movement: " We do not want to go into Parliament. He who steps into a morass is sucked under." And in August of that year Hitler gave this still more open expression in a confidential circular in saying that his movement did not possess more than half-a-dozen first-class speakers whose value was too great to allow of their being wasted in Parliament.

THE FORM OF THE STATE IS A MATTER OF PRIVATE OPINION

This contempt for the masses and for democracy indicates an indifference to the monarchical form of government that is more apparent than real. It was to the uninitiated that the *Völkischer Beobachter*, in November 1922, directed its words: " The question, monarchy or republic, is not in the least actual. To make use of a current phrase — it is a private matter." Nor did it indicate any objection on principle to monarchical government when the same newspaper called the former German Crown Prince the " Crown Prince of the Jews," because he had called upon his Jewish fellow-countrymen in his memoirs to co-operate in national work, or when it insulted Hitler's future supporters by exclaiming " How you have gone to the dogs, you Hohenzollerns! " For when is it to be found laid down that the future German Emperor must be a Hohenzollern or a Wittelsbach or indeed of princely blood? Whoever has ears cannot fail to understand what Hitler meant in April 1922, when he said that the form of the State was determined by the character of the people and by necessities of a nature so elemental and powerful that each individual would recognize them without opposition once Germany was united and free. Is it possible that a Hitler can look upon a republic as the form of government most in keeping with the character of the German people? At the time of his trial for high treason Hitler maintained: " I am in the last resort also a republican." But the words " in the last resort " are tantamount to " all the same, it is not true." A few years later Rosenberg was to avow his monarchist beliefs in a privately printed book. But in 1922 the *Völkischer Beobachter,* in treating of the monarchical problem, laid it down definitely: " We need national unity within and without. The overseer of this work will be the man who has accomplished it." And if Hitler accomplishes it? In that case he will become in accordance with the elemental needs of the German people their unchosen and lifelong ruler, with, in all probability, the right to nominate his successor. In his own words — " a benevolent despot."

OVERRATING OPPONENTS—A CAUSE OF VICTORY

The National Socialist theory of the State had passed through an astonishing series of changes in the three years of its existence. The Nazi Party began as a national Party representative of the masses — with thirty men. These men believed the masses to be the prisoners of a minority opposed to the national aims and of different blood. From this they deduced that Marxism was necessarily the result of clever leadership along a false and evil path. Nor did they deny that deeper causes such as social movements of elementary force were to be found. But what always remained of the greatest importance in their eyes was the influence of a ruling race, the plan of an autocratic minority, the activity of the Elders of Zion. Out of this arose a twofold decision: to win back the masses from this inimical minority, and for this purpose to imitate and improve upon the weapons of the enemy.

A want of historical knowledge was responsible for the firm belief of the Nazi leaders that the Marxist power was built up by an exceptionally cunning use of a profound knowledge of psychology in the service of propaganda. Although this was an ignorant and wildly exaggerated over-estimation of their enemies, it nevertheless proved advantageous to their own organization in as much as it caused them to create weapons which their enemy did not possess, to practice deceptions for the purpose of outdoing non-existent enemy deceptions, and, finally, thanks to this error, enabled them to create a mass propaganda on a scale that had never before been known in Germany. Thus National Socialism became a far more artificial and mechanical organization than Marxism with its decades of development behind it. Moreover, this Nazi machine derived its power from a source of political passion hitherto untapped in Germany.

If the masses blindly followed the Marxist enemy, why should they not also follow the Nazi leaders? The famous principle of leadership was, in fact, derived in the first place from the enemy. Lenin and Trotsky gave the idea of a dictatorship to Germany. The idea gradually developed that the great crime was not the enemy's leadership over the masses so much as the fact that that leadership was in the hands of an inferior race. Leadership was indeed necessary. The masses who were susceptible to Jewish influences were not only poisoned by these influences but were in themselves infirm of purpose. Nietzsche, Gobineau, Lagarde, Houston Stewart Chamberlain, and Madison Grant propounded the doctrine of a governing race. Thousands believed in this doctrine long before Hitler's time. The great orator who so swiftly made the tiny German Workers Party famous was also a receptive pupil. Dietrich Eckart and Rosenberg were his teachers. Hitler was little more than their mouthpiece for some years to come. Rosenberg taught him facts. Eckart polished his style.

CAPTAIN HERMANN GÖRING

Meanwhile, the SA had become the instrument of Röhm's militarist policy. At the instigation of the Reichswehr the so-called defence organizations throughout Germany were given proper military training during the troubles in the Ruhr. Owing to this training the popularity of the SA and with it of the Nazi Party increased enormously. At the same time, Hitler found himself in danger of losing his control over the Party itself. The very instrument which he had himself created to assure his control — the SA — was taken out of his hand by the military authorities. Moreover, the man who was responsible for this change was his own best friend — Captain Röhm. Röhm indeed hardly realized what the result of his policy must be for his friend and leader. He forced him to turn the Party into a horde of mercenaries with whose aid the Reichswehr could one day accomplish whatever they wished.

The increase in the numbers of the SA was another cause contributory to Hitler's loss of control over them. In March 1923, the SA in Bavaria comprised three "Standards," each of which numbered from three to five thousand men. Subsequently the designation "Standard" was changed at Röhm's request into "Regiment." The Reichswehr officers trained these men as well as other defence associations by means of great parades and night manœuvres. Thus Hitler found his political activity curtailed by innumerable military regulations and orders. It was a stroke of good luck for him that at this juncture he acquired a new SA leader who possessed great capacity for the conduct of civil warfare. This was the former Flight Captain, Hermann Göring, who had led Richthofen's famous "Circus" after Richthofen's death, and who possessed the highest German decoration for bravery under fire — the Order *Pour le mérite*. Göring was four years younger than Hitler, and had worked as a pilot and director of aviation companies in Denmark and Sweden since the War. He had also studied in Munich. Moreover, Göring was wealthy and money was specially welcome to Hitler in those days. Göring has indeed spent not only his personal energy but also his wealth unstintingly in the service of National Socialism. His is one of several cases of men who "bought" their way into its leadership. He was able to inspire the SA with enthusiasm. But he was too nervous for the ordinary task of training recruits. Röhm has always looked upon him with sceptical eyes. A stronger if less brilliant personality than Göring was his Chief of Staff, Captain Hoffmann, who had formerly served under Ehrhardt. He was even more sceptical of Hitler's political activities than was Göring himself, and entertained much sympathy for Röhm's militarist ideas.

The growing army escaped from Hitler's control in the ensuing months to such an extent that he was compelled to organize a special body for his own private aims. In August, Lieutenant Berchtold, who had been among the original founders of the Party, organized a sort of Staff Guard to which he gave the name of "Storm Troop Hitler."

Out of this personal bodyguard of Hitler's there subsequently arose the present SS.

INFLATION

Meanwhile the Nazi Party would not have found it possible to acquire the strong influence over the masses that it actually did, but for two events that turned out in its favour. The first was the inflation in Germany. The German currency had been seriously depreciated, even during the War, owing to the policy of the Government which sought to avoid taxing the large estates, and had been further weakened by the confusion of the State finances after the Revolution. When the Ruhr was completely occupied by the French in January 1923, and a so-called passive resistance was organized by Cuno's Right Wing Government, the Mark fell into the bottomless abyss. In order to finance the resistance immense quantities of new notes were printed which thus grew to have progressively less value. By November 1923, one billion paper Marks were paid for the value of a gold Mark — a depreciation which is simply impossible for the human mind to grasp. Innumerable people whose small capital was invested in Government Stocks and in Savings Banks were rendered penniless — those whose property was in goods and real estate were less hardly hit. Hitler's doctrines, therefore, made a great impression upon the smaller investors by telling them that the great "banking and Stock Exchange magnates" had used their influence over the Government to bring about the depreciation in order to enrich themselves. As a matter of fact, the inflation had been encouraged mainly by great industrial magnates like Hugo Stinnes, who by this means were able to export more, to liquidate their debts, and who were in addition directly financed by the State as "Ruhr fighters." Agriculturists also profited by being able to pay off their mortgages. The mass of small *rentiers* could not be expected to realize these facts. Whoever possessed a few pence became a speculator in those days. Never before or since have the stock and share reports of the newspapers been scanned so carefully by the general public. The tiny speculator knew from the movements of his stock that he was at grips with unknown Stock Exchange powers — those Stock Exchange powers against whose machinations Hitler had for years past delivered a great speech twice weekly. The small investor began to listen to Hitler. In November 1922, Hitler spoke to ten gatherings in the largest halls in Munich on the same evening. All these meetings were crowded out. The small investor understood at once when Hitler told him that " Jewish Stock Exchange swindlers " had cheated him of the little he possessed.

FASCISM

The second circumstance that turned out to Hitler's advantage was the triumph in October 1922 of Fascism in Italy. Mussolini's March on Rome took place nearly two months after the Bavarian Reichswehr had almost marched upon Berlin, and it had the effect of attracting attention to the leader of the Bavarian SA. Esser said to a meeting in November of that year: " We have no need to imitate an Italian Mussolini. We already have our own. His name is Adolf Hitler! "

The deep impression made upon public opinion in Germany by the March on Rome was in large part due to the smoothness and quietness with which the Italian State machinery functioned. There was no street-fighting, no strikes, no attack on the Crown, and no heads were broken — that was a revolution after the heart of a German citizen. Hitler promised to deal with Parliament exactly in the same fashion as Mussolini had just done. He echoes Mussolini's ideas in saying that "political freedom will always be a question of power," and followed that up by declaring somewhat doubtfully that "power is only the outflow of the will." In any case Mussolini's *coup d'état* strengthened the belief that a Fascist Revolution was a pleasant revolution from the standpoint of an onlooker. In his rôle as the German Mussolini Hitler became a popular revolutionary.

THE ABANDONMENT OF SOUTH TYROL

In Hitler's eyes the immediate aim to be accomplished by the Nazi movement was the destruction of German Communism. Rosenberg saw its final objective in the destruction of Bolshevism in Russia. What about a settlement with France? A feeling of uncertainty prevailed in the Nazi attitude towards England. Was it already enslaved by the Jews or was it still the home of the governing Anglo-Saxon race? In consequence of this uncertainty its attitude towards Italy was more pronounced.

A few months after the Fascist triumph in Italy, Hitler in addressing a small meeting let fall a few heretical words on the subject of South Tyrol. In those days the Fascisti had marched into Meran and were engaged in terrorizing the German population. At the beginning of 1923 Hitler was of the opinion that this state of things was not to be taken too tragically. On June 18, 1923, Rosenberg laid down the policy of the Party in this matter on lines along which it has ever since continued to follow: " The question of the liberation of South Tyrol will only become practical when we have once more established a German State." It would only become a matter of practical politics when " Ruhr and Rhine, when Posen and Danzig, these vital centres of German life, are again restored to us. There are many places that are of far greater value to Italy than South Tyrol. In the approaching new international situation it will suffice for a resuscitated Germany to speak the word and to exercise a friendly pressure for Italy to attain her wishes and for the South Tyrolese to regain their liberty." Germany is therefore in the future to buy back South Tyrol in return for political help to Italy.

The Nazi policy in the South Tyrol Question was laid down at the time of the Ruhr occupation and constitutes a corner-stone in Nazi foreign policy: an alliance with Italy against France with the possible inclusion of England. In conjunction and also in contradiction to this policy there exists the Nazi anti-Bolshevist plan of uniting the world in a crusade against Russia — a plan that must logically lead to an understanding with France. It was only after embittered domestic strife that the men responsible for Nazi foreign policy came with the progress of time to see that this political edifice with its interchangeable corner-stones was anything but solid. After attaining to this knowledge they were for long in favour of leaving Russia to her own fate. Since the Nazi victory in the 1930 election, however, the German policeman's sword with which the civilized world can be defended from the Soviet Union has once more been taken down from its peg and held up to the gaze of those parties who might have an interest in seeing it put to this use.

Foreign policy is a field that is better left untouched by doctrinaires. And it must be admitted that Nazi foreign policy has largely ceased to become the playground for their ideas.

THE STRUGGLE WITH THE CHURCH

In the popular sense of the term the Nazis were not even in those days good Christians. " Tear in pieces that lascivious bible of Satanism — the Old Testament! " Dietrich Eckart wrote in the *Völkischer Beobachter* on August 11, 1921. And Hitler, who had derived many of his ideas from Eckart, was only echoing his teacher's views when he said: " Luther's translation of the Bible may have been of use to the German language; it irreparably injured the German people's power of judgment. God in heaven! what a cloud of glory now hangs over the satanic Bible! Luther's poetical gifts sparkle so brilliantly that even the defamation of Lot's daughter is enveloped in a veil of religious glamour! " This remark was subsequently struck out from the article in which it appeared. Nevertheless Eckart's brochure in which it had been published was still being recommended to its readers by the *Völkischer Beobachter* as late as 1927.

For the Nazis the Cardinal Archbishop of Munich, Dr. von Faulhaber, constituted a rock of offence from the very beginning. In appearance and thought the Cardinal is a true Prince of the Church. As an intellect he may have been inferior to the present Cardinal Secretary of State, Pacelli, who was then Papal Nuncio in Munich. But as a coiner of political phrases Cardinal Faulhaber has no equal in the choice of word, place, and time of delivery. The Cardinal was a convinced monarchist and an enemy of the Revolution. At the same time he was as a Catholic the enemy of Nationalism and a Bavarian wearer of the purple possessed simultaneously of a world-embracing and patriotic ultramontanism. It was not long before the Nazis made this discovery. It was the Cardinal who invented a phrase that is still in current use: The Revolution was perjury and high treason. At a

Catholic Congress in Munich in August 1922, Cardinal Faulhaber attacked the " lies " contained in the " Jewish Press." While the Bavarian and patriotic Right Wing associations made use of these phrases as propaganda, the Nazis were troubled in their consciences by other words which the Cardinal had let fall on the same occasion. As a defender of the " Roman " peace, the Cardinal protested against military festivals, condemned political murders, and placed the responsibility for their occurrence at the door of the agitatist activity carried on in the radical Right Wing newspapers. This was in effect a direct attack upon the Nazis.

For this reason the Nazis did not make use of the Cardinal's words about perjury and high treason. Moreover, these words sounded too little inspired by an inborn sense of duty towards the nation and too much by a belief in monarchy. " Good and evil are mingled in the speech of the Munich Cardinal," Rosenberg declared at the same time as he came forward against the mistrusted Prince of the Church as the prophet of a new religion. " A new philosophy of life is arising in all classes and all confessions. A philosophy that is young and joyous and irrepressible. This philosophy will one day form the dome beneath which all the German peoples, but not all races, will come together to fight for their common cause. This philosophy is the national and democratic ideal." This " dome " theory of Rosenberg's was later to be elevated in Nazi circles to the dignity of a dogma. Hitler expressed it in a form which made it intelligible to the masses. " We do not want any other god than Germany itself. It is essential to have fanatical faith and hope and love in and for Germany."

THE PARTY BENEFACTORS

In November 1923 the Nazi Party numbered some fifteen thousand members in possession of membership cards and probably paying a subscription. But no Party could exist in those days from subscriptions paid in paper Marks. Hence donations became a matter of course. At the beginning of 1923 the *Völkischer Beobachter* had expressed itself on this subject as follows: " It must be definitely understood that if a German were to be found ready and able to lay one or two hundred million Marks upon the table without attaching any conditions to the use made of them, we should not hesitate for a moment to utilise this money for the benefit of our nation."

The acceptance of this principle by the Nazi Party was tantamount — even when carried out honourably — to its placing a halter round its neck permanently. Money — especially money that is regularly given — compels submission to the donor's wishes, even though he may give no direct commands, because he discontinues his gifts as soon as the Party embarks upon a course which is unwelcome to him. The early history of the Nazi Party is characterized by the subjection of its policy to the wishes of the Reichswehr or — better said — to a particular group of Reichswehr officers. Subsequently Hitler was fortunate in finding a few patrons, and especially patronesses, who were more devoted to him personally than is customary in the history of the relations between Party leaders and their financial benefactors. His control over the Party finances came to him as the result of this personal success. At the same time his own personal requirements were modest. At Easter, 1923, he borrowed a few Marks from Göring to enable him to take a holiday. If his material existence was more comfortable than formerly, Hitler was indebted for this to the hospitality shown to him by certain wealthy followers. Of these the most important was his personal friend, Ernst Hanfstängl, who to-day is at the head of the Foreign Press Department of the Nazi organization. Hanfstängl was the son of a respected and cultured family of art publishers in Munich, among whose members are many resolute opponents of Nazism. In March 1923 Hanfstängl made a loan to the Party of one thousand dollars — a fabulous sum for those days and for the comparatively small Party membership. The *Völkischer Beobachter* was mortgaged to him in return for this loan. The mortgage was subsequently disposed of to Hitler's old friend and comrade-in-arms, Christian Weber, who gave his Leader much trouble on its account.

An important rôle was played by the donations given by the wife of the famous pianoforte manufacturer Bechstein, and by a German woman named Frau Gertrud von Seidlitz, who was employed in a factory abroad. These donations enabled Hitler to turn the *Völkischer Beobachter* into a daily newspaper. Moreover, they were typical of many others that came to the Nazi Party from well-to-do private individuals who were actuated by no other motive than enthusiasm for the cause.

The evidence of Commercial Councillor Hermann Aust — a great industrialist in Munich — before the Court of Inquiry held prior to Hitler's trial throws a colder and clearer light on the motives which inspired financial aid from other sources. " For the purpose " — he told the presiding Judge — " of ascertaining Hitler's hitherto unknown intentions in regard to economic policy an interview took place with him in the office of Privy Councillor Dr. Kuhlo (Director of the Association of Bavarian Industrialists), at which were also present Dr. Nöll and the Chairman of the Association of Bavarian Industrialists, as well as myself. The conversation in the office of the Association led to the holding of a small meeting in the Herren Club (whose membership is not composed exclusively of members of the Association) and a much larger meeting in the Merchants' Hall. At this latter Herr Hitler delivered a lecture on the subject of his aims. He was listened to with much applause. Moreover, appreciation for his remarks showed itself in the fact that several gentlemen unacquainted with Hitler personally, but who knew that I was acquainted with him, gave me donations for the movement with the request that I would hand the sums in question to Hitler himself. I believe I am right in saying that Swiss francs were included among the various sums which passed through my hands."

The difference between these donations and those coming from private sources lies in the renouncement of " unconditional " financial assistance. It is possible that before these donations were accepted Hitler or Dietrich Eckart had seen in the " conditions " attached to a political money transaction a sort of pact with the Devil in which the receiver would have to bind himself by his signature to the pursuit of a particular political line of action. Lo and behold! a signature was not even asked for — only a short lecture! This meant the avoidance of anything disreputable. As a matter of fact, Hitler went as far as a political leader can go in deciding to reveal his economic policy to industrialists before he had so much as given the public a hint of its nature. The lectures which Hitler delivered in the National Club in

Berlin also helped to introduce him to further sources of financial supply. It was there in 1922 that Hitler became acquainted with the great locomotive manufacturer, von Borsig, who was also the leader of the German industrialists. Among Hitler's earliest benefactors was a factory-owner in Augsburg named Grandel.

These were the days of inflation. Hence all recipients of money regarded the worth of that money as a matter of the greatest importance. For this reason Hitler had also his collectors in foreign countries. One of the most zealous among these was a Dr. Gansser in Switzerland. It is true that enough care was not always taken in the choice of these agents. An attempt was at least made to extract money from Henry Ford. The deceased Labour M.P. in England, Mr. Morel, declared to Herr von Kahr that French money was pouring into the hands of the Nazis without their being aware of its source. Morel further declared that he knew this as a fact from a French Cabinet Minister. It is possible that certain French politicians may have thought that the success of the Nazis would prove of assistance to French separatist designs in the Rhineland. Those ignorant of the true state of affairs found it easy to confuse the anti-Berlin Hitler policy with Bavarian particularism. Hence it is also possible that some of the French money which flowed into Bavaria in the post-War years may have been intended to reach Hitler's hands. Probably no one in Germany knows whether it did in fact reach him. In any case, it is certain that it would not have influenced him in France's favour.

The Party officials, or at least those of the SA, were in part paid in foreign money. For example, Kriebel received two hundred Swiss francs monthly. The actual SA leaders were more moderate in their demands. Thus a former major received ninety, many other officers only eighty francs — a quite respectable sum for those days.

All this money flowed into Hitler's hands, and into his hands alone. Out of regard for the donors, Hitler dare not breathe a word about the sources from which he received money. His business manager, Amann, was his sole confidant. A violent quarrel broke out between Hitler and the second deputy chairman of the Party, Jacob, who had demanded to know the sources from which the Party was in receipt of financial assistance. He never learnt them.

"HEADS WILL ROLL"

Hitler was possessed of self-confidence to a degree unequalled by any German Party leader before his day. "What have you got to give to the people," Hitler shouted in reproach to the old Right Parties, "except traditions to which they attempt to hold fast? Absolutely nothing. You yourselves do not believe in your own prescriptions. That is the greatest aim which our movement shall achieve; to give a new faith to these questing and erring masses that they will each of them once more find a place where their hearts will be at peace. And that we shall achieve!" But this prophet of a new faith was forced to wait in the anterooms of generals anxious about their careers, of stupid civil servants, and cunning police officials. Faith cannot enter into places where there is no faith. In these anterooms Hitler was regarded as half-mad and just about fitted to deal with the masses. In daily intercourse with this cold-blooded society all that was evil in Hitler was aroused daily to new life. It was then that he spoke the famous words to his own immediate followers: "Heads will roll in this struggle — either ours or those of the others. Let us see to it that it is the others which roll!" These terrible words in their cold-blooded ferocity proved too much even for many of Hitler's own followers. Hence he insisted that they were unquestionably to be taken in all seriousness. "We are often asked," he said on another occasion, "if we really believe that we shall be capable of putting this into practice on attaining to power. Let there be no doubt of it. We shall be capable!" A deadly stillness reigned in the room after these words. "Mercy is not our affair," he said. "It is the affair of a Higher Power. We have only to see that justice is done." And again: "We can be comforted that we can be as inhuman as we like if only in doing so we make the German nation prosperous again."

HITLER'S PUTSCH

In the autumn of 1923, on the collapse of German passive resistance to the French occupation of the Ruhr, Nationalist and Communist disturbances occurred throughout the country. The movement was strongest in Bavaria where the Bavarian Government Commissioner, Herr von Kahr, who was armed with dictatorial powers, was planning a *coup* against the Reich Government. Afraid of being outdone by Kahr, Hitler seized the opportunity to act on his own. He surprised Kahr while he was making a speech at a large meeting in the Bürgerbräukeller, took him prisoner with all his friends, and forced him at the point of a pistol to proclaim then and there a new Reich Government. Once Kahr had regained his freedom he denied all that he had said, collected troops, and crushed Hitler's revolt, in which General Ludendorff had also taken part. A few dozen police summoned from the country districts easily overcame Hitler's and Ludendorff's armed forces, numbering several thousands, in a short and sharp encounter at the Feldherrn Hall in Munich, on November 9. Ludendorff was captured. But Hitler, who had thrown himself upon the ground at the sound of the first volley, fled from Munich by car and was only taken prisoner some days later in the country house of one of his friends.

The failure of Hitler's Putsch must be ascribed to lack of preparation and courage. The first mistake was that it should have been launched without previous military preparation; the second was the mistaken psychology shown in the handling of the Reichswehr; and the third the want of courage displayed on November 9. So brave a soldier as Röhm allowed himself to be surrounded by the enemy because he could not bring himself to turn his machine-guns on his former comrades. Ludendorff did not want to fight but to work miracles. When Hitler himself, at the head of the column, showed signs of anxiety in exclaiming, "They will shoot at us!" Ludendorff could only answer stupidly and heroically, "We will march on!" The citizens of Munich continued to show their willingness to demonstrate even after the Putsch had been defeated by thronging the streets for two days, insulting the Reichswehr, threatening Kahr's offices, smashing up those of moderate middle-class newspapers, and giving expression to their feelings in cries of "Down with the traitors!" Their fury was not stilled by repeated charges on the part of the mounted police. The students gathered in the university, where they demonstrated against Kahr and threatened to throw the Rector from the gallery into the hall below. Howls of abuse greeted even Captain Ehrhardt's attempt to call them to order.

It is obvious that great things could have been achieved with the aid of a populace in such a state of revolt. But then the "Fighters' Association" would have had to live up to its name and fought instead of taking to flight after the first shots. Every hour would have seen the position of the Government rendered more desperate in the midst of a rebellious people. The people indeed continued to demonstrate bravely and uselessly for two days whilst their leaders were seeking safety in flight. How differently the Communists behaved in Hamburg, and Berlin, Munich, and Central Germany, on the occasions of their risings! The "Fighters' Association," on the contrary, deserted Ludendorff, who advanced dauntlessly in face of the enemy fire. The leader of the Oberland Association, Dr. Weber, was for hours dissolved in tears. Hitler was the first to take to flight in a motor-car without troubling himself about what became of his followers. The fact that the majority believed Ludendorff to have been killed may excuse their conduct inasmuch as it broke their *morale*. Nevertheless Ludendorff's supposed death cannot excuse Hitler's hasty flight. For Hitler must have known that he was the sole leader left if Ludendorff were really dead.

The leaders of the Putsch subsequently sought to defend their conduct on November 9 by declaring that it was incomprehensible to them that Germans could kill Germans. Nevertheless, in the Ruhr, as also in the suppression of the Soviet Republic in Munich, they showed that they could comprehend such an action even against unarmed men. The truth is that they were unable to find adequate words to express what they really wished to say: that revolutionary warfare is only possible between classes in the nation who regard each other rightly or wrongly as foes. Among those killed at the Feldherrn Hall were four workmen. The others were business men, bank clerks, and former officers.

This bloodstained Ninth of November was nevertheless a blessing in disguise for the Nazi Party. It brought about the final breach between the Party and the Reichswehr. Hence November 9, 1923, is the real birthday of the National Socialist German Workers Party.

CHAPTER V

THE ROAD TO POWER

THE TRIAL of Hitler for high treason was the greatest political trial which had hitherto been held in Germany. Hitler was not alone in the dock. Beside him stood General Ludendorff, Dr. Weber, Captain Röhm, Dr. Frick, and others. Nor were all the accused present. Göring, Esser, and Rossbach fled the country. His death on December 23 released Dietrich Eckart from the hands of justice.

Hitler knew that his first duty must be to secure that he became more famous through his trial than even through his defeated Putsch. Reporters were present from all over the world. Before this world-wide audience Hitler's egotism rose above even the pinnacle on which stand princes and their ministers.

" Be assured " — Hitler said to his Judges — " that I do not look upon the achievement of a position in the Ministry as worth striving for. I do not consider it to be worthy of a great man to be content that his name should merely be recorded in history as having been a Minister. The vision that stands before my eyes was of far higher value to me from the very beginning. I wished to be the destroyer of Marxism. I will achieve this task, and once I have done so the title of Minister will be ridiculous in my sight. As I stood for the first time before Richard Wagner's grave, my heart was filled with pride at the thought that here lay a man who had forbidden that his tombstone should bear the inscription 'Here lies his Excellency Privy Councillor and Music Director Baron Richard von Wagner.' I was proud that this man, like so many other men known to German history, had been content with leaving his name alone to posterity. It was not modesty that caused me to wish to be the ' drummer.' That is the highest, and all the rest is nothing."

This is not wholly true. At first Hitler was really modest. Nor has false pathos been restrained by good taste; but then greatness is not troubled about good taste. And these words — it is due to the " drummer " that this should be emphasized — were inspired by true greatness. Hitler was courageous enough to admit the greatness of his self-appointed task at the risk of making himself ridiculous.

Hitler was condemned to nine months' detention in a fortress. In the case of Ludendorff the Court could not bring itself to condemn the greatest German of his day. At the same time there could be no dispute that the General had been present when Hitler deposed the Reich Government in the Bürgerbräukeller. Hence the Court took refuge in a most remarkable verdict. It found that Ludendorff on the evening of November 8 was so affected by emotion that he neither saw nor heard what was happening around him. It was hardly an honourable verdict of " Not guilty," and Ludendorff pathetically protested that it was a disgrace to the uniform he wore. It was nevertheless deserved.

While Hitler was sitting in the fortress at Landsberg where he was free to receive delegations, hold conferences, and issue proclamations as though he were in his office in Munich, the " Popular Movement," as the now prohibited Nazi Party called itself in association with other groups, increased largely. In the Reichstag elections in May 1924, it captured thirty-two seats. But it collapsed again with equal rapidity for reasons that cannot be entered into fully here. Perhaps the most important among them was Ludendorff's political short-sightedness in involving himself and the movement in a fierce quarrel with the Catholic Church. Hitler had scarcely regained his liberty before he separated himself from Ludendorff, and reorganized the Party on new lines on February 27, 1925, when he first announced the now famous principle of autocratic leadership.

THE FÜHRER (LEADER) PRINCIPLE

For years to come Hitler's most important task was to be the creation of a body of leaders capable of directing the Nazi Party and movement. The solution of this problem will doubtless prove itself to be a life-or-death question for the Nazi movement. On the day on which he refounded the Party Hitler promulgated the principle of a successive supply of leaders chosen from all the very various elements in the movement. The definition which he gave to this principle in the *Völkischer Beobachter* on February 20, 1925, is of such importance for a right understanding of the character of the Nazi Party that it must be reproduced here:

" I do not consider it to be the task of a political leader to attempt to improve upon or even to fuse together the human material lying ready to his hand. Individuals differ so widely in temperament, character, and capacity that it is impossible to unite in a single whole even a large number of completely equal and similarly educated individuals. Furthermore, it is not the duty of a political leader to seek to make good this want through an ' educational system ' designed to achieve unity. Every such attempt is condemned to failure. Human natures in their diversity are given, and factual phenomena that are unalterable individually, and are only able to change their character in the course of a century-long process of evolution. And changes in fundamental racial elements are in general presuppository to changes in the individuals composing the race.

" If a political leader should seek to attain his aim along this path, he must be able to think and plan in terms of perpetuity instead of in years or even decades.

" Hence his task can only consist in finding after long search those qualities in the individual man which will in co-operation with other qualities in other individuals enlarge themselves to form an entity.

" Moreover, he must reckon upon being able to bring into his movement not only ideal ' universal ' men, but men of the most widely differing temperaments and capacities who are only able to form a harmonious entity in their entirety (their conjunction of qualities).

" If a political leader departs from this knowledge, and if he seeks instead to find only those men who fit into his preconceived notion of the ideal man, he will not only see his plans come to nought but also leave a chaos instead of an organization behind him in a very short space of time. The blame which he will then place upon his individual supporters or subordinate leaders is in truth due to himself for his lack of understanding and capacity."

Hitler ends by saying: " Hence I see my task in pointing out to the most divergent temperaments, capacities, and qualities of character contained in the movement the path in which in conjunction with each other and supplementing each other they can work together to the profit of all."

In this definition Hitler professes his belief in a chosen leadership based on the principle that the aim sanctifies the individual. The practical reason which gave rise to this unpleasant profession of belief were the personal accusations made during his imprisonment by the leaders against each other, and particularly against Esser and Streicher. His success proves Hitler to have been right. The masses have taken no exception to the leadership of the Nazi movement. Although the Nazi Party has many excellent and honest officials, their presence does not as a matter of principle exclude that of very different persons. It is indeed difficult to understand how Hitler can in accordance with his own definition describe his Party as that of honest men. The Nazi Party has been uncommonly prolific for a political Party in serious — indeed very serious — scandals involving even its highest officials.

The presence of men of dubious character in the leadership of the Nazi Party has been among the greatest of its misfortunes. It may some day cause it to dissolve of itself. Hitler's indifference to the moral character of his subordinates can perhaps be explained by the superiority of a personally irreproachable character devoted solely to the cause itself. Unfortunately the supply of leaders affords by no means the sole example of Hitler's thoughtlessness in the choice of his co-workers. The movement originated amongst men who looked upon political murder as almost a sacred duty. These were the armed gunmen organized by Röhm who were responsible for a number of still unsolved political murders in Bavaria. Hitler's whole career is shot through with his avowed connexion with political assassination beginning with his approval of Rathenau's murder and continuing through the appointment of Schulz and Heines to positions of leadership up to his telegram to the Potempa assassins. This is not a question of the sacrifice of conscientious scruples for the sake of a cause. Hitler has often enough declared openly that human life has no value in his eyes. That pursuit of an ideal that cannot be denied to Hitler might excuse moral delinquencies. It cannot justify the readiness with which such delinquencies are condoned and forgotten. Moreover, these despisers of political and moral normality regard their actions as tantamount to a revolution in ethical outlook. Perhaps Röhm has given this aspect of the question most unmistakable expression, where he says:

"Nothing is more false than this so-called social ethic. I declare straightaway that I am not one of the morally upright and entertain no ambition to become one. I will on no account be reckoned among the 'moral men,' since I learnt by experience that the 'morals' of these 'moral men' do not as a rule go very far. . . . If so-called statesmen, leaders of the people, &c., act out of moral consideration, it is usually a proof that they can think of nothing better. . . . That this should be the case with a certain type of 'popular' writers who for the most part were never in the trenches and only 'experienced' the war from a safe place is small cause for wonder. . . . When the State claims the right to — and still more believes it can — regulate or turn into other channels human passions, the attempt appears to me to be ignorant and injudicious. . . . Madness, madness, everywhere madness! to quote the words of Richard Wagner's Hans Sachs."

The cry for unrestricted liberty for the individual to indulge his desires can only be a cry of evil. The old principle must always remain true: that only that is permissible to the individual which does not hurt his fellow. The best that can be said of this unscrupulous leadership is that the breakdown of civilization imposed upon it a guilt which was greater than it would otherwise have earned for itself. It is possible that these leaders and their guilt have their purpose in the universal plan of history. Nevertheless nation and State alike can only regain their lost morality when this generation which has been sacrificed in its guilt lays down the leadership.

OLD COMRADES DEPART AND NEW LEADERS ARRIVE

Old comrades parted company with Hitler in these days. Drexler founded a "National Social Peoples Union" which disappeared after a brief existence. Röhm quarrelled with Hitler over the use to be made of the SA, and went out into the wilderness without so much as a word of thanks from the Leader who called himself his friend. For years after his departure the Party lacked a proper SA. Röhm wanted to exclude party politics from the SA and to forbid the political leaders of the Nazi Party from issuing instructions to the SA leaders. In this demand Hitler saw a limitation placed upon his own personal authority. For his part he demanded of Röhm that the SA should be completely subject to the Party leadership. At this point Röhm broke off the conversation, and on the next day handed to Hitler his resignation as leader of the SA. The personal break with Hitler must have been one of the most bitter disappointments of Röhm's life. He wrote to Hitler that he thanked him from the bottom of his heart for his friendship in good hours as in bad, and concluded by asking him not to deprive him of his friendship. He never received an answer. His official letter of resignation remained unanswered. Röhm published a final order of the day to the SA which the *Völkischer Beobachter* printed without a word of comment. Hitler kept silence both in private and in public. Neither a word of thanks nor any public testimony to his services were accorded to the man who was the true organizer of the Nazi Party.

Among the new recruits in these days were three men who were destined to exercise an important influence upon the future destiny of the Nazi movement. Gregor Strasser was for long years the best known of the Nazi leaders. A huge man with the voice of a lion and the strength of a bear, Strasser stood out from among his companions in the Nazi Party by the sheer power of his personality. As a politician he is a brilliant example of that post-War type which has brought the Nazi movement to the pinnacle of power — a private individual who does not understand why only old and well-known men should become members of parliament. He is the nameless German from the trenches who is now resolved to take charge of affairs himself. Hitler is a bundle of nerves by comparison with him. Strasser came from Lower Bavaria and was a chemist by profession. It was chiefly due to Strasser that the Nazi ideal was spread abroad beyond the Bavarian frontiers into Northern Germany. He became District Leader and SA Leader for Lower Bavaria. He was never one of Hitler's intimates, exercised no perceptible influence upon the leadership of the Party, and on the day of the Putsch was abandoned to his fate and left to defend a hopeless position on the bank of the Isar. He was returned to both the Reichstag and the Bavarian Diet in the elections of 1924, and from thenceforward was prominently before the eyes of the public. The other recruit was of still greater importance. An attempt will subsequently be made to draw the portrait of the young journalist from Elberfeld, who is now world-famous as Reich Minister for Propaganda and National Enlightenment — Dr. Goebbels. For a time these two men sought to undermine Hitler's personal ascendancy in the Party councils. At the beginning of 1926 Hitler cannot have felt certain that he would still have a Party behind him at the end of the year. On paper the Party numbered some thirty thousand members. But these members looked to his untrustworthy subordinates even more than to Hitler as their leaders. He could only be certain of the support of Southern Bavaria. In Northern Germany Strasser had organized a Party within the Party, and was considering whether or not he should finally break with Hitler or depose him and relegate him to the harmless position of an honorary president.

It was at this juncture that Count Reventlow made the discovery that on nearer inspection Hitler was only a demagogue and not a politician or statesman. The ablest men in the Party were also aware that Hitler's persistent avoidance of decisions in political issues and his philosophical rather than political speeches rendered collaboration with him almost impossible. It is necessary to remember that all these Party leaders and members, comrades and conspirators, were not experienced politicians but private individuals who had been thrown, as it were, accidentally into political life. Hence their hopes and ideas were untutored and exaggerated, and they lacked a proper sense of the realities of a political situation. This led them to evolve the wildest plans on paper. Throughout 1925 Strasser had achieved success after success in winning over the masses who were avidly searching for an ideal. He who gains the support of tens of thousands can easily overlook the fact that these are only a small part of millions. Moreover, Strasser had not as yet known defeat, and therefore thought that the Party itself could be as easily captured as the masses. Meanwhile,

Hitler busied himself in strengthening his hold upon the Party organization.

The chief newspaper of the Nazi Party was the sole material and juridical support which Hitler then possessed in the movement. He was successful during 1926 in making the newspaper financially independent. His propaganda in 1926 was devoted less to gaining new members for the Nazi Party than new readers of the *Völkischer Beobachter*. The SS (*Schutzstaffel*) were forced to become touters for advertisements. A small body of SS had already been in existence in Munich for some months. In January 1926, SS groups were organized throughout the entire Nazi Party and took over the duties of the defunct SA. Their task was to dissolve and absorb all the innumerable SA groups, Rossbach groups, &c., as the sole official Party troops. The organization of the SS was therefore a matter requiring great circumspection. At the time of the establishment of the SA the proclamation had run: " The Party expects that you will all join." Now it was emphasized that " The Party leadership is convinced that a small number of the best and most determined is more valuable than a vast crowd of supporters lacking the power of decision. In accordance with this belief the regulations for the recruitment of the SS have been laid down with great strictness and the strength of the SS will be restricted as far as possible." In later years, when the Party had grown to vast dimensions, the SS constituted the Guards as compared with the line regiments that were the SA. For the time being their numbers remained small because it was necessary to ensure that they were faithful to Hitler personally. Their task was to form a centre in all the district organizations that would be loyal to Hitler and would uphold his rule as against Strasser. Their leader was Hitler's old friend and former leader of the " Storm Troop Hitler," Berchtold. At the Party Congress in Weimar in May 1926, Hitler presented these new troops with the " Flag of Blood " that had been borne in the fighting at the Feldherrn Hall on November 9, 1923.

NATIONAL SOCIALISM AND WOMEN

On January 21, 1921, the Party had resolved that no woman could at any time be a member of the Party Leadership or any controlling

Party organization. All the women present had enthusiastically voted for this resolution. This unanimity was now a thing of the past.

The Party did not possess any women's organization. An " Order of German Women " (*Deutscher Frauenorden*), led by Elsbeth Zander, was sympathetic to the Nazi movement. But it was itself of no importance. The motto of this Order was that the German woman should not insist upon her rights but upon her duties. This conception of feminine submissiveness was now violently attacked by a woman Nazi — Dr. Hadlich. She declared that in early days German women had often taken a decisive part in the men's councils. Moreover, it was no longer sufficient nowadays to educate children to be men and women; they must all be educated irrespective of sex to be German citizens. It no longer sufficed to hold up motherhood and marriage before a German girl as the sole ideal worth striving for. A woman must be accorded the right to occupy responsible positions in every department of public life. The lack of understanding of the racial problem displayed by the modern State was largely due to the fact that men were the rulers. Rosenberg retorted fiercely that this was nothing more than humanitarian democracy, and could only lead to the production of the " third sex." The rule of the man was natural to the early Germans, as is clear from the examples of Siegfried, Baldur, and Loki. The duty of the woman was to complete the lyrical aspect of life while the man directed its architectonical side. Conrad Hadlich found this antithesis both too beautiful and too meaningless. She replied that the Nazi men were " hopelessly orientalized National Socialists, because the subjection of women was a Jewish idea." Rosenberg rudely answered that Frau Hadlich's notions were those of an out-of-date Darwinism, and that in any case the Party leaders would make known their attitude to this question " at the given time." Goebbels expressed himself prophetically on this problem. " An intellectual warfare will break forth in our midst," he said in 1925, " between the Nationalists and the Socialists, and of the outcome of that struggle will be born the ultimate National Socialism."

Hitler cleverly disposed of the danger threatening his dictatorial rule from the side of Strasser and Goebbels. He attached Goebbels to himself by giving him an independent position as District Leader of the Berlin Nazis, while Strasser in his new capacity as Director of Propaganda continued to be indisputably the most powerful influence in the Party councils after Hitler himself. It was Strasser who made the Ninth of November into a day of mourning for the Party in remembrance of the defeated Putsch and those who had fallen in the fighting round the Feldherrn Hall. It was also Strasser who ordered every member of the Party to wear prominently his Party badge with the swastika on all occasions outside business hours.

PORTRAIT OF A PROPAGANDIST: DR. PAUL JOSEPH GOEBBELS

In entrusting the Berlin District to the young Dr. Goebbels, the Leader was not actuated solely by the desire to reward his services in Bamberg and Weimar. Goebbels had shown himself both an enthusiast for the cause and a man in whose eyes the person of his Leader came before all else. "Dear and honoured Adolf Hitler," Goebbels flatteringly wrote to him after the meeting in Bamberg of the Party leaders, "I have learnt so much from you. You have shown me in the most comradely fashion new paths in matters of principle. . . ." And he concluded by asking to be included among the "General Staff." "The men are there. Summon them. Better still — call upon them one after the other as they are found worthy in your eyes. . . . The day may come when everything breaks in pieces and the mob foams with rage round you and shrieks and yells 'Crucify him!' Then we shall stand there like iron and sing and shout 'Hosanna!'"

This singer of hosannas who was now so anxious for employment could not undo what he had once done in sitting at the same table with Strasser and the rebels to make plans for Hitler's deposition. He sought to rehabilitate himself by casting the blame upon others: "Now I recognize you for what you are — revolutionaries in talk. . . . I did not mean that. . . . Don't talk so much about the ideal, and stop thinking that you alone are the originators and guardians of the ideal. Learn and trust! And believe in the victory of the ideal! It is not a Damascus when we stand united behind our Leader. For we do not bow before him in a Byzantine manner but with the old-time manly pride before the royal throne, with the feeling that he is more than you and I, and that he is only an instrument of the Divine Will which shapes History in a new creative desire." In addition, Goebbels sought to be of one mind with the Leader in matters of detail no less than of principle. Hence he also adopted Hitler's attitude towards the problem of the Party participation in parliamentary elections. When Dr. Frick declared in the *Nationalist Socialist Year-Book* for 1927 that even a small Nazi group in the Reichstag could accomplish much by assiduity and cleverly thought-out questions designed to serve agitatorist ends, Goebbels attacked him violently in an open letter:

" To the devil with your questions! What has our mission to do with questions? " Goebbels then proceeded to draw a picture of how the Leader would one day send all these deputies a silken cord: " At an election the Leader alone decides what names appear on the list. The possession of a mandate does not entitle its holder to anything more than to wait to see if he is summoned. The best boxers will change places with the best agitators in the movement. . . . On the occasion of a great debate the twenty will appear in a body. Upright as oaks they will stand before the tribune of the Reichstag: ten orators possessed of every trick of speech; ten boxers skilled in the tactics of the ring. Ten clever cat-callers would alone suffice to disturb Herr Stresemann, and whenever an attempt is made by the red or pink Democrats to give expression to the ideas of Freedom, Equality, and Fraternity, a few knock-outs will teach them respect."

According to this division of labour, Goebbels could only supply the cat-calls and not the knock-outs if he were to enter parliament. For he is small of stature and has a crippled foot that rendered him unfit for military service. As almost the only civilian among his soldier comrades, Goebbels has to make his way by cunning like a dwarf among giants. Although his intelligence is above the average of Nazi politicians, he is lacking in purposefulness and character, and sways between systems and methods. He is only certain and steadfast in a single aim: his own personal success. In his brochure, *The Nazi-Sozi*, Goebbels depicted a future National Socialist State ruled by a dictator and possessing a parliament for economic questions composed of representatives of the several corporations and industries. This State was also to have a Senate composed of two hundred life Senators. In event of death the Senate chose the deceased Senator's successor. It also elected a Chancellor whose influence was " predominant " in the conduct of policy. In this daydream Goebbels had in mind the Nazi Party, in which a " Chancellor " Goebbels would control affairs under a " dictator " Hitler.

Goebbels is not a born politician. He lacks a sense of cause and effect. Nor does he possess Hitler's logical mind. But he has a rare understanding of men and the uses to which they can be put. His own staff consists of far more loyal supporters and far better co-workers than Hitler has been able to gather about him. In reality Goebbels possesses the intuition that is so falsely ascribed to Hitler, whose habits of thought and speech are far more intelligible to the masses than are those of Goebbels. Distance lends enchantment. Goebbels understands very well how to attract and dazzle the masses by the very fact that he is farther removed from them in thought and speech than the Leader. His greatest agitatorist achievement has been to raise Nazi propaganda to the level of an heroic epic. Hitler demands heroes for Germany; Goebbels finds them. When he described in the *Angriff* the march of the SA through the wet and silent streets of the still-sleeping Neukölln, the march becomes that of the Ten Thousand, and not one of the Nazi martyrs has been raised to such heroic heights as the murdered Berlin student Horst Wessel. Simplicity forms no part of his character. At the time of his removal to Berlin he wrote a farewell address to his former district in the Ruhr, in which there is no mention of his having been transferred to Berlin. On the contrary, he says that the dice have fallen and " decided against you and against my wishes." Moreover, Goebbels does not simply buy a ticket for Berlin like other travellers and arrive there at the Zoo Station at seven-forty. " With a silent regret in my heart I fold up my tent and by the time these lines have reached you racing steam will have already borne me into the asphalt desert that is Berlin." Here speaks a man who is determined to appear a hero even with a kit-bag in his hand. It is not chance that Goebbels's style is a mixture of archaic and glittering words. It is intended to furnish the vocabulary of the future. He who merely concerns himself with daily affairs must make speeches, write articles, collect money, and do a multitude of other petty jobs. But History leads her heroes through colonnades of immortal substantives.

It is possible that this is to do injustice to Goebbels the Man. It is certainly true of Goebbels the Agitator. At the urgings of conscience Goebbels was first forced to emancipate himself from his intellectual surroundings. He was born in 1897 in the Rhineland. A scholarship given to him by the Catholic Albertus-Magnus Association aided him to pursue his studies. Seven universities can count this unruly intellect among the students who listened in their halls to lectures on German philology and literature. He is a born man of letters whose intellect is more informed than deep, and who is wholly lacking in an inner harmony together with all that springs from it — tact, taste, and poise. In the very depths of his nature Goebbels is a seeker who is prone to scepticism rather than belief. He is a man who has never yet found anything in life with which he can sincerely agree. An unhappy temperament — perhaps his physical deformity — made him self-seeking and wavering. His talent is concentrated even more upon himself than upon the personality of Hitler. " And then I spoke at the end, in a breathless silence, the words about the unknown SA man." Without blushing, Goebbels can thus praise himself in a speech as the author of a coined phrase.

Goebbels has declared that as early as 1923 he had organized a local section of the Nazi Party in the occupied area and was thrown into prison by the Belgians. That is one version. Another time he claimed to have been sent to prison for his agitatorist activities on behalf of Hindenburg and to have been beaten with horse-whips. Former friends of his in the Party have openly and repeatedly declared this statement to be a lie. Goebbels has never brought an action for libel against them. As to the reputed founding of the local branch of the Party in 1923, it suffices to say that the *Völkischer Beobachter* for that year never mentions it or its founder; and at this time that newspaper invariably recorded the minutest progress made by the Party anywhere. In 1924 Goebbels edited a popular paper in Elberfeld. At first he was a supporter of Ludendorff. Then he was introduced to National Socialism by the District Leader Karl Kaufmann, and subsequently discovered by Gregor Strasser. His plays and novels are of little value from a literary standpoint, and are so many witnesses to his fight with religious and moral doubts — the revolt of a self-conscious personality against intellectual inhibitions. His writings are not only non-Socialist but are entirely unpolitical.

Goebbels has studied much and obtained his doctorate in the customary fashion. Nevertheless, he excels Hitler himself in his lack of acquired knowledge. His writings and speeches are the richest in ideas and the poorest in solid thought in the whole literature of National Socialism. At least, Hitler has acquired knowledge of a special subject — foreign policy. There is not a trace of any real and fundamental knowledge to be found in Goebbels. Such is the man who is the greatest agitator in the Party after Hitler, and, like Hitler, a Bohemian — though Goebbels differs from Hitler in having remained one to a far greater extent. He is the Public Orator of the Nazi Party. At times he makes clever and striking remarks, as, for example, that a type of working man is developing to-day who can claim with a good conscience to be the social equal of the lower middle class — " the lower middle-class working man." For not only satiety but also hunger is a levelling force. Goebbels cries to his working men: " Arise! Young aristocrats of a new working class! You are the nobility of the Third Reich and the seed you have sown with your blood will produce a magnificent harvest! Clench your fists! Square your jaws! Destroy the equalitarianism of democracy which closes the door to the advance of the new working class in the fulfilment of its historic mission! " But does that sound sincere? When Goebbels calls working men his comrades and talks of " moulding the brutality of the proletariat," it is as if a beautiful actress were to kiss a crossing-sweeper.

Goebbels has not indeed made life easy for himself, and cannot comfortably enjoy his fame after the fashion of many of his Party fellows. An inner sensitiveness that was ill-treated by Fate has concealed itself beneath a casing of brusqueness which causes it discomfort. Hence it is that everything Goebbels writes or says is sincerely meant and still not sincere. " So long as a man holds on to life he is not free! " True. But then Goebbels should add that he himself, in common with his fellow-men, is not free. It was not long before his supporters in Berlin were saying among themselves that " The Doctor " was not always very courageous. " I do not go about wearing a Party badge. It is seldom that I feel called upon to intervene in a political conversation." Nevertheless, the Reich Director of Propaganda had ordered the wearing of the Party badge as the best of all possible means of propaganda.

An article which appeared in the *Völkischer Beobachter* in February 1927, and which would seem from its style to have been written by Goebbels himself, described with hair-raising vividness the dangerous life led by the Berlin District Leader. After visiting a hospital Goebbels found that " the street had been occupied in military fashion by the guards of the Marxist money-coffers. In other words, the enemy had requisitioned bricks from a neighbouring building-site and piled them up for the purpose of stoning Dr. Goebbels to death in ritualistic fashion. It was a tense and fateful moment. At the very moment when Dr. Goebbels hesitated as to whether he should conceal himself in one or other of the buildings of the Virchow Hospital amidst the jeers of the Jewish doctors and nurses or let himself be stoned to death on the street to the accompaniment of cheers for freedom coming from the mouths of weak-minded fellow-countrymen — at this fateful instant there appeared the symbol of the Republic: the policeman's baton. The street was clear! " Another glaring example of this type of journalism is the description from the same clever pen of a motor-trip, during which the Berlin District Leader apparently revealed his possession of psychic powers. " All at once Dr. Goebbels rose from his seat. ' Stop, Comrade Chauffeur! Stop! ' The car stopped. ' What is the matter, Doctor? ' ' I don't know. We are in danger! ' We put our hands in our pockets and sprang out of the car. There was nothing to be seen nor heard. We went round the car and inspected it. All four tyres were sound. But — what is that? Actually — four bolts were missing from the left rear-wheel. Four bolts out of five. A mean and devilish piece of work. Traces of misapplied force told the rest of the tale. That is the way in which the Jews and their slaves fight. Intellectual weapons."

Other Nazi leaders have also experienced danger in the course of their agitation. Gregor Strasser was forced to lie in bed for weeks after a beating. Nevertheless they have never shown traces of possessing highly strung nervous systems that are alive to the least possibility of danger. And not a single one of them has so assiduously recorded his experiences in the history of the party. It is easy to understand why an enraged Strasser wrote towards the end of April 1927, in his *Berliner Arbeiterzeitung*, that it was not customary among soldiers in the trenches to make propaganda out of their actions and to appear continually in the public eye by means of self-commendatory newspaper articles. Another man, who knew Goebbels well in Elberfeld, published in the same issue of Strasser's newspaper an article entitled " The Consequences of Racial Intermarriage." It was apparently a harmless scientific essay devoted solely to proving that people with crippled feet are objects for suspicion. " Beware of the Marked Ones! " runs a Lower Saxon proverb. This truth is the result of experience. It points to the consequences of racial intermixture and serves as a warning against those who display these consequences in their own persons. Richard III of England was a hunch-back and lame. The court jester of Louis XIII was also crippled, and the club-footed Talleyrand possessed a notorious character. " One can hardly use the word ' character ' in speaking of him," wrote Erich Koch, who was the author of the article and subsequently East Prussian District Leader. " He knew how to fascinate, to exaggerate, to spread sensational reports abroad, to make use of others regardless of their feelings or interests, to squeeze them like a lemon and then throw them aside in order to obtain for himself the credit that rightly belonged to them. Moreover, he was a pastmaster in the noble arts of lying, intrigue, and duplicity. He betrayed his Emperor Napoleon as well as his King Louis XVIII in regular alternation."

All this parade of historical learning is nothing more than a lampoon at the expense of the Berlin District Leader, whose Aryan origin was questioned in the Party, and whose character was detested by his fellow-members. " An end to examples! " Koch concluded. " They all serve to teach us the appalling consequences of racial intermixture — racial degeneration. The bearers of the mental and bodily lack of harmony which is the consequence of racial mixture often display at first sight qualities and capacities that have an attractive power that resembles the brilliant light of an electric lamp before eternal darkness results from a short-circuit. These men are indeed clever. At the same time they are always inordinately ambitious and unfeeling egoists who have invariably brought injury upon the people as a whole."

In Berlin, Goebbels employed his undoubted talent as a propagandist energetically, but for a long time comparatively ineffectually. Although he surpassed even Hitler in the abundance of his propagandist inspirations, Goebbels was never his equal in popular appeal.

NEW OPPORTUNITIES

Meanwhile the SA was reorganized by Captain Pfeffer von Salomon. As Hitler's confidential agent in the Ruhr District, of which Strasser was the Leader, Pfeffer had kept watch upon Karl Kaufmann and upon Dr. Goebbels, who had both been conspiring with Strasser to depose Hitler from his pre-eminence in the Party councils. Nevertheless, promotion to the leadership of the SA was to prove Pfeffer's downfall. His insubordinate manner and lack of deference irritated the Leader and led to frequent quarrels between them. His influence in the Party also grew too swiftly for Hitler's liking. At the close of 1926 Pfeffer managed to secure control over the Hitler Youth (*Hitler-Jugend*), whose leader, Kurt Gruber, now found himself subordinated to the supreme SA Leader (Osaf). In alarm, Hitler issued an instruction that no orders or regulations would be binding upon the SA unless they bore his signature in addition to that of the Osaf. Pfeffer ignored this challenge. Thereupon Hitler returned to the charge with an order which declared that the responsibility for any regulations or orders bearing only the signature of the Osaf would fall upon the Osaf alone. Meanwhile Pfeffer was arming and training the SA to be a military force. It was a recurrence of the old quarrel between Hitler and Röhm — the civilian versus the soldier.

These continual internal crises prevented the Party from making any real progress. Nevertheless, it sent twelve deputies to the Reichstag in 1928, among whom was Göring, who had been allowed to return to Germany in consequence of an amnesty, but who was not reinstated in his former position as SA Leader. Göring had since his return been one of Hitler's closest political and social advisers. After 1928 the Nazi Party once more saw better times. Its membership now comprised sixty thousand divided into innumerable organizations. There was a Nazi Teachers' Association. There was the Union of German Nazi Lawyers and the Union of Nazi Physicians. The German Women's Order was transformed into the "Red Swastika" Order and incorporated with the Nazi Party. In addition to the Hitler Youth there was also a special organization for the pupils at higher schools known as the Union of Nazi Pupils (*Nationalsozialistische Schülerbund*). The growth of the Party had become slower. In 1926–27 it rose from 17,000 to 40,000 members. In the succeeding years the Party membership increased rapidly. If this small Party covered itself with such an overgrowth of organizations, it is not astonishing that as early as 1929 Strasser declared in dismay that the Nazi Party was in a state of over-organization. In 1930 Hitler was complaining that the Party organization was threatening to become an end in itself. This situation has not improved with the passage of time.

The increased prosperity of the Party was at least in part due to an agreement which Hitler concluded with Dr. Alfred Hugenberg, the leader of the German Nationalist Party, in the autumn of 1929, for the purpose of organizing a popular protest against the Young Plan. This alliance with Hugenberg brought the Nazi Party the most powerful means of propaganda which it had hitherto possessed. Hugenberg was the greatest magnate in the film and Press world. All his news services and film factories were now placed at the disposal of Nazi propaganda. Hugenberg thus gave Hitler the chance to make the Nazi Party a really popular Party. The membership of the Party numbered 120,000 in the summer of 1929, and by March 1930 it had already attained to the figure of 210,000. A contributory cause of this success was its obtaining a ministerial portfolio. In January 1930 Dr. Frick became Thuringian Minister of the Interior. A still more powerful contributory cause to the Party's increase in numbers and influence was the economic crisis which had already begun in Germany in 1928 and was now reaching its height. This crisis resulted in an increase in 1930 of three millions in the numbers of the unemployed. In 1932 this figure rose to six millions. The real figure was still higher — probably round about eight to nine millions. A the unemployed were not only workmen but also many employees had occupied so-called higher posts, and men who had been i pendent traders or industrialists whose businesses had failed because the unemployed and those whose wages had been cut were unable to afford to buy anything. Once again, however, this economic connexion of cause and effect was not immediately obvious to the broad masses of those who had been so sorely hit. They preferred to lay the blame upon the machinations of a clique at the head of which were the great combines, such as the department stores behind which they suspected the existence of the " Bank and Stock Exchange magnates." In consequence of the lowering of the buying power of the urban masses, agriculture also experienced a depression, and more especially since the farmers immediately after the inflation had loaded themselves with debt at incredibly high rates of interest. Thus the middle class, which was daily growing more impoverished, the heavily indebted agriculturists, and the unemployed part of the working class, became the reservoir from which — thanks to his clever agitation that laid stress upon the immediate and obvious and totally neglected underlying causes — Hitler took his followers.

CRISIS AND VICTORY IN 1930

It made no difference to the public success of the Nazis that a number of the members and officials of the Nazi Party grew dissatisfied with Hitler's tactics, and openly criticized them. Opposition centred round the person of Gregor Strasser, who had established his seat in Berlin, where he published a number of journals, including a daily newspaper. The most outspoken among these malcontents was Gregor's brother, Dr. Otto Strasser. He accused Hitler of having betrayed the revolutionary aims of the Party, and was rewarded himself by expulsion from it. The discussions on May 21 and 22, 1930, at which Hitler demanded from Otto Strasser that his publishing activities in Berlin should cease, began with a debate over the nature of art. Hitler's Wilhelmian aversion to modern forms of art was anathema in the eyes of the Strasser group. " Everything you say shows that you have not the least idea of art." Hitler retorted to their criticisms. " There is no such thing in art as ' old ' and ' new ' any more than there is such a thing as a ' revolution in Art.' There is only an eternal art, namely, Nordic-Grecian art. And it is all nonsense to talk of Dutch art, Italian art, German art, just as it is nonsense to look upon Gothic as a special art-form. That is all Nordic-Grecian art; and, indeed, all that can at all lay claim to the name of art must always be Nordic-Grecian." After defining the principles of art, Hitler went on to discuss Socialism:

" The great masses of workmen want nothing else than bread and amusement; they have no understanding of idealism; and we can never count upon being able to gain any considerable support among them. What we want is a picked number from the new ruling class, who — unlike you — are not troubled with humanitarian feelings, but who are convinced that they have the right to rule as being a superior race, and who will secure and maintain their rule ruthlessly over the broad masses."

Hitler added that an understanding with England was in the interests of Germany, because it was necessary to establish a Nordic-Germanic hegemony in Europe, and in conjunction with Nordic-Germanic America over the whole world.

In the course of this discussion Otto Strasser revealed his dislike of " so-called progress," while Hitler came forward as its champion. Humanity has developed enormously from the Stone Age to the present mechanical civilization. This progressive movement always received its impulsion from great men alone. When Strasser expressed doubts as to the importance of the individual great men in this connexion, Hitler asked him sharply if he denied that he (Hitler) was the creator of National Socialism. Strasser said that he did deny it: National Socialism was an idea which was still in evolution, and in that evolutionary process Hitler certainly played a specially important rôle. The " idea " itself was Socialism. Here Hitler interrupted Strasser by declaring that this so-called Socialism was nothing but pure Marxism. There was no such thing as a capitalist system. A factory-owner was dependent upon his workmen. If they went on strike, then his so-called property became utterly worthless. At this point Hitler turned to his neighbour Amann and said:

" What right have these people to demand a share in property or even in the administration? Herr Amann, would you permit your typist to have any voice in your affairs? The employer who accepts the responsibility for production also gives the workpeople their means of livelihood. Our greatest industrialists are not concerned with the acquisition of wealth or with good living, but, above all else, with responsibility and power. They have worked their way to the top by their own abilities, and this proof of their capacity — a capacity only displayed by a higher race — gives them the right to lead."

After this confession of his belief in the superior race of factory-owners and directors, Hitler went on to declare that rentability must always be the standard of industry (how differently Gregor Strasser thought on this point!), and when Otto Strasser contradicted him and praised the autarchy of a nationalist economist system, Hitler abruptly interrupted him and said:

" That is nothing more than wretched theorism and dilettantism. Do you really believe that we can ever separate ourselves from international trade and finance? On the contrary, our task is to undertake an immense organization of the whole world in which each land shall produce what it requires most and in which the white race — the Nordic race — shall take the leading part in administering and carrying out this vast plan. Believe me, National Socialism would not be worth anything if it were to be confined to Germany and did not secure the rule of the superior race over the whole world for at least one or two thousand years."

At this point Gregor Strasser, who had been listening to the discussion, declared that economic autarchy must unquestionably be the aim of National Socialism. Hitler beat a retreat. Yes, he agreed that autarchy must be the ultimate objective in, say, a century. To-day, however, it was impossible to cut loose from the international economic system. Once again Strasser let fall the word " Socialism." Hitler replied: " The word 'Socialism' is in itself a bad word. But it is certainly not to be taken as meaning that industry must be socialized, and only to mean that it could be socialized if industrialists were to act contrary to the national interests. As long as they do not do that it would be little short of a crime to destroy the existing economic system." It is hardly necessary to mention that this discussion did not lead to any agreement.

Soon after this discussion took place, a mutiny broke out among the Berlin SA as a result of Otto Strasser's expulsion from the Nazi Party after this abortive attempt at reconciliation between him and Hitler. Hitler was forced to come to Berlin to quell the revolt in person. He drove from one SA house to another, dissolved into tears, and besought his " boys " not to fail him in this decisive hour. Money accomplished more than tears. Every member of the Party was required to contribute twenty pfennigs SA tax. The entrance fee to the Party was doubled, and the local groups were forced to give up half their election funds to the SA. From this time onwards the SA did not have to carry out their laborious duties out of pure idealism alone. A fateful step had thus been taken that was to influence the future development of the SA, and to result in turning at least a fair proportion of them into nothing better than mercenaries.

In a professional army, mutiny is punished with death. In this instance it cost the leaders, who were for the most part helpless to prevent the revolt, their rank. Hitler seized the opportunity to rid himself of Pfeffer. He was honourably removed from his post, and retired to Munich to live in comfort with a pension. Hitler himself now became the supreme SA Leader and thereby the ruler of his Party who held in his hands the reins of both military and civil government. Since it was obviously impossible for him, personally, to control the SA, it became necessary to appoint a Chief of Staff — nobody dared as yet to use the expression " Chief of the General Staff." For a time Göring seemed to be the favoured candidate, and his candidature was supported by Goebbels. But Hitler did not appoint Göring. Instead, he appointed Röhm, who had just returned from Bolivia. Röhm had been officially reconciled to Hitler in 1927, and in the following year had been compelled for financial reasons to accept a commission in the Bolivian Army, to which he is still theoretically attached. In October 1930 Hitler recalled him, and, in January 1931, he was appointed Chief of Staff to the SA. Since Hitler himself became commander-in-chief (Osaf) of the SA, there has never been any criticism of the leadership principle in the movement.

These internal disturbances did not impede the triumphal progress of National Socialism any more than a stone holds back a waterfall. The Right Wing Government of Brüning, which had been placed in office by Hindenburg in May 1930, after the resignation of Hermann Müller's Cabinet, dissolved the Reichstag in the summer of that year in the belief that the consequent election would bring them large gains. In this belief, Brüning was proved greatly mistaken. The change of government had only served to make public opinion still more distrustful of all government. It only recognized the collapse of what was old, and did not notice the existence of something new. Brüning's start was unlucky; he dissolved the Reichstag and appealed to the nation — for a budget which he put into force by emergency decrees. The most unskilful propaganda gave the people words instead of bread. Speakers busied themselves with Conservatism, Liberalism, and Parliamentarism in the belief that the electorate was opposed to democracy. In reality it was only opposed to unemployment and taxation. At the same time Brüning recognized the existence of a negative factor: this election was not to be won by the old type of election promises. A part of the electorate was indeed discontented with rational methods by which the Government promised material performance in return for votes. The tendency, still more the feeling, to repose confidence in some one individual grew and influenced the election of this or that candidate. Nevertheless, Brüning and his friends did not know how to win this confidence for themselves.

The Right Wing electorate, inclusive of the German Nationalists, began to go over to Hitler in large numbers. On September 14, 1930, Hitler received 6.4 million votes and gained 107 seats in the Reichstag. He himself, of course, being still of Austrian nationality, was not among the Nazi candidates; and indeed he had no wish to be. The Right lost 111 mandates, of which the greater part fell to the Nazis. After this tremendous triumph Hitler was more than ever before the absolute ruler over the National Socialist German Workers Party.

"At the moment when the masses come over with cries of 'Hurrah' to our side we are lost," Hitler had said two years before. Now they had come over to his side. And not only the fact that they had done so, but also why they had done so, gave the Nazis cause for anxiety. The

6.4 million voters on September 14, 1930, did not support the Party out of enthusiasm but out of disappointment with the fallen Republic. Were these 6.4 millions, of whom more than the half had never previously troubled themselves about politics, really Germany's best citizens?

In the following chapters an attempt will be made to show how National Socialism has destroyed the Weimar Republic since the Reichstag election of 1930. Although itself lacking in any very definite political conceptions, the Nazi Party has been the only non-Marxist Party to reckon with the proletarianization of the middle classes. Without calling it by this name, the Nazis have recognized it as an irrevocable fact which will produce new social forms and new values. The middle-class Parties promised their supporters to restore to them their lost standard of life — and very rightly were met with incredulity. The Nazis promised them new means of livelihood, new esteem, and a new position in the State — and were met with credence. The future alone can prove whether or not the middle classes were right in placing their confidence in the Nazi Party's promises.

CHAPTER VI

HITLER IN OPPOSITION

BY September 14, 1930, the Nazi Party had become a factor to be reckoned with. The problem was now one of using that factor to the greatest advantage.

Hitler continued in his course of opposition and agitation. He wished to grow stronger before taking over the government. He intended the Party to become far more than a factor to be reckoned with. It was to become the most potent part of the whole of German public life. By about 1934 or 1935, he reckoned, he would be in control of a majority in the Reichstag. He was prepared to wait until then, but no longer. He had quite renounced his old idea of taking the position by storm, now that he had a good prospect of starving the enemy out.

LENIENCY TOWARDS THE "MONEY MAGNETS"

At first he extended, elucidated, and expounded his programme in order to bring it more into accord with the increased importance of the Party and the changed requirements of the time. He allowed the letter of the law to stand, but by sundry explanations gave a new interpretation to various sections.

One important problem which National Socialism had to resolve very thoroughly was that of their social and economic policy. The vital point of the Nazi programme was, of course, Feder's famous slogan, " breaking the bondage of interest." When Hitler as a young soldier in the Reichswehr attending the educational course of the Epp brigade first heard this new theory from Feder's own lips, he felt that scales had fallen from his eyes. It appeared to him to be the key to the whole social problem. Meanwhile Hitler had come to think on a much bigger scale. Various experts had taken trouble to instruct the National Socialist leader in certain general economic truths, or to win his sympathy for particular projects of their own. Now that Hitler had friends and advisers like Dr. Bang, a German Nationalist member of the Reichstag, and Dr. Wagener, an ex-officer, who enjoyed a great reputation at the Brown House, Feder's influence was on the wane. In addition, Gregor Strasser had his own economic views, which made a strong impression not only within the Party, but, thanks to their telling phraseology, also upon the public in general, and thus in time came to be a strong factor in the Party propaganda.

The economic ideology of the early days of National Socialism came once more to the fore in a motion which the Party members brought before the Reichstag on October 14, 1930, and which had been signed by their best men. One of its most pregnant sentences ran: "The entire property of Bank and Stock Exchange magnates, of Eastern Jews who have come into the country since August 1, 1914, and of other aliens and their families and relations, in addition to any increase of property due to war, revolution, inflation, deflation, or other profiteering, is to be sequestrated for the good of the German community without compensation of any kind. Large banks are to be taken over by the State immediately." Furthermore, the maximum rate of interest was to be fixed at four per cent.

The motion caused no small stir in that part of the Press which was normally well disposed to National Socialists. They were gently admonished not to make fools of themselves by showing their " simplicity " in economic matters. Professors Herkner, Adolf Weber, Eckert, and Götz Briefs demonstrated taking point for point in an open letter to the National Socialist Reichstag fraction that their demands were economically impossible. When, however, the Socialists and Communists threatened to support the motion and thus help to get it passed, Hitler's financial backers intervened, and it was quietly withdrawn.

HITLER'S POLICY TOWARDS WORKMEN AND EMPLOYERS

A second problem that grew much more pressing after the victory in September was the attitude of the Party to the working classes. The German employers were at that time beginning an extensive campaign against the Trade Union rates of wages. A wave of social unrest swept through Germany. About the middle of October 1930 there was a strike of metal workers in Berlin, which affected more than a hundred thousand workmen. What did the National Socialist Party do? Hitler announced in the *Völkischer Beobachter* that he would support the strike in order to make it clear to German industry that it was time the policy of concessions came to an end.

Obviously calling the men out on strike infuriated the employers. The number of employers supporting Hitler and his Party had grown considerably since the September elections. No doubt they were still inclined to regard the National Socialist Party as a friendly Power with whom they were in alliance against the common enemy, Marxism. As a constructive political factor, National Socialism of the Hitler type promised encouragement to the progressive employer, a designation which probably each one took to himself. In practice the Nazis would be accounted opponents of the Trade Unions. They did not actually throw overboard the Trade Union idea, but did, in fact, attack practically all the Trade Union organizations worth mentioning, on account of their political sympathies. National Socialism did not hold very closely to economic formulae. There was no real fear that it would nationalize everything. A far reaching understanding thus seemed within the realms of possibility when all at once the Berlin strike darkened the skies. The economic experts at the Brown House set to work to calm agitated feelings. Major Wagener explained to some Saxon industrialists that it had been impossible for the National Socialist Party to forbid its members to take part in the strike, because otherwise the working men would have left the Party and have gone over to Socialism. In other words, he tried to make the employers see that Nazis, even when on strike, were still preferable to Social Democrats.

THE PLEDGE OF LEGALITY

Finally, Hitler took advantage of the opportunity to declare that he no longer intended a *coup d'état*.

Soon after the September elections, three young Reichswehr officers — Lieutenant Wendt and Second Lieutenants Ludin and Scheringer — were arraigned before the Supreme Court in Leipzig. The three had been in touch with the Nazis, and were accused of political agitation in the Reichswehr. The fact that most of the Reichswehr officers belonged to Right Wing Parties had long been recognized by the Republic. It now became evident that many of the younger officers were Nazi in sympathy. The question was whether the National Socialist Party was making an organized attempt to win over the Reichswehr. That it had actually happened was undeniable. But Hitler was emphatic that the Party did nothing unconstitutional with his consent. He had no doubts that in any case he had plenty of friends among the officers of the Reichswehr. His assurance that he proceeded along constitutional lines was challenged during the Leipzig trial, because he had described himself as a revolutionary. He replied: " If we have another two or three elections now, the National Socialist movement will have a majority in the Reichstag and will then prepare for the National Socialist revolution."

President (ironically): " You imply a moral revolution? And if any one understands anything else by it you will say: ' We can't help that '? "

Hitler: " Germany is strangled by Peace Treaties. Every law that is made in Germany to-day is an attempt still further to grind down the German people under the Treaties. The National Socialists do not regard these Treaties as natural, but as something that has been forced upon the nation. We do not agree that future generations who are absolutely innocent should be burdened with them. By striving against them with every means in our power we are preparing for revolution."

President: " Even by illegal means? "

Hitler: " I am assuming that we shall be successful. Then we shall strive against the Peace Treaties with every possible means, even those that may appear illegal to the rest of the world. . . ."

President (growing more and more sarcastic): " What is your idea of the Third Reich? "

Hitler: " The Constitution gives us the ground on which to wage our battle, but not its aim. We shall become members of all constitutional bodies, and in this manner make the Party the decisive factor. Of course, when we possess all constitutional rights we shall then mould the State into the form that we consider to be the right one."

President (highly sceptical): " So you intend to work only along constitutional lines? "

Hitler (sharply): " Yes."

This was Hitler's famous undertaking to use only legal methods, which aroused surprise in the public at large, and dismay in considerable sections of the Nazi Party. People asked themselves whether Hitler really believed that he would ever gain 51 per cent. of the electorate. Numbers of SA officers, in particular, were astonished; for in face of so much legality they appeared to themselves to be somewhat superfluous. Many expressed the opinion that their leader's oath was no more than a matter of tactics — in other words, perjury. Quite a number, too, lost heart and regretted not having turned their backs on the movement with Otto Strasser.

"HEADS WILL ROLL"

This mood of gloom was somewhat dissipated by a second word that Hitler had let fall at Leipzig. One of those concerned in the trial had endeavoured to entangle him in contradictions and referred to some of his earlier sayings, amongst others one which had been much quoted about " heads rolling." Hitler was able to *put a legal interpretation* on this too:

" If the National Socialist movement is victorious, a National-Socialist Court of Justice will also be set up; November 1918 will be avenged, and *heads will roll.*"

Hitler's threat re-echoed in Germany like nothing else that he had ever said. By means of a ghastly simile it made clear what most people had felt at the back of their minds — that the revolution which had begun in 1918 had not yet come to an end, and would still bring forth all the glamour and all the horrors which had then been lacking. Hitler was announcing that he would set up the guillotine that, to the surprise of the bourgeoise, had been foregone by the revolutionaries of 1918. Possibly Hitler himself or one of his associates had been present at the mass meeting in Munich in the Spring of 1919 when some one had hysterically demanded that the social problem should be solved by setting up a guillotine in the square in front of the town hall. In answer to which Ernst Toller, the poet, who was at the time one of the leaders of the people, had leapt from his seat in a fury, saying that the guillotine was an out-moded instrument, unworthy of the twentieth century, and that we lived in a humanitarian age. Hitler now condemned this age to death, and the frenzied applause of his followers showed how much brutality existed in the world that could rejoice at its end.

As propaganda the threat had a tremendous effect. It showed the Nazi leader's ruthless self-confidence, and his opponents seemed to be in a sense paralysed with horror. A Socialist member of the Thuringian Diet protested against the fearful idea, whereupon a Nazi cried: "Your head is as likely to roll as any one's!" The abominations that Hitler's words called up from the depths of many a man's soul are perhaps best typified by an article published a year later in the *Angriff* by Dr. Von Leers, a Nazi educationalist and politician. He describes the Leipzig trial as the occasion "on which Hitler uttered the wondrous message that finds an echo in all our hearts, the glorious pledge of atonement: 'Heads shall roll!'"

In any normal State a man who had uttered a threat like Hitler's would have been arrested at once, especially since he was still in point of fact a foreigner. Nothing of the kind happened in Hitler's case. No responsible authority seems even to have given it a thought. And this fact showed more plainly than anything else that Hitler was working along the right lines in insisting upon everything being done "constitutionally." A State that was so weak must one day be destroyed by the growth of so determined a power as that represented by National Socialism, however closely it clung to the Constitution. And so it came to pass.

SA, THE STATE WITHIN A STATE

What with the appeal to constitutionalism and visions of carnage, a crisis occurred in important sections of the Party itself. The centre of the trouble was mainly in the SA. After the comparatively innocuous results of the unfortunate affair with the Berlin group during the September elections, the SA was reorganized under Röhm and its strength greatly augmented. This led to a dangerous increase of its feeling of self-importance, and it tended more and more to regard itself as the only really essential weapon in the struggle for power. The temper of the corps may perhaps be best shown by a quotation from the SA supplement to the *Angriff*: "We are superior to others. Hence our duties also are greater than those of others. . . ." By "others" were meant the ordinary rank and file of the Party.

This arrogance was countered by the new regulations, running into several hundred pages, that were drafted under Röhm's direction. In an introduction, Hitler narrowed down the sphere of the SA considerably. He said that it was "that part of the total organization which kept vigilant watch and supervised the propaganda." More important than the general remarks was the definite statement: "SA leaders are not to be regarded as subordinate to political leaders, nor *vice versa*." And section 133 of the regulations carries the division still further: "SA leaders, except those who are members of the Reichstag, shall in general only appear as speakers in public meetings when anything has to be announced concerning the SA or military matters. . . . Moreover, SA leaders shall not normally occupy political leaderships at the same time."

Nevertheless, the SA is on no account to live a life of its own within the Party. Hence Hitler in a proclamation on February 20, 1931, ordained: "The district leader shall lay down in broad outlines the political course, objects, and methods to be followed by the leader of the secondary group, (i.e. the SA unit of the district). Moreover, in principle, he shall determine every public appearance of the SA, and shall make the necessary arrangements with the leader of the secondary group. I wish these arrangements to be communicated by the district leader to his political subordinates and by the leader of the secondary group to the leaders under his command, so that there shall be uniformity of regulations within the district, and any possibility of dissension between the leaders is precluded."

THE ORGANIZATION OF THE SA

In externals the structure of the SA is similar to that of the old German army. There are, however, two essential differences: the lack of arms and the lack of any effective disciplinary power.

The smallest SA unit is the Squad, and consists of four to twelve men. The next above it is the Troop, consisting of three to six Squads, and containing not less than twenty or more than sixty men. The next and most important unit is the Storm Detachment, which contains two to three Troops, and thus numbers seventy to one hundred and twenty men. This is comparable with the Company in the old German army. Several Storm Detachments go to make a Storm Column, the strength of which varies from two hundred and fifty to six hundred men. The next unit, the Standard, numbers one thousand to three thousand men, and is equivalent to a regiment. Recruiting for a particular Standard is still to some extent confined to one locality. On the other hand, this is no longer absolutely true of the Brigade, a unit newly created in 1933, and not at all true of the next higher unit, the Group (formerly Lower Group). The highest unit of all, the Higher Group (formerly the Group) already bears the character of an Army and comprises some hundred thousand men. At present the total numbers of the SA are officially given as eight hundred thousand (and no more are being enrolled). The depôts of the eight Groups are Königsberg, Stettin, Breslau, Dresden, Hanover, Frankfurt-am-Main, Munich, and Linz (Austria). This fact proves that the alleged independence of the Austrian organization does not exist.

The Standards were in many cases given the numbers of regiments which had formerly been stationed at their depôts.

The regulations for the formation of the various units show great psychological insight. They are all founded upon Hitler's principle that there must always be a leader before the creation of any organization is attempted. Hence Hitler's above-mentioned edict directs:

" In the first instance, only he who forms a Squad can and shall be leader of that Squad." The Squad itself " shall consist of friends who join themselves together because they are of the same mind and are united by common interests founded on early friendship, on being old schoolfellows, or being engaged in the same kind of work." If possible, they should all come from the same place. The Squad is known by the name of the leader who forms it and not by a number. The original leader announces the formation of the Squad to the nearest higher SA leader (preferably a Storm Detachment leader) who takes the Squad under his leadership and confirms the Squad leader in his rank. If the latter is obliged for any reason to relinquish his post, successors are appointed by the leader of the Storm Detachment. These principles for the constitution of the smallest SA cell may be regarded as a model of organizing wisdom.

THE SPECIAL DEFENCE SECTION (SS)

A most curious and interesting section of the SA is the so-called special guard, known as the SS.

It may be recalled that it was derived from the first defence sections which were brought into being under Berchtold's leadership when the Party was reconstituted. More is expected of them than of the SA, their numbers are correspondingly less, and their sphere of activity greater. Above all, they are expected to be intellectually on a higher level. The present Chief of the SS is Gregor Strasser's old colleague, Heinrich Himmler, who became chief of police in Bavaria after the revolution of 1933. The best description of the SS can perhaps be gleaned from a speech made by Himmler on the occasion of a conference of leaders in the middle of the year 1931. He said:

"The SA is the Line, the SS the Guards. We are no wiser to-day than we were two thousand years ago. In the history of former wars, in the history of the Prussian armies of three or four hundred years ago, it is seen over and over again that wars are waged with armies, but that every leader has about him a particular organization of men of specially high quality, who go wherever things are at their worst; and those are the Guards. There have always been Guards — the Persians had them, the Greeks, Caesar, Napoleon, Frederick the Great, right up to the time of the World War. And the Guards in the new Germany will be the SS. The Guards are the elect from among picked troops."

Thus the SS form a body, possibly of the highest performance, certainly of the greatest arrogance. Part of a regulation of June 1931 runs as follows: "Every company of the SS shall attend the first meeting of the month as a body and in full uniform. No member of the SS shall ever take part in discussions at Party meetings ('aristocratic silence'). No member of the SS shall smoke, nor shall he leave the hall during the speech. Every month there shall be two special SS evenings. Any carelessness in equipment is punishable by a fine of one halfpenny to be paid into the funds of the SS."

Thus the leader of the SS requires his men to be the aristocracy of the Party. That is to be taken literally; for they are not only to be an aristocracy of action for this generation, but are to found a hereditary nobility for the future. SS men, in case of marriage, must submit themselves and their chosen brides to an examination to ensure that both parties are racially sound and suited to one another. Thus in place of natural selection is put a rational eugenic one.

Among the special duties of the SS are: defence of the leaders, liaison work within the corps, and observation and reportorial duties. By this is to be understood observation of oppositional organizations. Important oppositional newspaper articles are to be notified, and also opposition leaders. Every SS man shall always carry about with him three propaganda numbers of the *Völkischer Beobachter* or of the *Illustrierter Beobachter*, as well as a certain number of Party admission papers. One of the rules runs: " No SS man or SS leader ever meddles in affairs which do not concern him (local political leadership, SA) and is silent. . . . The SS man is the most model member of the Party that can possibly be imagined."

Even before 1933, but especially since Hitler's seizure of power, one of the most important duties of these ideal members of the Party was spying on and not seldom suppressing untrustworthy units of the SA.

At every meeting of the SS the song, " Though all should prove unfaithful," must be sung, and the last verse standing:

> " We shall keep faith for ever,
> We are not children blind,
> Our glorious land shall never
> Be absent from tongue or mind."

Is it by chance that the SS song was composed by that Conservative romantic, Max von Schenkendorf?

Here is a clear demonstration of the intellectual dissonance in National Socialism which combines within it the old — and according to the old views — irreconcilable antitheses of conservatism and revolution, and thus seeks to show that something fresh has been brought to life by a creative act. The SA embodies the revolutionary principle in it, the SS the conservative. The old dissension between the two principles sinks slowly back into the obscurity of History, while the earth turns towards the light of fresh revelations, and, alas! fresh dissensions. Only the over-vigilant, nervous consciousness with which this historical creative process is experienced and proclaimed by the participators in it leaves a doubt as to whether a new phenomenon is really coming into existence or whether it is not only another new illusion.

THE RISING OF OSAF STENNES

That difficulties should from time to time occur in the vast army of the SA was natural. The impetus for the greatest convulsion, as far as outsiders could judge, was given by Hitler's oath to act constitutionally. Numbers of SA leaders suspected that " Adolphe Légalité," as they called the Party Chief, was only trying to find some good means of getting rid of the SA, even if it were by a police prohibition. The leader of the Berlin SA, an ex-police captain named Stennes, who controlled the whole of the SA in eastern Germany and who was thus, after Röhm, the most powerful man in the organization, was a centre of conspiracy. The conspiracy was not indeed aimed directly against Hitler. The conspirators did not wish to dispute the position of the chief Party leader, but they hoped to compel the bestowal of greater freedom of movement on the SA. In the process the constitutional idea might and was intended to come to grief and the revolutionary to come to the fore once again — that a revolution could take place without machine guns was an idea that never dawned on these warriors. Even Goebbels seems to have fostered the confidence of the rebels by certain careless utterances. At all events, Stennes and his friends were convinced that the Berlin District leader was in principle on their side.

The details of this palace revolution are no longer interesting. The important thing is that Hitler was the quicker, and deposed Captain Stennes on April 1, 1931, before he had even thought of acting. A few agitated days followed. Several of the highest SA leaders joined Stennes, and the revolt for a moment looked dangerous. But only the very smallest number of men followed them. Once again it was seen that in the National Socialist Party no authority is obeyed that does not derive directly from Hitler. And even if a hundred thousand fell away to-day, Hitler by his personal magnetism would collect another hundred thousand to-morrow. And the new hundred thousand would be a solid rock of obedience, while the others would be as scattered dust.

Stennes and his men occupied the Berlin District office, declared Goebbels, whom he regarded as a traitor, to be deposed, and spread ugly stories about him. Thereupon Hitler took the oft-tried course of setting Goebbels the task of cleaning the Augean stable. Lieutenant Schulz, whose name had become well known in connexion with the Vehm murder trials in 1932, was placed under Göring's supervision to restore order into the SA of eastern Germany. The revolt was quelled within a few weeks, thanks to Hitler's promptitude and Stennes' lack of purpose — and, perhaps, it is also true to add, thanks to the historical destiny which put the German opposition into the hands of the leader Hitler and not of such unstable natures as Stennes.

HITLER AND HIS CONTEMNERS

As a lasting remembrance we shall only preserve here a single almost touching open letter of Hitler's which diverges into the personal, and in which he dissolves partnership with Stennes and defends himself against the under-estimation of his own person:

" I was not," says Hitler poignantly of himself and of his fate, " the child of well-to-do parents, did not enjoy a university education, but was brought up in the hardest school of life, in want and misery. The superficial world never inquires what a man has learnt, and even less what he really knows, but, as a rule, unfortunately only what he can show certificates for. The fact that I had learnt a great deal more than many of our intellectuals was never heeded, but only the fact that I had no certificates."

The lack of certificates — the ever-open intellectual wound. One is tempted to wonder how often Hitler looked suspiciously over his shoulder to see whether all the Doctors and Lieutenants were not whispering behind his back.

CHAPTER VII

THE CRISIS IN GERMANY

REVOLUTIONS wear a different aspect according as they are looked at from before or after their occurrence no less than from one or other side of their barricades. Future generations may perhaps see in the events of the years 1931 and 1932 the history of the National Socialist struggle for power. The contemporary reporter who is anxious to preserve as much as possible of the abundant material of the present for future objective study will regard as even more important and instructive the fact that the Weimar Republic collapsed owing to intrinsic defects.

The great positive achievement of this dying epoch was the economic restoration of Germany after the War and her reconciliation with her former enemies. The genius of National Socialism will be put to the test in the furtherance of these admittedly incomplete attainments, and it will be interesting to see whether it manages to retain its advantages. The re-entry of Germany into the company of the Powers had, it is true, not brought her the position which the nation at large and even so experienced a politician as Stresemann had expected. The Franco-German problem remained unsolved — and it is not proposed to examine the reasons here. Economic reconstruction was meanwhile retarded by the weakness of agriculture which was among the first to be seriously affected by the world crisis in grain, and caused the industrial market within Germany to shrink slowly but surely. However, neither the distress in agriculture nor the confusion caused by a superfluity of coal, by over-production of nitrates, and by other difficulties contingent upon raw materials, were misfortunes peculiar to Germany.

Nevertheless one special burden did weigh upon Germany's shoulders — the burden of reparations. The idea that it is possible year after year to transfer one and a half to two milliards of gold Marks from one country to another without any return is probably not taken seriously by many people nowadays — whether it is a question of German reparations or of inter-allied debt payments. And, in fact, Germany did not before 1930 attempt such transfers, but balanced them by foreign loans. Not until September 1930 was Germany forced to make actual transfers, when, as a result of Hitler's victory in the elections, foreign creditors called in the short-term loans and thus within a year some six to seven milliards of Marks capital were withdrawn from the country. German industry had ever since the inflation borne increased costs of production in the form of abnormally high rates of interest; but now capital flowed away altogether. And not only foreign capital, but large quantities of native capital which was either transferred to foreign countries or was withdrawn from productive investments to lie idle in the German banks.

INDUSTRY VERSUS TRADE UNIONS

A second critical manifestation presented itself. In the economic revival in which industry had taken the lead, the great organizations of workers had also played their part in various ways — by obtaining higher wages through the Trade Unions; by building up a great system of social insurance with at times considerable property in real estate; by establishing large blocks of dwelling-houses and welfare institutions through official and semi-official associations. Not only the Trade Unions but also the world of industry and banking conducted their affairs with the greatest optimism.

During this period of reconstruction the political situation remained stable for so long as manufacturers and the Trade Unions each kept peacefully to their own side of the line, even though governments might change and Socialism might for a long time remain in reasoned opposition. The great industries to some extent occupied a position of leadership against which opposition was only organized very slowly on the part of agriculture, while the middle class never succeeded in doing so at all. The attempt to create a middle-class economic Party proved after a certain initial success abortive.

When, however, the Trade Unions, more particularly since 1927, inaugurated a new campaign to bring wages into some accord with the higher profits, a certain tenseness entered into the political situation. Not only German business affairs, but those of the whole world, drifted into the beginnings of the credit crisis, which looks like capital cutting off its nose to spite its face by protesting against high wages and high social burdens.

In Germany the unwritten treaty of partition between industry and the Trade Unions went by the board, and the Socialists were turned out of the Government in the summer of 1930. The question now confronting this Party—which had hitherto been the largest Party in the country — was whether it should go into opposition. This implied also the question whether it was willing and able to come out of the system of irresponsibility of all participants in the power of the State which had up to the present falsely gone by the name of the parliamentary system in Germany. Should it do what it had not dared to do since 1918, and try to take over the command? This is not the place to inquire whether Socialism was fitted for the task of leadership. But it is certain that only such Parties as were ready to take it over were now fit to persist. Socialism preferred to continue to support the existing system even when it was forced into a position of apparent opposition. The word " toleration " was fixed upon to express this kind of support. In order not to give up the principle of parliamentary government, the Socialists tolerated Brüning's Government without belonging to it by always giving it their votes on the few occasions when decisive divisions were taken in the Reichstag. Thus the position of the Socialists in the Reichstag was very much like that of the king in certain democratic countries, in which the Crown has the formal right to veto but hardly ever exercises it. The only difference was that the king in such a country is in accord with the people in the voluntary limitation of his power, while the electorate of the Socialist members of the Reichstag were violently though unsuccessfully opposed to the policy.

THE FICTION OF GERMAN DEMOCRACY

This internal extinction of Socialism, which instead of a political purpose left behind it a handsome Party shrine, was all part of the desiccation of the whole system of parliamentary democracy in Germany. The drawback to the Weimar Republic was that it had no great political aim, because there was no leader nor leading party capable of giving it one. The working class called itself Socialist, but except as regards the name there was practically no general agreement about Socialism. No body of leaders having authority over their followers and an intellectual grasp of the problems of the revolution had grown up out of the Socialist Parties. Social Democracy had in pre-War times slowly but surely won to a more secure place in politics, apparently as a harmonious constituent of the general economic rise of the German Empire. His Imperial Majesty's loyal Opposition reckoned fundamentally with the idea that for a period that then seemed unlimited, Imperial Government and Opposition would continue to play the game of politics together, and that the day for a readjustment of responsibility was still distant. And if ever the day were to come, then no doubt — it was supposed — the Crown would appoint a few Socialist Ministers. There was certainly no idea that the State would be taken over by the working classes, that there would be a Republic, and that the military powers would be dethroned.

Everything turned out differently from the way in which the Socialists had anticipated. There was the War and its disastrous outcome, which the Party did not and could not desire. The clear purposefulness of the Russian Bolshevists, who accepted military downfall as part of the bargain in exchange for the victory of the Revolution, was quite alien to the German Socialist; and equally so was that of the German Conservatives, who were prepared to shed the last drop of their blood in fighting the external foe. These latter were, it is true, incapable of visualizing such a fight without the Emperor, and went miserably to pieces before the internal anti-monarchist revolt. The Socialists, for their part, unwillingly made the best of a revolution that they had not wanted, while the middle classes saw events happening around them that seemed to them to be an outbreak of subterranenan forces, whereas it was really only their own collapse. Thus the Weimar Republic was conceived in repugnance, and after its unhappy birth passed fourteen years of sickly life.

The most profound reason for the unfruitfulness of the German

Socialist Parties was that their foundations had crumbled. The proletarian class disintegrated. New class-consciousness from various directions permeated it and broke it up. This process (which was not confined to Germany) made an end to the Weimar Republic, whose maxim it was to educate up a working class to State-consciousness, while that working class was already falling asunder.

STRESEMANN'S FORLORN EFFORT

A State must be ruled either autocratically or by the consent of the majority of the people. Both were wanting in the Weimar Republic. It could not be a Dictatorship on account of its constitution, and could not be a Democracy because of the aims of the Parties. The Constitution assumed tacitly that in the nation there would always be a majority united, in spite of differences of detail, by a common desire for the good of the country. Thus it had invented a political aim capable of satisfying the majority, which, in fact, did not exist. The Parties, again, seem to have tacitly assumed that a State authority would in case of necessity always appear to overrule any egotistical attitude and to guard the interests of the community at large. That is to say, a government that might at any moment ignore the lack of co-operation among the Parties in the contemptuous dictatorial words that the then Chancellor Dr. Luther, who afterwards became President of the Reichsbank and German Ambassador in Washington, uttered on one occasion in the Reichstag: " Germany has got to be ruled by some means or other! " It was now obvious how fatefully dependent the German nation had for decades been upon the existence of an autocratic monarchy.

Both assumptions were self-deceptions. The two most important men produced by the Republic both tried to convert one of the fictions into truth. Dr. Gustav Stresemann, the creator of the " Great Coalition " which stretched from Social Democracy to the bourgeois Right Wing German People's Party, wore himself out in the vain endeavour to develop a republican spirit, and to this endeavour sacrificed health and life. Resigned, and altogether deserted by his own Party, he at last turned his attention entirely to foreign policy. Possibly he felt that it would be an easier task to arrange a tolerable agreement between Germany and her late foes than to bring the German Parties together.

BRÜNING'S ARTIFICIAL AUTHORITY

An experiment in exactly the opposite sense was undertaken by Dr. Heinrich Brüning, who had advanced by means of the Catholic Trade Unions, but who was, none the less, not by temperament a man of the people. In 1930, when the contesting forces consisting of Parties of equal strength had rendered one another powerless, he endeavoured to build up a Government of pure autocracy above the Party struggle. Its connexion with the mass of the electors really lay only in the confidence of the President of the Reich by whom the Government was appointed and on whom it was in fact dependent. By a very daring interpretation of the Constitution legislation was carried out by the President in the form of "emergency decrees," although that power had only been conferred upon the President for use in states of emergency lasting for (presumably) short periods. These emergency decrees were forced on the acceptance of the Parties by a kind of parliamentary sanction in making the Reichstag decide by a very narrow majority not to demand their repeal. This game, regularly repeated, did not, of course, give Brüning's Government the support of the National Socialists, of the German Nationalists, or of the Communists; but it did afford it that of the Social Democrats, of the Democratic State Party, of the Centre, of the German People's Party, and of various other Right Wing Parties. In so far as it was intended to create the illusion of parliamentary government, the whole process was a farce. On the other hand, it was politically important that within and without the parliament a number of forces gathered together which gave some measure of stability to the government authority by mutually supporting one another.

These forces were: first, the Reichswehr which, under General Groener and his first collaborator, General von Schleicher, supported the Government, or rather the President, more as a matter of duty than from conviction; secondly, the President himself, who represented the strongest authority in the country, not only because of the personal respect in which he was held but also because of the loyalty of the

Reichswehr. A third factor at that time was the Centre Party, which was supported by the Catholic Church during Brüning's experiment, and which was politically the decisive factor in Bavaria and Württemberg, the two largest States in Southern Germany. The fourth factor, finally, was Social Democracy, which in this connexion must be mentioned simultaneously with the Prussian police. As a consequence of the curious constitutional structure of Germany, a very important part of the State machinery is not under the control of the German Government, but under that of the individual States forming the federation, of which the most important, as comprising two-thirds of the whole country, is the State of Prussia. In Prussia, as distinct from the country as a whole, the most important Government posts, such as the supervision of the police, the internal administration, and the schools, were in the hands of the Socialists. Thus Otto Braun, the Socialist Prussian Prime Minister, and his Minister of the Interior, Carl Severing, formed a second important support for Brüning's policy. If the Reichstag division was a farce, the support of the Prussian Government was a political factor of the first importance.

Brüning's system of government, which was really carried through by one man for two years under the most difficult conditions and surrounded by foes, must be admired as a remarkable political achievement and not merely as an act of political strength and sleight of hand. It is a most positive result for the Chancellor to have held off anarchy in Germany for two years, and in foreign affairs to have achieved the settlement of reparations, even though the fruits of this success were only gathered by his successor. But Brüning's system suffered from being artificially built up on too many assumptions, and from the fact that the Chancellor did not manage to impose his political will upon those who supported him unenthusiastically and of necessity. He was, as Hugenberg, his most determined opponent, once expressed it, juggling with too many balls at once, and one or another was bound to fall. And then the game would be at an end.

The greatest misfortune, however, that attended Brüning's Government was that it came more and more between the upper and nether millstones of the great social and economic crisis. The crisis undermined confidence in the Governments of many other countries too. But in Germany it destroyed confidence in the Weimar Republic, or, as a most effective Nazi slogan had it, in the "System." In the great attack on the working class, Brüning was in point of fact on the side of the employers, because he was convinced that only by this means could he hold the social key-positions. He believed it to be a necessary concomitant evil that he must thereby forfeit the confidence of the masses. Thus it was Brüning who carried through all the unpopular measures which otherwise his more fortunate successor would have found himself obliged to carry through now. The cleverness of Brüning's policy lay in his assuring himself of the support of the Socialists even for the most unpopular measures by hinting at a dictatorship of the Right. Thus the Chancellor and the largest political Party steadily became more and more unpopular.

SOCIALISM AND REICHSWEHR

Passionately and almost masochistically as Brüning enveloped himself in his unpopularity and doled out better medicine to the nation, he did not manage to bring about any change in the crisis. The crisis had gone far beyond a mere loss of confidence; the essential of capitalist dealing — confidence — was called in question as a practical factor in commerce. The crisis raised constructive problems the solution of which could no longer be a mere reconstruction of what had previously existed.

Germany went through the world economic crisis in 1931 under Brüning's leadership. This year of catastrophes began with the crash of the Austrian Land Credit Bank, was continued with the Hoover-moratorium for political debts, and ended after the fall of the pound with the collapse of the Kreuger concern. And almost exactly in the middle of the year the greatest convulsion in German affairs took place, namely, suspension of payment by the Danat Bank and the failure of the Dresden Bank, which led to the reorganization of these two as well as of various other financial institutions throughout the country. These events very deeply affected every one in Germany who was concerned in economic affairs, and strongly encouraged the tendency towards State Socialism. An anti-capitalist, indeed Socialist, spirit now ran more powerfully through large sections of the people.

Among those affected by it was, most unexpectedly, the Reichswehr. It will be remembered that three officers had been condemned at Leipzig to detention in a fortress on account of Nazi activities. It was found that the three lieutenants, whose views were undoubtedly shared by many of their comrades, were inclined to extremes not only of Nationalism but also of Socialism. In March 1931, Kippenberger, a Communist member of the Reichstag, read a declaration by Scheringer, one of the three condemned men, in which he renounced his allegiance to Hitler and subscribed to Communism. Scheringer had been deeply disappointed in his personal experiences with Hitler and Goebbels, especially in their unwillingness to make any definite statement on the subject of Socialism. When Scheringer referred to Feder's idea of bursting the bonds of interest, which must surely be regarded as a part of Socialism, Goebbels replied contemptuously that the one likely to burst was any one who read Feder's nonsense. And in Munich Hitler had put off Scheringer with generalities, had with great demonstrations of enthusiasm shown him the magnificent new Party Palace, the Brown House, and said that Scheringer must just have faith in him and must believe that he, Hitler, would make everything come right. Scheringer, however, did not believe it, and joined the German Communist Party. When Kippenberger read the declaration in the Reichstag: " Only in alliance with the Soviet Union after the destruction of the capitalist system can we be emancipated " — it is to be noted that the aim is national emancipation, and the means the crushing of capitalism — the editorial office of the *Angriff* sent anxiously to inquire at the fortress of Gollnow, where Scheringer was imprisoned, whether the declaration was genuine. Scheringer telegraphed back concisely: " Hitler revolution betrayed. Declaration genuine. Publish it. Scheringer." The *Angriff* did not publish it, but the public had received an uncomfortable impression of the lack of veneration on the part of young lieutenants of the Reichswehr for the sacred possessions of the existing economic system.

This episode has a permanent value because it gives a glimpse into the hidden soul of the Reichswehr. The profession of arms in Germany no longer invests an officer with the same glory as in former days, but makes greater intellectual demands. Many of the officers of the

Reichswehr may be reckoned among the most cultured sons of the nation. Thus the army, which in imperial Germany had the reputation of being a hotbed of out-of-date prejudices, is to-day freer from such prejudices than perhaps any other profession. The present, or rather the now waning, economic order, which under William II and with his encouragement had undermined even the army with gold, is to-day regarded with a proper soldierly mistrust. Among those surrounding General von Schleicher, then chief of the Reichswehr Ministry, ideas of State Socialism were favoured. One exponent of these ideas was Major Marcks, who gave the General his mental ammunition. This particular movement used humorously to be known as "General Socialism."

THE BISHOPS AND NATIONAL SOCIALISM

Among all the powers who were at that time occupying commanding positions in German politics, the Catholic Church must receive special mention on account of its curious attitude towards National Socialism. The Church was offended by the dogma and doctrines of the Nazi Party. Its censure was directed at Point 24 of the programme, which contained the religious confession of the Party and introduced mention of the ethics and moral sense of the Teutonic race. The disposition of the Church, however, is to be tolerant in racial questions. Point 24 alone would probably not have proved the occasion for a quarrel had not Alfred Rosenberg, the theorist of the Party, written various articles containing statements that were dogmatically questionable. It is true that Rosenberg's articles were several times expressly stated not to be semi-official Party utterances, but that did not help matters. In March 1931 all the German Bishops issued strongly worded protests against National Socialism. The Bishops of the Diocese of Paderborn declared expressly that "membership of the National Socialist Party was not permissible for a Catholic Christian for so long and in so far as it propagates political and educational theories that are irreconcilable with the Catholic doctrine." The Bavarian Bishops said that what National Socialism called Christianity was no longer the Christianity of Christ. The Bishop of Mainz in

September 1931 denied Peter Gemeinder, a National Socialist town councillor, Christian burial, because "no Catholic may be a professed member of the National Socialist Party."

The Brown House was, of course, very anxious to live at peace with the Church, although it might possibly have joined battle with the hitherto mightiest ruler of souls — with some chance of at least temporary success — for the souls of its members. By way of composing the quarrel, Göring, though himself a Protestant, went to Rome in the spring of 1931, and talked, among others, with the Pope and Archbishop Pizzardo. He was able to assure them that National Socialism, which stood on a footing of positive Christianity, must not be confounded with certain religious sects or even with an imaginary cult of Wotan which is attributed to some popular movements. The conference had no immediate success. The Church and the Centre Party maintained a chilly attitude towards Nazism.

UNDECIDED CAPITALISTS—UNDECIDED COMMUNISTS

Industry is one of the forces to which public opinion in Germany tacitly attributes political influence. During those years it did not make the use that might have been expected of its right to mould political opinion. It is true that industrial influences grew stronger in Brüning's cabinet by the removal from his office in the autumn of 1931 of Warmbold, the Minister for Trade. But there was never any question of the leading industrial groups taking up a position of real influence either before or behind the scenes. The political and still more the moral revolution in the nation took place so rapidly that the old organizations were not capable of adjusting themselves equally quickly. Moreover, a change of leadership was impending in the National Association of German Industry. Privy Councillor Duisberg, who had hitherto been its President, was succeeded by Dr. Krupp von Bohlen und Halbach. When, in January 1932, Hitler, at the instigation of his old follower Fritz Thyssen, made a speech to all the leading industrialists of Western Germany at Düsseldorf, he failed to carry with him the greater part of the audience. When Thyssen closed the meeting by calling for cheers for Hitler, only one-third of the audience, according to an eye-witness, responded. The effect produced upon the majority was slight or actually negative.

This want of consistency, however, in the political opinions of so important a social group is characteristic of the mental attitude of most of Hitler's antagonists. In addition to the Conservatives, the Communists were also opposed to him, and this Party also won adherents during the crisis, though considerably fewer than did National Socialism. The Communists suffered, and presumably will continue to suffer so long as they work above or below ground in Germany, from their dependence upon tactical orders from the Moscow central authorities. These can never judge of the German situation with the same certainty as the man on the spot. What is still worse is that the Moscow policy naturally never can nor will be a German Communist policy. Moscow revolutionary specialists are obviously lacking in the medium for apprehending the intellectual tendencies of important sections of the German people. Until well on in the year 1932 German Communists were obeying the strange order that Hitler's seizure of power must be actually encouraged, because the path to Communism must go by way of the rule of Fascism and its collapse. Hence the German Communist Party right to the very end did not direct its fiercest attack against National Socialism but against Social Democracy.

Thus the Communist Party added its quota to the lack of cohesion among Hitler's opponents. In this very fact lay Hitler's greatest strength. The material and moral forces ranged against him were, taken all together, much stronger than his own. But they were aiming at different goals, were striving against each other, and so to some extent nullifying one another. Only a mimimum of political purpose remained among the political opponents of National Socialism, and this was easily overcome even when Hitler's impetus had actually begun to wane. The story of the struggle and the unexpected victory of Nazism shortly before an apparently unavoidable collapse is full to the point of monotony with dramatic events. Its end is a fairy tale that outdoes even the fairy tale with which it had been inaugurated fourteen years earlier.

CHAPTER VIII

THE WITHDRAWAL FROM THE REICHSTAG

On October 13, 1930, the hundred and seven Nazi deputies appeared in the Reichstag for the first time. Their spokesman and undisputed leader was Gregor Strasser. A few days later he made a speech which would certainly have created a great stir, if it had not been that the lively street demonstrations of the Nazis on October 13 created an even greater stir. The windows of sundry Jewish shops were smashed. Hitler informed a foreign newspaper correspondent that these excesses were mainly the work of rowdies, shoplifters, and Communist *agents provocateurs*. The culprits were at once expelled from the Party. The *Beobachter* added that in the Third Reich the shop windows of Jewish business would be much better looked after than they were by the present Marxist police.

In February 1931 the Party changed its parliamentary slippers for hiking boots again. Its Reichstag deputies decided not to take part in the Reichstag debates any longer, since the Party was systematically kept out of power, and in any case Brüning took no account at all of the Reichstag. The German Nationalists attached themselves to the National Socialists — thereby admitting perhaps for the first time that they had relinquished the leadership of the Right Wing to their stronger colleague.

And Brüning, whom Hindenburg had in the sight of all Germany given the power and the mission to be its absolute ruler, was solemnly abandoned by that part of the nation which really stood nearest to the President at heart.

FRANZEN'S RESIGNATION AND FRICK'S FALL

Soon after the Reichstag elections in 1930 the Nazis were given the chance of a second ministerial post in one of the German States. In Brunswick, where they had won an electoral victory, Dr. Franzen, a police court magistrate of Kiel, was made Minister of the Interior. Franzen was a comparatively unknown figure in the Party. His appointment aroused a certain amount of disapprobation, and as it turned out Hitler lived to be disappointed in him. In July 1931 Franzen's Nazi gorge rose at the thought that as a powerless provincial Minister he was obliged to obey the orders of Brüning's hostile central Government, and especially at being expected to administer the emergency decrees that were so contrary to his Party's views. Groh, the leader of the Nazi group in the Brunswick Diet, encouraged him in these ideas, and one day without asking the Party authorities, Franzen resigned his portfolio. Groh followed suit, and vanished from the Nazi ranks. It was a matter of some difficulty to keep the post open for the National Socialist Party. Franzen's successor eventually was Dietrich Klagges, an elementary school teacher.

Hitler's vexation over Franzen's defection was particularly acute because the Party had a short time before this been obliged to sacrifice Frick's strong position. It was on the day of the Stennes crisis, on April 1, 1931, that Frick was deposed by his former colleagues in the Thuringian Diet. Various measures introduced by the National Socialist Minister had shown the Centre Parties of the Thuringian Diet that there was no hope of discrediting the impetuous Nazis in the eyes of their electors by putting them into positions of power and then exposing them. Frick had acted too energetically, too eccentrically, and with too great an understanding of the curiosity of the political public. If, for example, he introduced prayers in the Thuringian schools that exhorted openly to hatred against internal political enemies, clergy and pedagogues might take exception to them; the local electorate thought it rather clever of him. Günther, the anthropologist, whose theories regarding the Germanic race are the bible of many German anti-Semites, had been made by Frick a professor in the famous old provincial university of Jena. Günther's induction, at which Hitler had been present and which ended in a torchlight procession by the students, had been one of the memorable occasions of the rising movement of National Socialism. His academic colleagues might protest against Günther as a scientist — the educational world was greatly mistaken if it believed that the protests of authorities that were losing their hold on the people had any particular effect. The leaders of the German People's Party in the Thuringian Diet at all events soon realized what von Papen and Hugenberg still did not know on January 30, 1933 — that Hitler's following is not subject to the normal parliamentary ebb and flow; that the possession of power does not weaken the propagandist force of this Party, but strengthens it. In this realization, they suddenly turned against Frick whom they had previously hoisted into the saddle; the Diet passed a vote of no confidence by twenty-nine votes to twenty-two, and his post went begging.

PRINCES AND PEOPLE

The ministerial post in Thuringia had been won by the National Socialists while they were still Germany's smallest Party. It was hard to lose it when they were practically the largest. It now became fashionable to be a member of the Party.

Most illustrious among prominent figures, Prince August Wilhelm of Prussia, one of the sons of the ex-Emperor, had joined the Party in the spring of 1930. With such a man as Hitler as leader, the prince had admiringly declared, any one might be proud to be in the ranks. The Hohenzollern prince appeared as a speaker in a brown shirt at National Socialist meetings. In the spring of 1931, during a riot, the Königsberg police attacked him with rubber truncheons. As far as History is concerned, it is perhaps less memorable that Severing's police should have hit a prince of Prussia than that a Hohenzollern should have submitted to being belaboured for Hitler's sake. Even the aged ex-Kaiser in his exile in Holland appeared to share in that opinion. At a meeting in Munich, the Prince read aloud part of a letter from his father: "You may be proud that you have been permitted to be a martyr in this great national movement."

Among those who joined the National Socialists was also Dr.

Schacht, the former President of the Reichsbank — the same Dr. Schacht who had helped to draw up the Young Plan and had defended it against National Socialist criticism. He probably did not get an official membership card at that time; but from then on he was one of the economic advisers upon whom Hitler placed great reliance. Prominent persons who scented success, and adored it from a feeling of their own impotence, rushed in ever greater floods towards National Socialism, which now became the centre of gravity of the Right Wing.

THE STAHLHELM PLEBISCITE, AUGUST 9, 1931

Rival institutions were alarmed and pressed tumultuously forward. The Stahlhelm remembered the old tactical axiom of the Right Wing: "Who holds Prussia holds Germany." They considered that since Brüning, being under the protection of the President, was at present unassailable, it would be simpler and more efficacious to take away his Marxist support in Prussia. They therefore contrived a plebiscite, permissible under the Constitution, by which a majority of voters was to declare that the Prussian Diet should be dissolved. And they calculated that a new election would leave the Braun Government without its majority. It was necessary to mobilize more than 50 per cent. of all the electorate. The Right Wing had some difficulty in doing that in Germany even in March 1933; and the attempt was hopeless in the summer of 1931. The National Socialists themselves had perforce to take part in this undertaking with which they did not sympathize, and which — one might almost say according to plan — ended in failure on August 9. Nine million eight hundred thousand, that is 37 per cent., of the voters went to the polls. And even this result was only achieved because the Communists had participated in conformity with their theory that Fascism must first come to power and prove itself to be a failure. Thus the 37 per cent. could hardly be regarded as a *succes d'éstime.* And Goebbels said testily after the voting that they would see to it that they did not waste time again upon such a hopeless quest.

BRÜNING AS "POOR JONATHAN"

None the less they did. For, two months after the Stahlhelm had made its abortive attack upon Brüning's Prussian support, Hugenberg,

Hitler's other rival, decided to force the strongest stone out of the Chancellor's position. He endeavoured to exercise moral pressure upon Hindenburg, and once again — at the beginning, at all events — Hitler supplied him with the best material for his Press propaganda. Since then the political struggle for Hindenburg's favour has been one of the most curious political dramas ever witnessed even in this land that is so rich in political curiosities.

Among the President's personal friends was a German National member of the Reichstag, the old Herr von Oldenburg-Januschau, from East Prussia. Even in the Emperor's time he had been prominent as a bluff *frondeur*, who played the reactionary boor not without intelligence and wit, and who, at a time when public opinion was already comparatively Liberal, had created a considerable stir by declaring that the Emperor should always be able to dissolve Parliament by a Lieutenant and ten men. His reactionary views had not, however, dimmed his political foresight. In 1917 he infuriated the Crown Prince by prophesying in broad East Prussian dialect: " Take my word for it, your Royal Highness, there will be no Throne for you! " The old man who, even before the War, represented an apparently obsolete type among the ruling class, now suddenly reappeared, and, chiefly owing to the influence which he was believed to exercise over the President, played a remarkable rôle in the State.

Through Oldenburg's astuteness Hindenburg had become the largest landowner in Germany. The President came of a family of impoverished gentle-people, who had hitherto played no very great part in the country. He himself had no property, had been no more than a professional infantry officer, and had expected to end his days with a General's pension. Then Herr von Oldenburg-Januschau came on the scene to make the old gentleman in his last years a member of the landed aristocracy to which his family had once belonged. The German Industrial Association was induced to organize a collection and to buy the estate of Neudeck in the south-western part of East Prussia that had once been the seat of the Hindenburg family. It was presented to him in 1927 on his eightieth birthday. Thus he became a landed proprietor. Or, to put it more accurately, his son and most influential adviser, Colonel von Hindenburg, did. The idea was to save the death duties, which must be expected to fall due at a not-too-distant date. This evidence of business capacity is, to say the least of it, not a proof of strong public spirit. At all events Colonel von Hindenburg, the real owner of Neudeck, has since then shown himself to be a politician who, consciously or otherwise, is very apt to regard the interests of the landed aristocracy as being identical with those of the State.

As far as the President himself is concerned, he certainly believed that he was honestly doing his duty by protecting so loyal a class as the landed proprietors against " agrarian Bolshevism " on the part of the State. By this term the landowners understood, for example, any demand that they should pay their debts. At the head of the *Preussenkasse*, one of the two most influential concerns for short-term agrarian loans, was Otto Klepper, a cold and clear-headed man, Prussia's last Finance Minister with any Socialist leanings. He saw that large numbers of the estates were hopelessly overloaded with debt and impoverished by bad management, and urged that they should be partitioned and peasants settled on the holdings. Even Brüning, who at first had treated Klepper with scant attention, at last had to admit that a part of the entailed estates could not be maintained. Though in 1931 he had tried by means of an immense gift, the Eastern Relief Fund (*Osthilfe*), to save the old owners, he and his advisers realized in 1932 that many of them could not possibly be saved.

This was the reason why in 1931 he had had the support of Oldenburg-Januschau and in 1932 no longer enjoyed it. It had been interpreted as a favourable sign that after some months of Brüning's Government the old gentleman had declared that the Chancellor was " the best since Bismarck." Not long after, however, he retracted the praise, and, being an old East Prussian noble who knew his Bible, was heard to exclaim sorrowfully: "I am distressed for thee, Jonathan my brother."

The signs were not propitious for Brüning.

THE HARZBURG FRONT

By the autumn the time appeared ripe to Hugenberg to get poor Jonathan into disfavour with King Saul himself by impeaching him to the President in the name of practically the whole of the Nationalist Right. The dock was erected in the little town of Harzburg in the State of Brunswick. Here, under the protection of a Government that was half German National and half National Socialist, large forces of SA and Stahlhelm gathered on October 11, 1931, for a meeting by means of which Hugenberg, together with Hitler and the leaders of the Stahlhelm, Seldte and Duesterberg, planned to organize a " National Front " against Brüning's Government. At a somewhat forcedly ceremonial meeting with numerous gentlemen in frock coats and uniforms, the German Nationalist leader read his declaration, which, aping the preamble to the Weimar Constitution, began:

" The National Front, united in its Parties, Associations, and Groups, and inspired with the will to act in unison and concord, declares as follows. . . ." And what did it declare? Substantially this: " We demand the immediate resignation of the Brüning and Braun Governments." The essential part appeared to have been written in blood, since it continued: " We declare that in the troublous times to come, while we shall defend the lives and property, houses and homes and workshops, of those who freely vote for the nation with us, we refuse to defend the present Government and the system at present in force or to sacrifice our blood for it." In other words: Make ready for civil war.

Meanwhile the impression made by Harzburg was weakened by information leaking out concerning quarrels among the confederates. Hitler had gone to Harzburg half-heartedly and for tactical reasons. Only a few hours before the joint declaration, the sub-leaders had voiced the strongest doubts as to whether the Party Leader should go at all. The great conference had not been far off a collapse. Frick finally decided for co-operation, partly by using the argument that Mussolini had also begun with a coalition government and had afterwards thrown over his allies. The Nazis often spoke as openly as this, and their present confederates have therefore possibly a moral, but certainly no intellectual, right to complain of their untrustworthiness or lack of public spirit.

Thus the grim ending to Hugenberg's announcement: " Any one who breaks our line will be considered as an outlaw," was at that very time applicable to the National Socialist leaders. For Hitler read a declaration of his own and disdained to watch the march past of the Stahlhelm at the joint parade. With the meeting at Harzburg, Hugenberg's part as intellectual leader of the German Opposition was at an end.

A few days later this was made clear by important political negotiations on Hitler's part. For the first time in his life he was received by President von Hindenburg. It appears that his verbosity, which was not checked by his having an audience of only one, made a certain impression upon the old Field-Marshal. It was not a positive one, as will be seen, but neither was it a negative one. More important still were two visits paid to General von Schleicher, Chief of the Secretariat of the Reichswehr Ministry, the man who from that time on became for more than a year the secret organizer of the political game in Germany. Schleicher had in his time already overthrown the last Socialist Chancellor, Müller, and put Brüning in his place. Now he gradually abandoned him and thus withdrew from him that support without which — even if it be only implied — no statesman can govern, namely, machine guns.

SENTIMENTAL GERMAN SOCIALISM

The longer the economic crisis lasted in Germany the more widespread did the conviction become among the people that it could only be ended by political means. Faith in the power of the capitalist system to cure itself is, even in normal times when the question is only raised theoretically, not generally very strong. And now, when on top of the industrial crisis of 1930 came the great financial crisis of 1931, it faded entirely. The growing wish to deal with the crisis politically may in the widest sense of the word be called Socialistic. But in no sense did it correspond with the Socialism of the Marxist Parties, who dogmatically and in accordance with their sentiments fixed their eyes only upon the purely economic event of the destruction of capitalism, and drew no constructive social inferences from it. The Communists saw a process of destruction which did not go far enough to please them and which must be forced still farther — while manufacturers in Moscow watched the collapse of the old Russian markets with very mixed feelings. One section, again, of Socialist theorists were surprised and unwilling to admit that the Golden Age of capitalism, in which they had believed, was over. Only the National Socialists, with their doctrine of the precedence of State interests over economic, in any way satisfied the feelings of the masses who were demanding vigorous action on the part of the Government in matters of profits, security of credit, and, in case of need, even of material property.

The national will, which was one of the mightiest motive powers of the movement, was strengthened by this economic disintegration. To the opposition to the Government's foreign policy were now added motives from the economic sphere in which the idea of national self-sufficiency was coming to the fore. Agriculture, especially, took a foremost place in the struggle for national self-sacrifice, which was voluntarily to sacrifice the cheaper prices and in many cases better quality of goods in the world market, and to prefer national productions not because they were better but from motives of patriotism. A movement in this direction swept through most countries. The high protective tariff in America, the fall of the English pound in 1931, and especially the abandonment of the free trade policy of Great Britain for one of tariff reform, gave a powerful impetus to the German autarchical movement. Nowhere except in Germany, however, was the movement fused with a nationalist political philosophy. The idea that to buy dearly was a patriotic duty, was only the beginning of the larger general concept that buying, building, and investing altogether, even in defiance of economic reason, might be a national duty. Thus the interests of particular groups of wage-earners became one with the great Nazi doctrine that economic happenings of all descriptions right down to the limited economic transactions of individuals must be guided by higher political considerations.

How greatly the confusion of political aims weakened the power of Hitler's opponents is shown by the history of the year 1932 in Germany. A detailed description of the never-ending play of intrigue during these thirteen months would certainly be a most vivid example of the inability of most people to see the simple thing in a complicated situation and to deal rightly with difficulties. Such a detailed account, however, cannot yet be written. It has been shown that the Republic was bound to collapse; it only remains to show, with the important dates, how amid its fall Hitler remained to his no small surprise upright — and victor.

THE HINDENBURG CAMARILLA

Until the beginning of 1933 General von Schleicher was at times Hitler's ally and at other times his opponent in this game of intrigue.

This General, who had in responsible positions proved himself to be only a very mediocre statesman, was a politician of the kind that prefers the background and the twilight, where the outlines of political character are not clearly defined, but where shining epaulettes and the gleaming scarlet of a General's stripes exercise their awe-inspiring fascination. Schleicher's official position was that of Head of the Secretariat of the Reichswehr Ministry. This made him the confidential, all-powerful, and dangerous adviser of the Reichswehr Minister, General Groener. His influence in the Government, which soon exceeded that of Groener or Brüning, was due partly to his being an old friend of Colonel von Hindenburg, the son of the President. The Chief of the State, now in his eighty-fifth year, was mentally no longer fully capable of carrying out his political task. Only in occasional situations, in which the personal element predominated, did he still show a stubbornness that was hard to break. In general, it had come to this, that if President Hindenburg, his views and his decisions, were referred to, it actually meant those of a group of people including the old Field-Marshal's son; Dr. Meissner, the Secretary of State; Dr. Gereke, a young Conservative Reichstag deputy; General von Schleicher; and, finally, a number of politicians and landowners from east of the Elbe, most prominent among whom was old Herr von Oldenburg-Januschau. Differently as individual members of this group might think on many subjects, they were all united on one point — to preserve the waning power of the old President and if possible to increase it, which did not seem to be a hard task in view of the paralysis and self-immolation of the Reichstag. Thus the political strategy of the Hindenburg group was similar to that of the Hitler group — to be the winning third between two struggling opponents. Politically the most ingenious and active brain in this camarilla, General von Schleicher, the former comrade-in-arms of Colonel von Hindenburg, intended that one day the Nazis, wholly or in part, should become a prop of this Hindenburg Dictatorship. He thought too little of his opponent and too much of himself, just as many another politician of the bourgeois Centre has done in Germany. This clique now taunted Brüning with being unable to persuade the Parties of the Right with their leaders, Hugenberg and Hitler, to adopt a friendly attitude to Hindenburg. Brüning thereby destroyed, so they said, the popularity of the President among the " nationally " minded sections of the people. Hints of this kind had their effect upon the President, who was nervous and vain of his popularity. If Brüning wished to maintain his position, he must give proof that he was determined to reconcile Hindenburg with the leaders of the Right.

BRÜNING'S OFFER TO HITLER

From this arose a farcical political plan. After the declaration at Harzburg, Schleicher once more threw himself into the breach for Brüning and gained time for him. True, the Chancellor was obliged to agree to throw out of his Cabinet certain of his ministers whose sympathies tended Left-wards, including Dr. Wirth, the Minister of the Interior, who was loyal to the Republic, and Dr. Curtius, the Foreign Minister. The latter had put himself in an untenable position through an abortive attempt to bring about an unwritten alliance between Austria and Germany in the form of a Customs union. It is true that Brüning did not succeed in getting the industrialists to support him any further despite his efforts to win them by his policy of wage-cutting, and though Professor Warmbold, a representative of the I. G. Farben trust, had after lengthy negotiations entered his Cabinet as Minister for Commerce and Industry. Nevertheless Brüning's ship was for a time set afloat again, especially since General Groener, the Reichswehr Minister, had at Schleicher's instigation declared himself ready to take over the Ministry of the Interior in addition to that which he already held. This seemed in a sense to indicate that the Reichswehr would stand or fall with Brüning. Thus strengthened and upheld, Brüning was able to start on the difficult task of negotiating a political peace and gaining the friendship and confidence of Adolf Hitler in order to be able to lay these trophies as the most precious outcome of his policy at the feet of the aged President. Through the intermediary of Schleicher, he invited Herr Adolf Hitler to come and see him.

The meeting took place in January 1932 and was of incalculable consequence for German politics. The ostensible reason for the conference was the Presidential election, which was due to be held in the spring owing to the expiry of Hindenburg's seven years' term of office. Brüning now suggested to the Nazi leader that he might save the nation an election at that difficult time by declaring that he agreed that Hindenburg should be re-elected. The Reichstag could with the help of the National Socialist votes prolong Hindenburg's term of office by an amendment to the Constitution. In return, Brüning offered to retire and to suggest Hitler's name to the President as Chancellor. Hitler must be prepared to wait for about a year until Brüning secured an object at which he had been aiming in his foreign policy for years — the abolition of the reparation payments that Germany was expected to make under the Treaty of Versailles. Brüning considered quite rightly that Germany's ertswhile foes might possibly make such a concession to him, but never to Hitler as Chancellor. It is, of course, also very questionable whether they would have done it for Brüning if they had known that he was already secretly working to clear Hitler's way to power. Brüning would with this policy have deceived the Powers just as much as by it he bamboozled the German Parties of the Left. And, finally, a third player at the game might have become the dupe — Hitler himself. For much might have happened in the year that he was to wait. Above all, if he suddenly supported Brüning's policy semi-officially, he might lose the confidence of a good part of his electorate.

Hence among the leaders of the National Socialists as well as in Hugenberg's camp violent opposition arose. The sub-leaders clearly saw the danger of being entrapped, but do not seem to have troubled much about what the consequences might be if Hitler were defeated in an open election. Röhm, the Chief of Staff of the SA, accompanied the Party Leader as spokesman of this Opposition when Hitler paid a second visit to the Chancellor. His presence was likely to cause Brüning embarrassment on many grounds. In Catholic circles objections were raised to the SA leader because of certain personal inclinations which had recently become publicly known.

Hitler realized that to agree with Brüning's plan implied support of the Chancellor himself, inasmuch as it would enormously increase his personal importance with the President. When Hindenburg's confidential adviser, Dr. Meissner, the Secretary of State, asked him directly, Hitler declared that he could only agree to a prolongation of Hindenburg's term of office if Brüning were dismissed.

That was a mistake. No political leader, however powerful, could demand of the aged President such a political tribute in return for his goodwill. Hindenburg was angered by Hitler's demand, and prepared for the struggle. One thing, however, Hitler had achieved — another cloud had drifted across the sun of favour whose rays still fell dimly upon Brüning. A Chancellor who forced the President into an open fight against the Right Parties could in no circumstances now appear to Herr von Hindenburg as the " best since Bismarck."

HITLER BECOMES A BRUNSWICK OFFICIAL

It turned out to be a contest not only between Hindenburg and Hitler, but one in which Hugenberg also presented a candidate — Lieutenant-Colonel Duesterberg, the joint leader of the Stahlhelm. Finally, the Communists also put up their Party Chief, Thälmann. Until the very last, Hitler had hesitated to enter the forlorn struggle. Finally Goebbels had announced him as candidate in the Sports Palace at Berlin, possibly against his own wish. In order that he might become a candidate at all, Hitler had to be naturalized as a German as quickly as possible. It was now seen how important may be a Ministerial post, however small, in one of the German States. The Brunswick Government, which was controlled by the National Socialists, appointed Herr Adolf Hitler a member of the Brunswick Legation in Berlin. It is an irony of history that the Pan-German Centralist Hitler should have acquired German nationality by the help of such a relic of German Separatism.

HINDENBURG'S VICTORY

The election was in truth a fierce contest between Hitler and the Chancellor Brüning, who was in reality waging a desperate fight to retain Hindenburg's waning favour. Hitler accomplished a colossal physical achievement by following out a terrible time-table planned by Goebbels, and spending two weeks travelling back and forth across Germany in an aeroplane, speaking several times daily to audiences composed of tens, indeed hundreds, of thousands. The personal success of this wild rush was as flattering as Hitler's numerical chances were poor. The leading groups of the Right Wing supported him. The Reichsland Association, which was by far the greatest industrialist association, recommended, with all due respect to Hindenburg, the election of Hitler; and even the ex-Crown Prince declared himself in his favour. All traditional affinities were torn asunder in this extraordinary contest. Behind the Protestant Hindenburg stood the majority of Catholic voters, whose Ministers had recently been obliged to retire before Protestant suspicions. Behind the Catholic Hitler appeared the upper classes of Protestant North Germany. And Hugenberg tried vainly to put a spoke in the Austrian's wheel by denouncing him publicly as a "Roman Catholic." In addition to the Centre, the Social Democrat working class supported the imperial Field-Marshal von Hindenburg with tremendous zest, while the Conservative Agrarian Party largely went with the revolutionary Hitler.

The result was that at the first election on March 13, 1932, Hindenburg had 18.6 million of all recorded votes, or 49.6 per cent., Hitler only 11.3 millions, or 30 per cent. That was less than he himself, even at a conservative estimate, had expected. The Communists got a bare five, and Duesterberg only about two and a half million votes. The solid mass of the people had decided for Hindenburg, though not in such numbers as to give him an absolute majority. And it remained a political fact of the first order that the agrarian districts voted for Hitler, especially in the east, which was peculiarly dear to the Field-Marshal. It was a rather uncomfortable surprise, too, that at Dietramszell, Hindenburg's summer residence in Bavaria, the majority should have decided for Hitler. Hindenburg has avoided the place ever since.

There was obviously no further chance of Hitler's being elected. Nevertheless, on the very morning after his defeat, he called up his followers for a second attempt. It was the only possible course for him to adopt. The Party must be held together, must not yet be given time to think. At the second polling, on April 10, in which Duesterberg withdrew his candidature, Hindenburg gained his objective with 19.3 million votes, or 53 per cent. In comparison, however, Hitler had increased the number of his votes much more largely. He now received 13.4 million votes, or 36 per cent.; while the Communists lost roughly a quarter. Hindenburg still had the majority, but Hitler was approaching it — Which was the better result? It would have been hard to say who was the real victor in the struggle. The loser, at all events, was Brüning.

The Field-Marshal could not get over the feeling that he had been ill-advised by his Chancellor. He may, moreover, have felt that it was his duty to prove his superiority to Party interests. In 1925, after the Right had elected him, he immediately disappointed his electors by expressing his belief in the brotherhood of peoples and in the Republic. A more profound political sense might be ascribed to this system of disappointments by supposing that the President was handing on the confidence of those who had elected him to those who had not, and was thus seeking to form a link between the contending factions in the nation. Hence he destroyed bonds of confidence if he feared that they might turn to fetters. Possibly there was a secret reservation in his mind, to show one day that he had never abandoned his position but had only done his duty by giving every man his chance. The German Right had after seven years of disappointment experienced this unexpected piece of luck. Certain remarks, however, might give reason to suppose that in regard to these Parties, too, the President has made a mental reservation to let them feel the weight of his super-Party position if they do not solve the problem " that I have set them," and which consists in their dealing with unemployment.

CHAPTER IX

THE BOXHEIM DOCUMENT

In view of this being the President's frame of mind, it must have cost him no small effort to decide soon after his election to direct a great blow at Hitler by prohibiting the SA and SS.

This measure had been planned for a long time by the opponents of National Socialism. The Socialists had striven to show the illegality of Hitler's private army; a demonstration that would have been considered superfluous in any normal State jealous for its sovereignty. Even a man like General Ludendorff, who had for years brusquely turned his back upon Hitler, had lived amid strange religious ideas, and more particularly had devoted himself to fighting the Jesuits and Freemasons, had violently disapproved of the Brown Army and had described Germany as territory occupied by the SA.

At the end of November 1931, the Socialist Government in Hesse had been startled by the coming upon some plans of the local National Socialists at the manor of Boxheim. These documents contained a plan of action for the Hessian Nazis in the improbable case of a Communist rising. The author of the greater part was Dr. Best, the agricultural expert of the Party in Hesse. The State was to be taken over by the SA, all revenues confiscated, private incomes were for the time being no longer to exist. The population was to be fed at the public expense, and agricultural products were to be requisitioned for this purpose. And in monotonous succession, paragraph by paragraph, the document announced for every case of opposition: ". . . will be shot; . . . punishable by death; . . . will be shot."

The plan was genuine and was never disavowed by the Nazis; but they denied that the Party Headquarters in Munich knew of it. That immediately raised the question as to whether other district offices might not also harbour plans of which Headquarters " knew nothing " — which was all very contradictory to Hitler's repeated assurances that nothing happened in the Party against his wish or without his knowledge.

It was, indeed, quite possible that details like the suggested confiscation of peasant property might not be in accordance with the wishes of the Party Leaders. But in fundamentals Hitler's political strategy was well formulated in the Boxheim plans. The forcible intervention of the SA in case of a Communist riot was the great secret political stratagem of the Party. In a sense — the sealed orders that accompanied every Party order. The Communist rising was the point over which Hitler wishes to nail down an undecided Government to a definite yes or no. It was for this great day that he had spun the net of his constitutionalism, and it was to be Communist rioters who were to force the Government to call for Hitler's help, or — failing to call on him — merely to accept him. Just as once a Herr von Kahr had planned to erect a federalist Germany according to a Bavarian model upon the corpse of Thuringian and Saxon Communism, so now Hitler planned to become master of Germany by saving it from Communism. He had announced this as early as 1923 and had not wearied in repeating it. Goebbels had conducted a lecture tour on the subject, " Lenin or Hitler," and it has been shown how Hitler made even foreign countries realize the inevitability of the decision. And when in 1933 National Socialism came into power without any previous Communist revolution, the strategy that had been planned for years proved stronger than the events which had not been provided for in the programme. Hence, shortly before the Reichstag election on March 5, 1933, an astonished world was informed that Germany had stood on the brink of a " Communist revolution," and in proof of this the Reichstag went up in flames. Thus Communists have exercised a stronger influence over German politics than perhaps they themselves realized. Their presence caused the bourgeois Centre Parties to keep the Socialists in power for years as a bulwark against Bolshevism, and their destruction, or more properly their disappearance from the public scene, made Hitler's power finally secure.

SEVERING'S REVELATIONS

A few months after the discovery of the Boxheim documents, Severing, the Prussian Minister of the Interior, produced a further supply of awkward material. Houses had been searched and plans for great gatherings of the SA had fallen into the hands of the police; the blockade of Berlin had been arranged for as well as a carefully worked out service of transport and communication with motor-vans and cycles. Moreover, it had become known that on the day of the first polling for the presidential election the SA had been assembled at their depôts. True, Röhm had already told General von Schleicher, and had represented it as an innocent proceeding — that they had only wanted to get the SA off the streets so as to prevent any possible clash. But a Government that was openly referred to by the SA as its worst enemy was surely entitled to regard such a gathering from its less harmless aspect; especially when once again the old code words for the attack appeared in the plans. " Grandmother dead " was to be telegraphed if the explosion came.

The documents of which, on April 6, 1932, Severing revealed a part to the public and the whole to the Judge of the Supreme Court at Leipzig, contained yet another particularly nice revelation which caused the Prussian Minister to accuse the SA of treason. If the Prussian authorities had really known Nazi tactics thoroughly, they would have realized that there was nothing new in this. It will be remembered that according to Hitler's announcement of 1928 the Nazi " is not required to raise so much as a finger to help the present State." Corresponding orders from sub-leaders were now interpreted as treason, and might no doubt be looked upon as such from a moral — though hardly a legal — standpoint. These discoveries were also not without influence upon the President.

SUPPRESSION OF THE SA

On April 14 the SA and SS were prohibited. It was the heaviest blow that the Government had directed against National Socialism since 1923. The blow was the heavier since it was not levelled by political opponents but by a Government which was really more in sympathy with National Socialism than with Social Democracy. Severing had not dared alone to undertake their suppression in Prussia, but had induced the Reich Government to accept the responsibility. In giving their reasons, Brüning and Groener used words that for the first time for many a long year showed that sound common sense was being applied to the question. " It is exclusively a matter for the State to maintain an organized force. As soon as such a force is organized by private persons and the State permits it, law and order are endangered. . . . Hence every private organization of troops is of its very essence an illegal organization."

The obvious rightness of this attitude made it seem all the more incomprehensible that the SA should have been permitted to exist for so many years. What was true to-day had been true yesterday. The Government was incapable of explaining why it had chosen this time to suppress the SA, or, rather, why it had not suppressed it long ago. It might indeed have alleged Reasons of State, but hardly the Reason of a Constitutional State.

The prohibition of the SA might have been one of the great turning-points in German post-war history; and indeed must be one if it were to be enforced. The policy of toleration that had hitherto been regarded as a national necessity by nearly every Government from Right to Left was defeated when confronted by the largest of the German armed forces. For even Socialist Ministers had clung to the idea that these military organizations were necessary for the cultivation of those manly virtues which had formerly flourished under the discipline of universal military service. This conviction always induced the Government to act with a leniency that was quite incomprehensible to outsiders towards organizations by which it was attacked most firmly. The Left was in this matter more forthcoming than the bourgeois Right. For the latter replied to the prohibition of the SA not with the demand that it should be cancelled but that further prohibitions should be issued. It demanded the prohibition of the Socialist Association " State Banner Black-Red-Gold," and even President von Hindenburg was in favour of this demand — although the State Banner was no less intended for, and if cleverly managed by the State equally capable of, promoting the aforesaid virtues. At all events, toleration of the military associations assumed such a gulf to yawn between the strength of the Associations and the strength of the State that there could never be any question of danger for the latter. The feeling of this gulf had been lost in the course of time and had left only the obedience of the authorities to the national Terror, which branded as criminal every attack on a military association — only, of course, in so far as it had leanings towards the Left. This terror had also paralysed the strength of the State in its fight against the Right extremists.

STORM OVER PRUSSIA

It would suffice, however, more than suffice, if the State should at last realize what must be its aim — victory. An electoral contest had been fought, and the Conservative State authority had triumphed over a powerful revolutionary element. This was not the time chivalrously to bewail the fact that there were many good men among the enemy. A fortnight after the presidential election new elections for the Prussian Diet were held, and the result showed once more how much opportunity there still was for strong government. The Nazis obtained exactly the 36 per cent. of votes that they had polled in the presidential election, and were the strongest Party, having won one hundred and sixty-two out of the four hundred and twenty-three seats. They were able to get one of their agitators named Kerrl, who held some small legal position in the State of Hanover, elected President of the Diet; and finally — their greatest achievement — they were able to overthrow the Braun-Severing Socialist Government by a vote of no confidence. Their power did not reach so far as to be able to set up a new Government in place of that which had fallen and which therefore — just as had for years been happening in Bavaria and Saxony — quietly carried on. And if the results of the Prussian election were examined carefully, they were seen to be no proof of a further increase in Nazi strength. There had at the same time been elections in Württemberg, Bavaria, and several other States, in which the Party had polled only 32 or even 26 per cent. of the votes. Thus on the average over the whole country it had not even quite kept to its highest point. In any case it was very far from having an absolute majority.

Now the Government had made up its mind to a counter-attack, had abolished the SA, and with the concurrence of the majority of the nation had thus for the first time for many a long year restored normality. National Socialism stood upon a peak whence by a decided push it would not have been difficult to make it stumble; and if it stumbled it might one day fall. If there had been a Government at that time which understood how to talk to the people, which had announced a constructive programme of economic recovery, which had used metaphors and promises only half as cleverly as National Socialism did later when it came to power — such a Government would probably have overthrown Hitler for all time. But in order to achieve this, it would have been necessary to unite all available forces; to aim all these forces at one goal: the recognition that since National Socialism was the enemy of them all, they must all be the enemies of National Socialism.

THE "IRON FRONT"

In an attempt to bring about such a union the Socialists made a very interesting move during those months. A military association had for a very long time existed under their aegis known as the *Reichsbanner Schwarz-Rot-Gold* (State Banner Black-Red-Gold). It had been founded in 1924 as a republican counterpoise to the military associations of the Right, since the Government did not prohibit their existence. It was an immense force — on paper. Practically, however, under its very incapable leader, Hörsing, it did not constitute a dangerous rival to the Right. It is true that on the whole the men in the *Reichsbanner* were better physically than those in the SA, and probably equally loyal. Its political leaders, however, failed to keep it at such a high pitch of enthusiasm, owing to a lack of popular aims. The collapse of the old Labour ideals, which was shown by the cleavage among the Socialist Parties, had left a gap which the pale symbols of the Weimar Republic filled very inadequately. Their military training was poor, because they lacked proper instructors. Ex-officers of the old army and those of the Reichswehr were interested in the military associations of the Right, and large numbers of them gladly gave their services, but only very few would have anything to do with the *Reichsbanner*, especially since it was supposed to be " pacifist." At length, in 1931, a few energetic people in the *Reichsbanner* tried to put an end to this unsatisfactory state of affairs by removing Hörsing, and putting his assistant, Karl Höltermann, in his place. As an organizer and agitator, Höltermann was on a much higher level than most of the members of his Party, and was also much shrewder than they were in realizing what was politically necessary and opportune. Whether he also possesses the hardness and stubbornness that are necessary in a great leader he has not yet had a chance to show. He came too late and has in the meantime been outstripped by the force of circumstances. At all events, he showed remarkable power by inspiring the weary and despairing Socialist working classes to a few months' passionate counter-attack on Hitler. He united the *Reichsbanner* and other workers' associations under the somewhat ostentatious title of the Iron Front, organized well-equipped bodies of picked men; and by sonorous speeches gave the Labour Parties' propaganda something like a new tone. His ideology was definitely not pacifist but militarist. It was a revival of the dormant Socialist military ideal. He was thereby enabled, though the time was really past for it to be any use, to win favour in many places in the Reichswehr Ministry. The strategic bases of the new organization were so-called " Hammer Groups " (*Hammerschaften*), or storm battalions. The *Reichsbanner* united its members in the various industries under this name, and made them cadres in case of a general strike. It may be called an idea born of creative despair. For there seemed little prospect that the working classes would for any length of time be able to stand up against a National Socialist Government that had come into power by constitutional means, and which was supported by the Reichswehr, the police, and possibly also the Stahlhelm. But it was a fact to be reckoned with that in case of the Shock Troops putting up a last desperate fight, immense material damage would be done; such damage that, in the eyes of influential industrial circles, the loss must outweigh the gain, which they might at that time still have seen in Hitler's accession to power. This juggling with the idea of internal political risk had an element of bluff in it; and in point of fact this form of resistance was not attempted, although at the time the workers might have had the help of sections of the Reichswehr and of the police. The bluff, however, was not at times without its political effect, and might have been of the greatest help to the Brüning-Groener Government, if that Government had been really determined upon resistance to Hitler instead of continuing to play with the extraordinary idea of " curbing " the might of National Socialism by giving it still more power.

SCHLEICHER VERSUS BRÜNING

Reflections of this description may appear as worthless lamentation to some people, but they contain the most useful lesson that can be drawn from the events in Germany during the year 1932, both by those who were concerned in them and by those who were not. For every informed person in Germany to-day knows that both General von Schleicher and the Socialist leaders would be only too thankful to have one of the many critical episodes in 1932 over again, so that they might act very differently from the way in which they did act. The reason why they both consistently did the wrong thing was their total lack of understanding of their Nazi antagonist. A boundless self-deception in the one case regarded National Socialism as nothing but a collection of demagogic rubbish, and in the other as a fine wine in process of fermentation which might at will be poured into any vessel provided by the Reichswehr and sealed up in it. The tactics of the Conservative State authority in the year 1932 with regard to Hitler afford one of the finest examples of the hopelessness of that form of diplomacy which loses sight of what is in broad daylight by inquiring after dark secrets, of the broad highway in its search for bypaths, of its own natural forces by delight in intrigue.

General von Schleicher, who from now on came well to the fore on the political stage, has become a classic example of such historical blindness. To the Chief of the Secretariat of the Reichswehr Ministry the prohibition of the SA, which he had originally supported himself, suddenly appeared too dangerous, too direct, possibly merely too simple. He would perhaps have preferred to achieve the desired result by some diplomatic sleight of hand, and, suddenly, at the last moment, demanded that, before prohibiting the SA, another conference should be held with Hitler, so that he might afterwards be made responsible for what happened. Evidently he felt, as did the eighteenth-century strategists, that the elegance of the solution to a tactical problem was of greater importance than the victory itself. The General does not seem to have realized that the time for negotiations was over, and that the Government must at last cease making itself ridiculous. When he was outvoted at the Cabinet meeting, he left the room and banged the door after him.

What General von Schleicher imagined that he was really going to do about the National Socialists, nobody has ever quite succeeded in discovering. Whether he intended honestly to make an alliance with them, or to engineer their fall and finally their destruction by refined diplomacy, may not be quite clear even to the General himself. His policy was, of course, not without a plan, indeed it might rather be said that it suffered from too much planning. The Brüning Government had at that time almost succeeded in solving one of its two problems in foreign policy — the cancellation of reparations. As Brüning once expressed it, he was a hundred yards off the finish, which Brüning's successor, Papen, then easily made. Then the Reichswehr began to set up a second aim by its insistence on equality of armament. To some extent it did this on its own initiative, and has never, at least as regards methods, quite had the support of the Foreign Office. For beside this Army policy there has been all these years the effort, varying in intensity, to come to a real understanding with France. Herr von Papen as Chancellor made the attempt, in agreement with the ideas of certain sections of French opinion, to bring together in a diplomatic negotiation the understanding with France and the ideal of equality of armament — an attempt that to-day (1933) was made barely a year ago, and yet already seems to lie centuries behind us.

THE FALL OF GROENER AND BRÜNING

General von Schleicher naturally looked upon the armament question as the more important. Possibly his view was that he would find allies more eager for the fray among those who followed Hitler's flag, not only under their former leadership but also after the reconstitution of the Party, than among Socialists. He either did not realize or did not take seriously enough the new martial spirit with which the *Reichsbanner* was informing the Socialist ranks. At all events, he hastened after the prohibition of the SA to express his regret to Hitler's representatives and said something very similar to the President. To crown all, at this moment German Justice once more came to the help of the Nazis. The Attorney-General decided that the documents discovered by Severing were not sufficiently serious to warrant an accusation of treason. This put the President, who had signed the decree for the suppression of the SA, into an awkward position. He wrote a cold letter to Groener indicating his desire that the *Reichsbanner* should be dissolved. And when Groener, a sick man with a failing voice — the scene is rather reminiscent of Bülow and William II over the *Daily Telegraph* affair — had the courage to refuse the demand amid the raging of the Nazis in the Reichstag, Schleicher stabbed him in the back. He went to his chief on the ministerial bench after the speech and declared, more or less in the name of the army, that it did not approve of him as Minister for War and that he must resign. Groener was thunderstruck. He had loved Schleicher as an adopted son, and had intended in the most self-sacrificing manner to open out a splendid future for the talents of his protégé. After his appointment as Minister of the Interior in October 1931 he had purposed voluntarily resigning the War Ministry to Schleicher in order that the ambition of that clever man might find a sphere of action. But he had not been prepared for desertion and treachery.

Abandoned by both Hindenburg and Schleicher, Groener was obliged to resign the Reichswehr Ministry. Unless the situation changed, the Brüning Cabinet was, morally speaking, wounded to death. The old President was at this time staying on his estate at Neudeck, in East Prussia, where complaints against Brüning were continually poured into his ears. The Chancellor's plan to break up some of the bankrupt big estates to the east of the Elbe and turn them into peasant holdings was denounced as "agrarian Bolshevism." Probably the old Field-Marshal's attention was chiefly caught by the word "Bolshevism." Stegerwald, the Minister for Labour, an ex-working man who became head of the Christian Trade Unions and was formerly Brüning's political teacher, and now Minister under him, was particularly stubborn in carrying out these plans and had taken a part of the work of settlement into his own hands. The old Field-Marshal was suspicious.

Brüning made up his mind to defeat the intrigue. He decided to ask the President openly whether he still had his confidence, in the hope that Hindenburg would lack the courage to say no. But he did not know the aged Field-Marshal as well as did General Groener, who had seen him part with the insensibility of a concrete block from Ludendorff, from William II, from those who had elected him in 1925, and from Hermann Müller. " The one thing you can rely on for certain is the inconstancy of the old gentleman," so people said.

As soon as Hindenburg returned from Neudeck, Brüning put the question to him. It happened in an interview that extended over two days — the first day for an hour, the second for a quarter of an hour, because the old gentleman could not stand long conversations. Hindenburg had made notes of what he intended discussing on scraps of paper, and he read them out. " It is said that you have Ministers with Bolshevist ideas in your Cabinet," was one of them. Brüning tried to explain, but the old gentleman was not to be parted from his notes. On the second day he suggested that Brüning might perhaps resign from his post as Chancellor and stay in the Cabinet as Foreign Minister, as Stresemann had once done. But Brüning refused. With the words: " I have some pride in my name and my honour too! " he left the room. It was on May 30, 1932, that the " best since Bismarck " succumbed after more than two years' tenure of office to the attacks of National Socialism, the discontent of General von Schleicher, and the machinations of the landed proprietors from the east.

A mixture of paladin and schoolmaster, Brüning had for the first time introduced into German post-War politics that touch of ascetism which the Nazis are carrying on with greater fervour but less selflessness — the idea of standing firm and suffering for the sake of independence. Having probably a more profound realization of the greatness of the sacrifices made by the people, he renounced easy palliatives for the sake of achieving great aims; and he deliberately made the sacrifice that the world is still waiting for from Hitler — the sacrifice of his popularity.

CHAPTER X

A MAN OF SHADOWS: FRANZ VON PAPEN

THE NEW Chancellor was Franz von Papen, a member of the Centre Party, whom Hindenburg appointed on Schleicher's recommendation. Papen was a scion of the Catholic Westphalian nobility, had formerly been an army officer, and during the World War had been military attaché to the German Embassy in Washington. In this post he had not only compromised himself but had made himself ridiculous by political conspiracies against the United States, whose early entry into the War the German Government had every reason to fear. Political intrigues that are brought to light by means of a stolen attaché case cause more amusement than indignation. He had acquired considerable industrial interests in the Saar by his marriage. And he used coal and iron, as also the keys of St. Peter, as arguments for a policy of Franco-German *rapprochement* that should guarantee permanent peace in Europe. His emotions can be roused impartially for a somewhat barbaric Nationalism and for a polite Catholic Universalism that pretends to great culture; and his intellect does not appear to be capable of realizing the incongruity any more than of enabling him to come to a decision one way or the other. He personally should not be made responsible for his political blunders to anything like the same degree as those who dragged him forcibly from his obscurity after years of political insignificance. For years " Fränzchen " (Frankie) had been trying to loose the bond between his Party and the Left and to induce it to follow a Conservative Catholic policy; all to no effect, and answered rather by a contemptuous than an indignant echo. He had also sought vainly to return to the diplomatic service, even if it were only as Minister to Luxemburg. He is a passionate amateur, but not a very fortunate lover, of politics. In speaking, he gives the impression of a little man standing on tiptoe.

Schleicher had brought Papen out of political obscurity and had recommended him to the President because he hoped through him either to win over or to destroy the Centre Party. The idea of winning it over proved at once to have been founded upon a false hope, for the Centre turned suddenly and indignantly against those who had formerly been members of the Party but who had allowed themselves to be used to help overthrow Brüning, whom it honoured. Neither did a dissolution of the Party take place immediately. On the contrary. The number of votes for the Centre was increased by its opposition to Franz von Papen.

For the moment, indeed, a truce on another front loomed larger. For Hitler promised both General von Schleicher and Dr. Meissner, Hindenburg's adviser, that he would tolerate Papen's Government. In return, Papen repealed the prohibition of the SA. That body reappeared with a promptitude that showed that even during the so-called suppression it had never really ceased to exist. The uniforms had in the meantime been slightly altered and had acquired a more military cut.

A second concession on Papen's part was that he dissolved the Reichstag in order to enable Hitler to increase his parliamentary representation proportionally to the increased number of his followers. Both concessions represented so desirable a gain in power that for his own sake Hitler was willing to preserve a benevolent neutrality towards a Government that showed itself so decidedly Conservative, illiberal, and reactionary. The fact that all the Ministers except two bore aristocratic names was perhaps only chance. At all events, it was a chance that was very closely connected with the views and the personal friends of Herr von Papen. A number of these Ministers, including Papen himself, were members of the *Herrenklub* (Germany's most exclusive club), a Conservative political association, the very name of which was a challenge thrown down to a democratic age, even though its active political significance has been exaggerated.

Moreover, Papen began his tenure of power very unfortunately by a proclamation that smelt of the candle, and which, among other things, unbraided former German Governments with having tried to turn the State into a sort of charitable institution, thus weakening the moral fibre of the nation. At a time when six million persons were unemployed through no fault of their own, it would have been hard to say anything more tactless.

None the less, much as men like Strasser and Goebbels might disagree, Hitler accepted the "Barons' Government." A change had come over German internal politics — for the first time National Socialism was not altogether in opposition to the Government. Since Hitler had made his secret offer of alliance to Held, the Bavarian Prime Minister, in December 1924, such a thing had never happened. Now at last he had got back on to the path towards which his tactical instincts had always led him — the way of alliance and friendship with the State authorities, who by this means insensibly grew less effective in their opposition. The Trojan horse had got one foot inside the wall.

As regards the election, Hitler had not much to fear from his alliance. The state of feeling in Germany was such that the fall of any Government — Left or Right — weakened the authority of the State. This was one of the facts that apparently no government realized. The change over from Brüning to Papen, just as that from Müller to Brüning in 1930, benefited National Socialism, which appeared in a sense to be the one stable thing in the whirl of changing governments.

Papen's first achievement was in the sphere of foreign policy and was a legacy from Brüning. An agreement was come to at Lausanne on the question of reparations, which provided that Germany should make a final payment of three milliards of Marks. Meanwhile Papen had got no nearer to a permanent understanding with France. To come to such an understanding was one of his dearest wishes, in pursuance of which he sought contacts among Catholics and his industrial friends in France. It was a policy which aimed at the solidarity of Christian Europe against the Antichrist of the Soviet.

SEVERING YIELDS TO FORCE

More independent and more original in tendency was the great measure of internal policy that Papen next introduced — the forcible removal of the Braun-Severing Socialist Government in Prussia. Notwithstanding Hitler's professed "toleration," the new Chancellor was not going to miss any opportunity of taking as much wind as possible out of the National Socialist sails. To do this it was essential before everything to carry on a determined fight against Marxism in both its forms. An attack on Communism and Socialism jointly could be explained by all manner of reasons. Papen censured the Braun-Severing Government — which the Communists reviled as a deadly enemy — for not being sufficiently energetic in attacking the partisans of Moscow. Diehl, one of Severing's higher officials, who later under Göring became Chief of the State Secret Police in Prussia, was brought in as principal witness for this assertion. The chief aim of the attack was, no doubt, to give as popular an appearance as possible to the campaign against Prussia. A more far-reaching and sounder political argument was the allegation that in Prussia a Government was conducting affairs without parliamentary authority, having been formally overthrown and furiously attacked by the majority of the Diet. Not but what Papen himself seemed quite content to work as Chancellor on a still smaller foundation, and to be evolving vast political schemes.

It was, of course, this latter that Braun and Severing were omitting to do. They confined themselves to the maintenance and conduct of routine business; they had, indeed, done so since long before their fall, and out of consideration for the many conflicting interests of the majority Parties had done nothing constructive apart from issuing a few police regulations and settling minor Church disputes. Moreover, Braun, the Prime Minister, was opposed to a continuance of the Government which had been formally overthrown in the Diet by a vote of no confidence, and had gone away for a holiday. It had for some time been mooted that the Reich should put a commissioner into Prussia to oversee the activities of the Government. Severing had mentally adjusted himself to the idea and seemed to think that he might none the less continue to hold office.

Then on the morning of July 20 Papen invited the three Prussian Ministers who were politically most obnoxious to him, namely, Severing, Klepper, the Finance Minister, and Hirtsiefer, the Minister for Public Welfare, to come and see him at the Chancellery, and announced that both Severing and the absent Prime Minister, Braun, were to consider themselves as dismissed. He, Papen, would, as Commissioner, take over the duties of the Prime Minister, while Bracht, the Lord Mayor of Essen, a man belonging to the Right Wing of the Centre Party, and a permanent candidate for high office, would become the Minister of the Interior under the Commissioner. Severing replied that he would yield only to force; whereupon Papen inquired what form of force he preferred, in the belief that it was only for the sake of appearances and to save his face. Severing replied that it was not a mere matter of appearances, but of justice, and the interview came to an end. The three Prussian Ministers went straight back to their offices, and Papen, with the consent of Schleicher, immediately proclaimed a state of emergency.

In the afternoon Papen's new Minister of the Interior, Bracht, appeared at Severing's office in person and demanded possession. Severing repeated that he would only yield to force, and Bracht went away again, regretting that he would now be obliged really to use force. Meanwhile, at the offices of the General Association of German Trade Unions were collected the political leaders of the German Socialist Party, of the Trade Unions, and of the *Reichsbanner*, debating whether or not the moment for armed resistance had come. This was surely the occasion for which the key-positions in Prussia had been held in spite of unpopularity, for which the police had been schooled, and, finally, for which the *Reichsbanner* had been expanded into the Iron Front. In retrospect it may be said that resistance would probably have been unsuccessful; that the workers for want of arms would have been defeated and a large part of the police would have refused to fight against the Reichswehr — the former would have been routed, and the latter would at best have stood with arms grounded. Politically, no doubt, the Socialist leaders reflected that though to give way before Papen was bad, it would in the long-run turn out to be less dangerous than to hold their ground, for this would probably mean that the SA would be called out, and that would turn the *coup* of the reigning " aristocratic clique " into a National Socialist Revolution. Opposition to Papen, who had no followers among the people, might have some hope of success, but not to Hitler with his thirteen millions. Finally, the elections of July 31 must not be jeopardized, and Papen must not be given an excuse for postponing them on account of political unrest.

All these considerations were perfectly correct and quite consistent with the mentality of the Socialist leaders. Of course, it would have been equally possible to regard the whole affair from a different angle. They might have preferred to perish honourably rather than to capitulate disgracefully. They might have made the day of the Republic's downfall a day of pride and defiance that, like March 18, 1848, would have been a splendid beacon across the years, the memorial of a glorious defeat that would have eclipsed all the ignominious half-measures of the previous thirteen years. Only such a death ensures immortality in history and prepares the way for resurrection.

But what is already dead can no longer die gloriously. The men who met on July 20 at the Berlin Trades Union offices were too prosaic for such conceptions. They did not even achieve Severing's gesture. When Bracht appeared at his office late in the afternoon with a few policemen and asked him very politely to give up his place, he went unprotesting to his private rooms. In the same way, Grzesinski, the Berlin police president, with his vice-president, Weiss, and Heimannsberg, the Chief of Police, submitted quietly to being arrested. The courtyard of the Police Prefecture resounded to the farewells of the men who were in political sympathy with their arrested chief. They shouted " Liberty! " — the greeting of the Iron Front. It was a farewell to the liberty of Weimar.

The three arrested men were politely taken to police cells and well looked after. There they seem to have decided that there had really been no reason why they should have let themselves be locked up, since not even Severing had been detained. To round off the comedy, they signed a declaration that they would not interfere in police affairs until the Supreme Court in Leipzig should have given a decision. For Braun and Severing, having judiciously yielded to force, had remembered that there were such things as judges in Leipzig and had lodged a complaint against Papen. The case, which dragged on for months, and which finally resolved itself into a discussion about offices and service cars, was a worthy last act to a régime that had intended to be democratic and had turned out to be more bureaucratic than the old imperial government.

July 20 saw the end of that degenerate Socialist rule that in its last days was nothing more than police Socialism. This government had for years sharpened and polished the police sword in readiness for a futile struggle for power of which it could make no reasonable use, and when at last the time came for this sword to be put into action, the wielders were afraid to sully the beautiful blade.

HITLER'S PACT WITH SCHLEICHER

Meanwhile Hitler was carrying on a curious and ambiguous electoral campaign. He had, as will be remembered, and as future events will make still more memorable, promised Schleicher and Meissner to tolerate Papen. It is certain that he did not do that in order to perpetuate the Papen Cabinet. It is much more likely that he hoped that Papen would himself one day resign the Chancellorship in his favour. It is true that such generosity is not what is generally to be expected of human nature, but the political decisions that had been made in Germany during the past few years had been more usually than not the result of unusual motives. Brüning, too, had played with the idea of sacrificing himself for the sake of Hindenburg's popularity in offering Hitler the Chancellorship. Groener had been prepared to give place to Schleicher out of pure magnanimity. It is not easy to make up one's mind whether Hitler was actually promised anything of that kind by Papen, or whether he took hints and indications of possibilities too seriously. It is known that those in power had definitely made up their minds that in certain eventualities much apparent power might be allotted to the National Socialists, while at the same time clever hands in the Cabinet and the various Ministries would hold them in bounds, since they were obviously inexperienced in the conduct of government. It does not very much matter now how far these illusions had matured by the summer of 1932. At all events, by January 1933 they had evidently gone so far that it was thought possible to restrain Hitler, even if he were given full power as Chancellor, by means of a Vice-Chancellor and a majority of individual Ministers.

In any case Hitler wished for reasons of diplomacy to spare Papen during the electoral contest. When, however, this born agitator faced the masses of the people and saw the demagogic talents of Goebbels blazing beside him, he found himself incapable of relinquishing the slogan, " Down with the Barons' Cabinet," entirely to the Socialists. But he did not yet throw all the force of his personality into the attack, and one person was very noticeably spared at this election — General von Schleicher. It is possible that he looked upon him as a friend at that time. At any rate, he knew that he would have to make the best of him as Reichswehr Minister in his Cabinet, for Hindenburg would certainly cling to Schleicher. He had long since ordered his Press to spare Schleicher. One district leader who did not do so was relieved of his post. And indeed the wielder of the military power in the Reich, who had overthrown Brüning and Groener for the sake of the SA, did not give any cause for attack.

AN ELECTORAL SKY FULL OF ILLUSIONS

The electoral campaigns of the year 1932 were swayed by a single great desire which Gregor Strasser had called an " anti-capitalist " desire, and which in popular parlance was simply and forcefully stated: " Things have got to be different." This subterranean slogan, the small coin on which Hitler's ardent programme circulated, " made " the elections of the spring and summer of 1932. And while the simplest of all magic formulae was handed on by word of mouth down below, the National Socialist propaganda fired rocket-like Utopian ideas into the air. Feder published an economic programme that appeared in the *Völkischer Beobachter* on April 2, and that as far as the faithful — and they were many — were concerned, painted a dry and withered land in the most glorious colours of fantasy.

The great new system that was in prospect, so said the author of the programme, could not be carried out over night, and could not immediately provide work. But: " What will instantly be done when

National Socialism crosses the threshold to political power is to provide means of employment. A great number of plans have already been made to this end, which cannot and must not be explained in detail now. At all events so much may be said that any one who takes the trouble to familiarize himself with these matters will see and be convinced how seriously and conscientiously the central authorities of the National Socialist Party will treat the problem of the provision of work. . . . One of the first measures will be the practical realization of the idea of compulsory labour corps. Without any difficulty worth mentioning, at least half a million men can be called up for this service in a very short space of time. . . . A second measure, which will again incorporate at least five hundred thousand in the economic advance, is a simple matter of taxation technique: the revenue from the house duties is to be diverted into industry in such a manner that those who fall under the duty will have up to 75 per cent. of the tax remitted if they can produce receipted bills for repairs carried out on their own premises. The whole of Germany will from one day to the next be filled with the sounds of hammering and knocking, of cleaning and roofing, of floor-laying and installation, of painting and whitewashing."

A still greater impression was made on the electors by a brochure that was published and circulated to the extent of sixty thousand copies all over the country as the official " Immediate Economic Programme " of the National Socialist Party. This pamphlet, which runs to thirty-two pages, will remain as a permanent record of what unscrupulous propagandists will offer to a desperate people. The first promise concerned the improvement of the soil, which was to increase the annual yield from German arable land by two milliards of Marks. What could the people think? Two milliards more every year for German agriculture — and an evidently criminal Government had hitherto neglected even to begin on this useful work. And it was apparently the suggestion of the best qualified experts, for according to a footnote the plan was based upon the publications of the Association of German Agrarian Societies. What the nation did not realize was this — that these Agrarian Societies were organizations of landowners and of those who had money invested in land, and that their suggestions, which had been published a year earlier, had been laid aside with a sigh by all real experts as a well-meant Utopian scheme. The Immediate Programme also announced that the work would entail a total expenditure of ten milliards of Marks; and only forgot to mention that if German industry could produce ten milliards of Marks from anywhere, it would at once flourish as never before, without any Immediate Programme, without Agrarian Societies, without even the National Socialist Party.

It continued in the same tone. Within a year four hundred thousand houses for single families were to be erected, which would at once give a million men work for a year. The undertaking was to be partly financed by an artificial creation of credit. An even more important point in the programme was an extensive industrial autarchy. The necessary raw materials were preferably to be obtained from friendly European Powers. Along the same lines was a demand for the abandonment of the gold standard after the English example. The conclusion and in a sense the intellectual crown of the programme was the compulsory labour service to which all young men of a particular age were to be liable: "there will be no exemptions for university men or other propertied persons. Every one will wield a spade."

Thus the programme closed with the avowal of those new ethics of labour that contain the social intention of National Socialism, and which do it more credit than its highly imaginative economic promises. It was, however, these material promises that enticed the voters, although their serious parts are so vague and ambiguous that they inspire little respect for the attainments of the National Socialist Economic Council that pretends to such wisdom.

And what was the reaction of the electorate to this juggling? On July 31 Hitler got 230 seats in the Reichstag out of a total of 607, that is, nearly two-fifths. And what was more important, or at least more threatening as far as Papen was concerned, was that this number — together with the Centre Parties — gave Hitler an absolute majority. That was the greatest triumph that he achieved on constitutional lines. He could by purely constitutional means overthrow any opponent such as a constitutional Government that tried to put a spoke in his wheel. That was the negative side of his success. On the positive side he now derived from it the claim that the repository of State authority should, even against the law and the Constitution, appoint him to the Government and retain him in it.

THE UNGOVERNABLE SA

With the most ingenuous air in the world Hitler based his demand upon the proposition that if he were not put into a position of power, he could no longer keep the SA in check. And by this argument, which actually only betrayed his weakness, he was always able to impress the men with whom he was dealing, because they did not understand and were secretly afraid of the masses. Hitler first showed his cleverness in rising from so low to such a height; but that he should be able in the face of all the Presidents, Generals, and Princes to dive down again to the bottom at will, like a fish in water, seems to be his inimitable strength.

The nervously excited state of the SA, which had for years been stimulated by bloodthirsty speeches, was noticeable even during the election campaign. Sub-leaders had promised them a "night with long knives" in case of victory. And even a responsible man like Frick had observed that no doubt a few thousand Marxist functionaries would "be damaged."

The SA gradually became convinced that it was they who had been attacked by the Communists, although regarded historically it had been Hitler's old SA which first began fighting in the streets, and although Goebbels at his entry into Berlin had instructed his men to use force in overcoming resistance. It is human nature always to throw the blame on to the opponent, and so it may also have been human nature, though of a singular kind, that led Göring to exclaim, on July 15, 1932, at the Sports Palace in Berlin:

"The murderous mob is still reckoning on the discipline of the SA. And it knows, too, that there is an order that no member of the SA shall carry arms. I tell you, this is the end. In a day or two, when the Leader comes back from East Prussia, I shall go with the other Party leaders and ask him — and I know that he will grant our request — to take back this order. When the right to bear arms in an emergency has been admitted for thrice twenty-four hours, when once the brown-shirts have been given their liberty — the cowardly mob will creep away into any dark corner."

And Strasser said much the same thing in Bielefeld: that if the Government could not or would not act, then the National Socialists would clean up the streets themselves.

RUMOURS OF RIOTS

" Cleaning up . . ." was the expression used by the Nazis when they talked of the destruction of their enemies. After the Reichstag elections the SA began very seriously to " clean up " in various parts of the country on its own responsibility. Many human lives were sacrificed to this cleansing process, which was sometimes — in East Prussia, for example — carried out by means of bombs. And a part at least of the forces equipped themselves with lorries and machine-guns for the march on Berlin. The Reichswehr Ministry found it necessary to make it clear that it would not capitulate out of any soft-hearted shrinking from spilling blood; but that the Reichswehr would shoot. And they were all the more determined since they believed themselves to have been deceived by Hitler. Shortly after the elections Hitler had made a speech to his sub-leaders at Berchtesgaden, in which, amongst other things, he had exhorted them to be loyal to the Reichswehr. He had officially sent this part of his speech to the Reichswehr Ministry, and the Ministry had caused the contents to be officially communicated to the troops. It was a very significant episode. The temper of the men was evidently such that the Ministry considered it admirable to let them know how good were the relations between Hitler and themselves, and that the troops need have no conscientious scruples on this score. But when the SA denied and disturbed these good relations by their insubordination, when they threatened rioting and cleaning up the streets, the higher Reichswehr authorities might very well feel that they had been deceived; and the occasion was favourable for communicating something of these hostile feelings to the ranks.

In order that there should be no possible doubt of their determination, the Government on August 9 issued an emergency decree against terrorization that provided for the most rigorous punishment of offenders. Misdemeanours that had hitherto only been followed by imprisonment were now threatened with death. The emergency decree had a double purpose. It acted as a barrier between Communist terrorization and the SA's lust for revenge, and was intended to take from the brown-shirts any pretext for proceeding against the " Red Murderers " themselves. The State authority said " Revenge is mine " ; and thereby took a certain amount of wind out of the sails of Hitler's anti-Bolshevist propaganda. At the same time — and this was very necessary — it set bounds to the restlessness of the SA, whose deeds of violence on and about July 31 had undoubtedly roused far greater alarm in Germany than anything their opponents had done.

It may be imagined what sort of temper was kindled in the SA by this emergency decree. The theory of two kinds of justice was very strong in these men; a distinction must be made between persons who were nationally minded and those who were not nationally minded. It was the theory that Hitler had postulated at the very beginning of his career in saying that the country must cherish more those people by whom it was loved than those by whom it was not loved. The *Angriff* demanded that those should not suffer under the emergency decree " who snatched at any weapons in self-defence and despair " — thus admitting two kinds of justice, one against the Right and the other against the Left. Hitler hoped at last to finish forging the sceptre of his might in the fire of these words. Once more there were rumours of a *coup d'état* in Germany. But Hitler was now sufficiently well known for it to be quite certain that he intended nothing against the Reichswehr. He never did intend anything of that nature — not even on November 9, 1923. A *coup d'état* means something quite different to him, means much the same as a Bolshevist terror. It must be remembered that in accordance with the chief tenet of Hitler's strategy the Bolshevist terror is a state of affairs out of which only National Socialism could find a way of escape. Hence it must be evolved.

THE MEMORIAL TABLET

Alertly, cheerfully, confident of victory, Hitler approached the goal — Power — which had at last come in sight. He had no intention of taking it by force; it would be given him, in the glamour of the suggestive power of his success, for the good of the Fatherland. Upon the parade ground in Fürstenberg he met General von Schleicher, and found the Chief of the Reichswehr ready once again to be the intelligent ally who would use his whole influence to give the people's tribune the Chancellorship. Hitler was so well satisfied with this conversation that he suggested to the General that a tablet should be affixed to the walls of the house: "Here the memorable conference between Adolf Hitler and General von Schleicher took place, in consequence of which . . ." Memorable! Hitler's life flows through time as a sluggish, undisciplined stream, every now and then bursting into tremendous cataracts. In his own eyes it evidently consists entirely of a chain of memorable events.

CONVERSATION WITH PAPEN

In this sanguine frame of mind Hitler went to Berlin on August 13, whither a telegram had summoned him to an interview with the President. He would become Chancellor — Schleicher had promised it — Schleicher, the only member of the Cabinet who enjoyed respect in Nazi eyes since he was the only one who had a hundred thousand soldiers behind him. But what a cruel disillusionment awaited Hitler! A conversation with Papen made it quite clear that neither he, nor evidently Hindenburg, had any idea of making Hitler Chancellor. And the reasons? There were so many. One thing was certain: that the President regarded "the Austrian" as a very curious personality. Great as was his interest in the national movement, he would heartily dislike to see it controlled by a "Bohemian corporal." For the present he regarded him as an ambitious man who was not easily repressed, and who might be kept quiet by being made "Postmaster-General if the worst came to the worst." In the shelter of his knowledge of these feelings on Hindenburg's part, Papen felt perfectly secure.

He explained to Hitler discreetly that Hindenburg's views were such and such, and would not Hitler be content with the post of Vice-Chancellor? And, in addition, the post of Prussian Minister of the Interior, which meant control of the police force of the largest State. With hysterical temperaments like Hitler's, particular catchwords will always induce an explosion. In Hitler's case, one of these words was "Vice-Chancellor," which he had so often heard during the last few months, and which was at the time synonymous for him with scorn and rejection. The floodgates of his eloquence were opened, and Papen discovered what Lossow, Hugenburg, and Brüning had discovered before him — that it is hard to discuss anything with a man who is only capable of talking and not of listening.

He told Herr von Papen that he claimed for himself the position in the Cabinet that Mussolini had had after the March on Rome. Papen, who had not studied the history of the Fascist *coup d'état* as minutely as had the denizens of the Brown House, could at the moment only think of something like dictatorship. Hitler, for his part, never dreamt that his parables needed to be explained to this unsuspecting bourgeois. Mussolini had at first ruled as chief of a coalition in which only a minority was in his favour. Of course, privately, he would also have remembered that Mussolini threw out his allies after a time and became an autocrat. Aloud he began by saying something else: that he regarded it as one of his first duties to "mow down" the Marxists; advanced the demand "three days clear for the SA" — whether the massacre of St. Bartholomew was mentioned or only implied is immaterial. Horror filled Papen, as it had once done Herr von Kahr when he heard of Göring's bloodthirsty speeches. Coldly he advised Hitler to try his luck with the President; to do his best to convince him. And when Hitler saw the trap and swore at Papen saying, not he, Hitler, but Papen should win over the Field-Marshal in Hitler's favour, Papen did not laugh in his face at the idea that he should overthrow himself for his rival's sake. No, he stuck to his plaintive and not quite convincing attitude of patriotism, on the strength of which the lord over thirteen million votes demanded to be honoured as a national hero. The hero must go that afternoon and see the President, and with a handshake and "after all, we all want to do what is best for Germany," Papen set the net about his feet.

REJECTED BY HINDENBURG

Hitler was filled with fury on leaving the Chancellor's Palace, and certain only of two things — that Papen had not resigned so as to leave the way clear for him, and that Hindenburg was evidently not going to make him Chancellor. He went straight to Goebbels's house, where he also found Göring, and listened to their talk of "baiting traps." Meanwhile, there were agitated telephone conversations, the upshot of which was that there had been a mistake, the President had not by any means definitely made up his mind. Hitler took fresh heart. He appeared with a certain feeling of confidence at the President's Palace at 4.15, with — a gesture of defiance — Röhm accompanying him. It was feared that this companion would so upset the old Field-Marshal that he would cancel the interview. The Field-Marshal, however, who had taken a personal dislike to the Chief of Staff of the SA on account of his much discussed idiosyncrasies, controlled himself and reserved his energies for the scene which now followed.

Hitler was still hoping that this was to be only a ceremonial occasion; hoping that the proclamation was already prepared: "The President has entrusted Herr Adolf Hitler, the leader of the National Socialist Party, with the task of forming a Government that will have his confidence and be supported by the national forces. . . ." In his propagandist mind's eye he already saw himself mounting the steps, watched with bated breath by the whole of Germany, and showing the world how a crown should be accepted.

Instead of which he found a haughty, almost contemptuous, old gentleman, who immediately began to interrogate him without offering him a seat. Hitler was obliged to listen to an address by the old gentleman, telling him his plans for a Cabinet — under Papen — and at the end asking him almost sternly whether he was willing to co-operate. Hitler replied angrily that he had already told Herr von Papen and Herr von Schleicher his condition; that he held to it: only as Chancellor . . . that he must reply in the negative to the President's question. Silence. The bystanders expected that Hitler would burst into a long speech according to his usual custom; this time the not-always-opportune talent might have saved the situation. But the Leader was exhausted. Hindenburg, who had already heard something of the story from Papen, asked: "So you want the whole power?" Hitler wanted to say no, to adduce the example of Mussolini, but Hindenburg refused to be diverted from his idea. Hitler was silent in rage and disappointment. Hindenburg continued the conversation in a firm tone (which was afterwards reproduced in the official *communiqué*) to the effect that he definitely refused Hitler's demand because he could not reconcile it with his conscience and his duty to the country to hand over the government exclusively to the National Socialist Party — a Party which would use its power one-sidedly. Hindenburg loathed the idea of anything like a St. Bartholomew's Night. Therefore he recommended Hitler in conclusion to learn a little chivalry for use in his future campaigns. In other words — the eighty-six-year-old Field-Marshal gave Hitler a thorough dressing-down, and sent him home.

After less than fifteen minutes, Hitler left the Palace in the eyes of his followers, of his opponents, of the whole German nation, and especially in his own eyes, a beaten man. He went away with burning and well-founded doubts in his mind as to whether he had handled the situation aright. Perhaps there were only two men who were perfectly satisfied with the result of the interview — Göring and Goebbels. They had warned the Leader of Papen's trap — and they had been justified. Now he was more than ever in their hands.

BREACH OF FAITH?

And this was not the end of his humiliation. Hindenburg, who had not liked the National Socialist leader before, now regarded him as a man who had broken his word. He said so to him quite bluntly, and had it bluntly inserted in the official *communiqué:* that he regretted that Herr Hitler did not see his way to supporting the national Government appointed by the President, in accordance with the promise that he had given in the Reichstag. How terrible it sounded! Breach of faith, he has broken his word, resounded throughout the Press.

What promise had he broken? Hitler had promised General von Schleicher and Dr. Meissner that he would tolerate Papen. Schleicher and Meissner were now informed by the National Socialists that Hitler's promise had only been valid until the time of the election. The forms of Kahr, of Lossow, of Seisser, emerged from the shadows to remind the present-day men that Hitler's promises were always wrongly interpreted. These men who vanished from the public eye in the year 1923 have no reason now to rely on Hitler's promises. One cannot say if they would still do so. Schleicher, Meissner, Papen, and finally Hindenburg, will still have plenty of opportunity of showing how little use man makes in an emergency of even his own unfortunate experiences.

NEWS FROM POTEMPA

Having been turned out of the Presidential Palace ignominiously, Hitler returned raging to his house at Berchtesgaden, and decided to stir up Acheron against the arrogant men in Berlin. He had been beaten, there was no doubt of it. His luck had not held, his ascent was impeded. The limits of his potentiality had been touched, and amid sparks that had been visible at great distances, had given him an electric shock. Nothing is more dangerous for a mythos than to be seen through; and the mythos of Hitler's success was now exploded. He was not the equal of these gods. There were still, however, unexplored and vasty deeps below. Perhaps the National Socialist movement, having been cast from the heights, might dive down into the depths of the proletariat into which it had hitherto failed to penetrate.

If they thought they did not need him to still the seething populace, they should learn to their cost who would burn to ashes all resistance and all State authority by means of the fiery spirit of the people. The Conservative classes and their government had still not realized the hellish laws obeyed by this power that had grown up from the people. They were now to discover it.

Soon after the issue of the emergency decree against terrorism on August 9, five Nazis had murdered a member of an opposition Party, a workman called Pietrzuch, in an utterly brutal manner at his home in the Upper Silesian village of Potempa. A special court at Beuthen condemned all five to death. This sentence roused the whole SA, including Hitler, to fury. He sent the following telegram to the five condemned murderers at Potempa: " My comrades! In face of this ghastly and sanguinary sentence I feel myself bound to you in limitless loyalty. From this moment your freedom is a question of our honour. To fight against a Government that could allow this is our duty."

It must be remembered that the Potempa murderers were not honest lads who had gone farther than they intended in self-defence. One at least of them had not even acted on the spur of the moment, but had coldly and deliberately egged on the others to the crime — and these were the kind of men to whom the Nazi leader felt himself bound in unlimited loyalty. He was in this obeying the law of his movement in which the ideal of personal loyalty played a part not generally accorded to it in modern politics — a law according to which moral lapses, political faults, and even crimes are easily pardoned so long as faith and obedience are rendered to the leader. Hitler may have thought that it was a good opportunity of showing the outside bourgeois world in a serious case how far this " Nibelung loyalty " could be carried; how in the old Teutonic manner loyalty between men and their leader cloaked every sin. There may be a touch of Nordic greatness in this attitude, but at the same time there is a will to barbarity which at that time, it must be admitted, was rejected and abhorred by the majority of the German people.

Hitler's hate was now directed against two men — Papen and Hindenburg. Not against General von Schleicher. He probably still regarded him as to some extent an ally who was doing his best to bring about good relations. But the President and his trusted adviser who had not been willing to resign voluntarily from his Chancellorship — these two appeared to him as two conspirators who were trying to refuse what was his due to the man who was called by Destiny.

His hatred of Papen exploded after the judgement at Beuthen in a furious announcement to the National Socialists, in which he raged:

" German fellow-countrymen! Whoever among you agrees with our struggle for the honour and liberty of the nation will understand why I refused to take office in this Cabinet. The justice of Herr von

Papen may perhaps in the end condemn thousands of National Socialists to death. Did they think to cover this procedure, which is a measure inspired by ignorance and is a challenge to the whole nation, with my name too? They were mistaken. Herr von Papen, I understand your sanguinary 'objectivity' now! I wish that victory may come to nationalist Germany, and destruction upon its Marxist destroyers and spoilers. But I am not fitted to be the executioner of nationalist fighters for the liberty of the German people! . . . Let Herr von Papen set up German tribunals of blood over us. By the force of the national uprising we shall as certainly deal with this system as we shall do away with Marxism in spite of all attempts to save it!"

Strange language to use to the man who had the President's confidence. Could not even consideration for the Field-Marshal subdue Hitler's voice? No, it could not. He made speeches at this time in which he quite openly pointed out that he was young enough to wait for the next presidential election — reckoning with the probable early decease of the eighty-six-year-old man in his hearing and in that of the whole of Germany. And some of his friends were not content even to await the natural event.

TO DEPOSE HINDENBURG

Let us consider for a moment the outraged Centre Party. In all the struggles for power during the summer it had, practically speaking, taken no part. Since Brüning's resignation it was nothing but a Party, and from now on Parties had very little concern with power in Germany. The Centre had even been obliged to watch its own Ministers in Prussia, who had formed a Coalition Government with Braun, being removed. The loss of a portfolio might indeed be borne in the ups and downs of the political game, but the continuance of the Papen Government was another matter — it was directly dangerous to the existence of the Centre. For the more Papen's power increased, the more did also the danger increase that the renegade would one day form a new Conservative Catholic Party and by means of it dissolve the Centre. Hence Brüning especially carried on a campaign against Papen, and carried it on with all the passion of a man who has been thwarted and deceived. His passion, however, was not equal to that of the National Socialists with whom he now found himself in alliance to compass Papen's fall. In the coalition conferences of September 1932, a Nazi suggestion actually came up to depose the President by means of a motion in the Reichstag followed by a national plebiscite. This proposal of the Hitler Party speculated on the disaffection with which Hindenburg was regarded by the whole of the Left, since he had so cruelly disappointed his electors and had overthrown Brüning who had suffered so much for his sake. Brüning, however, refused with very good reason to join in the hazardous undertaking of the National Socialists. Apart from the fact that an attack on the hero of the World War who had been elected by the majority of the people would always be unpopular, the only result that he could expect would be in place of Hindenburg to raise Hitler to the Presidential chair — and that was the last thing Brüning wanted.

DRAMATIC END OF THE REICHSTAG

Acheron could, however, be kept in a state of turbulence by many other means. At the beginning of September the Reichstag met. This body, consisting as it did of two hundred and thirty Nazis and eighty-nine Communist members, was no longer an active part of the State machinery and not an executive of the will of the people, but a kettle of seething popular fury. Papen — it is true — managed to keep a lid on it. The Nazis might make Göring President of the Reichstag; Göring and Frick might discuss the overthrow of the Chancellor with the Centre; but Papen had a strong weapon against them in his traditional red portfolio — the order of the President declaring the Reichstag to be dissolved. For the prorogation of Parliament is the privilege of the Head of the State, and the somewhat dilatory practice of the past years has made it possible to bottle the lightning by the President's giving the order for dissolution into the faithful hands of a Chancellor in whom he has confidence. He keeps it in a red portfolio and if necessary brings it out — a potent spell that will at once reduce the most fractious parliament to order. For some time Herr von Papen had had this magic formula in his red portfolio in case of emergency, and he would have been wise if he had taken it out at once as soon as the Reichstag met on September 12. For it was believed that the Centre and the National Socialists were planning in their furious hatred to overthrow him with the help of the other Opposition Parties. But is it certain that they were planning this? It is not absolutely certain, and Herr von Papen seems to have counted a great deal on the uncertainty. The situation was thus: the Nazis might try to overthrow Papen out of sheer revenge. But if the Chancellor anticipated them and dissolved the Reichstag, then they would be faced with an election campaign in which they would certainly be the losers.

August 13 had given their reputation among their electors something of a jar, and not without reason did Hitler rage over the defeat out of which Papen had made a great show before the world. In grasping at power, he had slipped, and that meant not a short but probably a long fall, so awkwardly was the Party placed between the heights and the abyss. Its policy of continually collecting fresh votes had in fact made it not more powerful but more in need of power. It could no longer afford to wait for power. It was not possible for this Party to say to the electorate like other Parties: "Give me more votes and I will fulfill your desires." The attractive power of this militant Party rested not only in the hopes of its electorate for future achievements, but just as much in its certainty of victory. The Party could not first try out its talents in office but must prove them by winning the victory. If this did not succeed within measurable time, then its prestige would fade and votes would fall off like leaves in autumn. And once the falling off began there was no saying where it would stop.

Since this was the case, the Party dared not risk another election so soon, but must avoid a dissolution of the Reichstag by every possible means. That seems, in fact, to have been the intention of Dr. Frick, the leader of the Party in the Reichstag, to judge by his attitude on September 12, when the Communists proposed a vote of no confidence, and demanded an immediate division. Papen might by this means be overthrown, but even after his fall he might as *locum tenens* dissolve the Reichstag by means of the President's order — an interpretation of the Constitution which, though not edifying, was hardly refutable.

At Frick's request the sitting had been interrupted by half an hour's recess. The Party leaders wanted time for discussion. Papen, however, made the most of the opportunity to arm himself — he dashed over to the Chancellery and fetched the order for dissolution in its red portfolio. If they saw the red portfolio lying on the table — he reckoned — the National Socialists would take good care to run no risk of overthrowing the Government. He never guessed at the remarkable ambush that Göring was preparing for him.

The House reassembled. Before any one had time to think, Göring announced that the division would be taken. Only then did the Chancellor, who was sitting beside him on the Ministerial bench, realize the game that was being played. He demanded the right to speak. Göring either did not or would not hear him. They were voting, he said afterwards, and he could let nobody speak. Then Papen, silent and trembling, drew from the red portfolio the scrap of paper on which the order for dissolution was scrawled in a simple line of writing, rose and laid the creased scrap on the table in front of Göring. It is possible that in his haste he laid the note face down, and Göring maintains that he had no idea what it was that lay before him. He continued in his duties as President of the House; and rustling and scraping their chairs, the Government supporters rose and left the hall. From this moment on, the sitting of the Reichstag was unconstitutional. The House continued to sit completely illegally. All the members from Right to Left (except the German Nationalists) carried out their functions illegally and amazedly according to Göring's illegal directions. Illegally the solemn division was taken, and provided for the Chancellor a shadowy fall that signified nothing at all.

It was a useless gesture that would probably never have been made if Göring had had a better understanding of constitutional law and practice. The fact that Papen had the majority in the Reichstag against him had been known before. What made the decisive impression upon the public was the fact that the whole great National Socialist Party with all its allies could still not overthrow him, simply because the Chancellor was able to lay on the President's table an insignificant piece of paper that he had hastily fetched. Hitler had been beaten for the second time, and Papen had been victorious for the second time. It was this which counted in the eyes of the people; and the fact that the National Socialists, above all that relentless fighter, Göring, published flaming declarations throughout the land about the sacred rights of popular representation during the following weeks — that popular representation which they had always abused as a gossip shop; that Göring ferreted his way through an investigation by a parliamentary committee with the wretchedest excuses, such as " did not see," or " failed to hear," in order to explain his conduct; that the grossest ignorance was proved against him of the duties of a Reichstag president, and that the better-instructed Socialists led him up and down like a captive bear on the floor of parliamentary procedure — all this showed the National Socialists to be in the toils of a run of bad luck such as they had not had since the unfortunate year 1924. Hitler was, needless to say, not wholly pleased with the inferior performance of his Reichstag president.

CHAPTER XI

NSBO

THE INJURY which the Party had sustained on August 13 was only aggravated by this parliamentary massage. In vain did the sick movement now transfer its whole weight on to the proletarian side, hissing and fulminating against the " aristocratic clique " of Herr von Papen and his *Herrenklub.* In vain did Strasser make speeches to the German working men which are some of the highest intellectual achievements of National Socialism; and in vain did the Nazi cells agitate in the factories.

This " National Socialist Industrial Cell Organization " (N S B O), brought into being by Reinhold Muchow in 1928, was reorganized at the beginning of 1931 and had long since found its way from the small workshops into the large factories. Under the leadership of Muchow and Schumann it had become a considerable organization with a large central bureau in Munich, but still carefully avoided making an appearance as a Trade Union, or making any attempt to interfere with wages. Hitler consistently forbade this because, as he says in his book, he regards the foundation of a National Socialist Trades Union as a task for an outstanding genius, and such a genius had up till then not appeared in the Party. He feared, moreover, that the active militant power of the movement might be enfeebled by participation in economic questions. Hence the N S B O had to rest content to be a recruiting body for the Party; the sluice that lay before the great reservoir of the Party. Their members were at first to be kept separate from the Party. The N S B O worked on the assumption that the Third Reich was inevitable; that it would be the particular duty of the N S B O, as Muchow expressed it in his maxims of the organization, to train the working classes to be the ruling class in the new State. Thus any one who wished to collaborate must join a cell in good time.

"ANTI-CAPITALIST SENTIMENTS"

The intellectual chief of the social wing of the National Socialist Party, Gregor Strasser, made great efforts to win over the working-class mind during that year, 1932. An imperishable witness to these endeavours was the great speech he made on May 10, 1932, in the Reichstag, which can hardly be equalled by anything Hitler or Goebbels has ever done. Let us listen to it carefully, including all its absurdities, " unto the Jews a stumbling-block, and unto the Greeks foolishness," as the Apostle said: let us listen to it, for it is the most complete expression of the National Socialist point of view; any one who wishes to know what National Socialism really is cannot do better than read it:

" The rise of National Socialism," said Strasser, " is the protest of a people against a State that denies the right to work and the revival of natural intercourse. If the machinery for distribution in the present economic system of the world is not capable of properly distributing the productive wealth of nature, then that system is false and must be altered. The important part of the present development is the anti-capitalist sentiment that is permeating our people, that has by now laid hold of something like 95 per cent. of our people, consciously or unconsciously. This anti-capitalist sentiment is not in the least a refusal to recognize property acquired by personal labour and thrift and morally justifiable. Above all, it has no connexion with the senseless or destructive tendencies of the International. It is the protest of the people against a degenerate economic system; and it demands from the State that, in order to secure its own right to live, it shall break with the demons Gold, World Economy, Materialism, and with the habit of thinking in export statistics and the bank rate, and shall be capable of restoring honest payment for honest labour. This anti-capitalist sentiment is a proof that we are on the eve of a great change — the conquest of Liberalism and the rise of new ways of economic thought and of a new conception of the State."

The significance of this speech certainly did not lie in its ideas or suggestions, which were neither new nor of undisputed value. Its importance lies rather in the absolute and unqualified nature of its demands, in its tragically great realization of the seriousness and the pregnancy of this denial of former economic thought, which even Marxism had not denied. Hence the Socialist, Dr. Hilferding, was on the wrong track when, amid the laughter of his colleagues, he demonstrated learnedly to Strasser that a great part of his ideas were derived from Marx. The importance of Strasser's speech lay in something quite different. It lay in his convincing expression of popular thought. The robust common sense of the people, which " demanded " from the State that it " should be in a position " to provide " remedies," was more highly rated by Strasser than any amount of debatable book-learning. Economic capacity is required, and in case of necessity enjoined. " Decretinism," educated Marxists had called this faith in the omnipotence of the State, which had also occurred in the Marxist movement. But in this case it was being raised from a fallacy to an ideal.

Strasser's speeches caused long-rusted metal to shine brightly again in the heart of many an old Trade Unionist. Here was once again a piece of Utopianism, gleaming as once did Bebel's State of the Future, only with this difference, that Reason was no longer adduced in proof, but was pushed aside as a superfluous and contentious monitor. Conferences were set on foot between Strasser and the leaders of the German Association of Trades Unions, which had hitherto been clearly allied with the Socialists, but which had for some considerable time disassociated itself from the moderate foreign policy of the Socialists by violent utterances on the subject of reparations. There could be no doubt about Strasser's seriousness on social questions, and was there any law to prevent the independent Trades Unions from following in the tracks of Stresemann and Breitscheid in matters of foreign policy? Were German workers who hated especially the Jews among capitalists, any the less German anti-capitalist workers? At such moments, when under the pressure of an overwhelming situation — which the situation in the summer of 1932 undoubtedly was — what is in common to men who have hitherto been antagonistic comes to the fore, their fundamental differences are easily forgotten.

The independent Trades Unions probably felt increasingly that the differences were unimportant, since they became more and more undecided about their own aims. The spiritual barrenness of Socialism had become notorious, especially its incapacity to suggest constructive solutions. National Socialism of Strasser's brand was, in its bearing at all events, full of projects. Its key idea — that the State could be ordered to be in a position to look after anybody — this key idea was really part of the ideal wealth of the Labour movement, only buried under the erudition of decadent leaders who had come from capitalist universities. In a second great speech that he made to the industrial cells in the Sports Palace at Berlin, Strasser introduced a compliment to the Socialist Trades Union leader, Leipart, and thus gave some indication of what had been planning in secret. The reason why Strasser's rival and successor, Dr. Ley, later arrested and prosecuted this Labour leader who was so highly thought of by Strasser, lay probably simply in the alliance that existed between Leipart and Strasser and in the political projects that had finally resulted from it.

THE COLLAPSE OF NOVEMBER 6, 1932

While, however, Strasser was doing his best to attract kindred spirits from the Left Parties — not in order to include them in the ranks of National Socialism, but in order to get into line all political enthusiasts without regard for Party — the sails of his own vessel were rent. The attempt to incline towards the Left cost the Party more than it gained. At the beginning of November a strike of transport workers broke out in Berlin, which partially paralysed the town for several days, and its effects looked uncommonly like a general strike. The National Socialists were obliged willy-nilly to join in this affray with waving banners, although the strike had been called by the Communists and rejected by the regular Trade Unions. The idea of their joining in a strike shoulder to shoulder with Communists roused horror in a section of the bourgeois electorate. But it is necessary to look deeper — into the great disappointment of August 13 — for an explanation of what followed immediately after the strike.

In the Reichstag elections of November 6, Hitler lost over two million votes and only polled 11.73 millions. Instead of 230 he had only 197 seats. It is true that the Socialists also fell from 133 to 121 — a belated retribution for July 20 — and the Centre from 97 to 89. On the other hand, the Communists rose from 89 to 100, and were thus about on the level that the Nazis had been on September 14, 1930, when they had just startled the world. And this run of ill-luck did not cease. At local elections during the next few weeks, the National Socialist votes decreased from Sunday to Sunday, so that it was reckoned that in the next Reichstag elections they would not win more than 150 seats. To put it in a nutshell: The Party was large, but no longer anything out of the ordinary. What was even worse was that it had once been phenomenal, and now it was doubtful whether it could keep up to a reasonable level, whether it would not, now that it had begun to sink, very soon collapse altogether.

On the other hand, it was clear that all the Parties supporting Papen were on the upward trend. The German Nationalists, for instance, the number of whose votes rose by nearly 50 per cent., obtained 51 seats to their former 37. It was the definitely Conservative forces that were now ranging behind Papen — the forces that will probably always set the political tempo in a bourgeois Germany. An analysis of the election results shows that it was in the agricultural districts that the voters had deserted National Socialism. And as regards parliamentary tactics — Hitler and Brüning, Papen's two bitterest enemies, had lost the majority with which they might in the defunct Reichstag have formed a Government.

PAPEN'S SECOND BLOW

Papen felt that the present condition of the National Socialist Party was very suitable for his launching a fresh attack on it. Since August 13 he had worked against National Socialism. He had pointed out to Hitler that an incident like the Potempa telegram was quite incompatible with his aspiration to the Chancellorship. When he announced that he would " stamp out " the fire of civil war in the country there was no question as to whom he regarded as the incendiary. After the Reichstag election of November 6, he determined on a bold stroke. On November 17 he resigned from his post. There was just as much or as little obvious reason for his resignation now as earlier. Papen had in fact achieved some notable successes. He had turned out the " Marxist " Government in Prussia, and had — long before Hitler — effected a real and decisive political co-ordination between Germany and its largest State. Further, he had made a not unsuccessful attempt to revive industry by giving it advances in the form of bills upon future taxation.

Hence it was not lack of material success that caused Papen's resignation. The fact that the majority of the people and the majority in the Reichstag still regarded him with distrust was certainly a serious drawback, and would have been a decisive drawback in normal circumstances. It had, however, been no different in the preceding months and had nevertheless not prevented him from governing as he thought fit. What reason was there for his suddenly losing heart? No reasonable person could have expected that Papen's tiny following in the Reichstag would suddenly be changed into a majority by the elections of November 6. It was, indeed, a triumph that his most determined opponents — the National Socialists and the Centre — were no longer capable of forming a majority.

This was the very reason why he resigned and invited Hitler to try his hand. He wanted to show the world that Hitler was incapable, and seldom has such a demonstration been more successful. It must even have convinced General von Schleicher, who was once again concerning himself with the making of Cabinets, and who had advised Papen " as a friend " to retire. Hitler now appeared in Berlin with a large staff and was received by the President. On this occasion there were no mean and humiliating circumstances attendant on his reception. The interview lasted over an hour, and everybody sat on chairs. He went away with the commission that he had vainly sought in the summer — the commission to form a Government as Chancellor. Had he not once asserted that he would succeed in doing so without violating the Constitution?

That, of course, had been in the summer, while in alliance with Brüning he still had a majority in the Reichstag. Now he no longer had it; he had grown weak and Brüning had grown weak — how weak the Nazis really were nobody guessed as yet. Hitler sat in the

Hotel Kaiserhof surrounded by his staff and wrote letter after letter for days on end, avoiding — no doubt at the desire of both Parties — verbal intercourse. They were letters full of cunning democratic opinions on constitutional law. What Hitler was aiming at was this — since he would probably not manage to get a majority in the Reichstag, he wanted the President to appoint him as a Chancellor enjoying his special confidence, that is, to give him full power to govern without parliament, and if necessary in an unconstitutional fashion. The Reichstag was to be dissolved. The President indicated, however, that if he were to appoint a man in whom he had special confidence, that man would certainly not be Herr Hitler. All that was expected of Hitler — and nobody knows what it cost Hindenburg so far to do violence to his innermost feelings — was to try to form a parliamentary Government. The President expressed himself in his letter to Hitler as follows:

"You know that I prefer a *Präsidial* Cabinet . . . that is conducted not by a Party leader but by a man who is above Party, and that this is the kind of man in whom I should have special confidence. You have announced that you will only place your movement at the disposal of a Cabinet presided over by yourself as the Party leader. If I agree to this plan, I must request that such a Cabinet should have a majority in the Reichstag. . . ." Blow upon blow. "First of all," says the President, "I do not want Herr Hitler at all, because I want a *Präsidial* Cabinet. You, Herr Hitler, are not the man in whom I repose confidence. I would much rather not agree to anything you want; and if I do it is only on one condition — and that is one that you will not be able to fulfil. . . ."

HITLER AGAIN FRUSTRATED

Thus the President commissioned Hitler to ascertain whether he was capable of obtaining a definite working majority with a constant and agreed programme. It was a commission impossible of execution; for it meant that Hugenberg and Brüning must agree to work together under Hitler's leadership. And that was impossible for many reasons. Everybody was too inimical to everybody else; Hugenberg was the enemy of Brüning and also, in secret, of Hitler, to say nothing of the opposition between Hitler and Brüning, who were really only united by a common hatred of Papen. Hitler did not even attempt the impossible feat, but kept on writing letters full of animadversions to the President from the Kaiserhof. Schleicher tried to mediate between them, but Hitler told him that if the President insisted upon his condition of a Reichstag majority, there would simply be no Hitler Cabinet. And he would refuse to have anything to do with any other Cabinet, whoever was the head of it. The Reichswehr Minister may have taken that as a warning that even a Chancellor von Schleicher would meet with opposition from Hitler. It was the logical but already somewhat abortive defiance of a man who had been beaten twice and thrice. Once again seriously wounded in his feelings, Hitler returned the President's mandate and retired to Munich.

One success he did achieve which had its importance in spite of the greater failure. He had got nearer to the President as a man, and he took with him the assurance: "Whatever happens, my door will from now on always be open to you."

PAPEN'S FALL

Papen had had his wish and had triumphed over Hitler. But it did not bring him luck. He now fell into the toils of the Reichswehr Minister, von Schleicher. Schleicher had apparently hoped that the negotiations with Hitler would lead to some sort of liaison being established with the Nazi leader, a gentleman's agreement that would permit of some kind of Government being set up that would not be attacked by the National Socialists. He himself had done his best to get Hitler's consent as he had done at the beginning of Papen's Government. This time he did not get it — Hitler was not going to be accused of breach of faith a second time.

Schleicher now regarded the Papen Government as finished. He was no longer anxious to join in the difficult game played out on a narrow ledge of authority that was upheld by only two props, the favour of the President and the guns of the Reichswehr. Amongst other things a sort of loyalty to his Ministry restrained him. He could not bear to hazard the Reichswehr in an internal struggle. As an expert at the Reichswehr Ministry he was too much concerned for the brightness of his sword, and dared not test the edge. He knew that there were certain Nazi sympathies in the Reichswehr. And possibly an even stronger impression was made on him by a shock that came from another direction — the Berlin transport strike at the beginning of November. He expressed the opinion that if a few thousand bus and tram conductors could paralyse the capital of a large country for days without the Government's being able to prevent it, a Government would be powerless if it were faced with a real general strike. A general strike in which the whole population would join with tacit sympathy and into which even the National Socialists would be drawn. This had already happened in the transport strike. In these circumstances the Reichswehr Minister did not feel himself to be strong enough to promise the Papen Government the unconditional protection of his machine guns.

It is not worth going into all the details of the intrigues. It will suffice to say that Papen resigned finally and definitely at the end of November, to the honest regret of President von Hindenburg. As a farewell gift, he presented the Chancellcr, whom he had liked best of all, with his portrait, upon which was written:

" I had a comrade."

SCHLEICHER AS CHANCELLOR

Perhaps not altogether to his own satisfaction General Kurt von Schleicher found himself called upon to be Papen's successor. There had been times when Hindenburg had heartily wished the difficult and politically dangerous officer out of the way. His former liking had waned to a noticeable coolness. The President now took a certain malicious pleasure in setting him the task over which his two predecessors had come to grief. Papen had had the President's order for the dissolution of the Reichstag in case of its proving refractory. Schleicher, on the other hand, was not given this mark of the President's confidence, and was therefore doomed from the beginning to fail. What was really most truly ironic about the whole affair was that Schleicher did not realize his own vulnerability, and only saw at the decisive and fatal moment how cruelly he, the tireless intriguer, had this time been deceived himself.

For the first time in the history of the German Republic a General had become Chancellor. His rule was very different from what the public imagined. General von Schleicher repudiated the idea of a military dictatorship. He was quite sincere in doing so. It was because he did not want such a dictatorship that he had overthrown the Papen Government, and not because of ill-timed personal ambition. For the idea of being Chancellor himself did not attract him particularly. He would probably have preferred a part like that which Marshal Pilsudski in Poland played with such success while merely Minister for War. Schleicher relied far more upon his political deeds than upon his machine-guns, and this arrogance which had a somewhat bourgeois tinge finally contributed not a little to his downfall.

He was obliged to face a double task — he had to be an actively nationalist Chancellor, and at the same time the architect for the social reconstruction of Germany. He may certainly be called a Chancellor whose spiritual home was National Socialism, and his duel with Hitler was not merely a struggle for power but actually a struggle to decide which of them was to carry out the National Socialist programme.

German Nationalism, which had grown more and more passionate during the post-War years, takes its origin in many springs of the national spirit which will not here be examined. It has already been said that in one aspect it was directed inwards against its own fellow-countrymen. It was a jealous nationalism that went about among the people and sought enemies. In foreign policies it whetted itself on the dilemma of Versailles, which may, perhaps, be most easily gathered from the two important and alternating methods of German post-War policy.

THE DILEMMA OF GERMAN NATIONALISM

It was impossible for the German people to agree permanently to the Peace of Versailles in the form in which it had been dictated in the year 1918. With the passing of the years this has also come to be recognized by many members of the victorious Powers. It was possible to maintain that the treaties of 1918 had in so far as they were untenable been the outcome of a passing mood of victory, and that when this mood was over the field would be free for revision. Nobody tried with greater success to awaken in the German people a belief in the psychological capacity for revision of the treaties, especially of the possibility of an understanding with France, than did Stresemann. There was, however, another possible view of the matter — that there was among the peoples a conviction based on principle of Germany's unfitness to be a voluntary partner in peace and a member of the League of Nations. If Germany was really regarded in this way by its neighbours, then there was no prospect of a friendly understanding; then Germany could only be permanently delivered from the insupportable terms of the Treaty by defiance and resistance — if not by force of arms then by means of one of those political miracles which are the foundation of all world history. The most convinced champion of this view is Hitler.

TIRED CAPITALISM

To find a way out of this dilemma which could be vouched for by a responsible statesman was the Chancellor's task in foreign policy. One success came to him unexpectedly in that the Disarmament Conference at Geneva recognized on December 11 the principle of the restoration of equality of rights to Germany. In internal politics, he had to help Germany to adapt herself to the great social upheaval due to the economic crisis by constructive measures. That a mere wait-and-see policy would prolong the misery indefinitely was the general conviction. It must be realized how utterly the moral rôle of the economic leaders who had formerly been so much looked up to was played out in Germany. In the year 1931 the great Banks had collapsed and had left economic authority a heap of ruins. In 1933 there came a crisis among the leaders of industry which was not so obvious except to the initiated. The most evident sign of this crisis was the collapse of what was then the largest trust in heavy industry as revealed in the sale of the great block of shares held in it by the industrial magnate Friedrich Flick. This man by a clever manipulation had made himself the actual owner of the largest heavy industrial concern in Western Germany, the United Steel Works, which had from the beginning been badly organized and had now been in difficulties for years. Its shares were quoted lower than any on the Stock Exchange, and Flick, who was only able to maintain his majority holding with the help of Bank credits, saw the day approaching when the Banks would refuse to give him any more credit on his increasingly worthless shares. There was some talk of disposing of these shares to French financiers, and the possibility gave rise to extensive political speculation in high places in France. It was, however, a plan which was entirely contrary to the efforts at political independence, one might almost say the Puritanism, of the Brüning Government. In order to prevent the sale to France, the Government took over Friedrich Flick's shares itself. Thus the State became owner of the largest mining concern — not on any Socialist principle, but for national necessity; not from any inherent constructive desire, but because of capitalist exhaustion. Flick's example produced a curious reaction. Other industrial magnates began to dream of being one day thus advantageously nationalized — and by the agency of the National Socialist, Hitler. So utterly had the once admired power and creative will of the coal and steel magnates been crushed by the crisis! From the Nationalization Commission of the Revolution that piled up protocols and accomplished nothing down to the cry of heavy industry for nationalization in 1932 — through what a parabolic flight of pride and fall had German industry passed in the post-War years!

General von Schleicher expressed opinions about this economic revolution that were regarded as Socialistic. That may have been a mistake. It is much more likely that, being a soldier, he did not apprehend the underlying philosophy in economic affairs, nor revere the creative principle of capitalism in existing capital. In the speech in which he outlined his programme, he pointed out that the Reichswehr did not exist in order to protect any particular economic system. On the whole, no doubt, the daily political tasks must have appeared to him the most important considerations. And the most important of all was to curb Hitler finally; and if he were not to be curbed or be made useful, then to destroy him.

THE MENDICANT SA

From the point of view of the Brown House, whose foundations suddenly did not seem to be laid on a very stable rock, the problem now appeared to be: which would prove the less weak in a clash—the National Socialist Party or the Schleicher Government? For Hitlerism had grown weak. This was now ominously clear. On the other hand, the whole of the non-Nazi public, including, really, the Socialists, was hoping at long last to find some signs of political firmness in Schleicher's Government.

Hitler's loss of votes after the set-back in November continued at a startling rate in the municipal elections in Thuringia in December. Still more pressing, however, were the money troubles of the Nazi Party. The numerous publishing bodies, ordnance depôts, departments for the provision of SA uniforms, various districts with their Brown Houses that had grown steadily more and more magnificent, were desperately in debt; they were obliged to write pathetic letters to their creditor Banks, to their innumerable large and small purveyors, some of which found their way into the opposition Press. The burden of debt which rested on the various Party organizations has been estimated from an informed source at twelve million Marks. So great was the lack of money that the Party members of the Prussian Diet even omitted the customary Christmas tip to the servants of the Diet. And tens of thousands of SA men infested the streets all over Germany and held out collecting boxes labelled by the Party to a compassionate public, like discharged soldiers to whom the Commander-in-Chief had instead of a gratuity given a permit to beg. Subleaders of the SA came in hosts to opposition Parties and newspapers offering to betray Party secrets for ready money.

This mendicant SA was a true child of the German economic crisis, and the Party now for the first time had the experience of not merely battening on the German collapse like a parasite but threatening to collapse with it. The most useful of the six hundred thousand SA men, and those who were always ready for action, were the unemployed, mostly young people who had often been driven into the SA clubs and to the food supplies of the movement by their want. These unemployed men were the first to make of the SA an efficient force, for they had all day to spare and made their training the chief occupation of the day. They would sit for hours over the dregs of their beer in the SA clubs, which at first were mostly small public-houses; later the clubs were to a great extent transferred to private houses, where the men spent their spare time sleeping on palliasses or playing cards. Every now and then those who lived in the large towns were taken out into the country to practice " country sports." The leaders of the movement took considerable pains to act up to the old military theory, to find as much occupation as possible for the men and not to leave them to get stale. In the evenings there was nearly always something for the SA to do in guarding the Party meetings. When they went on route marches they were fed by the peasants or landowners, and all over the country their appearance gave an impressive picture of Hitler's authority over Germany, beside which the sparse country police almost disappeared. The SA men hardly ever received any cash pay, but often — according to the means of the local organization — food and lodgings. The uniforms, which when carried out in the cheapest manner possible only cost a few Marks, were in theory supposed to be paid for by the men themselves. The Party, however — that is to say, the " regimental stores " — financed them in the meantime, and such loans probably often turned into gifts. The best of the SA men were certainly filled with high idealism, and nearly all of them had that indifference to personal danger which is a product of the mass soul. It must not, however, be forgotten that a very large section of the SA sought immediate material advantages, and above all expected permanent support when Hitler attained to power.

This mendicant SA was over and over again disappointed by Hitler, who always hesitated to seize power. It was no wonder that numbers began gradually to fall off. Later on, after Hitler's victory, the *Angriff*, with the comfortable sensation of a danger passed, described the temper of December 1932 as follows:

" A mood of despair soon began to make itself felt on the outskirts. Many feared openly that they would never achieve their aim, and saw no reason for living up to the rigorous demands of the Party. They felt that it would be better to accept every Ministerial post as it came along." Goebbels himself admitted publicly that there were times when even he feared that the movement might collapse.

GREGOR STRASSER'S EXIT

In this mood of depression two men were found who wished to save the movement by making a compact with Schleicher against Hitler's wishes. They were Frick and Strasser. And when Hitler forbade them both to have any further dealings with Schleicher, Frick submitted, but Strasser for the first time refused obedience. In his view the Party was faced with a decision that might prove fateful. Above all, he saw the financial collapse, and said to himself that the twelve million Mark debt that consisted of innumerable small ones must somehow be consolidated by a large financial transaction, if the local and central Party undertakings were not to go bankrupt. There were two possible ways of making such a consolidation. If the Party had some part in the Government the confidence of its creditors would be re-established, and thus the Party would have an extension of credit; it could moreover count on semi-official supplies that were at the disposal of the Chancellor for " education " or " labour service." The other method was by means of funds supplied by private industries, especially the Rhenish-Westphalian heavy industry. The first plan meant that the Party had to make friends with Schleicher, the man who had made the Socialist programme and who was alleged to scorn wealth. The second method would make the Party once again dependent upon large-scale industry and finance. Strasser realized that a breach with Schleicher must necessarily lead the Party to adopt the second alternative. This was no doubt one of the principal motives that led him to initiate the long-delayed, decisive discussion with Hitler.

Strasser went away after the discussion a shattered man. He regarded Hitler's plans as cynical, indeed anti-national, and expressed this view in a letter to the Party leader, which was worded as a resignation, but was also a witness to years of conscientious scruples. To begin with, he complained of the restrictions with which he was surrounded by the Party authorities, and which he evidently regarded as insulting to his political standing. And, furthermore, he explained that he no longer agreed with the conception of the State held by the National Socialist Party — that is to say, by Hitler. He felt himself opposed to the extremists who demanded the employment of physical force against political opponents, and was thus the first to admit that physical force was originally introduced into the political struggle by the SA and not by its opponents. Among these opponents, said Strasser, were plenty of valuable men who were anxious for reconstruction, both among Socialists and other democratic Parties; they should not be repulsed and suppressed. He considered that the practice of the National Socialist leaders was not at all in accord with their frequently proclaimed ideals — this was a shrewd personal hit. In place of leaders who were conscious of their responsibilities and clear as to their aims, had come the internally unsound demagogy of men like Goebbels; and the Party was carrying on a desperado policy with the sanction of the supreme leader. He regarded the Party as heading for chaos, for crime, and for a Germany laid in ruins.

Hitler's path is clearly described here. But it had always been like that from the very beginning. As far as Hitler was concerned, the way to power led across the Communist riot — that is to say, across a series of acts of violence the authors of which were to be alleged to be the Communists. Strasser forgot that once upon a time he had merrily gone along the road himself. A few years earlier he had rejected the idea of aiming at ministerial portfolios, because the Nazi Party had no reason for supporting the existing system by any kind of co-operation; its way, he said, lay rather through chaos. Meanwhile he had grown more law-abiding and parliamentary than Hitler himself. He was the technical and business manager of the Party, and it began to go against the grain to hazard the Party machinery thoughtlessly in the struggle for power. In this case, Hitler, who was still something of a Bohemian at heart, had fewer inhibitions. Strasser had put together a balance-sheet according to which Socialism would be increasingly unsuccessful and therefore would become more and more radical, so that it would become less and less acceptable as an ally to the intermediate Parties, especially the Catholic Centre. Then this intermediate section would be thrown back upon alliance with National Socialism, which would then be on the fringe of power. That there might be developments other than parliamentary had not, it is true, been allowed for in this reckoning.

The end of the quarrel was that on December 8, 1932, Strasser resigned his Party offices. For a moment Feder, too, considered rebellion, but was quelled by a threat of expulsion from the Party. Strasser vanished immediately from the political arena and retired into private life, though not with the intention of leaving the stage permanently. He kept in touch with Schleicher and was also received by President von Hindenburg. There were even rumours of a ministerial portfolio. It did not come to a Party split, although Strasser had many followers, such as Count Reventlow and the Königsberg district leader, Erich Koch, who remained faithful to him even after he had fallen from power. The influence of the Strasser Wing was, however, broken by the retirement of its chief. Hitler called a meeting of his officials and Nazi Reichstag members in Berlin, and with their help organized a thrilling demonstration of loyalty at Göring's, the Reichstag President's, palace. It was one of his really great oratorical moments; he shed tears and his audience wept too. "Never would I have believed it of Strasser," he said, and laid his head sobbing upon the table. "Abominable of Strasser to do such a thing to our leader!" exclaimed Streicher malevolently from his modest place in the background; his deadly enemy, who had put him to shame all these years in the matter of political decency, had fallen. It is one of the secrets of true leadership to be able to utilize the unrest arising out of such quarrels to weld the remaining followers still more closely together. Hitler might have gathered vanloads full of vows of loyalty from all over the country during the next few days.

The power hitherto enjoyed in the Party by Strasser was now carefully divided up by Hitler amongst various functionaries. He gave the post of chief organiser to Dr. Ley, the Cologne District Leader, who was fanatically devoted to him, and had in all the internal disputes with Strasser taken Hitler's side. The political organization and control of the districts — the transmission and circularization of policy — were made the business of a newly created "Central Political Commission" at the head of which was Hitler's private secretary, Rudolf Hess. After the seizure of power, Hess was officially given the title of "Deputy Leader." Thus a comparatively youthful favourite, who had hitherto held no position of importance in the Party, rose from being domestic confident to being Chief Vizier, and old combatants with famous names were expected to obey him. The appointment of his private secretary to the post of political deputy was an autocratic action by means of which Hitler once more proved his omnipotence over the Party after the Strasser crisis.

Strasser remained a member of the Party, and in the history of the Party he remains the leader who most successfully united political powers with sound intellectual sense and personal honesty. He is more intelligent than Hitler, more thorough than Göring, and more straightforward than Goebbels. The latter might, indeed, regard himself as victorious, for he remained master of the field after the fall of the former chief as well as of later rivals; doubly successful, because it was his and Göring's political strategy that was adopted as the official Party strategy as against that proposed by Strasser.

It was the strategy of harsh, radical, indeed chaotic opposition; a demonic game that could only end in absolute victory or utter collapse. The Party, in its negotiations with the Government, always boasted that it was the one stable moral value amid the disruptions of Germany. It affirmed — with some justice — that the social disorders in Germany were by the discipline of its members robbed of their worst manifestations, that famine riots were held at bay, and daylight robbery prevented by their political self-sacrifice. This counterfeit presentment of order, this Trojan horse, now threatened by bursting and scattering its contents to flood Germany with all the blood and terror that lay concealed within it. The new slogan was: "If the National Socialist Party collapses, there will be another ten million Communists in Germany."

Thus National Socialism by threatening suicide like a hysterical woman forced German industry and finance to save it by handing over the Government to it.

HITLER IS SAVED

The first thing that happened was that a group of industrialists in Western Germany under the leadership of an influential member of the Steel Trust made themselves responsible for a considerable part of the National Socialist debts.

It would be giving a false interpretation to the episode if it were regarded merely as bribery of National Socialism by capitalists, as being a method of giving a capitalist turn to Hitlerite Socialism. It is true that there was a certain admixture of private interest, but that was no new phenomenon and its intentions were peculiar. The " big men " from the west were, as has been indicated, not nearly as big and as self-confident as they had been. Instead of controlling and guiding Hitler, they felt that they needed some guidance themselves — a symptom of bankruptcy that was no longer only material but also moral. Their longing for strong government — after they had done their best in the good years to weaken the Government — was also the outcome of very human personal hopes. Hopes that the Government would relieve them from their economic troubles by taking over their shares at a suitable price. This " bankruptcy-socialism " had become the economic confession of faith of many an industrialist, and not only of those who were least important. It was also to be found among East German landowners. It was the final touch to that pernicious, degenerate Liberalism of post-War days, which regarded only the chance of gain as the sacred privilege of the private individual, while the risk of failure was tacitly handed over to the State — at least in so far as it was a case of very large undertakings, of very large projects, and very large failures.

Hence it happened quite logically that at the end of 1932 declining National Socialism and declining Capitalism spent their last effort in helping one another to rise anew.

In January 1933 a follower of Hitler's, the Cologne banker von Schroder, arranged a meeting at his own house between the National Socialist Leader and Herr von Papen. It resulted in a reconciliation over personal matters. Papen tried to make it clear to Hitler that since he had refused the invitation to form a parliamentary government in November he must join in the " national concentration " of all the forces with a tendency to the Right, beginning with the President and the Reichswehr and going by way of Stahlhelm to Hugenberg. Papen was to some extent acting as the spokesman of those industrialists who had been his most faithful adherents while he was still Chancellor, and who would rather have the Westphalian aristocrat and Saar industrialist than General von Schleicher with his vague Socialist ideas;

who, therefore, would prefer to see a new Cabinet with Papen at the head in which Hitler would be a pawn.

The conference did not lead to any agreement regarding positive future co-operation. In those days when Hitler's star seemed on the wane, he was incapable of taking up any definite standpoint. His great anxiety was in some way or other, by any partial success, however small, to restore his lost prestige. Hence the election campaign which he carried on in the tiny State of Lippe-Detmold was of greater importance in his eyes than any number of conferences. He travelled from one village to the next, and did not disdain on occasion to address a mere handful of people. He thereby managed to raise the number of his votes in this small State during November and December. True, it was only an apparent success; a forest had been razed for the sake of a bird's nest. Members of the Party, however, regained a certain amount of confidence. A few days before, Stegmann, the chief SA leader of Franconia, had renounced his allegiance to Hitler. He gave as his reason for resigning the abominable private life led by the Nüremberg leader, Julius Streicher, whom Hitler retained for no apparent reason. This reason, however, had existed for a good ten years. The fact that use was now made of it was a symptom of the general crisis. Even the Lippe elections did not end the crisis, but at all events they furnished an argument for holding out.

SCHLEICHER'S GREAT GAMBLE

While Hitler strove with the Party crisis, Schleicher dealt with one in his Cabinet. Suddenly, out of what looked like practically a clear sky, came a bolt in the shape of the Agrarian (*Land Bund*) Association, a powerful organization led by the great landowners, which launched an attack upon the Chancellor of unexampled violence.

The influence of the landowners upon the highest landowner in the country had perhaps hardly been taken sufficiently into account by General von Schleicher. Count Kalckreuth, the President of the Association, and his fellow-members were received with a positive flourish of trumpets by President von Hindenburg on January 12. At the same time the Association issued an announcement filled with fierce denunciations of the Schleicher Government. There was talk in it of

" despoiling agriculture for the benefit of the general financial interests of an export industry that looked at things internationally." In other words — self-interest against self-interest. And the refrain was the same that had been heard for fourteen years: a Chancellor hostile to agriculture! Unheard of for an ostensibly nationalist State! Utterly intolerable for a ruling General, for a ruling Field-Marshal, and a ruling landowner to boot!

The storm arose because Schleicher at the outset of his Chancellorship had announced his intention, like Brüning, of sequestrating a part of the bankrupt estates in Eastern Germany and dividing them up among peasant settlers. Thereby he — a non-landowning General — had signed his own death warrant.

Moreover, he did not succeed in identifying his Cabinet with the nation. Attempts were made which betrayed a poor knowledge of the labour world, and especially of a fatal over-estimation of the Labour bureaucracy that might rather be said to be passively than actively engaged in the Trades Unions. Schleicher, and still more his advisers, thought they saw in them forces behind the Parties that might be released from the automatic fractions in the Reichstag and made to help towards a permanent reconstitution of Germany. Some hope of this was given by the Trades Unions, who might perhaps allow themselves to be united with the constructive element in the National Socialist Party to form a support for the Schleicher Government. Although the person of Gregor Strasser played a great part in these plans, it had not been definitely settled that Strasser was to be set up in opposition to Hitler. Possibly it had been hoped to bring Hitler to heel by raising the bogy of a new opposition. There was a great deal of cunning and too little honesty in all the projects; and General von Schleicher proved in his own person the truth of Lassalle's saying that it might cost one one's head to be too clever in great affairs. He certainly saw many paths opening out before him and reserved to himself the choice of which he would follow. Thinking in Plans A, B, C, . . . on General Staff lines may be a form of strength, but not when it is a case of deciding for one principle or another.

THE FALL OF A GENERAL

Moreover, General von Schleicher's projects required time, and in order to gain time it was necessary to adjourn the Reichstag. The General hoped to be able to force the National Socialists to put through the adjournment by threatening them with another election at which they would lose still more votes — for in spite of what happened at Lippe, nobody had any doubt that they would lose in a Reichstag election. Hindenburg had given the order for dissolution to von Papen. Now General von Schleicher asked for it too — why should he not also have it? It was on January 28 that Schleicher found to his dismay that the President had no intention of giving him the required order. The reason was that Papen had been to him on the day before and had assured him that he had succeeded in winning over Hitler for his government of "National Concentration." Hitler would, of course, have to be made Chancellor. Hindenburg resisted this idea, but Papen believed himself to be capable of restraining Hitler by taking a few precautionary measures. Thus the Reichswehr and the Foreign Office were both to be untouched by the Nazis; the Nazis were to be a minority in the Cabinet; and Papen himself as Vice-Chancellor was to be the real link between the Government and the President. In this way Papen would become the repository of all real power.

The President might nevertheless conceivably have refused this solution if General von Schleicher had not thought he was being particularly clever, and had urgently warned Hindenburg against appointing Papen Chancellor. Schleicher explained that a Cabinet that was thus in conflict with the majority of the people not only could not last, but it could not permanently reckon on the support of the Reichswehr. Schleicher calculated that if a Papen Cabinet would not be formed, the President, whose dislike of Hitler was well known, would be forced to fall back on him. For behind Schleicher loomed solidly the Generals and the Reichswehr — the most terrible and most indispensable power in the State.

A great gamble was now attempted. The Reichswehr saw that their leader and friend had lost his former influence over the President to Papen; saw especially that Colonel von Hindenburg, Schleicher's former friend, had gone over to Papen's side. The President's influential adviser, the "son who had not been allowed for in the Constitution," had as legal owner of Neudeck driven him more and more into the adoption of a policy favourable to agriculture, and very likely regarded Schleicher's policy of small holdings, which was directed against the great landowners, as being an attack upon the political faith of the Hindenburg family. Possibly, too, Schleicher had unwisely neglected his personal relations with the son, while Papen had carefully cultivated them. It was now necessary to eliminate Papen at all costs. A plan, military in its ruthlessness, was evolved. Papen and Hitler were to be arrested for treason, and Hindenburg was to be confronted with the *fait accompli* of a small *coup d'état.* Whether Schleicher's diplomatic visits to the President and the martial prospects of his followers were quite in accord cannot — now that those who were concerned naturally deny it or say nothing at all — be definitely established. At all events, the projected *coup* had exactly the opposite result from what was intended. It was found out. An officious political busybody, Herr von Alvensleben of Neugathersleben, repeated the rumours, and is said to have told Colonel von Hindenburg that his own father was to be arrested.

At all events, Herr von Alvensleben's news warned Hitler that he must hurry if the gate to success was not to be shut in his face for good and all by the military hand. Seldom has a political speculation failed so utterly as that of the Schleicher clique in the last days of January 1933. The only thing that can be compared with it is the still more ghastly disillusionment later provided by the Hitler Government for its too cunning promoters. When Papen began to negotiate, Hindenburg did not wish to have Hitler as Chancellor beside Papen, nor did Hitler wish to be Chancellor in a government that included Papen and more especially Hugenberg. This dislike changed at one swoop into a ready willingness to co-operate when the plans of the Generals became known. In November 1923 it had been the Reichswehr that had beaten Hitler at the decisive moment. In 1933 he took his revenge by beating them.

True, he saw the trap that Papen thought to set for him in this Cabinet that had a bourgeois majority. But he avoided it by using a weapon that no hand could wield as he could. In return for his assent, he demanded the dissolution of the Reichstag and another election. He knew very well that, though he might be no more than a shadow Chancellor at first, the public now looked on him as the victorious popular tribune, a man of the people upon the throne, an insurgent whose cause success proved to be right. The great suggestive power of victory was on his side, and he now had at his disposal an instrument of which none of his predecessors had realized the value — the wireless. There was no fear at all that this greatest of German propagandists would be beaten, or even in any way approached, by his new colleagues, Papen and Hugenberg, in the race for popular favour.

One among the Ministers saw that very clearly — Hugenberg. The founder of the *Harzburg Front* now at last saw a *Harzburg Front* Government before him, but he also realized that it must be carried on by Harzburg methods if it was not to turn into a National Socialist Government. Hence, though he agreed that the Reichstag should be dissolved, he demanded that there should be no new elections, but that a state of " national emergency " should be proclaimed. This was a measure which had not been provided for in the Constitution, and which was for that very reason advocated by those members of the Right Parties who desired a dictatorship. They thought that it would give the President the power to disregard the trammels of the Constitution. Hitler, however, refused to hear of such a proposal, and the negotiations threatened at the last moment to come to nothing over his refusal. The President had already made up his mind to appoint a Papen Cabinet. At that moment the rumours of the projected arrest of Papen and of the *coup* that was being planned helped to bring the negotiators into a more amenable frame of mind. A formula was found. Hitler with great solemnity gave his word of honour that — as Duesterberg, the Stahlhelm leader, later described the scene — " whatever the results of the election might be, all the Ministers who were in this Cabinet should remain even after March 5 (the day of the elections)." Another word of honour — how many times had he given it in fourteen years?

It was at twelve noon on January 30 that Hitler and Papen appeared together before the President and told him of the success of their efforts for "national concentration." After referring to the "national concentration," the President gave Herr Adolf Hitler the commission to form a Government. He explained to him that he could not have appointed him as Party leader, but now Hitler stood before him as champion of a united national front — in parenthesis it may be observed that it is a front which then as later never was more than a few dozen Reichstag members ahead of the National Socialist Party. How the Conservative governmental powers are entangled in the net of their out-to-date formulae! Either the National Front must mean the Front of all or at least of most of the German people, equivalent to the National Socialist Party — which was Hitler's aim and which he had not by any means achieved on January 30. Or else the National Socialist Party did not win a majority — and then the National Concentration Government would be a Party Government, a government by force and of a minority. Hindenburg's national concentration was a form of self-deception; the Chancellor who received his office from him in the name of concentration knew this very well. The question was whether his Vice-Chancellor also realized it. There was a great deal of deceit and self-deceit mixed up with all the handshakes and vows of loyalty that were given at this time.

AT THE GOAL

Hitler was Chancellor.

The office of Vice-Chancellor, which had been known in very few cabinets, was filled in this case by Franz von Papen, who was also Prime Minister of Prussia. During interviews between the Chancellor and the President, the Vice-Chancellor was always to be present — the *enfant terrible* with its governess! Obviously a few important posts could not be withheld from the leader of the largest Party, so Frick became Reich Minister of the Interior and Göring became Prussian Minister of the Interior. Thus the supervision of the States and the control of the largest police force in Germany came into the hands of the National Socialists. But Papen still retained the highest power in Prussia, and, moreover, the Nazis remained in a hopeless minority both in the Prussian Cabinet and in that of the Reich. The Constitution indeed states that the course of policy shall be determined by the Chancellor. But was it to be expected that this curious person, Herr Hitler, who had no practical understanding of affairs, would prevail against — against whom? The President had stipulated that the Foreign Office should remain in the hands of the conservative Baron von Neurath, and that the Reichswehr should once more be confided to a professional soldier, General von Blomberg, from Königsberg. He brought with him his own chief of the ministerial secretariat. And who was there to observe that this man — Colonel von Reichenau — sympathized strongly with the Nazis?

The strange circumstances that brought General von Blomberg into the Ministry and thus the Reichswehr — though with many mental reservations — on to Hitler's side make up a curious story. An episode was enacted in Protestant Königsberg, in the prosaic offices of the military command, that has something of a Ruritanian background. It reminds one of indecisive kings clothed in ermine, and carefully directed by mysterious father confessers, who will one day receive a Cardinal's hat as a reward for their advice. The divisional padre of the East Prussian Reichswehr was the pastor Ludwig Müller. He played no small part in the events that led to the formation of the Hitler Cabinet. It is reputed to be his influence which induced General von Blomberg to join the new Government and thus to give it the support of the Reichswehr. Müller's name later became better known to the public in connexion with the political co-ordination (*Gleichshaltung*) of the Protestant Church, in which he gave no indication that he was a man of outstanding religious gifts. The secret moral support that he still gives his Party leader within the Reichswehr may be of greater importance. These services have not been too dearly bought — from Hitler's point of view — by the dignity of Reich Bishop which was later bestowed upon him.

The remaining posts in the new Cabinet mostly came into the hands of proved friends of Papen's. Graf Schwerin-Krosigk, universally recognized as able, remained Finance Minister; Baron Éitz von Rübenach remained Transport Minister; and Dr. Gereke, Reich Commissioner for Unemployment. This latter was a close confidant of Hindenburg's, directed the propaganda in favour of Hindenburg at the presidential elections, and was a few weeks later to be arrested for it by the Nazis. Further, there remained the Minister for Justice, Dr. Gürtner, a Bavarian. It will be remembered that he was a man whom Papen had brought to Berlin after he had fallen victim to the Party strife of a decayed parliamentarianism in Bavaria — the same Dr. Gürtner who had once so benevolently granted Hitler a cautionary period instead of imprisonment. Dr. Hugenberg was given two important portfolios — Trade and Agriculture. He also occupied the corresponding posts in Prussia and now had the opportunity for which he had been longing for testing his expert capacities. He was the first of the political Ministers of this Cabinet who did not think of propaganda but of actual work, and even managed to do some. Franz Seldte, the Stahlhelm leader, became Minister for Labour. In order that Göring should have a seat in the Cabinet, he was given the Air Ministry in view of his war record as a fighting pilot. One person remained temporarily without office — Goebbels.

Hitler in a hopeless minority? Hitler held in check?

On the evening of this January 30 the Nazis celebrated the day as a day of victory. The great Victory Propaganda began, which was largely responsible for the results of the elections of March 5. For hours twenty-five thousand torch-bearers marched along the Wilhelmstrasse. Hindenburg stood at a window in his palace, his face like wood, his body stiff as a ramrod. A few steps farther on, the restless, fidgeting figure of Hitler was framed in a window. He had never looked so happy in public since November 8, 1923, at the Bürgerbräu Keller in Munich. His bearing was one laugh of triumph; the upper part of his body jerked backwards and forwards as he bowed.

CHAPTER XII

THE REICHSTAG FIRE

"My task will be ended when I have raised up the German people." So Hitler had once said in 1924 before the Courts of Justice in Munich.

Was his task, therefore, ended on January 30, 1933? "We have won, but that is no reason for losing courage," said a leading Nazi of Jacobin tendency on the evening of that day. Serious journals, whose political opinions are respected throughout the world, declared that Hugenberg was the real victor. Taking the Reich and Prussia together, he had no less than four Ministries under his control; and these were the Ministries controlling trade and commerce, which in those prosaic days were regarded as the true source of all political power. Count Schwerin-Krosigk, who had very little sympathy with National Socialism, might be expected to keep a tight hold on the money-bags in his capacity as Finance Minister. In the Reichswehr Schleicher's influence was apparently still very great. Hence National Socialism's entry into the Government could hardly be looked upon as the great Nazi Revolution. In fact, this was only about to begin. In these days there began the greatest and most terrible—though not the most difficult—campaign that Hitler had as yet led.

The campaign was waged for two objectives and carried on by two different methods of warfare. Hitler must secure the support of a majority of the nation through an unwearying and intensive campaign of propaganda. It must be emphasized that this majority must stand behind Hitler himself and not his variegated company of Party leaders. This propaganda sought and found its most telling weapon in the fact that Hitler was now Chancellor. Success leads to success. The second objective was the removal of all Hitler enemies and rivals from the Communists to the German Nationalists. This objective was attained by the extraordinary clever and unscrupulous use of all available means, regardless of brutality. At the same time it must be remembered that Hitler did not then control all the forces of the State.

Chance came to his aid and helped him over the final obstacle to success. The President had made Hitler's appointment to the Chancellorship conditional upon his undertaking to respect the Constitution and maintain internal law and order. Hence it became Hitler's duty to endeavour after the precedent of the previous November to secure a majority for his Government in the Reichstag before that assembly was dissolved. Hitler negotiated with the leader of the Centre Party, Monsignor Kaas, with the ostensible purpose of securing his consent to an adjournment of the Reichstag for the space of a year. Instead of negotiating with Hitler personally, Kaas wrote him a letter on behalf of his Party Committee in which he required the Chancellor to answer ten very awkward questions that in effect constituted an entire Government programme, contained far-reaching demands, and amounted, in fact, to nothing less than a prohibition upon both a Conservative Restoration and a Nazi Revolution. As if this was not of itself sufficient, Pelion was piled upon Ossa by the publication of the letter which thereby acquired the character of a political ultimatum for Hitler's acceptance. But Hitler found little difficulty in inducing his Cabinet colleagues to agree to his absolute refusal of the Centre's demands. He wrote a courteous letter to Kaas in which he explained that further negotiation could not lead to any results, and might cause an embitterment that would be deeply regretted by him personally. Nothing — he added — now remained to him to do in accordance with his duty to God and the dictates of his conscience except to propose to the President the dissolution of the Reichstag. He hoped and asked that this action would not have the effect of severing the personal relations which bound him to Brüning and Kaas — relations which Hitler himself had established on his own initiative. In saying this, Hitler was doubtless sincere and animated by the respect which he entertained for the clever leaders of the Centre. Nevertheless it was these clever men who — contrary to their own innermost desires — freed Hitler's hands and thus enabled him to rid himself of the Conservative elements in his Coalition Government.

GÖRING MAKES HIMSELF AT HOME

The Nazis established themselves with amazing rapidity in their new administrative posts. The Ministries that had been given to the moderate German Nationals were heads lacking bodies. From the Prussian Ministry of the Interior Göring supervised the entire German administration. He brought with him a number of so-called honorary Commissars, such as the SS Leader Daluege, his aide-de-camps Hall and Sommerfeld, and, as his legal adviser, Hitler's own lawyer, Dr. Luetgebrune. A singular personality in the former jurist and public prosecutor, Herr Grauert, who had been at the head of the Employment Association North-West, which was the most ruthless and least socially inspired organization belonging to German heavy industry, became Director of the Police Department of the Ministry of the Interior. Grauert was a Nazi of long standing who had rendered the Party useful service in the acquisition of money.

All over the country dismissals and new appointments became the order of the day. All officials from the head of a provincial administration to a police sergeant who had been members of Left Parties were given leave of absence or placed temporarily on the retired list. Their successors were Nazis in the large majority of cases; and invariably so where political power was in question. Innumerable SA leaders or other Nazi officials became Police Presidents, even in cases where their predecessors had been known to be rigid Conservatives. Thus, for example, the Berlin Police President, Melcher, who had been largely instrumental in securing the success of Papen's *coup d'état* in Prussia on July 20, 1932, was replaced by the Nazi Rear-Admiral von Levetzow. Several hundred political officials lost their posts in Prussia alone before the Reichstag election on March 5. In a brief four weeks Göring built up an instrument of power that could not have been easily destroyed by the German Nationalists even if the subsequent course of events had proceeded less violently and more slowly.

"FOR THE DEFENCE OF THE GERMAN NATION"

In order that this machinery should work efficiently it was necessary to supply it with sources of power which finally and completely destroyed the political equality of all citizens that had already been severely curtailed under Papen's rule. For this purpose the President was called upon on February 4 to sign an emergency decree bearing the resounding title, " For the defence of the German Nation." This decree conferred upon officials the right to prohibit public meetings and the wearing of uniform. Every political meeting had to be announced to the police forty-eight hours previously, and could be forbidden if there seemed reason to fear that public security would be endangered. If government officials were abused at a meeting, the meeting could be at once broken up. Newspapers could be suppressed for similar reasons. All that was necessary to secure their prohibition was that they should have " incited " to civil disobedience or published false reports — this latter being something against which no newspaper can wholly protect itself. This decree placed in the hands of Göring's Nazi police presidents the necessary regulations that enabled them to suppress at will every oppositional newspaper or meeting. Full use has been made of these provisions. In the first few weeks of the new Government, and before the burning of the Reichstag, the principal newspaper of the German Socialists — *Vorwärts* — was twice prohibited and the prohibition twice lifted by the Supreme Court, and on one occasion the Supreme Court declared seven prohibitions of newspapers invalid at a single sitting.

Terror from above was supported by terror from below. It is indeed undeniable that the Communists provided an excuse for this terror in calling a general strike and organizing street demonstrations as soon as Hitler became Chancellor. Nevertheless, the subsequent course of events proves that the Nazis were already determined to take the offensive. Numerous riots occurred in front of Communist meeting-houses — a fact that in itself proves that the Nazis were the attackers. Nor was any distinction made as heretofore between the meetings which were broken up by the SA. In Krefeld the SA stormed an electoral meeting of the Centre, forced the audience to take to flight by firing pistols, and manhandled the chief speaker, the former Minister for Labour, Stegerwald. Indeed numerous Centre meetings, including one at which Dr. Brüning himself was speaking, were thus dispersed. According to the official reports of the German Information Bureau fifty-one opponents of Nazism were killed in these free fights before March 5, and the Nazis themselves admitted to losing eighteen of their supporters. It is scarcely to be believed that Göring himself was distressed by this conduct on the part of his followers. On the other hand, Hitler certainly found himself placed in an awkward predicament by the protests of Papen and Hugenberg. On February 22 Hitler issued an appeal to his followers in which he placed the responsibility for these excesses upon the provocative conduct of his adversaries without bringing forward any proofs to support his statement. He declared that the Nazis must maintain an unbroken discipline in the face of this provocation. Moreover, he added that Marxism and not the Centre Party was the enemy who was to be destroyed. This appeal to his followers is in so far of historical interest as it is the first of dozens of such appeals in which the Leader has sought to liberate himself from the thraldom of passions which he had summoned into existence.

GÖRING'S ORDER TO SHOOT

Appeals to moderation and to terroristic action have since then alternated in a swift and unbelievable succession. At the very moment when Hitler was seeking to impose respect for law and order upon his followers, Göring issued, on February 17, his celebrated order to all police officials to avoid even the appearance of a hostile attitude towards SA and Stahlhelm, and instead to support them with all their force and authority in whatever actions they might undertake for the national cause and for national propaganda. The most ruthless measures were to be employed against the enemies of the State, and especially against Communist attacks and terrorism. " Police officials who make use of firearms in the execution of this duty can count upon my support regardless of the consequences of their action. All officials who fail to do so out of a false regard for the consequences will be punished in accordance with the official regulations. . . . Every official must constantly remember that failure to carry out a regulation or order will be looked upon as a graver dereliction of duty than any mistake made in the execution of such regulation or orders."

Such a decree could only spring from the disordered brain of a man who demanded that his subordinates should allow themselves to be possessed by the same mania. Every policeman who came in conflict with members of the Left Parties in the course of his official duties had to ask himself: " If I do not shoot, I may possibly lose my daily bread. If I shoot, I will certainly not lose it."

THE "SPECIALS"

A few weeks later Nazism achieved its victory over the German police forces. On February 22 Göring published the following order:

" The existing police forces have for long been overworked and have often been unable to be at their normal place of duty owing to the necessity to withdraw them from their proper districts for special service elsewhere. It is at present impossible to increase their numbers. Hence it will no longer be possible to refrain from utilizing the voluntary services of suitable men as special constables in case of necessity."

The order went on to state that only honourable men of German nationality, living in Germany, and qualified to vote at parliamentary election could be accepted as special constables. These men were to wear their own clothes — Party or other uniform was permissible — and carry a white arm-band bearing the official stamp with the words " Special Constable." For their services these men were to receive three Marks daily, which had to suffice them for their living. Of greater importance from the Government standpoint was the fact that these " Specials " were equipped with batons and revolvers. Although they were ordered to return these arms on the expiry of their period of duty, the " Specials " were not thereby prevented from entering cafés in their off-time with their arm-bands concealed in their trouser pockets and their revolvers still at their sides, in order to sell post cards of Hitler to the affrightened public.

This order meant in effect the mobilization of the SA for the Nazi revolution. Only 20 per cent. of the " Specials " were to be recruited from the Stahlhelm, while 50 per cent. came from the SA and 30 per cent. from the much smaller but far more efficient SS. In Prussia alone 50,000 men were to be enlisted as "Specials." If it be sought to deliver judgement from a purely technical standpoint upon actions which aroused the horror of the entire civilized world, it must be confessed that the armed SA most efficiently performed what it had been called upon to do — to strike fear into public opinion in Germany to such an extent by a series of terroristic actions that there would be no longer any need to crush opposition on a large scale, inasmuch as no opposition would be capable of coming into existence.

THE COMMUNIST CATACOMBS

It was the Germany of the Weimar Constitution that Hitler wished to destroy. A Germany whose outstanding characteristic was that all political Parties from the Nazis to the Communists, and all shades of political opinion from those to whom the Constitution was anathema to those who wished to uphold it, were able to find a platform for their views. This Germany would cease to exist in the moment in which a majority of the electorate declared itself in favour of Hitler by constitutional means. Nor was it even then impossible that out of the ruins of this Germany there might arise new opponents of Nazism with new methods of warfare. These new opponents might prove more dangerous than the weak forces emanating from the Weimar Constitution. New coalitions, new fronts, might come into existence. The working class was still politically active and permeated by a sense of political realities. The Social Democrat workmen would have supported an alliance with the Reichswehr to overthrow Hitler's dictatorship, and the Communists would probably have placed no obstacle in their way. There were those in the Reichswehr who regarded this possibility without sentimentality and merely as one among many possibilities. It was discussed among German Nationalists who stood nearest to the Reichswehr generals. It is, however, typical of the German Nationalists that they only regarded it as a defensive possibility; they were resolved to die in the last ditch if their Nazi rivals were to risk everything on a desperate throw. Hence the offensive was left to the Nazis, and with it the possibility of making a surprise attack.

The Communists are strangely enough to be found among the supporters of this Conservative Opposition. The majority in the next Reichstag would depend upon the number of Communists returned to it. As a matter of fact the Nazis did not win an absolute majority in the Reichstag elected on March 5, 1933, and could only form one with the aid of the German Nationalists. If, however, the Communists were excluded, then the Nazis were in an absolute majority. For this reason it was of the greatest importance for the Nazis in the weeks before the Reichstag election to " trample " the Communists under foot. The events that are about to be described are only to be understood aright if this fact be borne constantly in mind.

On February 24 the police forced their way into the central organization of the German Communist Party in the Karl Liebknecht House on the Bülow Square in Berlin. The Party officials had left the building several weeks previously and had certainly taken with them all incriminating documents. It is also a matter of fact that it has never become known that the police did actually find lists of names, plans, or other papers affording an insight into the Party activities. Later on the police almost invariably declared after discovering an alleged Communist secret organization that they had found important documents relating to the extent and activities of Communist organizations. Nothing was said of the discovery of any such documents after a three days' search of the Karl Liebknecht House from attic to cellar. Their failure did not indeed prevent the police from publishing a dramatic account of their finds in this dangerous building — an account that deserves reproduction here as an example of skilful electioneering propaganda:

" In accordance with a report from the Conti Bureau in Berlin the Political Police on raiding the Karl Liebknecht House, which is the central office of the German Communist Party, and which has been closed for two days by police orders, found a number of subterranean cellars containing a vast quantity of treasonable material. A subterranean passage was also discovered through which persons sought by the police escaped on the occasion of police raids. It was discovered that the German Communist Party, and its subordinate associations, had developed a second and illegal existence and an extremely intensive agitatorist activity whose source remained unknown to the police authorities. In former years it had been remarked that persons wanted by the police for participation in street fights took refuge in the Karl Liebknecht

House, and were no longer to be found there when the police subsequently raided the House. Although searches had been repeatedly made by the police, the means of exit used by the wanted persons had never previously been discovered by their pursuers. . . . In the subterranean chambers lay hundreds of tons of treasonable material which had doubtless been printed on the printing-presses in the Karl Liebknecht House itself. This material consisted of leaflets summoning the populace to armed revolt and to bloodstained revolution. Text-books on the Russian Revolution served for training the leaders of Communist cells. These text-books emphasized the necessity on the outbreak of revolution for arresting and shooting well-known citizens."

This scanty information was supplemented by certain details which Göring published three days later through the Official Prussian Press Bureau. He declared that the result of the police discoveries was to show that " Germany was to be hurled into the chaos of Bolshevism. Assassination of individual popular leaders and statesmen, attacks on vitally important industries and public buildings, the poisoning of whole groups of persons who were peculiarly dreaded, the slaying of prisoners and of the wives and children of well-known public men — all this was to bring horror and terror upon the nation and paralyse all opposition. The Reich Commissar for the Prussian Ministry of the Interior, Reich Minister Göring, will bring the documents in question before the public in as short a space of time as possible."

All who have a regard for truth will allow that the final sentence is the most important. The official police *communiqué* gives the impression that the police had found documents which for the most part had been printed on the premises and whose contents were obviously designed for publication. Certain secret documents, on the other hand, which were unknown to the public, Göring promised to bring before their notice at as early a date as possible. Up to the present these documents have never been published.

The Communist documents also contained plans for the assassination of Nazi leaders and for attacks upon public buildings. Hence Göring must have been aware that he would have to reckon with such attempts. From the Communist standpoint, however, if indeed such actions were regarded as useful in the weeks preceding the Reichstag election, it must have been obvious that the assassination of Göring or Hitler would have a far greater political value. Nevertheless, if the official story is accepted, the Communists unexpectedly contented themselves with carrying out the least utilitarian of their aims — the attempted destruction of public buildings.

THE BURNING OF THE REICHSTAG

On the evening of February 25, about eight o'clock, firemen stationed in the Palace in Berlin discovered a fire in an office beneath the roof above one of the main gates. This fire they immediately put out. On the window-sill and beside the central heating lay so-called firelighters which had seemingly caused the outbreak. The public was kept in ignorance of this fire in the Palace for two days. It was not until February 27 that the public was informed of what had occurred in the Palace. Meanwhile the evening of that day had brought more thrilling news. Late that night the following message reached newspaper offices throughout the world:

" Towards 9.15 on Monday evening the Fire Brigade was summoned to the Reichstag where a fire had broken out in the dome. A brigade alarm was sent out and ten fire brigades responded to the call. The police also arrived in large numbers and formed a great cordon around the Reichstag. On the arrival of the fire brigades the great golden dome of the Reichstag was already a mass of flames. A shower of sparks rained down on every side of the building. Firemen and police forced an entry into the building and captured a man who at once admitted his incendiary act. He declared himself to be a member of the Dutch Communist Party."

Early in the morning of February 28 this first hasty report was followed by a second emanating from the official Prussian Press Bureau. It ran:

> " On Monday evening a fire broke out in the German Reichstag. The Reich Commissar for the Prussian Ministry of the Interior, Reich Minister Göring, on arriving at the scene of the fire immediately took charge of operations and issued the necessary orders. On receiving the news of the fire Chancellor Adolf Hitler and Vice-Chancellor von Papen at once betook themselves to the scene.
>
> " This is unquestionably the worst fire that has hitherto been experienced

in Germany. The police inquiry has revealed that inflammable material had been laid throughout the entire building from the ground floor to the dome. The material was composed of preparations of tar and torches which had been placed on leather seats and concealed beneath piles of paper. These were then laid by doors, curtains, wooden panelling, and other places of a highly inflammable nature. A policeman saw people carrying torches moving about in the dark building. He immediately opened fire upon them. One of the criminals was arrested. He was a twenty-four-year-old mason named van der Lubbe, from Leiden in Holland, and was found to be in possession of a properly-visaed Dutch passport. He stated that he was a member of the Dutch Communist Party.

"The central portion of the Reichstag has been completely gutted and the chamber in which the Reichstag held its meetings has been destroyed. The damage runs into millions. This act of incendiarism is the greatest terrorist achievement of German Bolshevism. In the hundreds of tons of pamphlets found by the police in the Karl Liebknecht House were instructions for carrying out a Communist terror after the Bolshevist pattern.

"According to these instructions government buildings, castles, museums, and vitally important factories were to be set on fire. Instructions were also found ordering that women and children, and wherever possible the wives and children of policemen, were to be used as cover by the Communists, in cases of rioting and street fighting. The discovery of this material prevented the Communists from systematically carrying out their revolution. Nevertheless the burning of the Reichstag was intended to serve as the signal for bloodshed and civil war. Raids on business houses and shops had been ordered for Tuesday at four in the afternoon. It is clear that it was intended that to-day should see the outbreak throughout Germany of a terror directed against well-known individuals, property, and the lives and persons of peaceful citizens. This terror was to signalize the commencement of civil war."

The evidence given at the trial of van der Lubbe before the Supreme Court in Leipzig has proved this official narrative to be false in at least three particulars. Since, however, this trial is still in progress as these lines are being written, it is not yet possible to express a final opinion upon the as yet unknown causes of the Reichstag fire. At the same time this much can be said definitely: The official report declares that the police found incendiary material throughout the entire building. This has been shown to be false by the testimony of all the witnesses at the Leipzig trial, including the police and the firemen. Preparations of tar and torches were not discovered in any part of the building. The official report further states that van der Lubbe admitted to being a member of the Dutch Communist Party. This is also false. Van der Lubbe expressly declared that he did not belong to any Party. In another report it was stated that a membership card of the Communist Party was found upon him. The evidence of the police who arrested him demonstrated the falsity of this statement. Van der Lubbe had no membership card upon his person.

The official report nevertheless claims that evidence is available to show that the burning of the Reichstag was only a part of a general Communist Putsch. The documents found in the Karl Liebknecht House — the report states — show that the Communist Party had planned for the day following the Reichstag fire ("Tuesday at four o'clock," runs Göring's *communiqué*) a revolution to be carried out by means of incendiarism, capture of hostages, and even, as another official report states, by poisoning the food in public restaurants. If any such plan actually exists, the documents found in the Karl Liebknecht House could undoubtedly be produced as evidence that the Reichstag fire was planned and carried out by the leaders of the Communist Party. It has already been stated above that Göring promised the publication of these documents in " as short a time as possible." At the time of writing these words the documents have not yet been laid before the Supreme Court. If they are indeed brought before it as evidence for the prosecution, then it remains to see whether the Supreme Court will declare them to be genuine and valid. It is at least remarkable that the police reports of their raids upon Communist organizations throughout Germany contain no word to show that they found any material indicating even an intention to commit these terrorist actions.

The foregoing does not exhaust the list of errors contained in the official report of the Reichstag fire. It says in another place that " the incendiary captured in the Reichstag admitted in his confession the existence of an understanding with the German Socialist Party (Social Democrats). This confession reveals the existence of a common front on the part of the Communists and Social Democrats." This imputation is also false. At the preliminary inquiry the Presiding Judge Vogt published through the Reich Propaganda Ministry a statement which ran: "There has been no evidence whatever to prove that non-Communist circles had anything to do with the Reichstag fire." In deliberate defiance of the truth, the official report associated Social Democracy with the responsibility for the Reichstag fire merely and obviously in order to furnish an excuse for the suppression of Social Democrat newspapers and electoral propaganda.

Four men were accused before the Supreme Court in Leipzig in addition to van der Lubbe of complicity in the act of incendiarism. Two were well-known group leaders in the Communist Party organization — the Reichstag deputy Torgler, and the Bulgarian Dmitroff. The other two were a Bulgarian student named Popoff and a cobbler from Macedonia named Taneff. A great part of the evidence brought against them has already been proved to be false. Dmitroff was able to prove an alibi to show that he was absent from Berlin on the day of the fire. Nevertheless there remains the evidence of the Nazi deputies, Karwahne and Frey, as also that of an Austrian official, Kroyer, which states that these men saw Torgler talking to van der Lubbe and Popoff in the Reichstag. The value of such evidence scarcely needs demonstration. Is it likely that the leader of a Communist incendiary band would discuss his plans with his followers in public in the corridors of the Reichstag? Moreover, the prosecution might also have asked themselves the question, What reason would induce two clever Communist leaders, fully capable of foreseeing the consequences of their action, to set fire to the Reichstag? It is possible that a van der Lubbe might not be capable of realizing that such an act could only bring destruction upon the Communist cause. Torgler and Dmitroff could not have been under any illusions on that score. It is in any case too much to expect that prosecuting counsel, who did not hesitate to bring forward criminals from prison as witnesses for the prosecution, would trouble themselves with any such common-sense considerations.

On the night of the fire Karwahne betook himself to the then Commissar — later General of Police — Daluege and drew his attention to Torgler as the possible incendiary. It is easy to understand that this clue was at once followed up. What is far more remarkable is that it should have been pursued, in spite of its obvious improbability, and notwithstanding the fact that no further evidence of guilt was forthcoming, up to the time of the trial. At times it is indeed difficult to avoid the impression that this very doubtful clue was pursued in order to divert attention from another that might have led to the discovery of the perpetrator.

A great deal has been written and said on the subject of this other clue. The news of the burning of the Reichstag had hardly become known to the world before the Press in foreign countries was expressing doubts as to the responsibility of the Communists for the deed. These doubts were subsequently strengthened by opinions emanating from German sources with intimate knowledge of the whole circumstances. These opinions came from a quarter that had been even more seriously affected politically than had the Communists by the Reichstag fire. The Communists were forced to admit that — Reichstag fire or otherwise — the days of their public and legal activity had come to an end. On the other hand, the German Nationalists saw in the fire a superbly conceived piece of propaganda intended to benefit the Nazi Party alone. Moreover, their position was weakened in consequence of the exclusion of the Communists from the Reichstag. Hence the German Nationalists had no interest whatever in preventing the publication of facts that absolved the Communists from guilt and possibly placed the responsibility for what had happened upon other shoulders.

It is true that the German Nationalist leaders were not in agreement among themselves on this subject. Hugenberg declared on March 2, in his electoral address at Bielefeld, that the burning of the Reichstag was not only a declaration of war on the part of the Communists but also on that of their Social Democrat allies. In doing so he publicly proclaimed his agreement with the Nazi interpretation of the political meaning of the Reichstag fire. It is impossible to determine whether Hugenberg still believed in the truth of the official version of events or whether he knew that what he said was false. At least it is certain that he must have known that doubts of the truth of the official version were current among his own friends.

At the beginning of May a memorandum containing sensational revelations on the subject of the Reichstag fire was circulated amongst political circles in Berlin. This brochure was subsequently declared to have been the work of a German Nationalist Reichstag deputy, Dr. Oberfohren, who had formerly been chairman of the German Nationalist group in the Reichstag. It is unquestionable that Dr. Oberfohren verbally communicated his revelations to others besides recording them on paper. Nevertheless it is not known whether the version of these revelations which has become public emanates directly from him or not. The present writer has been told by a customarily well-informed source that the originator or at least author of the brochure was a Right Wing journalist possessed of excellent sources of information and moving at that time in similar political circles to Dr. Oberfohren.

This brochure declared that the burning of the Reichstag was the work of the Nazis themselves, and was inspired by Dr. Goebbels's desire for a resounding " electoral bomb." It placed the responsibility for its initiation upon Goebbels and Göring, and gave the name of the Reichstag deputy and Police President of Breslau, Heines, as the actual incendiary. The brochure does not bring forward any evidence in support of these accusations. Moreover, it must be remembered that its genuineness has never been submitted to proof. Towards the end of March the Prussian police searched the houses of Dr. Oberfohren and his secretary and found incriminating documents. These documents were subsequently declared to be in the nature of anonymous attacks upon the chairman of the German Nationalist Party, Dr. Hugenberg. At the end of March Oberfohren resigned his seat in the Reichstag, and on May 6 he was reported by the police to have shot himself in his house in Kiel. It is, of course, possible that the authorship of this brochure was ascribed to him falsely on the ground that his death placed him out of the reach of harm. Although the authorship of the brochure cannot be determined, it at least reproduces with tolerable exactitude the opinions as to the cause of the Reichstag fire that have found publicity since the beginning of March 1933, and have emanated from non-Nazi circles of the Right. In the Conservative review *Der Ring,* edited by the secretary of the Herren Club, Heinrich von Gleichen, the following sentences appeared in the second number for March 1933: " Are we a nation of blind hens? Where are to be found the promoters of this attempt of which the results show with what certainty of aim they went to work? In order to give a single answer to all these questions we must emphasize clearly and soberly the fact that we (Germany) do not possess a secret service like the English and other nations. . . . If we had had it, one would know to-day in what direction to seek for the Reichstag incendiaries — indeed one would know the names of the men themselves. They are, perhaps, members of the best social circles in Germany or of cosmopolitan society."

These are the words of a man who obviously regretted his inability to speak more openly. Perhaps his use of the word " hen " (*Hühner*) was intended to be a play upon the name of the criminal. In any case neither Heinrich von Gleichen nor Dr. Oberfohren nor the anonymous Right Wing journalist were the sole members of their circle who gave voice to these opinions. On February 28 — the day on which the Reich Cabinet deliberated upon the Reichstag fire and its effects — an official *communiqué* of the discussion at the Cabinet was published in the *Frankfurter Zeitung* and other newspapers. The version in the *Frankfurter Zeitung* ran as follows: " As material for its deliberations the Reich Cabinet made use of a detailed report from the Reich Commissar for the Prussian Ministry of the Interior, Göring, on the course of events at yesterday's fire, at the fire in the Palace, and, above all, on the nature of the documents discovered in the Karl Liebknecht House. On the subject of Reich Minister Göring's report the following is communicated by the competent Government authority. . . ."

What does that mean? It means that somebody in the Government took pains by carefully wording the *communiqué* to throw upon Göring the entire responsibility for all that had happened and might still happen. The writer of the *communiqué* says in words of which the meaning is unmistakable to all who are willing to understand it: " I do not say all this. Göring says it."

There follows a recital of all the terrorist actions planned by the Communists. Then comes the following paragraph:

" With regard to the fire in the Reichstag, incontrovertible testimony was forthcoming [it is to be remembered that the writer of the *communiqué* is only paraphrasing Göring's report and not giving his or the Cabinet's opinions] that the Communist Reichstag deputy

Torgler had spent many hours in the Reichstag together with the Dutch incendiary. Other persons were also seen in his company, and among them some with torches, who could not be arrested by the police because they escaped apparently through the subterranean passage bearing the central heating apparatus from the Reichstag to the palace of the President of the Reichstag. Two men were also arrested who made an attempt yesterday evening to telephone from the Reichstag, and in their conversations declared that the burning of the Reichstag was the work of Reich Minister Göring. At their cross-examination these men admitted their association with the Social Democrat Party and Press. Inasmuch as the inquiry is still in progress, it is impossible to say more at present about this incident."

Among all the other official announcements on the subject of the Reichstag fire this *communiqué* works like a bomb thrown by a mysterious hand. Up to the time of its publication all mention of the subterranean passage connecting Göring's house with the Reichstag had been regarded as idle chatter. Such carelessness exceeds the bounds of probability. On the contrary, it is necessary to inquire whether this *communiqué* was not inspired by the desire to give the public at least a hint; and this suspicion is only strengthened by the detailed account of the two men who endeavoured to telephone from the Reichstag. The Union Telegraph — an information bureau belonging to Hugenberg — knew enough to be able to say that they had spoken with the Social Democrat newspaper *Vorwärts*. The Union Telegraph also declared that they had mentioned Göring as the real incendiary, and that they had been ordered by *Vorwärts* to circulate this news. The Editor-in-Chief of *Vorwärts* immediately and categorically denied the truth of these statements, and was able to prove that nobody had held a telephone conversation with his newspaper office on the subject of Göring's having set fire to the Reichstag.

Of these two mysterious callers-up on the telephone nothing more was ever heard. Their names did not appear in the list of accused before the Supreme Court in Leipzig. If these unknown figures of such importance for unravelling the mystery of the Reichstag fire, and they must be regarded as such in the light of the official *communiqué*, were in reality only figments of somebody's imagination — who was their discoverer? Is it not likely that it was somebody who wanted to associate the words " Göring " and " incendiarism " in the public mind? In the official announcements this implication was naturally stigmatized as " libellous." But that did not prevent it from exercising an influence upon the public. Indeed, the result was the coining of the phrase " Firelighter Göring." The most inexperienced beginner in the art of propaganda must have realized beforehand, must indeed have known by instinct, that such would be the effect. For this reason alone it is difficult to believe in the existence of a mistake due to carelessness. The *communiqué* only serves to strengthen the impression that a group which had its representatives in the Cabinet was at pains to indicate the true incendiary by all the means lying ready to its hands.

A hint from this particular quarter cannot be lightly neglected. It is a clue; and a very important one. Although it is not evidence in the truest sense (which must be emphasized), nevertheless it acquires the force of evidence in the movement when an inquiry into its essential truth is refused or prevented by a Court of Justice. A former member of Brüning's Government said to his Cabinet colleague, Göring, in the course of a somewhat heated telephone conversation: " For goodness' sake, shut up — you and your Zinovieff fire." (This latter a reference to the famous " Zinovieff Letter," published by the Conservative Party prior to the General Election in England in 1925, which caused the Labour Party to lose the election and was subsequently proved to have been a forgery.)

The wrong witnesses appeared before the Supreme Court in Leipzig. The Nazi leaders appeared — men who were guilty of complicity in the crime in the eyes of the world. It would have been wiser to have invited Herr von Papen and cross-examined him as to what he knew of the origins of the Oberfohren Memorandum. Perhaps he would have known the identity of the author. Perhaps, indeed, that of the man who set fire to the Reichstag.

On the whole, it is possible to say that the probability that any particular Nazi group set fire to the Reichstag is at least as small as is the probability that it was the work of the Communists. The indictment, however, did not mention any special group of Communists. It spoke of the leaders of the German Communist Party itself as those responsible for the crime. This seems to cause the scales to fall against the Nazis. It is more likely that an action which could be of great service to their Party would be committed by unscrupulous Nazi incendiaries than that responsible Communist leaders should lay their hands to a work which could only bring destruction upon their own Party.

The composition of the — unknown — Nazi incendiary column, and the identity of those members of the Party organization with which it was connected, are matters that it might be dangerous to know too much about. The mystery surrounding the murder of the clairvoyant, Hanussen, has never been officially solved. But the murder has been associated with Hanussen's knowledge of what happened at the time of the Reichstag fire. It would at least seem interesting to examine the circumstances of this murder more closely. For reasons as yet unknown, Hanussen possessed great influence with the then Chief Leader of the Berlin SA, Count Helldorf, and he had endeavoured to make use of his influence for business purposes. The superstitious Count believed for a long time in the clairvoyant powers of this — at least by descent — non-Aryan soothsayer. Moreover, Helldorf was one of Röhm's intimate friends — a group of men accused in the Oberfohren Memorandum (which mentions the name of Heines) of having carried out the burning of the Reichstag. Originally Helldorf had hopes of becoming Police President of Berlin instead of Levetzow. His expectations were disappointed through Papen's claiming the post for one of his supporters. Towards the end of March 1933 Hanussen was arrested by the SA, brought to Spandau, and on April 7 was found murdered in the neighbourhood of Zossen. After Hanussen's death Helldorf was recalled to Munich, lost his Berlin post in favour of his former deputy, Ernst, and was forced to content himself with the less important position of Police President in Potsdam. If Helldorf knew anything about the history of the Reichstag fire, it is at least probable that Hanussen also learnt certain details. And that Helldorf knew what was afoot is rendered more than likely by his conduct on the night of the fire.

At the time of the outbreak of the fire Helldorf was seated in a restaurant in Berlin. According to his own evidence before the Supreme Court in Leipzig, Helldorf left for home on learning of the fire with the intention of going immediately to bed. This seems strange conduct in the case of the Chief Leader of the Berlin SA, who must have known from the documents found in the Karl Liebknecht House that the Communist Revolution was due to break out at the latest at four o'clock on the following afternoon! If Helldorf had not been a witness, but one of the accused, he would have been reproached with having done something utterly improbable — a not uncommon happening in criminal history — in order to secure a sound alibi for himself. If one is Chief Leader of the SA in Berlin, and knows that a Communist Revolution accompanied by incendiarism and the poisoning of food supplies is imminent, one does not retire to bed immediately on hearing that the Reichstag is in flames. If Helldorf, despite this knowledge, still retired to his bed, it was because he knew that the Reichstag fire was *not* the signal for a Communist revolt. He also knew that the very contrary to that which the official propaganda was inculcating into the German nation as truth was in fact the truth. Moreover, if Helldorf knew what the Reichstag fire did *not* signify, it is more than probable that he knew its real significance. At this critical moment whose interest was it to remain in bed? Was it that of the Chief Leader of the Berlin-Brandenburg SA who was responsible for political order in the capital of the Reich? Never. It was only the interest of somebody who was in some fashion implicated in the fire and who wished to conceal the fact.

On April 3 an international adventurer named Dr. George Bell was shot dead on Austrian soil in the village of Durchholzen, near Kufstein, by unknown men who came in two motor-cars from Bavaria. Bell's murder is another testimony to the dangers attendant upon too great knowledge. He was a former associate of Röhm, and his name first came before the public in connexion with the so-called Tscherwonzen Forgery Case. He was then accused with others of having forged Soviet Russian banknotes for political purposes. He must have been possessed of extraordinary diplomatic skill to have been able as he did to maintain his friendship with the various inimical groups in the Brown House. His relations with Rosenberg were no less friendly than with Röhm. Indeed, Bell's influence over Röhm was at times so great that he was able, for example, to induce him in 1932 to meet the then influential leader of the *Reichsbanner*, Major Mayr. At this interview Röhm opened his heart to Mayr on the subject of certain circles in the Nazi Party, and let him see that his own ideal was that the soldiers in all Parties should join together to counteract the overwhelming influence of the civilians. This and other secrets of Röhm's, and also those private habits of life which were so strongly criticized by the public, were no secrets from Bell, who in consequence went in terror of his life — as he told his friends — after he had quarrelled in 1932 with Röhm. His murder can thus be explained without reference to the Reichstag fire. At the same time persons are known to whom he is said to have admitted his knowledge of this as well.

To sum up: it is impossible to bring forward evidence outside a Court of Justice which would satisfy an impartial judge. Nevertheless, as has been shown, there are numerous facts and also the evidence of witnesses which at least go to prove Torgler's innocence.[1] Since the Supreme Court of Justice has refused to admit foreign counsel for the defence, i.e. counsel who could feel themselves free from the inhibitions under which the German counsel suffer, it is impossible to do full justice to this evidence. In such circumstances, moreover, it is equally impossible to speak of a thorough investigation of the suspicions of guilt that have settled upon other persons. In view of the serious accusations made against Göring from many responsible foreign sources, and especially in that very England which is so admired of the Nazis, the refusal to admit foreign counsel to the trial is inexplicable. If, indeed, there was nothing to conceal, it would surely have given the German Government satisfaction to have confounded in a Court of Justice those same foreign counsel by exposing to them the falsity of the accusations which they themselves had brought forward. Why did it deny itself this pleasure?

THE UNSUCCESSFUL COUP D'ÉTAT

One thing is certain: the Reichstag fire broke forth at the time when Hitler's Government was experiencing its first serious crisis. Conservative circles were contemplating a *coup d'état* for the purpose

[1] The trial ended in the condemnation of van der Lubbe on his own confession of guilt. All the other accused were acquitted [Tr.].

of appointing a Hohenzollern as Regent. The Bavarian Prime Minister, Dr. Held, referred to these plans in a speech which he delivered on February 19 in Amberg in the Upper Rhineland. Nevertheless his insinuation that the plan emanated from Nazi sources and that the Hohenzollern in question was Prince August Wilhelm was founded on a misunderstanding. It is true that the opposing parties frequently attempted to surprise each other with such projects. On the day before the election the Nazis organized mass parades of the SA in every German town, and their announcements bore the resounding title "The Day of National Awakening." It was feared that Hitler was contemplating seizing the person of the President in similar fashion to the manner in which he had dealt with Herr von Kahr nine years previously. Papen began to think of removing Hindenburg to the security of the Reichswehr Barracks in Döberitz, and mobilized the Stahlhelm. But the fact that both opponents were on the watch prevented either of them from taking the offensive. The SA contented itself with its "Day of National Awakening," and on the following Sunday the Stahlhelm paraded in imposing numbers and formed a cordon round the Wilhelmstrasse where Hindenburg had quietly continued to live. He was now protected from any surprises on the part of the SA.

The connexion between these events and the burning of the Reichstag finds mention in the so-called Oberfohren Memorandum, which refers to the strong feelings of disapproval felt by the Reich Cabinet after the fire. As yet it is too early to ascertain the whole truth. From an historical standpoint the fact of greatest importance cannot be controverted: the burning of the Reichstag caused the "National Socialist Revolution" to reach its zenith.

"IN DEFENCE OF THE NATION AND STATE"

The revolution from below and from above joined hands. Göring and Röhm became successful collaborators.

On the evening of February 28 Hindenburg was called upon to sign a further emergency decree "In Defence of the Nation and State" that suspended the most important fundamental rights of the German Constitution and that has ever since functioned as the constitutional law of Hitler Germany. The first and most important paragraph runs: " Articles 114, 115, 117, 118, 123, 124, and 153 of the Constitution of the German Nation are suspended until further notice. Hence restrictions on personal liberty, freedom of speech and of the Press, of association and assembly, as well as interference with the secrecy of the postal, telegraph, and telephone service, and also confiscation of property and the right to search private houses are permissable beyond the limitations placed upon them in law." This provision is followed by a list of Draconian penalties. The death penalty was employed as a deterrent in innumerable cases. Since the publication of this decree sentence of death can be imposed, for example, for a serious breach of the peace if committed by an armed person, or in association with an armed person, no matter whether the deed results in dangerous consequences or not.

A second decree against "treason to the German Nation and treasonable behaviour" enforced the death penalty in cases of treason, and penal servitude in those of treasonable conduct.

The situation thus created was similar to what had formerly been known as a state of emergency — a state of siege. In former days on the occurrence of any such state of siege the State authority was placed in the hands of the army. The Nazis were clever enough to prevent this happening on the plea that the army must not be involved in domestic political struggles. Hence it was the police who were given full authority to act under these decrees. And that meant in Prussia — by far the greatest State in Germany — that power came into Göring's hands.

Göring lost no time in placing the whole Communist Reichstag group, as well as a number of Social Democrat deputies and other Left Wing politicians and journalists, under protective arrest. He dissolved their associations, prohibited their newspapers, and suppressed not only the Communist but also the entire Social Democrat Press for two weeks on the ground that van der Lubbe had admitted that he had had relations with the Social Democrats. A few days later it was officially conceded that this statement of van der Lubbe's was false. Nevertheless, Göring continued to prohibit the Social Democrat Press until he had rendered it bankrupt, and its property was in consequence officially confiscated. SA men wearing the official badges of the "Specials" drove in lorries through the towns, raided the homes of the " Marxists," dragged them away to SA headquarters and there beat them nearly — or sometimes wholly — to death. These incidents are deserving of a chapter to themselves. Within forty-eight hours of the Reichstag fire more than four thousand persons were taken into " protective " custody in Prussia alone. Since this number increased many times over in the course of the succeeding days, the SA established " Concentration Camps " in which, as Frick put it, Marxists were to be trained to become useful members of society once more.

A MINISTER VERSUS JUSTICE

On February 27, 1933, the Nazi Revolution from above joined forces with the Nazi Revolution from below. From that day onwards it swept like a cyclone across Germany. Not since the Peasants' War has any domestic German upheaval cost so much in property and human lives as has this storm.

In an election speech on March 4 in Berlin Göring said: " I do not need the Reichstag fire to enable me to attack Communism. I am betraying no secrets when I say that, if things had gone as Hitler and I wanted, the perpetrators would already be hanging on the gallows." In this last sentence Göring revealed the existence of a difference of opinion in the Reich Cabinet of which mention was made in the Oberfohren Memorandum. The Nazis would indeed have preferred summary justice to a legal trial before the Supreme Court. A speech which Göring delivered on March 3 in Frankfurt-am-Main constitutes what may be called the " Shorter Catechism " of the Nazi Revolution in three sentences. It ran:

" My measures were not weakened by legal or bureaucratic considerations. It is not my business to administer justice but to destroy and uproot. This is a war against chaos. I will not wage such a fight with only police methods. The fist that I shall set upon these criminals' necks is the Brown Shirts — the living embodiment of national strength."

A statesman and police commandant lacking in a sense of justice is in truth an ultra-revolutionary figure. For up to the present revolutions have always been conducted in the name of Justice. At the same time, Göring has admitted that in quiet moments doubts — can they be called twinges of conscience? — have crossed his mind.

"When work is finished, when nerves begin to tremble, when the load of responsibility suddenly looms up vast before the eyes, then one asks oneself again and again: 'Will it succeed?' 'Will God send His blessing upon the work?'"

Those words were spoken in the Town Hall of Aachen on July 27, 1933. They came from the mouth of a man labouring under a curse, a damned soul given a day's holiday from Hell who relates what happens there when the torturer starts back in horror from his own deeds.

THE STOLEN REICHSTAG MAJORITY

At first Göring enjoyed mundane rewards and the pleasures of power to the full. Large masses of the people believed him when he said the Communists had set fire to the Reichstag and that they had been aided in the nefarious work by the Social Democrats. These supporters came to Göring from the German Nationalists, for whom they would probably have voted in a less excited state of feeling. The German Nationalists joined with the Stahlhelm to form a "Fighting Front Black-White-Red" for the purposes of the election with Hugenberg, Papen, and Seldte, as the first names on their list of candidates. Their prospects were encouraging in many parts of the country — if the election of March 5 had not simultaneously been a revolution.

Other voters were affrighted, and believed that the secrecy of the ballot could no longer be relied upon, despite assurances to the contrary, now that letters were opened and telephone conversations overheard. The Left Parties could no longer hold electioneering meetings. The Social Democrats and Communists no longer possessed a Press, and distributors of leaflets risked at least a beating. Not a single Social Democrat stood before many of the balloting centres on March 5 to distribute voting papers or to display election placards. Nevertheless, the ballot officials at least in the towns were appointed in accordance with the regulations. The Communist Party was not prohibited as a Party, and votes cast for it were therefore not regarded as invalid. If they had been, many Communist voters would probably have cast their votes for the Social Democrats, and thus strengthened the Party that was as yet less persecuted than was the Communist Party. The wireless, however, both on the days preceding the election and on the election day itself, was reserved almost exclusively for Nazi use. On the day of the election the report was time and again broadcast that Otto Braun, who still looked upon himself as the legal Prime Minister of Prussia, had that day fled to Switzerland. Of the happenings on that day it is impossible to give any detailed and accurate account. The suppression of public opinion in Germany at least justifies belief in rumours until they are proved to have been false. It is certainly impossible to look upon the election on March 5 as a free expression of national opinion. Moreover, the Nazi philosophy built up upon propaganda makes no demand for the support of an untrammelled popular opinion.

The number of votes cast was unusually large. External pressure and inner conviction were probably equally responsible for the attainment of the high figure of 88 per cent. of the total electorate. As the first name on the Nazi list of candidates, Hitler received 17.2 million votes, or 43.9 per cent. of all votes cast. He thus not only made good his disappointment on November 6, 1932, but actually increased the total of votes which he had received on July 31. The Social Democrats received 7.1 millions, the Communists 4.8, the Centre 4.4, the German Nationalists only 3.1, and the Bavarian Popular Party, which was allied to the Centre and whose candidates came forward in Bavaria alone, one million votes.

The 647 seats in the Reichstag were divided up as follows:

	March 5.	Nov. 6.	July 31.
National Socialists (Nationalsozialisten)	288	196	230
Social Democrats (Sozialdemokraten)	120	121	133
Communists (Kommunisten)	81	100	89
Centre (Zentrum)	73	70	75
German Nationalists (Deutschnationale)	52	52	40
German People's Party (Deutsche Volkspartei)	2	11	7
German State Party (Deutsche Staatspartei)	5	2	4
Christian Socialist People's Service (Christlich-Sozialer Volksdienst)	4	6	3
German Peasants Party (Deutsche Bauernpartei)	2	3	2
Württemberg Peasants Union (Württembergischer Bauernbund)	1	2	1
	647	585	607

In the simultaneous elections to the Prussian Diet the Nazis gained 211 out of 474 seats, while 43 fell to the German Nationalists.

Thus the " Government of National Concentration " obtained a bare majority in the two greatest parliaments in the Reich; and in the Reich itself the total votes cast in its favour did not reach 52 per cent. of the total electorate. If the votes cast for the German Nationalists are deducted, the majority vanishes into thin air. Was Hugenberg therefore the real victor in this election?

It is probable that Hugenberg would have been the victor if it had not been for Göring and the emergency decrees. Göring placed Hugenberg's tacit allies, the Communists, under lock and key, and in so doing deprived the German electorate of one-eighth of its legal representation. The new Constitution of the Third Reich gave Göring in its six paragraphs the necessary power to do this. In consequence, only 566 deputies instead of 647 were able to be present to vote in the Reichstag. Moreover, Göring was left free to decide how many Social Democrat deputies should be removed from the Reichstag and placed in concentration camps. This gave the Nazis a certain majority and the real victory in the election. Already on March 6 Papen had made haste to express to the Chancellor in the name of his Cabinet colleagues their admiration and gratitude.

The bourgeois elements in the Hitler Government endeavoured to make the best of a situation from which nothing more was to be hoped. They desired peace and order and found themselves confronted with a revolution. They had expected triumphal marches of the SA; but not the burning of the Reichstag and the establishment of concentration camps. They hoped that these latter would prove temporary, and in the meantime pretended not to be conscious of their existence. If certified evidence of brutalities was brought before Herr von Papen, he exclaimed in horror that it was impossible to believe such stories. The flood rose steadily round these men in the German Nationalist Front. All they did was to place their top-hats firmly on their heads and comport themselves with dignity as though they were making a pleasant excursion by water.

CHAPTER XIII

BAVARIA'S LAST EFFORT AT RESISTANCE

THE GREATEST political surprise of the elections of March 5 was the triumph of National Socialism in Bavaria and in the Rhineland. Both States were accounted the indubitable political property of the Catholic Parties. They appeared to form a safeguard against any too obvious encroachments by the Central Nazi Government. The Rhineland, although it had for over a century been a part of Prussia, had always cherished certain longings for independence. It is true that no serious-minded person thought of a separation from the Reich, but they certainly did of a separation from Prussia and of the erection of a barrier which should be impassable to Göring's police force. In order quickly to crush such tendencies, the National Socialist Minister of Police had soon after taking up office organized the western police into effective units under high police commands. The South German States, on the other hand, and especially Bavaria, remained until March 5 centres of resistance and the cause of much anxiety to Hitler. They were regarded as being so safe from the Nazi flood that the Social Democrat Party transferred its head offices to Munich.

A hatred of Prussia has long been traditional in Bavaria. Nevertheless, Papen's attack on Prussian independence on July 20, 1932, inspired hardly less fury in Munich than in Berlin. The Bavarians feared that if the Reich allowed itself to take such a liberty in the case of Prussia, it might all the more readily do so in Bavaria. Moreover, the Hitler-Papen-Hugenberg Government was looked upon in the South simply as the creature of an East Elbian Junker clique, trying to seize afresh the sovereignty over the German West and South. The popularity of Hitler and the Swastika, however, could in Bavaria be opposed with a person and a symbol that were even more familiar to the inhabitants — Prince Rupprecht and the Bavarian Crown.

It is a fact that at the time a variety of well-known Bavarian personages approached Prince Rupprecht and sounded him as to a proclamation of the monarchy.

The conferences, which were conducted by intermediaries, even got as far as discussing the civil list which would have to be granted the future king. Since July 1932 there had been, moreover, plans regarding the union of an independent Bavaria with the racially and confessionally allied State of Austria. They had arisen in connexion with a conference of the Danubian States which was then being held in Munich, and the idea took a new lease of life in February 1933. Both the Held and the Dollfuss Governments were agreed in their dislike of the Hitler régime. Hitler had quite ineffectually sent a telegram of greeting to Dollfuss as one of his first acts after his rise to power. There had even been talk of the new Southern State coining a new currency.

The projects, however, were very artificial and went far beyond the limits of Bavarian nationalist sentiments, the existence of which is not to be denied and which stirred again later, protesting, under the National Socialist rule. A new young generation has grown up in Bavaria that is more attached to the Reich than were its fathers. Moreover, northern Bavaria, which is to a great extent Protestant, would certainly not join in any secession. Hitler, therefore, knew very well what he was saying when he told the Bavarian plotters in a speech on February 24 that if they were to threaten him with the Main line, i.e. with separation from the north, the attempt would be foiled and crushed by Bavaria itself.

"POLITICAL CO-ORDINATION"

Hitler was right. The Bavarian Nazis ejected the Party that had hitherto been the most powerful in the State by getting a far greater number of votes at the elections of March 5. In Lower Bavaria, for example, they doubled their poll.

Much the same thing happened in the other States. The Nazis waited for one day and then the SA stepped in and swept away the existing Governments. All over Germany they marched through the towns in mighty columns, occupied the Government offices, plundered the Trades Union buildings, and smashed up the printing presses of the Social Democrat newspapers. And they never forgot to run up the swastika flag. The malcontents who were the noisiest members of the Nazi groups in the urban councils in Prussia headed SA processions to remove the mayors from office or demanded telegraphically of Göring that he should remove them and set up National Socialist State Commissars in their place. Göring had had the forethought to advise the Lord-Lieutenants and the Presidents of the Government Boards in Prussia on March 6 not to resist any such excesses, and especially to suffer the SA swastika flags to be run up on public buildings. He had politely conceded to his official superior, Papen, that the black-white-red flag should also be flown if any one wished. It was for the Stahlhelm to see how far their flag could prevail beside the SA swastika.

This was the Prussian Revolution as sanctioned by the Prime Minister. A certain constitutional resistance had still to be overcome in other States. In these cases again violence came from below and legality from above, and both complemented one another admirably. While the SA set siege to the Government buildings, Frick on March 8 telegraphically appointed Nazi Party functionaries as Reich Police Commissars in Baden, Württemberg, Saxony, and Schaumburg-Lippe. In Baden it was the District Leader, Robert Wagner, who had taken part in the Hitler *coup* of 1923; in Württemberg, the SA Leader, von Jagow; and in Saxony, Manfred von Killinger, the leader of the National Socialist fraction in the Diet, an ex-member of the Ehrhardt Brigade, and an accessory to the murder of Erzberger. In other places things were done in a more business-like manner. In Hamburg, for instance, the existing Senate under pressure from the National Socialist District Leader resigned together with the Lord Mayor, and the National Socialist, Karl Vincent Krogmann, was elected Lord Mayor by the new Senate.

As early as May 11 Wagner announced in Baden that he would assume governmental power as provisional Prime Minister; National

Socialists were appointed to all five Ministries. The first act of the Government was to ratify a Concordat between the Holy See and Baden which had not yet been signed. Schmitt, who had up till then been President of the State, was arrested together with a number of Social Democrat politicians. In Württemberg, too, the National Socialist, Murr, took over the Government as Prime Minister on March 10. The Police Commissar von Jagow, soon disappeared again.

The most brilliant success of this admirably planned and timed revolution was scored in Bavaria. Here the Nazis demanded on March 8 that the Held Government should, without formally resigning, hand over the whole power to a National Socialist bearing the title of General State Commissar. " Any Reich Commissar sent down to us will be arrested at the frontier," had hitherto been the attitude of Bavaria. Such a Commissar had always been imagined as a " Prussian," i.e. an emissary from Berlin who was not known in Bavaria. Now the Nazis produced a Bavarian, General von Epp, whose familiarity to the people no Minister in the State could dispute.

The Bavarian Cabinet refused, discussed the matter and telephoned to Berlin, while the SA poured into the streets on March 9. They ran up the swastika flag on the Town Hall, and the Nazi President of the Diet did the same at the Parliament House. The Bavarian Government meanwhile received soothing promises from the Reich Chancellery, which afterwards proved to be a fresh proof of how little Papen knew what Hitler was planning.

There were, indeed, reasons for the speed and secrecy with which Hitler conducted his attack. After the elections of March 5 the Bavarian royalist plans had revived again in a modified form. Prince Rupprecht was first to be appointed General State Commissar. March 11 had been decided upon as the fateful day, and so the Bavarian king-makers must have felt that the opposition was not observing the rules of the game when it acted on March 9. Hitler had concentrated non-Bavarian SA troops in Munich. Meanwhile the important members of the Bavarian People's Party, including the State Councillor Schäffer, Monsignor Scharnagl, and Dr. Pfeiffer, the Party secretary, were sitting playing a quiet game of cards in a back room at the Pschorrbräu. When a reporter called up Dr. Pfeiffer on the telephone and told him that everything was over, and that all resistance had been nullified, the Party Secretary told him not to make silly jokes. What had really been happening?

In the evening hours of that historic March 9 Epp received a telegram from Berlin handing over to him the chief police authority in Bavaria. He went to the Government building, which was empty, and entered upon his duties. The SA dragged Stützel, the Minister of the Interior, and Schäffer, the chief of the Finance Ministry, out of their beds and beat them. Epp appointed Commissars to the Ministries: Wagner, a member of the Diet, was put in charge of the Ministry of the Interior, Dr. Frank, Hitler's solicitor, in that of Justice, and Siebert, the Lord Mayor, in that of Finance. As so-called Commissars for Special Duties he appointed Röhm, and Hermann Esser, a man with a bad reputation and possessor of membership card No. 2, Hitler's oldest fellow-campaigner, whom the Leader had, after one of his numerous scandalous affairs, banished to the lower regions of the Party. Curiously enough Epp had kept up a close friendship with him all these years. As head of the Bavarian State-Chancellery, Esser applied himself with an unmistakable business instinct to promoting the Bavarian tourist traffic.

On March 16 the Held Government went, as it was officially called, "on leave." By March 12 Hitler was able to fly to a conquered Munich. On landing he made a short speech, in which amongst other things he said: "It was here that many years ago I began the campaign, the first part of which may now be regarded as accomplished. There has been a co-ordination (*Gleichschaltung*) in political life, such as has never before been known." And thereby Hitler adopted the word "co-ordination" for the internecine political struggle in Germany that was henceforward to cover every manifestation of force and every infamous action of National Socialism. That this co-ordination was a revolution Hitler had already emphasized in an address to the Party members, which began with the words: "An immense change has taken place in Germany . . ." and had extolled this change as the "National Revolution of 1933." Besides, he had in this same speech implored his people, wringing his hands, not to plunder shops, to steal motors, or to kill civilians, although it is true he delicately paraphrased it to not " annoying private individuals, obstructing cars, or interrupting business."

CONSERVATIVE CAPITULATION

In their triumphal speeches at this time the Nazis always referred to the destruction of Marxism, but their real victory was gained over their middle-class rivals. The true conqueror of Marxism, if one must use this word, had been Papen, and the day of his triumph July 20, 1932. On March 10, 1933, on the other hand, Papen had been defeated. On March 12 Hindenburg signed the attestation of the Conservative capitulation. He signed a proclamation whereby he determined that " from to-morrow until definite arrangements have been made as to the Reich colours, the black-white-red and the swastika flags shall be flown jointly. These flags unite the glorious past of the German Reich with the mighty rebirth of the German nation. United they will embody the power of the State and the inner unity of all sections of the German people. Military buildings and ships will only fly the Reich military flag."

The last sentence was the only blot upon Hitler's victory. The Reichswehr had not yet joined in the National Revolution.

While riding splendid charges all over the Reich, the National Socialist Revolution was obliged to smoke out nests of Conservative resistance by lengthy and determined efforts. On March 16 Dr. Luther, the president of the Reichsbank, after a conference with Hitler, retired, and the ambitious Dr. Schacht was reinstated in the post that he had vacated three years earlier. He was the Chancellor's personal candidate. Luther, who had hitherto been a most ardent champion of Germany's republican illusion, was sent as Ambassador to Washington, and has since then been an enthusiastic servant of the National Socialist State.

GOEBBELS ON THE HEIGHTS OF PROPAGANDA

A further stage of the National Socialist Revolution was the appointment of Goebbels to the Ministry on March 14. In order to utilize the particular talents of the Berlin District Leader, a special

"Ministry for National Enlightenment and Propaganda" was formed. This Ministry made at times excellent propaganda during the next few months for National Socialism, and for Hitler as well as for itself and its chief. Goebbels, who knew the value of the most insignificant little scrap of power, kept in addition to his new dignity both the Berlin District Leadership and the propaganda machinery of the National Socialist Party. As Propaganda Minister he ruthlessly usurped large portions of the functions of not only his middle-class but also his Nazi colleagues. He took away the Press Department from the Foreign Office, the Wireless from the Postal Ministry, the Film from the Ministry of the Interior, and the *Hochschule für Politik*[1] from the Prussian Ministry for Education. He won over the Press and Film world by pleasant after-dinner speeches of mediocre intellectual depth but of courteous form, which contrasted favourably with the oratorical trumpet-blasts during those weeks of the National Socialist leaders who were drunk with victory. When he spoke of the "wonderful steely romanticism" of our times, or sent telegrams expressive of admiration (which elicited no response) to Stefan George, he appeared among the somewhat rough figures of his fellow-campaigners like a youth with a lute, and gradually played his way into the rôle of a favourite revolutionary of high society.

For Goebbels is in his personality altogether a child of "Asphalt Democracy," a positively sycophantic son of modern mass society. The little man, who behind an apparently indolent exterior is very explosive, is much more at home in the "imaginary world" of film and rotary machines than in the legendary domain of "blood and earth." However much he may have abused it, he was happier than almost any of his companions in the Berlin of the "Jewish Journaillez" and in the Kurfürstendamm,[2] and his advancement to the Ministry has acted as an elevation into the society that, though he attacked, he secretly aspired to join. Although he speaks of Jews more contemptuously than others, it sounds less credible from him, and as though it were an intentionally exaggerated adaptation to the methods of the Party. On the whole, he seems rather to be a philo-Semite gone

1 More or less corresponding to the London School of Economics.
2 The Montmartre of Berlin.

wrong than a true anti-Semite. These characteristics, which always seem a little odd in the sphere of Nazism (which is why Goebbels every now and then seeks to " prove " himself by verbal, though in tone exaggerated, imitation of Hitler), are the very ones that make him suitable to push his way into the pores of Society with propaganda by means of Press, Film, and Wireless.

His successes in this direction, however, have been greatly overrated. It is true that the heads of the middle-class Press without exception (there is no other now apart from the Nazi Press) have agreed to co-ordination, which necessitated far fewer changes of personnel than would have been the case if they had all been genuine democrats. Within the editorial offices, however, resistance has not been entirely overcome. The fact that, owing to stupid " cooling " of the news by official Press bureaux, the newspapers have become useless as sources of information and boring as literature, can hardly be regarded as a success by the Propaganda Minister himself. Whether the decline in the circulation of middle-class papers will be compensated for by increased circulation in the Nazi Press (the *Völkischer Beobachter* has a circulation of over a million, including a good many compulsory subscriptions) appears in some cases at least questionable. The " Press Law " of October 4, drafted by Goebbels, makes the profession of editor dependent upon being registered in an official professional register kept by a compulsory organization of journalists. In order to be so registered, certain demands are made which are to be welcomed in principle — such as the possession of civic rights, professional training, intellectual and moral qualifications — but which may also lead to wanton chicanery. In addition, Aryan descent is required; exceptions may be made, particularly in the case of editors requiring special technical knowledge, which is important above all in trade journalism.

Stronger even than in the case of the middle-class Press is the decline in the number of patrons of the theatres, where the audience can hardly be forced permanently to forgive bad quality for the sake of good intentions, apart from the fact that an audience that wants entertainment only partially appreciates the intentions of the concentrated form of present-day drama. It must, however, be said in fairness to Goebbels that his work in connexion with the theatres has been greatly hampered by petty jealousies, especially on the part of Göring. The commercial side of the film industry has been seriously upset by rash co-ordinations in regard to the personnel, and this is to be counterbalanced by help given through a " Film Bank " founded by Goebbels with a credit account of 10 million Marks supplied by the great Banks (that is to say, partly from the public funds). The news-films are, of course, entirely at the service of propaganda; the narrative-films, however, have not yet succumbed to the influence of the Propaganda Ministry. A film about the Nazi hero, Horst Wessel, was made against the wish of the Propaganda Minister. Goebbels then prohibited its performance on grounds that clearly showed professional jealousy — the whole affair did not shed any glory on the Minister for Propaganda. It should surely be his business to influence the production of films instead of destroying them financially by prohibitions.

National Socialist propaganda was carried through most unrestrainedly in the case of the wireless, which was completely reorganized by Goebbels assisted by the " Reich Broadcasting Leader," Hadamovsky, appointed by him. It is true that in this case, too, the public began to show signs of getting tired of propagandist monotony, but it cannot altogether escape from the effects of continuously having the same thing dinned into its ears, so that the political purpose is certainly to a great extent realized. It is difficult to give up a wireless set; it might have unpleasant consequences.

With his sure instinct for power Goebbels took care that the Propaganda Ministry should not, like so many of the other Reich authorities, remain a head without any body. At the beginning of August he organized a network of thirteen " State Divisions " and eighteen " State Propaganda Stations," the average personnel of which is a chief and two assistants. The sum of all these people gives quite a handsome bureaucratic total. It is, therefore, also improbable that the 14.2 million Marks ear-marked for the Ministry in the budget of 1933 will prove adequate. Perhaps the most interesting part of the Ministry is Section II, which is concerned with propaganda in the narrower sense — festivals, parades, poster campaigns. It is directed by Haegert, a professional advertising expert who has been appointed adviser to the Ministry, and who is the author of many of the propagandist ideas for which Goebbels has had the credit.

On the whole, it may be said that the Nazi propaganda has succeeded in filling the empty space of German public opinion — in which no critical voice may now be raised — to bursting point with its noise. Political independence having been taken from the people, even privacy of thought is intruded upon, and the individual is kept in a state of continual political tension which reaches into his very dreams. A positive philosophy of propaganda has arisen in which the nation appears only as the creation of sublimated advertising. There is, however, no doubt that the instruments of propaganda have suffered greatly by extravagant use, and it is easy to prophesy that the present policy will not be pursued for much longer.

THE POTSDAM CELEBRATION

The first great test of Goebbels's talents in his new post occurred on March 21, the day of the ceremonial opening of the new Reichstag. The place chosen for the opening ceremony was the Garrison Church at Potsdam where Frederick the Great lies buried. Hindenburg read a short speech in which he said that the people had "gathered with a clear majority behind the Government appointed with my confidence." Thus he emphasized firstly that this Government was his Government, and secondly that only this Government was — that is to say, that it was not a purely National Socialist Government. When he continued ". . . and have hereby given it the constitutional basis for its work," the word "constitutional" was intended to be specially stressed. Hitler replied that the upheaval of the past weeks had "re-established national honour." Now the Government would "re-establish the supremacy of politics which are called upon to organize a nation's struggle for life." It was a challenge both to the overrating of economics and of the individual. The unity of the spirit and the will of the nation must be re-established. The culminating point of the festivities occurred when the President went down into Frederick the Great's vault and stayed there for several minutes while the congregation waited in silence.

Some hours after this impressive scene the Reichstag met in the hastily prepared auditorium of the Kroll Opera-House, the chief ornament of which consisted of an immense swastika. Of the Communist members, most of whom were in prison, not a single one had, of course, appeared. Over twenty Social Democrats were also missing — most of them because they had been arrested.

THE ACT OF AUTHORIZATION

The chief political business of the Reichstag was transacted two days later, on March 23. The purpose prescribed for it by the Government was to pass an Act of Authorization which should cloak the naked despotism that had reigned in Germany since February 4 with the mantle of legality. Like all the laws of Hitler's government, it bore a resounding title. This time it was called " For the reduction of the misery of the Nation and Reich." It ran:

" The Reichstag has passed the following Law, which is hereby promulgated with the consent of the Council of States (Reichsrat), it having been ascertained that the requirements for the promulgation of laws changing the Constitution have been complied with.

" *Art.* 1. Laws may be enacted by the Government upon other occasions than those provided for in the Constitution. This holds good also for the Laws mentioned in Articles 85, 11, and 87 of the Constitution.

" *Art.* 2. Laws passed by the Government may diverge from the Constitution, in so far as they are not concerned with the constitution of the Reichstag and the Reichsrat. The rights of the President of the Reich remain untouched.

" *Art.* 3. Laws determined upon by the Government will be drawn up by the Chancellor and published in the *Reichsgesetzblatt.* Unless any other date is mentioned, they come into force on the day following the day of publication. Articles 68 to 77 of the Constitution have no application to the Laws determined upon by the Government.

" *Art.* 4. Agreements between the Reich and foreign Powers which affect matters of legislation do not require the assent of the legislative bodies. The Government will issue any regulations necessary for the carrying out of such agreements.

"*Art.* 5. This Law comes into force with the day of its publication. Its period of validity shall end on April 1, 1937. It shall, moreover, be considered as annulled if the present Government is replaced by another."

The last sentence aroused much comment. Hugenberg and his friends averred that under "present Government" only one could be understood in which they too were represented. National Socialism at the height of its power refused to admit this interpretation.

Each article of the Law demolished an important part of the German Constitution. Article 1 said that the power of legislation was transferred from the Reichstag, which was elected by the people, to the Government; parliament had thereby made itself superfluous. Article 2 extended this already enormous power of the Government to the point of allowing it even to alter the Constitution if it thought fit. It need only allow the Reichstag itself and the Reichsrat to exist in their present form, and the powers of the President of the Reich are also nominally not to be restricted. Actually, however, they are, for according to Article 3 it is no longer necessary for the President to ratify the laws, but only for the Chancellor. This abolition of one of the most important prerogatives of the Head of the State was announced in a semi-official publication that betrays Goebbels's sarcastic style to be due to a desire to relieve the President of unnecessary work.

THE REICHSTAG SUBMITS

According to the Constitution no law can be passed unless a two-thirds majority of the Reichstag agree to it. Not, indeed, a real two-thirds majority; the Constitution only prescribed that two-thirds of the members should be present and that two-thirds of these should vote for the law. Hence, if a sufficiently large number of members had stayed away — for they would probably not dare to vote against it openly — they could have forced down the number of those present below the statutory two-thirds. Since the eighty-one Communists had already been kept away forcibly, the hundred and twenty Social Democrats and about fifteen Centre Party members would have sufficed — and there must surely have been enough secret fury in the Centre Party to move fifteen men. The seventy-three members of the

Centre Party, together with the nineteen that went with them for the Bavarian People's Party, had it in their power by voting openly against it, or by simply staying away, to deny the Hitler Government the legal assent to its dictatorship. Hitler used promises and threats to bring the Centre to heel. He promised Kaas, the leader of the Centre, that all the Parties that voted for the Law should be united in an executive committee (*Arbeitsauschuss*), which would thus form a smaller and more select parliament to which the Government would be responsible for its actions. Hitler broke this promise, as he did so many others; and possibly Kaas only pretended to believe it. It was of greater significance that Hitler incorporated certain promises concerning the rights of the Churches, which stood out in relief by their definiteness against the rest of his speech which consisted mainly of generalizations. And since these assurances were in actual part made to a foreign Power — the Holy See — they seemed to be to some extent binding on the Government.

There was no need for Hitler to trouble about the Social Democrats, although at that time the Party had not been altogether excluded from political life, and according to the Nazi strategy was for the present to keep its rôle as an object for ill-treatment. After violent discussions among themselves, the members decided to go to the Reichstag and to vote against the Law, obviously considering that this was braver than staying away.

In his speech Hitler said, *inter alia:* " The National Government, in view of the misery at present rampant in the nation, regards the question of a monarchist restoration as closed to discussion. Any attempt at a separate solution to this problem in individual States would be looked upon as an attack on the unity of the Reich." Further: " It would be contrary to the character of the national uprising that the Government should be obliged each time to ask for and to obtain the assent of the Reichstag to its measures. The authority and thus the efficiency of the Government would suffer if the people were to entertain any doubt as to the stability of the present régime." Further: " Hardly ever in the history of the world has a revolution on such a scale proceeded in so disciplined a manner and with so little bloodshed as the uprising of the German people during the past weeks."

Further: "The Government purposes to make no more use of the powers given it than is necessary for carrying out absolutely essential measures. Neither the existence of the Reichstag nor of the Reichsrat is thereby threatened. The position and powers of the Reich President remain untouched. To come into perfect accord with his wishes will always be the chief aim of the Government. The continued existence of the States will not be affected, the rights of the Churches will not be curtailed: their relation to the State will not be altered." And then came the forcible conclusion in sentences that betray the real motive underlying the speech: "The Government offers the Parties the chance of peaceful development along German lines, and hence of coming to an understanding in the future. But it is equally determined and prepared for refusal and resistance. Now, gentlemen, the matter is in your own hands — to decide for peace or war."

War was Hitler's last word; his perpetual war against the other half of the nation. Since this other half was unarmed, Hitler was bound to win the first battles of the war. On the platform and in the passages between the rows of members stood heavily armed SA men. The possibility that the war might begin at once in the hall, or at all events in the anterooms, had to be reckoned with. The fact that in these circumstances the Social Democrats voted against the Bill must be accounted very highly to each one personally. It was a vote taken under grave terrorization, and if in spite of this resistance dared to raise its head, it was certainly not Göring's fault. The speech with which Otto Wels explained the reason for the opposition of the Social Democrats was in these circumstances brave; nevertheless it was not the smallest indication of the real state of feeling in the country. Hitler overwhelmed Wels in a reply, which was poor as regards content but which must certainly be one of the cleverest exhibitions of oratorical duelling that has ever been heard in the Reichstag. With a mixture of embarrassment and assurance Kaas explained why, in spite of hesitation, the Centre was prepared to support the Bill. He recalled Hitler's promises at the preliminary conferences, and the unprejudiced National Socialist Government rewarded with applause the leader of the — apparently — still powerful Catholic Party; even Hitler clapped. By 441 votes to the Social Democrats' 94 the Reichstag passed the Act of Authorization. The Nazis leapt to their feet and sang the Horst-Wessel song.

THE GOVERNORS

The political co-ordination of the States, that is to say, the absorption of important posts, continued after March 23. On March 31 the Cabinet published a "provisional law for co-ordination in the States" by which the local State Governments were made independent of their parliaments as the Reich Government had become by means of the Act of Authorization. The State Diets were, moreover, except for the recently elected Prussian Diet, dissolved and reconstituted without fresh elections according to the results of March 5; the Communist votes were simply left out of account altogether. It was left to the Parties to send as many representatives to the new parliaments as were due to them on this system. In the same way the local councils and other autonomous bodies were reconstituted. Thus at one blow the National Socialists had in most of the popular representative bodies, at all events in all the important ones, from the smallest village council up to the Reichstag itself, not only obtained the greatest number of votes but, after the Communists had been ejected, actually a majority.

Nevertheless the fate of the various States was not given into the hands of the parliaments which had thus been rendered submissive, but was made dependent on the wish of the Reich. On April 7 the Cabinet decreed a definite "Law to co-ordinate the States with the Reich"; and then the President appointed a Governor in each of the German States, with the exception of Prussia, upon the recommendation of the Chancellor. The Governor must not be confused with the Prime Minister, i.e. the leader of the Cabinet; he is in fact a completely new figure, not hitherto known in Germany. It is his business to see that the policy decided upon by the Chancellor is adhered to in the States. He appoints and dismisses the presidents of the local Governments (the Prime Ministers), and the remaining members of the Governments on the recommendation of the Premier. He has the right to dissolve the Diet and to order fresh elections (and in any case the dissolution of the Reichstag implies also a dissolution of the Diets). The Governor draws up local laws and puts them into force. At the recommendation of the local Government he appoints and dismisses the immediate State officials and the Judges (these officials are removable according to the new regulations). He has the prerogative of pardon. At meetings of the local Governments he can act as chairman in the absence of the Prime Minister.

An important special regulation has been made in the case of Prussia. Here the Reich Chancellor himself occupies the post of Governor. He may delegate his powers to the Prime Minister.

The official head of Prussian politics was still the Vice-Chancellor von Papen, with the title of Reich Commissar. The German Nationalists had hoped to make him Prime Minister and thus to put the power permanently into his hands in Prussia. The Nazis destroyed this hope by the law which created the post of State Governor — a law ostensibly made in the interests of unity within the Reich. The Reich Governor, Hitler, announced that Herr von Papen would not be his Prime Minister, and he had to resign his post as Reich Commissar. On April 11 Hitler appointed Göring, who had been Minister of the Interior, to be Prime Minister. For several weeks Kerrl, a minor legal official, had been Commissar of the Ministry of Justice; similarly in the Ministry of Education was Rust, a former member of an educational committee. The two National Socialists were now appointed Ministers. The Finance Ministry kept an expert who had been put in a year earlier by Papen, a Dr. Popitz, formerly Secretary of State in the Reich Finance Ministry. One block of resistance which the Nazis were not yet able to clear away entirely was Hugenberg, who on January 30 had occupied the two Prussian Ministries for Trade and Agriculture in addition to his Reich offices. Hitler refused, however, to raise him to ministerial rank, and he was obliged to content himself with the title of Commissar.

FOR THE GLORY OF PRUSSIA

The chief characteristic of Göring's governance has since then been that he has considerably retarded the co-ordination of Prussia with the Reich, and has carried on an arbitrary, independent, and ambitious Prussian policy. He started on this path in his speech to the Diet on May 18. Though he referred to his Leader in reverential terms in saying that he had sat at his feet for ten years, though he emphasized that he ruled " first and foremost as the true paladin of my Leader," yet his further statements were not at all consonant with Hitler's principles regarding the abolition of particularism. " An important mission devolves upon Prussia, which was already hers during the previous century — to be the basis of the German realm," said Göring. And then: " In no circumstances will I suffer Prussian possessions to be separated from Prussia." That was a blunt declaration of war against any effort to do away with the awkward State system prevailing in Germany. When a few weeks later the Thuringian Government dared to think that the Prussian enclave, Erfurt, which lay in the very middle of Thuringia, might at least enter into closer economic relations with the State of Thuringia, Göring said brusquely that Erfurt would in all circumstances remain Prussian, and that the Prussian Prime Minister would oppose its even being made an economic province of Thuringia. And when at the beginning of July it was suggested that East Prussia, which is completely surrounded by Polish territory, might be brought into closer internal relationship with the Reich by making it a Reich province, Göring indicated that he would put any one who spread such an idea in a concentration camp.

In order to cause the glory of Prussia, and especially of his own dignity to shine duly before all Germany, Göring destroyed the old Prussian State Council and set up something in its place that was more like a Crown Council. The former Council had consisted simply of the representatives of the provinces. Dr. Ley, the chief organizer of the Nazi Party, had managed to make himself its president at the end of April, hoping thereby to attain to power by combining one of the most important Party offices with one of the highest State dignities. Göring, however, would not tolerate a rival. On July 8 he promulgated a law which turned the Prussian Council into something quite different. Its members are in future to be nominated by the Prime Minister in so far as they are not *ex-officio* members like Ministers and Secretaries of State. Among those appointed are the typical members of all Upper Houses, the representatives of Church, Science, and

Art, but also of Trade and Labour — " Labour " being understood to mean leaders of the SA and N S B O. Göring has, moreover, deliberately sought out high-sounding names, including some from among the Conservative, not National Socialist, upper classes. Indeed he takes far more trouble than any of the other Party leaders to get into touch with these classes in society in the hope of securing their support in case of future struggles with rivals. The most important group in the Council, however, is probably that of the Nazi Party functionaries. Röhm, the Chief of Staff of the whole SA; Himmler, the Reich leader of the SS; Ley, the head of the Party organization; all Prussian District Leaders of the National Socialist Party, all higher group leaders of the SA, and all group leaders of the SS are members of the Council. The function of the Council as a body is simply to act as adviser to the Prime Minister, who is its president. The influence of each individual member of the Council, on the other hand, is immense. Lord-Lieutenants and presidents of Government boards in the provinces and governmental districts are obliged to ask the State Councillor of their district before taking any important decision. In case of important questions of personnel, especially appointments to offices, the State Councillor's permission must be obtained, and the Lord-Lieutenant can do nothing against his veto. He must himself obtain the decision of a Minister. Göring's intention in all these arrangements is to give a semblance of legality to the power actually and often unrestrainedly exercised by the powerful Party functionaries and by those of the SA over the weak officials all over the country, and to bring these satraps gradually under his own supervision.

The Council meets in the Palace at Berlin, and the resemblance to the Crown Council of Hohenzollern times will no doubt strike many. It embodies the glory of Prussia which Hermann Göring, a Bavarian, has caused to blaze up once more. Is it a last flare before it goes out altogether?

CONSERVATION OR LIQUIDATION?

In the other States, too, Hitler's faithful paladins soon developed into jealous and stubborn defenders of their new powers, maintaining their positions as fiercely as they fought for them. Despite all opposition the National Socialists carried through their determination always to make one of their own men Governor, who then appointed another Party member as Prime Minister. In Bavaria Epp became Governor, appointed Röhm as his deputy, and the Finance Minister Siebert as Prime Minister. In Saxony the influential District Leader Mutschmann became Governor; Killinger had to be content with the office of Prime Minister. Murr became Governor of Württemberg; Wagner of Baden; and the District Leader Sauckel of Thuringia; Brunswick and Anhalt were joined under one governorship, which was given to the SA leader Loeper. Even a little State like Oldenburg was given a Reich Governor in the person of the District Leader Röver. Mecklenburg-Schwerin, Mecklenburg-Strelitz, and the Hansa town of Lübeck were put under the governorship of the Nazi Agricultural Labour Leader Hildebrandt. District Leader Sprenger was made Governor of Hesse; and a settlement that caused more disputes than any other was at last made for Hamburg and Bremen, which were united under the District Leader Karl Kaufmann. Even the two dwarf States of Lippe were given a Governor in the person of Dr. Meyer, a member of the Prussian Diet.

Thus even the smallest State had instead of the former single supreme authority obtained two. In spite of their high-sounding title, the Governors — and that is indeed the only justification for their existence — are really Party bailiffs in the States. District leaders of the National Socialist Party have deliberately been made governors everywhere. They guarantee the decisive influence of the Party bureaucracy over the State, and thus in spite of their high dignity actually form a secondary government of the most disturbing kind. In the smaller States they have the same function as the State Councillors in the Prussian districts. They see to it that the Party rule is kept active and intact, and is not swallowed up in the super-Party life of the State.

It does not matter whether, as in Bavaria, the Governor has a strong influence, or, as in Hamburg, the weight of trade and hence of State affairs, tends towards the Lord Mayor — everywhere the private interests of the States come to the fore again in the course of time.

When the Hessian Prime Minister Werner alluded to the Hessian racial individuality in his inaugural speech at the Diet on May 16, when the Saxon Prime Minister von Killinger demanded preferential treatment for Saxony in the allotment of Reich taxation on the same day, or the Thuringian Governor Sauckel protested vehemently against a partition of the somewhat artificially created State among its neighbours — everywhere the old colours of federalist self-will burst through the swastika escutcheon. When the little State of Thuringia, for example, announces the simultaneous erection of three new palaces in its capital, Weimar — one for the Governor, one for the Government, and one for the District offices of the Nazi Party — then this extravagance sails under the flag that covers every folly, that of the provision of work; but the true purpose is, of course, to strengthen the glory of the State of Thuringia with concrete foundations.

In a State such as Bavaria the desire for independent State existence has remained very strong. The Bavarian Prime Minister Siebert characterized the peculiar rôle of the Governor best when he said at his first official appearance on April 12 that Herr von Epp would always be careful to champion the interests of Bavaria in his high office. Thus the classic Bavarian battlecry in its struggle with Prussia, the phrase about Bavarian interests, has not only survived the National Socialist Revolution, but has been taken up by it, and now resounds from the National Socialist mouth to Berlin.

National Socialism, it is true, believes itself to be in possession of something that robs this clash of interests of political significance — the fundamental separation of the idea of State sovereignty from any economic admixture. Let the districts defend their various interests; the allurement of sovereignty will none the less be taken from them little by little. What Hitler wants is exactly the opposite of what Göring wants. He took no part in the solemn opening of the Prussian State Council. And when the Party Leader exclaimed at the Nuremberg Party meeting that National Socialism had not come to preserve the States but to liquidate them, the Prussian Prime Minister knew very well what he was referring to.

Centralization is the strongest tendency in the movement to-day, and will seek to abandon words for deeds. The feeling of individuality, however, is not nearly dead yet in the different States. True, they must keep quiet about it at present and perhaps for some time to come. But it is like the Church, which can afford to wait and which outlasts many things. After the upheaval in Bavaria, Crown Prince Rupprecht avoided discussion, and possibly something more unpleasant, by a trip to Greece. When he came back, General von Epp paid him a ceremonial visit in his new capacity as Governor. The Crown Prince said only one word: " Traitor! " and left the disconcerted Governor standing.

THE MUNICIPALITIES

Besides the States, the German municipalities have of course also been co-ordinated. It has been seen how their administration was reconstituted. Nowadays there can hardly be a single one of the larger municipalities in Germany the mayor of which is not a National Socialist. The various municipal associations, the most important of which was the German City League, were on May 22 forced by the Party authorities under the leadership of Ley to form themselves into a united German Municipal League. Karl Fiehler, the Munich civic politican, whom his fellow-Party members had made Lord Mayor of Munich, became head of the association. It was not a specially good choice for the National Socialists; it should not have been difficult for them to find a rather better man. National Socialism has not brought any new features into the life of the German municipalities. On the other hand, large cities like Berlin have gone bankrupt; not that National Socialism can be held solely responsible for this, but it must at least bear a part of the blame. There seems to be no unanimity as yet about the principles upon which municipal policy is to be conducted in the future. While Florian, the Westphalian District Leader, announced towards the middle of August that the mayors would in future be appointed according to the Leadership principle, the Bavarian Prime Minister, Siebert, was animatedly championing the preservation of self-government.

THE DESTRUCTION OF THE PARTIES

(*a*) *Communism*

The revolution extirpated the Parties that opposed or competed with National Socialism very quickly, possibly more quickly than was altogether pleasing to the Nazi Party leadership, and certainly more quickly than they expected. The extremes — the Communists and the German Nationalists — were the most stubborn.

The Communists were best prepared for Hitler's and Göring's application of force, because they must have expected something of the same sort from any other Government more bourgeois in trend. The German Communist Party was made illegal on February 28, although for tactical reasons the Communist votes were reckoned in the Reichstag elections of March 5. Many of the leaders, including Thälmann, the Party Chief, were arrested. The remainder carried on their work underground — many went abroad. The illegal activity of the Communist Party, though it was in itself carefully prepared, suffered from the fact that it was unconsciously based on Russian experiences which were no longer valid as examples. In the Russian case, the opposition only consisted of the organs of a police State. Their preparations were not calculated with a view to a struggle with a power supported by a mass of fanatical partisans in every class of the nation, and therefore possessing a vast army of voluntary spies. The illegal apparatus of the Communists is too large, too loose, too permeable, to be able to cope satisfactorily with so vigilant an opposition that goes through the whole population. Moreover, the Communists, except for a small nucleus, are not dependable, and numbers of deserters have always gone over to the SA, though the opposite has also happened. In view of this natural fluctuation, betrayal is at present inevitable, and the police are able as often as they wish to report the discovery of a new secret organization. The support of the Communists by their Moscow Central Office was very ambiguous. Outwardly the Soviet Union was very careful to announce its neutrality by ratifying on May 4 the protocol which had been agreed upon a year earlier for the prolongation of the treaty of friendship with Germany concluded in Berlin in 1926. Nevertheless, treason and many arrests have not put an end to resistance, because the source cannot be touched — proletarian criticism, which is kept alive just as much by the brutal successes of the régime as by its defeats.

(*b*) *Social Democracy*

The opposition of Social Democracy collapsed more quickly, although it had put up a surprisingly good fight at the Reichstag elections on March 5. But it was not in the least prepared for the methods of the Nazi Revolution from above and below simultaneously, any more than were the mass demonstration forces of the *Reichsbanner*. This is shown, for example, in the statements made by Dr. Hertz, a member of the Reichstag, to the Copenhagen newspapers at the end of March. In the *Socialdemokrat* he said that the Social Democrat Press was prohibited all over Germany. The prohibition came to an end on March 28, and Göring had raised very sharp objections in his Reichstag speech to exaggerations, but not to objective criticism of the prevailing political system. In his, Hertz's, opinion, therefore, there was no reason for an extension of the prohibition. In the *Politiken* Hertz declared that false reports of National Socialist terrorization could only harm German Democracy in its fight to win back its liberty. German Social Democracy would conduct its campaign against Fascism exclusively by means of objective arguments.

The tactical intention of these remarks was clear; it was hoped that the régime would at least tolerate the existence of the Party. What political use an opposition, which thus existed by the grace of the Government, was to be is not altogether obvious. In the effort to save the Party apparatus Otto Wels, the Party Leader, resigned his post in the Second International on March 30, because it had published violent manifestos against the Hitler régime. Later he explained that his resignation had only been a tactical move, which had proved to be useless. On April 27 the Party made another effort to preserve its existence by electing its leaders afresh. There were indeed some names missing of those who had already gone abroad, but otherwise the composition of the committee was much the same as it had been. One resolution declared in favour of their continuing to work within the framework of legality. A fortnight later, on May 10, Göring showed exactly how far they could go in this direction by occupying the Party buildings and newspaper offices, locking up the offices and confiscating the Party funds. None the less, on May 17, the Party actually appeared at the Reichstag, and voted for a speech of Hitler's on foreign policy. Frick had previously threatened that if there were not unanimity in the House upon this occasion, the life of the individual would no longer be safe, nor the lives of those who were in the concentration camps. Thus the motives of the group were humane; they had already ceased to hope for any political success.

Most of the Leaders of the Party went abroad one after another. One of the first to leave was Otto Braun, the former Prussian Prime Minister, who had been so careless at the elections on March 5 as to overstep the bounds, and had thus given the most useful material to the National Socialist wireless propaganda. Some of the higher members of the Party with Otto Wels at their head founded a Party Committee at Prague. Others, like Severing, Löbe, the ex-Reichstag president, Stelling, a member of the committee, and Heilmann, a Reichstag member, stayed in Germany, showing commendable bravery but not being of any political use. As late as June 19 a new Party Committee, consisting of four persons, was elected. An announcement was made that: " The newly elected committee in Berlin is the sole responsible Party authority. Party members who have gone abroad have no warrant to speak in the name of the Party."

The courage of these members is as astonishing as their shortsightedness. Three days later, on June 22, Frick published a general " Prohibition of activity " against the Social Democrat Party, which stated that Social Democracy was the enemy of people and State, and could thenceforward expect no other treatment than Communism. Their representatives were at once excluded from all parliaments and municipal bodies, their offices closed, and their newspapers permanently suppressed. A large number of the parliamentary representatives who had remained were gradually rounded up and arrested, among them being Löbe and Heilmann. Johannes Stelling, a member of the Party Committee, was murdered.

Thus Social Democracy " within the framework of legality " no longer existed. What happens further belongs to a fresh chapter in

History. Whether it will be the introduction to something new or a mere episode will be for History itself to decide.

(*c*) *Liberalism*

The Liberal Parties faded away more quietly. On June 28 the leaders of the German State Party declared this once mighty Party to be dissolved in a notice consisting of three lines of print. On July 4 Dr. Dingeldey, the head of the German People's Party, did the same with the Party that had been Stresemann's; not omitting to admonish his friends to give their earnest and glad co-operation for the glory and liberty of the Fatherland, because Unity, Right, and Liberty were the pledge of happiness.

(*d*) *Centre*

The Catholic Centre cherished the belief for some time longer that it might be allowed some small say in the new State. True, its leader, Dr. Kaas, soon realized that the hope was forlorn. Brüning, on the other hand, allowed himself to be elected as Party leader in Kaas's place on May 6, and announced his belief in freedom of thought and responsibility before God. Hitler received Brüning twice, on May 17 and 31. The personal respect which the present Chancellor showed to the former, and no doubt a certain similarity of outlook, seem to have awakened hope in Brüning. But though Hitler himself may have played with the idea of finding some use for a Centre Party that was attached to him — whether against the Vatican or against Papen — the waves of the National Socialist Revolution simply washed away the whole edifice.

The fate of the remaining Parties was decided about the middle of June. Hitler summoned the National Socialist leaders to a meeting in Berlin and made two speeches announcing the continuance of the Revolution. "The Laws of the National Socialist Revolution have not yet lapsed," he said on June 15; "their dynamic power still guides the development of Germany." And on June 16 he added: "The German Revolution will only be over when the German nation has been wholly reconstituted, newly organized, and newly conditioned." In his speech on June 15, he also said that the last few months had strengthened his conviction that the National Socialist movement would overcome the difficulties of foreign and economic policy in the same degree as it was surmounting those of internal politics. He thereby announced that the Party no longer needed the support of the German Nationalists and of the Centre Parties. These Parties must therefore make their exit. He added that he was absolutely convinced that the mighty National Socialist movement would outlast many centuries and that nothing could now do away with it.

That gave the expected signal. On June 22 the SA fell upon the leaders and offices of the Bavarian People's Party — arrested, occupied, and confiscated. Even priests were taken prisoner. They excused themselves by alleging conspiracies of the Party with the Austrian Christian Socialists. Graf Quadt-Isny, the Party leader and Minister for Trade, was obliged to resign from the Cabinet on June 27. The Centre Parties outside Bavaria were treated less harshly, but Hitler intimated that the Party no longer had any justification for existence. On July 5 the Party leaders announced that the Centre had decided on its own dissolution, one day after the Bavarian People's Party had done the same thing for itself through an announcement by Graf Quadt. Dr. Hackelsberger, a prominent industrialist, undertook the liquidation of the Centre Party with Hitler's assent. Permission was given to a certain number of the Centre Reichstag members to join the Nazi Reichstag group as guests — a personal affair of no political significance. At all events, the Vatican no longer had a Party in Germany, and it recognized this fact in a public and contractual manner in the Concordat.

(*e*) *Stahlhelm*

The defeat of the Conservative opposition was achieved along two lines of attack. The German Nationalist Party was exterminated, the Stahlhelm, which was a rival of the SA, was deliberately weakened and at last brought to submission. A great part of the Stahlhelm leaders were dissatisfied with Seldte's taking office in Hitler's Cabinet, and especially with the contemptuous part which he played. The leader of these malcontents was the second-in-command, Lieutenant-Colonel Duesterberg. Moreover, he expressed openly what many of his comrades thought: that the violence of the SA against political opponents, which was often only the result of personal vindictiveness, was making the cleft in the community even greater than it need be. He spoke of the " invisible grey front " of the World War, which should bridge over Party conflicts, and warned them not to rebuff their fellow-citizens. With Duesterberg's knowledge and consent many local Stahlhelm groups took into their ranks large numbers of ex-members of the Social Democrat Party and of the *Reichsbanner,* who hoped to fight beside the Stahlhelm against National Socialism and for their ideas. Here a line of resistance was being built up which quite evidently reckoned upon a day of national crisis when the President and the Reichswehr would have need of a political force to help against the SA.

The result was that at almost regular intervals, first at the end of March, then again at the beginning of April, and at the end of June, Stahlhelm leaders were arrested by the SA and whole groups disbanded. This happened in Brunswick, especially, several times. Seldte wrung his hands and, though he had not much authority, deposed the accused Stahlhelm leaders, accepted the verdict of the SA in individual cases, and declared in general that co-operation between the associations must be strengthened and increased. Intellectually Seldte came more and more under the influence of Hitler, whom he genuinely admired.

The first great sign of his submission to the Chancellor was that on April 26 he arbitrarily deposed Duesterberg. There was no reason for it. It really was not only due to Duesterberg's opposition to Hitler's course. Duesterberg was also affected by the Aryan clause that now held good all over Germany, for his paternal grandfather had been a Jew. On the following day Seldte became a member of the National Socialist Party, and announced the submission of his association to the Chancellor over the wireless in the words: " God save Hitler! "

The accomplishment of this capitulation gave rise to many difficulties. A great number of Stahlhelm leaders had to be removed; while Röhm demanded that the Stahlhelm should be entirely under his command, which the pride of the " grey front " would not suffer. A compromise was made on July 21. The so-called nucleus of the Stahlhelm remained under Seldte's leadership and as ST beside the

SA and SS was subordinate only to the supreme SA leader — that is to say, to Hitler himself. The junior associations, the " Young Stahlhelm " and " Defence Stahlhelm " were to be absorbed into the SA. Members of the Stahlhelm were not allowed to belong to any Party but the National Socialist. At a meeting of leaders in Reichenhall on July 2 the submission was ratified, and Seldte in words expressive of admiration vowed to be true to Hitler so long as life was in him. This did not altogether settle the " Stahlhelm case " internally. The annual old comrades' meeting was not allowed to take place in 1933. At a meeting of leaders, which was held instead on September 24 at Hanover, Röhm took the salute, and Seldte marched past him with the other State leaders. This made it clear which of them was only a troop leader and which was Commander-in-Chief.

(*f*) *German Nationalists*

With the Stahlhelm Hugenberg lost a support which, however, had grown steadily more unreliable. The German Nationalist Secretary of State, von Bismarck, had tried in some way to compensate for this. Though he had only taken up his post at the same time as Göring, he was removed from it again on April 9; his successor was Grauert. One reason for the change was Bismarck's strongly monarchist views, which had led him to announce that the restoration of the Hohenzollern hereditary monarchy and the divine right of kings were " damned well our duty and obligation." Since his removal from office, Bismarck had devoted himself to the formation of a " German National Circle of Fighters," consisting of youths in green shirts, which was to stand beside the SA and the Stahlhelm as a Conservative factor. The German Nationalists also sought in other ways to adapt themselves to the fashionable political forms. In the middle of April they introduced the leadership principle, and no longer called themselves a Party but the " German Nationalist Front." One of the fashionable practices was that they should accept in their Circles members of former Left Parties, as the Stahlhelm did.

After this everything went, so to speak, according to plan. The Police Chief at Dortmund, who had formerly been an SA leader, struck the first blow, and disbanded the local Circle on June 14. On June 21 the SA made a surprise attack all over Germany. They and the police together occupied the clubs and offices of the Circles everywhere, and thus also of the German Nationalists. In some cases there were shooting affrays, and casualties occurred. Hugenberg made vain remonstrances at a heated Cabinet meeting; he dashed out of the room scarlet with fury and ordered that a courier should be sent immediately to Neudeck, where the President was staying on his estate well guarded by the Rosenberg group of the SA. Meanwhile the German Nationalist Front began to disband itself voluntarily all over Germany. On June 27 Hugenberg announced his retirement, and on June 28 Dr. von Winterfeldt and two others of the Party leaders went to Hitler, who dictated the dissolution of the Party to them. It was carried out at once.

A fortnight later, on July 14, the Cabinet decreed a law " against the formation of new Parties." Its first paragraph ran:

" There is only one political Party in Germany, and that is the National Socialist German Workers Party."

REICHSWEHR, GOVERNORS, AND SA

Was the State that only recognized one Party from now onwards this Party's State? The importance of the disappearance of the German Nationalists lay not in the fact that fifty-two opponents happened to be gone from the Reichstag, but that this Party had been the parliamentary foot of the Conservative Colossus which still existed in political space beside the new Nazi élite. The most important supports of this block from now on were the Reich President and the Reichswehr, which up to the present have not been " co-ordinated." With his back against this immovable force, Herr von Papen still makes some attempt to join in the government. Apart from large agriculturalists, industry, whether as employers or employed, is powerless beside it; it is capable of alteration and always ready to listen to the politically stronger.

No one who does not realize that General von Blomberg intends to be a completely unpolitical Reichswehr Minister can understand the rôle of the Reichswehr in the National Socialist State. Even Schleicher used the internal political force of the Reichswehr more as a form of bluff than as an actual factor. Since Schleicher's inglorious fall had completely revealed the lack of political aim and the weakness of this armed body of officials, the burnt child has been dreading the fire. The Reichswehr is once again devoting itself to its military duties and obediently follows the precepts of its Commander-in-Chief, who is Hindenburg to-day and may be Hitler to-morrow. One would have the strongest possible suspicion that matters were strained between the Reichswehr and the SA if it had not been proved by numerous small episodes and some more serious ones. In reality, however, neither men nor officers look upon the SA as equivalent to Hitler or Göring — it will be seen why. While jealously preserving its unique military position, especially as against the SA, the Reichswehr nevertheless does its best to give the National Socialist Government what it needs in the way of prestige.

Blomberg has emphasized the exceptional military position of the Reichswehr in various speeches since the beginning of the régime. On February 23 he said to the Munich garrison: "We are the sole armed force in Germany and shall remain so." At the same time, however, he called for cheers for the association that contained "millions of determined men who like ourselves live and fight for the Fatherland." On March 15 the Reichswehr assumed the black-white-red cockade and erased the black-red-gold corner from the military banner. There was, however, no mention of the swastika. That the old military jurisdiction was reintroduced on April 28 created no particular stir in a military nation. On the other hand, many suspicions have been roused by a second law promulgated on the same day, which runs: "The members of the SA and SS are subject to the common processes of law in accordance with the regulations laid down by the Chancellor as Supreme SA Leader." No regulations for the carrying out of this interesting law have so far come to light. One thing, however, is worth remembering. When, ten years ago, Röhm wanted to turn the SA into a military force, Hitler opposed it on the ground that no troops were any use unless their commander had disciplinary powers. Now he has them.

The military force was made accustomed to the new totalitarian State by small pedagogic doses. By an instruction dated May 20,

Blomberg arranged that officers and men " serving with the two national corps should salute one another to mark the friendly alliance subsisting between them." Three months later it was decreed that for officials and other members of the military forces wearing mufti, the salute was to be the Hitler salute, and as a matter of etiquette it was indicated that the younger should salute the older and the lower rank the higher. Thus a Lieutenant in the Reichswehr salutes an SA group leader. The Aryan clause of the officials law has in most cases been dropped for the Reichswehr, since nobody was anxious to have a second Duesterberg case in the officers' corps. A regulation dating from the beginning of August, however, prohibits marriage with non-Aryan women. With the bestowal of the rank of General upon Göring and an address by Blomberg expressive of loyalty to Hitler to the Ulm garrison early in September, the bonds were drawn even closer. One man was passed over on this occasion who, for sheer military performance, was much more deserving of general's rank, and that was Röhm.

An alteration in military law on July 23 empowered the Governors (hitherto the State Governments) to requisition the assistance of the Reichswehr in case of public emergency and unrest. This implies not so much an increase in the power of the civil authorities over the Reichswehr, which in principle already existed, as a guarantee of Hitler's authority against possible insubordination among the SA leaders. For the Governors are his confidential agents, and they are throughout officials of the middle-class organization of the National Socialist Party.

Here may be descried an element of unrest and a cause of continual small outbreaks — the repression of SA leaders by the Governors as also, as in Göring's Council, their being fobbed off and kept quiet with posts in which they are subordinate rather to Göring than to Röhm. Röhm has already in his decree against busy-bodies, forbidding the SA to interfere with women who smoked and with prostitutes, attempted to give direct orders to police chiefs, alleging that they are first and foremost SA leaders — a question of jurisdiction in which he will find it hard to be the victor. However, there is here to be seen the resentment of old soldiers that have been pushed aside, which is increased by Hitler's instability. On May 7 he promised before the Schleswig-Holstein SA in Kiel. "The hour of reckoning has come in which we coldly draw the logical conclusions. An eye for an eye, a tooth for a tooth." Towards the middle of June, as has been seen, he was still preaching the continuance of the Revolution. And suddenly only a fortnight later, on July 2, he announced at the leaders' meeting in Reichenhall that he would proceed ruthlessly against any so-called second Revolution!

And little by little the SA was forced into the background. On May 9 Göring had strictly forbidden his police officers to be members of the SA, SS, or Stahlhelm, to take part in political processions except as a unit, or to wear the swastika symbol, except officially on their new sharpnel helmets. At the beginning of August he even went a step farther and disbanded the SA special constabulary. In Bavaria, again, Epp asked and received of Hitler special powers to proceed against the excesses of the SA that Röhm would not control.

Röhm was not the man to swallow his wrath. While Hitler was holding another meeting of leaders at his country house in Obersalzburg on August 6, Röhm on the same day called up the whole of the Berlin SA, eighty-two thousand men, on the Tempelhof parade-ground and made an impassioned speech which culminated in the sentence: "Any one who thinks that the day of the SA is over must make up his mind to the fact that here we are and here we remain!" That was directed against Göring, against the industrialist Thyssen, and against Schmitt, the Minister for Trade. Possibly Röhm was also thinking of Hindenburg, to whose dislike is partly due the fact that Röhm remained in the background. In the Cabinet, too, attacks were at first made on Röhm because of his much-discussed private habits of life. Then Hitler made a speech about loyalty between leaders and men, his voice choked with tears, and amid general emotion it was resolved, in consideration of the comradely feelings of the Chancellor, not to pursue Röhm's case any further. Röhm referred over and over again to Hitler's saying in his Kiel speech that the SA men were the guarantee for the victorious outcome of the Revolution. At a meeting of leaders in Godesberg on August 20, he declined indignantly to allow outsiders to tell the SA what was its sphere of duty; that this sphere of duty still was to hold down the conquered enemy, and if need be to extirpate him.

GERMANY AND PRUSSIA

Amid all these acerbities, Röhm could comfort himself with the fact that he and his corps were still indispensable to Hitler, and that in case of any change they might even come to the fore again. The extension of the power of the Governors, it is true, strengthened the state of law and order that was desired by Hitler on economic grounds. But at the same time the Governors, who now confronted the violent guarantors of the Revolution as the cold bureaucrats of the Revolution, were growing too independent and might possibly some day become dangerous. As soon as the whilom agitator Göring was sure of his official police and his Conservative State Councillors, he no longer wished to recognise the SA. Hitler, however, still remained the supreme SA leader.

There is no need to underestimate the importance for the present time of the discord arising here, if it is looked at in the right perspective for the future. The barometer of the Party's temper is well known to be Goebbels, who is apt to be the first to scent such disputes. It has always been his advantageous, if not altogether creditable, fate to be the third person at a fight between two others, and to attach himself timely to the stronger. By open polemics against Göring he subtly indicated the decision which is now maturing. By stubbornly maintaining the Prussian State power and favouring the ruling class that is materially and morally allied with it, Göring is seeking to create for himself a political position among the props of which is the old President, if not consciously then at least by his sentimental attachment to the old Prussia. The policy that Göring is pursuing is a policy contrary to the spirit of National Socialism; and it is a violation of Point 1 and Point 25 of the Party programme. It has been shown how Hitler opposed these arbitrary particularists in public speeches. When on September 15 Göring held a ceremonial opening of his Council at the Palace in Berlin, Hitler stayed away.

Göring's whole policy, in so far as it deserves this name, has at all events a limit that is automatically drawing nearer — the natural decease of Hindenburg, which is bound to come. Then — at the latest — the centralization of the administration which is slowly approaching in isolated places without rousing any great attention will make a fresh start and do its best to include Prussia too. If it is successful Göring's semi-monarchical power will be made innocuous without any very serious commotion. Hitler, moreover, despite some qualms, is saving up the SA for this day — not in order to let them riot, but because on that day the eight hundred thousand guarantors of the Revolution will by their mere appearance become guarantors of the unity of the Third Reich.

In what form National Socialism will take over what it still has not got of governmental power after Hindenburg's death is probably only known to Hitler and possibly Goebbels. Shortly before Hitler took up his post the Reichstag had quickly passed a law that provides for the possibility that a new President might not be elected immediately, but that the President of the Supreme Court might deputise for the Head of the State even beyond the period already assigned in the Constitution. The practical importance of such a deputy has already been greatly lessened by the Act of Authorization of March 23, which excludes the Reich President from legislation. More important when this time comes will be a law of July 14, 1933, which gives the Government the power to take a plebiscite on any measure that it has in prospect. According to paragraph 2, " the majority of votes decides. This also applies in cases where the voting concerns a Bill embodying a change in the Constitution."

The Government might ask the people whether instead of the President a Regent should be appointed. It might bring forward for discussion the plan drawn up by Alfred Rosenberg in the newest edition of his *Myth of the Twentieth Century:* " It is the duty of the founder of the new State to form an association of men, on the lines of the Teutonic Order, consisting of personages who have taken a leading part in the reconstitution of the German nation. . . . The head of the State-president or king or emperor — will be elected for life from the Council or by the Council of the Order." That is to say, a lifelong Head of the State, perhaps an elected emperor — although this particular expression of romanticism does not especially appeal to the National Socialist Leader. At all events, the law says that Hitler can ask the people what he likes — and they will answer him what he likes.

Will he perhaps ask them one day whether the House of Hohenzollern shall in some way be brought back to take part in the life of the nation? William II, the ex-Kaiser at Doorn, has helped to finance Hitler. His eldest son in a private conversation alleged this as an excuse for supporting Hitler, although it went against his inclination. Gratitude, however, is not a political virtue. And indeed what possible use could there be for National Socialism in the restoration of the Hohenzollerns? In periods of safety it does not need the support of a monarchy or of an administrator sprung from a dynastic House; at times of uncertainty and danger it would be bound to fear that it would be sacrificed by the dynasts for the sake of popular favour. And if the dynast were not strong enough to throw off the National Socialist yoke in this way, then he would be too weak to help.

National Socialism neither requires nor likes princes. They are bogies put up in the internal rivalry between various groups that threaten one another with a return to the monarchy without being able thereby to frighten each other much. In general, National Socialism only recognizes those who were in its ranks before January 30, 1933. Of the former lords and princes there were very few among them.

CHAPTER XIV

INDUSTRIAL OPPOSITION

THE NATIONAL SOCIALIST revolutionary wave that swept over States and Parties also penetrated the innumerable associations and Trades Unions into which German industrial life was organized independently of the administration. The associations of employers, of employed, and of independent workers were within a comparatively short time sequestrated by National Socialism, being in some cases destroyed and in others reconstituted. The prevailing ideology in Germany demanded that the capture of these heights should be considered as "permanent reconstruction." Meanwhile there was no sign of any architectural plan. All that was visible was the process of co-ordination of all these organizations, which was, roughly speaking, carried out along three lines of attack — against the industrial associations, the Labour Unions, and the peasantry.

Of the three, the great industrial associations have survived attack best, and have escaped with a few changes of personnel. Thus the attack launched on April 1 by Dr. Otto Wagener, the expert adviser on economics of the National Socialist Party, against the National Association of German Industry ended in a tremendous defeat for the attacker, which not only deprived Wagener of his post but brought a number of his friends into concentration camps. The Association had coldly announced soon after Hitler's assumption of office that its attitude to the Government would be determined by the Government's actions. Wagener thereupon demanded not only that trusted National Socialists should be put into authoritative posts in the Association, but also that the President, Krupp von Bohlen, should retire, and that the manager, Privy Councillor Kastl, should resign. The powerful organization was as a matter of fact quite prepared to make reasonable concessions to enable the Government to save its face. It published a subduedly enthusiastic announcement regarding the national holiday proclaimed by Hitler for May 1; and when it was eliminating an ancient flaw in the structure of the German Employers' Association during the month of June by combining with the Union of German Employers' Associations, it adopted the fashionable nomenclature of the day and called itself from thence on " Reich Corporation (*Reichstand*) of German Industry." Moreover, Kastl, who in any case had not been intending to stay in office, retired. On the other hand, Krupp remained as President of the new Society. The Board had in the excitement of the moment resigned on April 6, but with the help of Fritz Thyssen, who had much influence with Hitler, it had soon got the better again of the Commissars of the Brown House. For a time Wagener and his colleagues, Möllers and von Lucke, continued their interference in the administration of the Association; but when at the end of June Dr. Kurt Schmitt, a man who had the confidence of the industrialists, was made Minister for Trade, this interference came to an end. Wagener had wished to weld together the Association with the Trades Unions into a " Corporation " Industrial Organization, and had taken it amiss of Krupp that he had dared to designate what was purely an employers' association as a Reich Corporation. This protest was one of his last acts. His successor as manager of the political affairs of the National Socialist Party was Wilhelm Keppler, a man trusted by the industrialists, and whom Hitler appointed on July 13 as Commissar for economic questions both at the Brown House and in the Chancellery.

The National Socialist tornado had rather more effect upon the most powerful employers' association of western Germany, which owing to its complicated name, " Association for the Preservation of Economic Interests in the Rhineland and Westphalia " was commonly known as the "Langnamverein" (Long Name Society). The chairman of this society, which had for many years had much influence in German politics, was now Dr. Schlenker, an ambitious man who had first been in political touch with the German People's Party and then the German Nationalists, wherein it proved, as things turned out, that he had backed the wrong horse. A rival of his had up to the present been chairman of the other powerful organization in this coal and iron district, the North-Western Employers' Association. This was the ex-public prosecutor, Grauert, whom Göring, as has been said, had made his adviser in his Ministry. The National Socialist attack was now directed against Schlenker. He was expected to allow a junior SA leader to be attached to him as fellow-worker, in other words, overseer, a situation which was quite untenable. Schlenker resigned at the end of June. The man who really came off best in these confused happenings was Fritz Thyssen, a large shareholder in the Steel Combine, that is to say, in the biggest concern in German heavy industry, a friend of Göring's and a man who had given Hitler a great deal of money. He was doing his best to get the Government to hand over to him the control of the Steel Combine which Friedrich Flick had once seized and had then sold to the Government. The Government, which at present possessed a controlling interest in the concern, was by a complicated system of amalgamation to be forced into a minority position and thus virtually to be done out of the 125 million Marks with which it had bolstered up the tottering concern a year earlier.

That Fritz Thyssen would be one of those who did best out of the National Revolution of 1933 was clear to everybody a very few weeks after Hitler's rise to power. After Schlenker's resignation the nominal president of the Langnamverein, Dr. Springorum, who was at the same time head of the Northwestern Employers' Association, also retired, and Thyssen became his successor in both posts. There was now no more talk of a corporative organization of industry. Any one who could not live without ideology might comfort himself with the thought that at least at present the pure leadership principle was in vogue without any kind of democratic machinery, and that the leader in the most important section of German Industry was the man who used to supply Hitler with money — Thyssen — and who thereby to all intents and purposes forced Krupp out of the picture too. To crown all, Göring also appointed Thyssen to his State Council, and thus he became by law one of the mighty men before whom even Lord-Lieutenants tremble. The chiefs of the four Nazi districts over which Thyssen's authority extends thereupon all hastened, towards the middle of July, to send to their new chief letters of allegiance which ran:

"You have become the highest State authority for our economic administrative district. In accordance with this I have instructed my subordinates to refer all economic matters with the exception of questions of agrarian policy exclusively to yourself, and to regard your decision as final."

Filled with pride, Thyssen published this letter, and warned the workers' associations not to presume to disturb the peace in their works. Although this was a good Nazi catchword, it annoyed the National Socialist Labour leaders, and called forth an irascible counter-manifesto from Seldte, the Minister for Labour, on July 21, which without mentioning Thyssen's name denied him all right to interfere in labour matters, and also reminded Göring that this was a question concerning the Reich as a whole, and not merely Prussia. The interests of the workers had meanwhile been taken over very firmly by the National Socialist Party — but of this more will be said later.

THE STUNNED MIDDLE CLASSES

The National Socialist attempt under middle-class influences to organize trade fared worst. It did not, however, end so badly for the chief protagonists as for the matter in hand. At the end of 1932 a "Fighting Association of the Industrial Middle Classes" had been founded, under the presidency of Dr. Theodor Adrian von Renteln, a former National Socialist Youth leader. This Association was for millions of National Socialist electors the great hope for the sake of which they gave Hitler their votes. Small tradespeople went about in 1932 in the big department stores looking at the places where they proposed to set up their businesses under the Third Reich in accordance with Point 16 in the Party programme which demands the "immediate communalization of the departmental stores and their lease at low rentals to small tradespeople."

The first "success" was won by the Association on March 28, when the Head Association of German Retailers allotted 51 per cent. of the seats on its board to National Socialist members. The Head Association then joined with other wholesale and retail trade societies to form a " Reich Corporation of German Trade." Dr. von Renteln himself became the chairman of this Corporation. He had also on the previous day had himself elected leader of the new " Reich Corporation of German Manual Labour," which was a rechristening of an association that was already in existence under the same name. His deputy and the actual effective head in the latter case was Dr. Zeleni.

After a somewhat stronger opposition, proceeding especially from Hugenberg, the Fighting Association also won over the " German Industrial and Trade Committee." This represents the union of all German Chambers of Commerce; these are legal corporations which represent the interests of the whole commerce of a district with the Government, but on the other hand have also certain supervisory duties in regard to this commerce.

On July 22 the Industrial and Trade Committee elected Dr. von Renteln as sole president, after the former president, Dr. Grund, had announced his resignation " in order to fall in with the demands of the time." Dr. von Renteln in his inaugural address promised to lead the institution of which he was now the head towards glorious times. His sphere of activities must be enlarged, trade must according to the National Socialists ideal govern itself, and the Chambers of Commerce would be the corner-stone in the coming edifice composed of Reich Corporations.

This was a mistake on his part, because there were mightier men than himself in the National Socialist movement who conceived the corner-stone of the coming edifice as something totally different. Dr. Ley, the leader of the Party organization, had planned that it should be the Labour organizations. In the end, however, Hitler, the mightiest of all, himself made the quarrel superfluous. For many reasons, notably the influence of capitalist-minded advisers like Dr. Schmitt, the new Minister for Trade, he abandoned the whole idea of Corporations, and put off the policy of protection for the middle classes *sine die*. This terrible disappointment, details of which will be discussed below, led to protests which did not always even preserve the outward forms of respect to National Socialism. Ley made use of this to get rid of his competitor by means of the full powers of the Party and with the consent of Hitler. On August 7 he declared the " Fighting Association of the Industrial Middle Classes " to be dissolved. He split it up into two different organizations. One was called " National Socialist Trade and Industrial Organization," and the other "General Association of German Manual Labour, Trade, and Industry." The first comprises those members of the former association who had joined before May 1, the second the remainder. In practice this bisection implied the expulsion of those who had become competitors for power within the body of National Socialism, but at the same time a definite weakening of the middle classes within the Party. Thus the middle-class movement within National Socialism was silenced by the leaders, because it was becoming a cause of irritation to them. Whether it is dead remains to be seen.

SUBJUGATION OF INDUSTRY

The attack made by National Socialism upon the labour organizations was conducted with greater vehemence. The Trades Unions of all shades of opinion, including those which inclined to Social Democracy, did their best to live in peace and amity with National Socialism. On the day when Hitler became Chancellor, Theodor Leipart, the president of the Independent Trades Unions, made a statement to the effect that though they were in opposition to the present Government, organization and not demonstration was the order of the day. After March 5 even this moderate opposition was forbidden. The SA occupied the Trades Union buildings. On April 7 Leipart said in a speech to the allied committees of the General Association of German Trades Unions that the Trades Unions might demand recognition from the Government, since they for their part recognized the great aim of the Government, which was to set the external and internal liberty of the people upon a foundation of the productive forces of the whole nation.

The weakest resistance was made by the associations of clerks, for here an anti-Semitic Society that stood very far over to the Right politically had always been master of the situation — the German National Association of Shop Assistants. On March 29 the Social Democrat founder and head of the General Free Association of Employees, Aufhäuser, a member of the Reichstag, resigned. A month later the Association dissolved itself. The manual labourers' Trades Unions, on the other hand, despite their policy of conciliation, showed themselves to be possessed of much greater innate vigour than the clerks who were sometimes politically wavering. An election for the works committee which took place at the Berlin municipal works on March 2 showed the power of the independent Trades Unions to be still unbroken. The nearest approach to them was the Communist opposition, while the National Socialists only obtained a very small proportion of the votes. On the other hand, similar elections in the Ruhr mining district on April 7 already showed signs of the change. In this case the National Socialist Industrial Cell Organization outstripped the Independent Trades Unions by polling 30.8 per cent. of all the votes registered. Meanwhile, of course, the National Socialist Revolution had passed over the Westphalian mining district. The workers had been informed that Social Democrat members would not be allowed to sit on the committees at all, and the presence of the SA ensured the threats being taken seriously. Hence it appeared to many of the men useless to vote for the independent Trades Unionists.

And what the Revolution did not achieve from below, was in this case, too, done from above. On April 5 the Government published a "Decree concerning Trade Representation and Economic Societies." It gave the employer the power to dismiss any employee upon "suspicion of an attitude inimical to the State." In part voluntarily, in part under pressure from the Brown Shirts, many employers thereupon threw out their "Marxists." This law broke the resistance of the workers.

There was, indeed, a tendency among certain of the National Socialist authorities not to put the Trades Unions on a level with Social Democracy, but to preserve them as a justifiable union of German workers. The only National Socialist Workers' Association was the Industrial Cell Organization (N S B O), which, as its name implies, simply gathered together the Nazi workers in any industry and used them to make Party propaganda in that industry. The structure of these "cells" precluded their being able, for instance, to take up any matter of wages for a whole branch. The leaders of the N S B O asked nothing else than what the Nazi middle-class leaders had already done — they wanted the Trades Unions to remain, but to occupy themselves the chief posts in them. Many hoped that this might be achieved peaceably, and tried to persuade Leipart as well as his colleague Grassmann to retire voluntarily and with all honour. Leipart came to no decision.

MAY 1

As a matter of fact Leipart did approve of the new political development. The National Socialists had had the brilliant idea of turning the old Labour Day, May 1, into a national holiday and thus making of it a legal day of rest, which the Social Democrats had never managed to achieve even in the days of the Republic. That made a tremendous impression on the workers. Even if no external pressure had been applied, the Independent Trades Unions could hardly have avoided passing the resolution that they did on April 20, in which they hailed May 1 as the legal holiday of national Labour, and exhorted their members " to take part in all the festivities decree by the Government, with the full consciousness of their pioneer service for the idea, for the honour of productive labour, and for the complete incorporation of the working classes in the State."

On May 1 the " national holiday " was kept amid tremendous pomp and unparalleled throngs. On the Tempelhof parade-ground near Berlin more than a million people gathered together. All the workers in certain industries were marched up in a body without having been asked whether they wanted to or not. However, great numbers certainly also came of their own free will, either out of enthusiasm or curiosity. Hitler's speech disappointed many. It was not one of his best, and, above all, it did not give what many had hoped for — a concrete programme of economic reconstruction and the provision of work. An indication of what was really a very secondary project — the building of motor roads — had an actually irritating effect. The basic idea of his speech was ideological — that manual labour must be raised from the condition of social contempt in which it was still held: " Honour the work and respect the worker! " On the whole this idea probably affected the non-manual workers more strongly — perhaps more romantically — than the actual labourers, who are more concerned with getting a job with a living wage and reasonable hours of work. Thus, in reality, the speech was no more than a means of eluding the social question; a very ill-timed affectation of superiority to the question of food and drink in favour of social dignity — or possibly merely of social courtesy. The *Völkischer Beobachter* had expressed it poetically some years earlier:

> " Brother in gold and silk,
> Brother in fustian,
> Shake hands with one another."

But why there should be this difference, why one should go in silk and another in coarse cloth — not even Hitler on May 1 could explain.

THE "GERMAN LABOUR FRONT"

Behind the splendid scenery of this national holiday, however, gangs were collecting to blow up the Trades Union edifice. On May 2, between ten and eleven in the morning, vans full of SA and SS men pulled up in front of every Trades Union building in the country, occupied the offices and arrested the leaders. Leipart, Grassmann, and the former Labour Minister Wissell were arrested, mishandled, and put into concentration camps. The affair was conducted under the direction of Dr. Ley, chief of the Nazi Party Organization. He published a manifesto in which he said:

" Worker! Your institutions are sacred and inviolable to us National Socialists. I myself am the son of a poor peasant and have known want. Worker! I swear to you that we shall not only keep intact everything that already exists, but we shall also extend still farther the protection and the rights of the worker, so that he may take his place in the new National Socialist State as a precious and valued part of the nation."

This act was a demonstration of considerable power on the part of National Socialism. The Trades Unions had been regarded as inviolable by every previous Government, and now National Socialism took them over without the slightest difficulty. It was an act of revolution without the smallest legal justification. Not the Government co-ordinated the Trades Unions, but the National Socialist Party as such attached them to itself without any opposition from the Government.

All Trades Unions were welded together as a " German Labour Front." It was a militant name, and a curious choice for an organization that was supposed to mark the end of class warfare. At the general congress of this Front in Berlin on May 10 Hitler made a speech in which he urged the workers " to eradicate the impression from among the millions that stood on the other side that they were in any way opposed to the idea of the German nation and its advancement." Then, he continued, those people in Germany who desired only the glory of their nation would find one another.

How simply the social question is then solved: " They will soon manage to understand one another, and if doubts should return and stern reality should play some trick, then it will be the business of the Government to act as an honest intermediary and join again those that were slipping apart."

In the Trade Unions, too, National Socialism has stopped short at the externals of conquest. The various duplicate organizations which resulted from the co-existence of different tendencies were gradually run together, so that by the end of June only fourteen Workers' Unions existed for as many branches. They formed the Workers' Column of the German Labour Front. Ley wanted even to include the employers in his Labour Front; but his one-sided " decree " on this subject had no practical result. The two other pillars of the Labour Front are controlled from above by a central bureau, which is more or less Ley's private office. The actual control is exercised by a " minor labour convention." The representatives of the various unions form the " Major Labour Convention." Ley's old fellow-worker, the Reichstag deputy, Schmeer, acts as his deputy, since Ley is also concerned with the work of Party organization. Besides the Trades Union machinery the old N S B O also remains extant, though with considerably diminished importance, and it is expected to continue its work of propagating the National Socialist ideals in the various trades. Its leader is the Reichstag deputy, Schumann.

Dr. Ley believed that he had made his position secure in the German Labour Front, and expected that it would make him the chief man in the realm after Hitler, possibly even raising him above Göring. In this hope he was thoroughly disappointed. Göring asserted his superiority in various ways. In many cases N S B O leaders who stood up too zealously for the rights of their trade, were sent off to concentration camps. True, the N S B O also sometimes succeeded in having a refractory employer arrested. Ley himself seems to have decided very early that he must compromise with the employers. In an article in the *Völkischer Beobachter* he promised the employers they should be masters in their own houses again if they would in return be servants of the nation. In other words: the National Socialist Trades Unions would not interfere with them so long as they supported the Government politically. He dreamt of making the Labour Front equivalent to the great edifice of Corporations, and of thus controlling the real political life of Germany.

These hopes were destroyed by two events. The Trades Unions lost a great part of their importance owing to a " Law concerning the Trustees of Labour " that the Government passed on May 19. These Trustees whom the Chancellor appointed on the recommendation of the local State Governments for large industrial areas, are to be the " honest brokers " of whom Hitler spoke. This law nullified a despotic action of Ley's who, together with Wagener, the Nazi Trade Commissar, had appointed so-called district managers. The National Socialist Party intended that these district managers should be the final court of appeal in labour disputes, and prevent open conflict. Now the Government reassumed these duties. The Trustees are to take the place of the Trade Unions and Workers' Associations in settling conditions of work " until society shall have been newly organized." Care is to be taken to avoid the two parties regarding one another as class opponents in future; the organizations then existing were not sufficiently mature for this ideal condition. That was serious evidence of Ley's incompetence; and towards the middle of June at the International Labour Conference he gave a second proof of incompetence by his rough and tactless manner, which roused in the hearers partly wrath and partly amusement. Everything that followed was really only the prelude to his inevitable downfall.

The ministerial bureaucracy temporarily destroyed the power of the Trades Unions by this regulation, and at the beginning of July the economic change, of which more will be said, destroyed Ley's hopes for the future. Various instructions were issued that the preliminary work for the organization of Corporations was to be suspended; in fact any discussion of the scheme was finally looked upon as sabotage. Since that time the German Labour Front leads a more representative existence. It has, of course, become a compulsory organization, which at present assures its members their jobs, and repays itself for this service by considerable subscriptions. It has not at present, however, any organic function in the structure of the State; the thirteen Trustees of Labour now do as dictators everything that the huge associations hitherto did by their living pressure. The absolutist and paternal State refuses to allow its workers to use their reasoning powers.

THE AGRARIAN STRUGGLE

In the sphere of agriculture, National Socialism remained in opposition for a considerable time, even after Hitler's coming into office, since the agricultural Ministry had fallen to Hugenberg. Even then the National Socialists had control of numerically the largest peasant organization in the country, the so-called Agrarian-Political Apparatus (*Agrarpolitischen Apparat*) of the National Socialist Party. It seems a curiously cynical name for a society composed of living human beings, and it unconsciously betrays something of the cold lust for power of its creators. At all events this struggle for the key positions was carried on with principles as weapons. Hugenberg wanted to ameliorate the indisputably serious position of German agriculture by raising the prices for agricultural produce. Darré, on the other hand, the leader of the Agrarian Political Apparatus, believed according to good Nazi tradition that the remedy lay in relieving the burdens of rural debt, which he proposed to do by lowering the rate of interest to 2 per cent.

At first Hugenberg carried out his plans quietly. By means of a revision of the system of taxation he forced up the prices for milk and fats sharply even before the Reichstag elections. At the same time he was able to have a regulation passed extending a protection against distraint which already existed in the east of Germany to cover the whole country. Forced sales of land and agricultural implements were — at first only until October 31 — simply prohibited. That the peasantry must be saved and that the rest of the nation must bear the cost was, as a matter of fact, the opinion both of the German Nationals and of the National Socialists. In a speech to the German Board of Agriculture on April 5, Hitler expressed the view that the peasants would be the most important support of the State because they represented the future of the nation. The German nation might exist without its townspeople, but not without its peasants. For their sake the Government must be prepared even to risk a certain unpopularity.

Meanwhile Hugenberg continued to raise the prices and to lighten the burdens as far as possible without destroying credit. By the end of April he had worked out a Bill to free agriculture from its debts, which according to capitalist principles represented nothing more nor less than a legalized breach of contract. Agricultural debts that exceeded a certain maximum were to be arbitrarily lowered by anything up to 50 per cent. of their capital value, and the rate of interest was to be reduced to 4½ per cent. Even this, however, did not satisfy Darré. At a meeting with Hugenberg and his colleague, the Secretary of State von Röhr, he demanded that interest should be lowered to 2 per cent. Hugenberg exclaimed that he had raised the price of milk by one Pfennig and this one Pfennig increase was worth more to agriculture than another 2½ per cent., less interest. They parted without coming to an agreement. Accidentally Schacht was also involved in the dispute, but without any intention of supporting either Hugenberg or Darré. In fact he regarded the drop to 4½ per cent. as too dangerous. Nevertheless, Hugenberg had his way, and his Bill became law on June 1. It was his most notable achievement as a Minister.

"PEASANT NOBILITY"

Meanwhile Darré had been successful in carrying out a plan that he had very much at heart in a place where he exercised more influence. The Prussian Ministry of Justice was in National Socialist hands, and it promulgated a "Hereditary Farms Act" (*Erbhofgesetz*) that had been worked out by him. Its purpose was to create a law of entail for old-established peasant families. The farms were to be kept in particular families indivisibly and inalienably. Thus Darré planned to put an end to the " nomadization of the soil," and to raise up from the peasantry on legally assured farms a " new aristocracy of blood and land " which he regards as the élite of a nation. One of the main purposes of the law was to make it illegal to sell the farms or to mortgage them. Hence it forcibly conferred a benefit upon future generations of peasants even against the wish of the present generation. The law was extended at the end of September to cover the whole of Germany.

This law created for the whole country a form of peasant proprietor which had already existed in some parts by the help of voluntary jurisdiction. It had early roused the interest of lawyers and economists. Lujo Brentano, the celebrated Munich professor of political economy, had in academic controversy proved that the idea of entailed farms was derived from Non-German, Norman influence, while the original German institution was a division of property with equal shares for the younger sons.

Nevertheless, as long as Hugenberg held the administration of agriculture in his hands, this form of law-making did no more than touch the edge of the problem. Darré's chief task was to foster the revolution from below against the German Nationalist Minister. On April 4 he forced the Reich Land Association, which was still the most important agricultural organization, and the Christian Peasant Associations together with his own Political Agrarian Apparatus, into a union at the head of which was a " Reich Association of Leaders of the German Peasantry." Its patron was Hitler; its president Darré, who thus became the leader of the entire German Peasant movement. A month later the National Socialists ejected the president of the Land Association, Count Kalckreuth, from his position for alleged corruption — which charge was afterwards proved to be false — and set Darré's colleague, Meinberg, in his place. The German Board of Agriculture, too, a legal corporation for agrarian affairs, comparable with the Industrial and Commercial Committee that has already been described, elected Darré as its president during the month of May. Thus the whole substructure of German agrarian politics was already in his hands at the end of June when on the field of politics in general the struggle between National Socialists and German Nationalists ended in the downfall of the latter, and Hugenberg retired from the Government.

DARRÉ'S AGRARIAN DICTATORSHIP

Hitler gave Darré , whom he regards as an agricultural reformer on a historic scale, the post of Reich Minister for Food and Prussian Minister for Agriculture. Willikens, a National Socialist Reichstag deputy, became Secretary of State in the Prussian Ministry of Agriculture. In accordance with Hindenburg's wish, Darré was obliged to have von Röhr, a colleague of Hugenberg's, as Secretary of State in the Food Ministry. Backe, a man who enjoyed Darré's special confidence, was made Commissar for special duties in the Food Ministry.

Darré's first act, which made his entry into office truly noteworthy, was his declaration that the promised lowering of interest would not take place. His, Darré's, attitude to Hugenberg's Bill for relieving indebtedness was known, but its immediate repeal was not possible. The truth was that Schmitt, who had been newly appointed Reich Minister of Trade, would never have taken up his post if his colleague on the agricultural side had said anything more about 2 per cent. interest. And the economic condition of Germany was so desperate at the end of June 1933 that Hitler could have more readily spared Darré the reformer than Schmitt the expert; and a Ministry appeared to Darré to be worth 2 per cent. interest.

R. Walther Darré, born in 1895, is like so many of the leading Nazis, a German who was born abroad. He hails from the Argentine. For several years he held posts in the Reich and Prussian State services as an expert on agriculture in the Baltic States. His observation of peasant customs in the northern lands stimulated him to studies upon a problem to which he has given fame as a catchword by his formulation of the connexion between blood and soil. He can almost compete with his colleague Goebbels in the matter of youth, and as regards vanity perhaps he surpasses him. A few days after he had taken office, he permitted the Nassau peasants in the neighbourhood of Wiesbaden, where Darré had written a book about *The Peasantry as the Source of the Nordic Race,* to put up a basalt memorial weighing six tons with the inscription: "R. W. Darré, from the grateful peasantry in his Nassau home." At the dedication of his own memorial, he himself delivered a speech. He takes his office very seriously and in a sentimental spirit. During his summer holiday he prohibited the performance of the operetta *The Jolly Peasant,* because the satirical representations in it were incompatible with the idea that the peasantry was the foundation for the new Germany.

Upon taking up office, Darré announced that it would be his task as a National Socialist to keep the people on the land, indeed to increase the peasantry; the towns were only "consumers of the people." The preservation of nationality was the first reason for which the peasantry must be saved; and the second was the independence of the national food supply. Attention must not be fixed exclusively upon agrarian forces, since by economic means there was no way of preventing the German peasantry from being in exactly the same state again in a few decades' time as they were to-day. In any case, according to the National Socialist conception, not economics but man and civilization were the first considerations. The safeguarding of the peasantry was not a matter of prices but of constitutional law, of peasant law. Thus Darré intends by legal fettering, of which the Hereditary Farms Act is a beginning, to keep the peasants on the land even at a sacrifice to themselves; to make them share in the sacrifices that the nation has to make in order to maintain itself. In other words, he wants to force men to remain peasants even if they no longer wish it. And the real reason is because Germany lost the War largely owing to her inability to provide her own food supply.

On assuming office Darré was under the impression that he could comparatively easily obtain control over the price fluctuations in the corn market. The abundant harvest and the resultant fall in prices in addition to the exclusion of the Jewish middlemen — which has not benefited prices — obliged him to take more forcible measures. A law passed during September gave him the power to unite into what is practically a coercive association as a "Reich Corporation of Food Producers and Consumers (*Reichsnährstand*)" not only the peasants but also the consumers. The Minister has, above all, the power to dictate the prices of rye and wheat and to limit the area to be put under cultivation. This power was so contrary to Hitler's favourite idea of the freedom of industry that at Schmitt's request the Government was obliged to make a soothing announcement to the effect that no such regulation was purposed for the rest of industry. Agriculture, whose debts have already been put into cold storage by the Government, has now also come out of the natural current of industry as regards prices.

Industry is to be free — but agriculture has a dictator.

"NO LAND SETTLEMENT"

Darré expressed himself carefully about peasant settlements and the ownership of large estates. He thought that many a landowner might prefer to be free of a debt-ridden estate and have instead a hereditary peasant property. But Hugenberg's protection against distraint and his mortgage laws have put many an estate that was *in extremis* on its legs again. Never has so little land been offered as in 1933 in the estate market of Eastern Germany, which was formerly flooded with land on which the mortgages were overdue. Hence the Pomeranian District leader of the National Socialist Party, State Councillor Karpenstein, shortly and sharply required his estate-owners voluntarily to put land at his disposal. The East Prussian landowners had providently declared themselves ready to do so without any public demand, but had made it a condition that the native tenant farmers should have first choice. On the whole, the National Socialist land settlement is not turning out according to the announcement of Kube, the Lord-Lieutenant of Brandenburg, who promised a settlement programme " more important than the peasant emancipation of Baron von Stein." Rather does the official policy follow the advice of Göring, who declared before the Pomeranian Land Association at Stettin that his common-sense view of the matter was: " There should not be settlements made on the one hand and destruction allowed on the other. The first care should be to preserve what already exists."

These were words that endeared Göring to the large estate-owners. He followed up his words by a symbolic act on August 28 in giving the Reich President Field-Marshal von Hindenburg, in addition to what he already possessed, the national domain of Langenau. It was a gift that Hitler then made doubly valuable by granting freedom from taxation for as long as the estate remained in the possession of the male line of the Hindenburg family.

FORWARD TOWARDS THE EAST

The settlement of Eastern Germany with peasants instead of landowners is one of the most popular economic ideals in Germany. The difficulties are generally underrated. National Socialist agitators have freely made use of the idea of settlement as a slogan. The authorities, however, especially Hitler, held back, though indeed for an unexpected reason. Thus Hitler wrote in his book:

" For us Germans any talk of ' internal colonization ' is deplorable, if only because it strengthens the opinion that we have found a means of making our living in a peaceful dreamy state, which accords well with the pacifist type of mind. This scheme, which was at first taken seriously by us, implies the end of all efforts to preserve the place in this world that beseems us. . . . Not that such a policy could be carried out satisfactorily in the Cameroons, for example. Nowadays Europe is almost our only possibility. The matter must be looked at coldly and with common sense. It can certainly not be the intention of Heaven that one nation should have fifty times as much land as another. In this case political boundaries must not distract our eyes from the boundaries of eternal justice. If there is really space on this earth for every one to live, then we should be given the ground that is necessary for us to live on."

Thus the " policy of settlement " of National Socialism does not consist in the development and parcelling out of Eastern German estates, but in the conquest of fresh land in Eastern Europe. Conquest is not an idea before which Hitler blenches. For he says in the same part of the book:

" Either the world will be ruled according to the ideas of our modern democracy, and then every decision will fall in favour of the numerically strongest peoples; or the world will be ruled according to the natural laws of force, in which case those nations will be victorious that have the more savage will-power; nor will it be those who keep within their own boundaries. Nobody can doubt that mankind will still have to go through fearful struggles for existence. Ultimately only the instinct of self-preservation counts. Beside it so-called humane feelings that are a blend of stupidity, cowardice, and priggishness melt away like snow before the spring sun. Humanity has grown great by perpetual warfare — it would perish in an eternal peace."

The whole train of thought proceeds from a false premiss, for Hitler is supposing that in the course of a century the German nation will increase to two hundred and fifty millions. Actually, however, the German nation is not increasing with such primitive fecundity, but is slowly decreasing. According to the calculations of the Reich Statistical Office it will only be about fifty million strong by 1980; thereby Hitler's land policy is deprived of all reason. And as regards perpetual warfare — possibly even Hitler has now realized that as a result of the most recent improvements in scientific warfare the German population curve would have a much greater chance in such a struggle of inclining sharply downwards than in a state of " unnatural " peace.

THE SMALL SHOP LOSES THE FIGHT

Only a few of the more salient points of the economic policy of the National Socialist State can here be touched upon. The most important event of the year for Germany as for the rest of the world was the failure of the London World Economic Conference at the end of July. It ruined the greatest economic chance of Hitler's government — the hope that its beginning would coincide with the natural revival of world trade. This revival neither appeared in the world market nor by means of a miracle in the German home market. German foreign trade fell off to some extent, partly as a result of political boycott, but probably largely as a result of increasing autarchic tendencies in the whole world.

Hence Dr. Schacht, the president of the Reichsbank, after unavailing conferences with Germany's foreign creditors, announced on July 8 a German refusal of payment, which was called a transfer moratorium. This meant in effect that Germany would no longer pay the interest on the greater part of her foreign debts. Individual debtors within the country were, nevertheless, expected to produce interest and amortization. The amount received was by means of the so-called "Script system" used to give the German exporters a subsidy in order that they might lower their prices and undersell their foreign competitors. This opportunity of dumping was further exploited by the formation of cartels.

In general, Hitler left the conduct of economic policy to Hugenberg during the first few months of his rule. The struggle for power at that time probably seemed to him more important than economic stabilization, and he was also acting up to his principle that politics are more important than economics. "Capital is useful to trade, and trade is useful to the people," was the somewhat banal statement of his economic doctrine in his Reichstag speech on March 23. The National Socialists applauded tumultuously. As regards economic methods, however: "In principle the Government will not push on the revival of the economic interests of the nation by means of a State-organized economic bureaucracy, but by the strongest encouragement of private initiative and the recognition of private property." After these words the Reichstag report no longer records a storm of enthusiasm among the brown shirts, but "lively applause from the Right and the Centre." Hitler was giving capitalism a chance to prove itself.

As long as Hugenberg was in office the economic activity of the National Socialists consisted mainly in an aggressive policy on the part of its middle-class organizations. Department stores and co-operative stores were boycotted and brought to the verge of ruin. Every now and then their managers were arrested and those who insisted on shopping there were exposed to the most severe terrorization. This destruction of live economic bodies was called the creation of Corporations — it was a serious jeopardizing of the idea. As late as May 31 Hitler promised representatives of the middle classes who were clamouring for results that a law outlining the principles on which the Corporations were to be organized should be promulgated immediately. Nevertheless, he indicated even then that too great hopes should not be built on it; that living things could not be pressed into fixed moulds; that these Corporations must grow organically from below. While the middle-class leaders wanted to destroy the department stores, and ignorant local Governments, regarding only popularity, were supporting them, the Reich Government was trying to preserve the posts of the employees, and gave the department stores credits from Government money to the total of many millions of Marks. And in this case, as in other undertakings, no one seems to have thought of dispossessing the erstwhile owners by taking over the shares at a greater or less compensation.

The desire of the National Socialist State not to come into conflict with the great powers of industry for the sake of the middle classes is reflected in the medley of laws and their application. A law for the protection of the middle classes that had already been submitted to the Trade Ministry by the middle of March, and which would have satisfied the small retailers, remained only paper. What actually came at the beginning of April was a law entitled "For the Protection of Retail Trade," the most important clause of which prohibited the establishment of new retail businesses as branches until November 1, 1933. Refreshment rooms and workshops in the department stores were closed down. A law dated July 15 empowered the various States to introduce a tax on department stores. Prussia, however, the largest of the States, made no use of the permission. And to round off the immeasurable disappointment of the middle classes properly, Hess, the deputy leader of the National Socialist Party and Hitler's most confidential fellow-worker, published an announcement on July 7, which ran:

"The attitude of the National Socialist Party to the question of the department stores remains unaltered in principle. A solution will be found for it when the right time comes in the sense of the National Socialist programme. In view of the general economic situation, the Party leaders feel that they are not at present called upon to proceed towards the destruction of department stores and similar undertakings. Hence members of the National Socialist Party are forbidden until further notice to engage in any action against department stores or similar undertakings."

Ley defended still more forcefully the co-operative societies that had before been exposed to such hatred. Since the "co-ordination" these belonged to the Labour Front. Thereby the National Socialists suddenly had an interest in them as in so many other things that they had cheerfully combated before their advent to power. As late as May 29, Ley asked his friends for nothing but a little time in which to " wind up " the co-operative societies organically. Meanwhile, he said, he had already done various things: " I have arranged that within a week all posts are as far as possible to be filled with convinced National Socialists." After this act of reformation everything followed logically as it was bound to. On July 5 Ley was already fulminating fiercely against the attacks on the co-operative societies by the Fighting Association of the Middle Classes: " That such actions would leave half a million people starving seems to be a matter of indifference to these selfish individuals." Finally, on July 19, the Reich Minister for Trade, in collaboration with the Chancellor, declared in an official circular to the local State Governments ". . . that there were now no political reasons against the continued existence of the co-operative societies." When the time came, measures would be taken to effect a compromise with the interests of the middle classes.

The co-operative societies and the department stores were saved for the time being; and the middle classes were the poorer of another hope.

FOOD IS MORE IMPORTANT THAN CO-ORDINATION

Meanwhile the great political change had taken place that cost Hugenberg his office on June 27. His successor as Minister of Trade was Dr. Kurt Schmitt, the managing director of the Alliance Insurance Company, who had not been a member of the National Socialist Party for very long. He certainly was more in sympathy with Hitler than many of the other representatives of industry, but might, nevertheless, be reckoned as one of them. A new man who enjoyed the confidence of industry had been urgently needed. After March 5 many industrialists had taken heart and looked forward to an approaching stability. This was proved by an activity on the Stock Exchange such as had not been seen for a very long time. Then, however, came a serious reverse. This was partly due to the hostility of foreign countries, which was particularly marked after the boycott of the Jews on April 1, of which more will be said; but more particularly was it due to foreign anxiety, to rumours of war, to the licence of the SA and the militarist associations, and to Hitler's obvious incapacity to keep his people in check. Confidence was shattered, and this was again shown by the quotations on the Stock Exchange. The entry of Schmitt into the Government, therefore, began with a general purgation of the Party's economic advisers and a solemn renunciation of the " Revolution."

Hitler announced the renunciation in three speeches that may be likened in significance to Lenin's declaration discarding militant Communism and introducing the new economic policy. At first Hitler declared at a meeting of SA leaders in Reichenhall on July 2 that there were four phases to the National Socialist Revolution: 1. Preparation; 2. Achievement of political power; 3. Creation of the totalitarian State (which was obviously to be set aside again); 4. Solution of the unemployment problem, upon which all forces must now be concentrated, for it was decisive for the victory. He would, however, he continued, oppose ruthlessly any so-called Second Revolution, for it would only lead to chaos — this was a reprimand to Goebbels and the Bavarian Minister Wagener, who had proclaimed the Second Revolution.

On July 7 Hitler told the Reich Governors at the Chancellery that revolution was not a permanent condition. And " an economist must not be dismissed if he is a good economist but not yet a National Socialist; especially if the National Socialist who is to take his place does not understand anything about economics. We shall not provide food for any worker by theoretical co-ordination. We shall not abolish unemployment by industrial commissions, organizations, constructions, and theories. This is not a matter of programmes and ideas, but of the daily bread of seventy million people."

That was a confession of faith in materialism; and the primacy of economics was thus casually recognized by Hitler. He then went on to call the revolutionaries germ-carriers who forced their way into industry — presumably he meant the germ-carriers of Communism — and continued: " Practical experience must not be set aside because it conflicts with a particular theory. If we come before the nation with reforms we must also show that we understand facts and are able to master them " — a consideration that might not have been out of place even before January 30, but certainly came too late after it;

for true dilettantism is not to be taught by adversity. It could not be tolerated, said Hitler, that certain organizations or positions in the Party should arrogate to themselves governmental functions, dismissing and appointing men — a sharp reprimand to Ley and Renteln. " The Party," Hitler concluded, " has now become the State. All power lies with the Government. The centre of gravity of German life must be prevented from being again placed in individual sections or organizations. No authority can any longer come from any individual part of the realm, but only from the German nation."

These last sentences were also intended to be noted by Göring, who was making such parade of his rule over Prussia. In a third speech to the District Leaders and the Trustees of Labour on July 13, Hitler repeated his commination, and said that it was a principle of the National Socialist Party " not to fill a post unless some individual of proved capacity was at their disposal." The existence of certain organizations was no proof of their capacity.

Schmitt then passed on these principles to the industrialists by way of comfort and reassurance in a speech which he also made on July 13. He informed them officially that the creation of Corporations " which must of course come to pass in our country, and whose non-existence is felt very severely at this particular juncture, has for the moment been stopped and set aside because of the danger that a great number of unauthorized persons were trying experiments in connexion with it." It was a series of humiliations that the National Socialist leaders of the middle class had to listen to in the presence of those whom they led. Schmitt also assured himself the decisive influence upon the Government's social policy. Seldte could do nothing now without his consent.

This was expressly stated in an announcement about the middle of July. In addition Seldte had to agree to an expressedly pro-employer official being sent over from the Ministry of Trade to the Ministry of Labour. This man, Dr. Pohl, took over the direction of Section IIIB (Social and Wages policy), which also controls the Labour Trustees. It is by far the most important section, indeed the heart of the Ministry. At the same time Pohl remained an official at the Ministry of Trade. This event, which was almost entirely suppressed from the public, is one of the most important in the National Socialist reconstructive policy.

FROZEN INDUSTRY

The romance of the "Corporative Construction" fell a victim to the troubles of the day. Nevertheless, the interests that lay concealed behind the catchword had their benefit of it. Industry, which was no longer fit for free competition, demanded that its existence should be assured. The new State was the less able to find fault with this demand, since it had expected it to employ an uneconomic number of people in order to combat unemployment. Industry hoped to balance it by guaranteed and, if possible, rising prices.

Hence on July 15 a law was promulgated concerning the establishment of compulsory cartels, which, in cases where the interests of the community demanded it, gave the Minister for Trade the power to form compulsory cartels, and to forbid the establishment of new undertakings as well as the extension of existing businesses in any particular branch of industry. On the other hand, he was also, by an alteration in the existing cartel regulations, given the power to dissolve existing cartels without a judicial procedure. This was a corrective to exaggeration. The first law, however, was of much greater importance. The Minister has hardly ever had to make use of his power; the mere threat of the law has practically always been enough to make the recalcitrant outsider come to heel. Thus from the time of the promulgation of the law until the late autumn some three hundred cartels have come into existence in all possible branches of industry, often with the avowed purpose of raising prices, as in the paper, building materials, and textile industries. There is even a "central station for the German Carp Market" in Breslau. The index number for the wholesale trade in articles of consumption rose from 109.2 in April to 113.3 in September. In the textile industry the prices of individual goods went up by 50 or more per cent. This grew so unbearable that trade and industry finally formed a committee to regulate prices, which succeeded for the time being in putting a stop to the rise.

"LABOUR WAR"

By concentrating all the forces of the Party upon the provision of work, Hitler and Schmitt thought they were deflecting them from revolution. Nevertheless, the Revolution of National Socialism remains revolutionary in every sphere, and turns everything that it touches into a piece of itself.

The National Socialist district lords hurled themselves into the "Labour War," formed "fronts" against unemployment, conquered "sections," and exhorted their men to bind their helmets more firmly after the "victory." As proofs of energy and idealism these Labour Wars are certainly marvellous. Moral pressure — and the idea of morality must be taken in a wide sense here — was brought to bear upon employers to employ workers even if the condition of industry did not justify it. Enthusiasts ventured upon investments that would have been rejected as impossible in normal times or even under the "November State." At a time when a full month's supply of coal and coke lay unsold at the pit heads, Thyssen began on the construction of a double pit at Walsum. Mines that had been idle were put in work, and on the other hand many machines were stopped so that hand-workers might be employed. This happened, for example, in the Thuringian bottle industry and — by an Act of Parliament — in the cigar industry. Real buoyancy was shown in the building industry, which was animated by the matrimonial loans, and which again gave work to many providers of raw materials. Employment was given in the textile industries by the demands for the new uniforms of the SA and N S B O men.

To a great extent employment was created by shortening the working week to forty hours — an old suggestion of the Independent Trade Unions, to which most of the employers had previously refused to accede. Now they did so under compulsion. The wages of those already in employment were, of course, thereby lowered.

The greatest economic high-handedness took place in the eastern provinces, where East Prussia, Pomerania, and Silesia vied with one another which should first be free of unemployment. The unemployed were partly used to reclaim land in swampy and loamy districts, and partly as labourers on large and medium-sized estates. Here they came in as cheap labour with no wages, sometimes even with financial assistance from the Government. During the harvest in East Prussia, since the nomadic Polish workers who had previously done it were no longer admitted, the need of workmen was so great that first-year and second-year students were compulsorily employed as harvesters. This explains the apparently brilliant results of the Eastern German provision of work during the summer weeks. An embittered struggle, which represents the new, in a sense National Socialist, form of class-warfare, will begin when the employers want to dismiss these agricultural labourers again and the National Socialist Party refuses to allow them to do so.

By means of " political dismissal " of " Marxists " many posts have undoubtedly been opened to workers who are true to the system, especially SA men. The local Party organizations have everywhere urged that the deserving Party warriors shall be given employment. A centralized Party activity at the same time was concerned with getting all SA men numbered from one to one hundred thousand into work at all costs. In the course of the summer the statistically proved number of unemployed fell by some 2.4 millions. There are certainly some sources of error in the calculation, but this says nothing against the formal good faith of the compilers: the removal of " enemies of the State " from unemployment insurance; severest application of the regulation that members of a family cannot all receive public assistance; artificial control of the fluctuations in the labour market, whereby dismissals that in normal times, even when there was a general increase in unemployment, occurred frequently are simply prohibited by the local authorities of the National Socialist Party.

To an overwhelming extent the provision of work in Germany in the year 1933 meant the occupation of the unemployed in work of small productivity and at correspondingly low wages; further, a distribution of what productive work there was among a larger number of people; and finally, to a small extent, simply the exchange of people in various posts. The attempt must be admitted to be reasonable up to a point, though this point was often not seen and far overstepped by those in authority. The very unseasonable ambition of the District Leaders and Lord-Lieutenants in the eastern provinces, with their "notifications of victory," such as "East Prussia free of unemployed," occasioned a sharp reprimand from the Minister of Trade, Dr. Schmitt. At a congress in Cologne of the Rhenish Labour Front he said on August 13 that such announcements of victory could not solve the real problem of the abolition of unemployment; that in industry there was no going from one victory to another; and that the worst thing that could happen would be a reverse, which the new German Reich could not survive. When Koch, the Lord-Lieutenant of Prussia, refused to be damped by this castigation, but telegraphed the complete abolition of unemployment in East Prussia to Hindenburg and Hitler, the Chancellor, it is true, congratulated him heartily, but added acidly: "I also wish you complete success in your work of safeguarding the object you have attained."

How completely former ideas on economics were destroyed during the Labour War is shown in an announcement by the Eastern and Western Prussian Employers' Union at the beginning of August, in which they state — perhaps a trifle forcedly — that the Unions "enthusiastically welcome the measures introduced by the Lord-Lieutenant. They are determined emphatically to urge all the industries within their control to let no petty hesitations prevent their engaging fresh personnel over and above what is at the moment necessary and economic."

The violent and overhasty pressing of workmen into a halting industrial concern which was done by the local authorities of the Party was in tendency and desire nothing more nor less than a continued rebellion against the cold and methodical economic thought of the Berlin central authorities. Koch was an old pupil and follower of Gregor Strasser's. Not only he, however, but also the great mass of the Nazi leaders regard economic matters as the Leader regarded them in his great Reichstag speech of May 1932: It should be possible to demand of industry to supply work and food for every one. Schmitt will also have to learn to think like this if he is going to be able to maintain himself.

INFLATION?

Hitler's acquiescence in capitalism is only an acceptance of a temporary expedient, but not of a dogma. For National Socialists dogmas exist only in the domain of politics and never in the subordinate domain of economics. The indecisiveness of National Socialism in economic questions originates in an idealistic and, in the deepest sense of the word, non-material point of view. It is also the reason why the calculating moderation of the Minister Schmitt and the positively destructive pugnacity of the District Leaders can subsist side by side and get on together in the Labour War. It is not only the promises of National Socialist Germany that are opposed to one another in an economic competition, and sometimes in actual economic hostility. The individual branches of industry and the Corporations demand besides special privileges special positions in the social reconstruction, such as, for example, is demanded by the compulsorily syndicalized agriculture. It is a division of Germany into economic provinces, spatially and materially, which is reminiscent of the struggle between Marshals and provinces in China.

On assuming office Schmitt had found in existence a programme for the provision of work which had been passed by the Cabinet on June 1. Its special points were: the granting of loans to married people, which would take money out of the labour market and would animate the building trade together with the related industries; further, freedom from taxation for those who have repairs done; and finally — Hitler's favourite plan, which probably has also some military purpose — the building of great motor-roads. The means for all this were to be supplied, according to the idea of Reinhardt, the National Socialist Secretary of State in the Treasury, by using national funds to the extent of one milliard Marks (fifty million pounds at par; at present nearly seventy-seven million pounds).

This milliard-programme, however, only comprises a fraction of the sums which have gradually been pumped into German industry by the creation of a credit account for the artificial provision of work. Under Brüning a programme of this description had been drawn up at the conservative estimate of 135 million Marks; Papen wanted 207; and Gereke, the Commissar for the provision of Labour (under

Schleicher and during Hitler's first few months), brought it up to 600 millions. The State railways entered upon the year 1933 with a programme of 280 millions, and the Post Office required 34 millions. Some 500 millions were supplied in the year 1932–33 from State finances and from the moneys of the Institution for Unemployment Insurance. To this was now added Hitler's Reinhardt's one milliard programme, and two new programmes from the State Railway for 560 millions and the Post Office for 76 million Marks. That adds up to a grand total of 3.39 milliards. If this is added to Papen's famous tax bills, which anticipate the prosperity of future years, then it comes to a round sum of four milliard Marks. The burden of this ambiguous blessing fortunately did not fall all at once upon German industry. It would otherwise already be struggling with an inflation. Nevertheless, no amount of manipulation and distribution will avail in the long-run if there is not a natural animation of artificial values which turns them into real ones.

Schacht applied the brake from the beginning. At the end of September Schmitt sent off his colleague, Gottfried Feder, who after long delay had become Secretary of State under him, and who was continually making plans of this description, on a research tour in Italy. Besides the public creation of credit, a more subtle credit support was now sought. The Reichsbank altered its statutes and bought up stock certificates which henceforward were to be used to cover issues of notes. The aim was to make prices go up on the Stock Exchange and to awaken public confidence; idle money would thereby be attracted and be turned into fruitful capital. The Reichsbank must indeed know from the example of America in 1932 that the result may be the exact contrary: that the public will sell its papers to the Reichsbank and thus increase still further the amount of idle capital. A protection against this is to be the tacit threat of inflation which is inherent in the whole procedure. For the Reichsbank is to be able to finance the new business indicated in the alteration of its statutes by the issue of notes. The plan was intended to tranquillize industry and to consolidate confidence. The most helpful thing, said Schmitt at Munich on September 26, was to know oneself to be under the firm leadership of Hitler.

Hitler's name covers many various financial adventures. While the revenue from taxation was going down, Goebbels, in a struggle on an imposing scale " against cold and hunger," tried to get no less than 300 million Marks out of industry as a freewill offering. No eastern potentate ever organized the system of compulsory gifts on so vast a scale as National Socialism. It is an achievement which nobody can deny. Even National Socialists, however, could not at the beginning of the autumn honestly deny that though the condition of the Labour market had been changed the people in general were no better off. The statement published by the Treasury regarding the income of the Reich from April to August 1933 tells its own story. According to this, the yield from the tax on turnover compared with that during the same period in the previous year went up by 54 million Marks, that on the forwarding of goods by 2.6 millions. On the other hand, the income tax went down by 35.7 millions, the tobacco duty by 13 millions, and the beer duty by 15.7 millions. The deduction is obvious: there was increased activity in business but it was less lucrative. Production and turnover increased, but the total income, the spending power of the people, diminished. Upon the deceptive increase in the production of textiles in the summer followed, as is shown in the departmental reports, a reaction. The final buyer, the consumer, failed to materialize; the retail traders had their stores full, could give no further orders, and production should be lessening. But this is impossible, because the system has announced that no man shall lose his job.

Hence things must inevitably go from bad to worse. A strong State, however, can survive a great deal of misery in its subjects. Whether prices rise in Germany and thus decrease the participation of the consumer in the social product; or whether the prices are forcibly kept down and thus wages are lowered — in any case, Germany, which has been seriously shut off from the flow of world trade, is steering towards a form of life which Schacht — the only one among the responsible men to do so — has described with some frankness as: " Industrial self-denial and a readiness to do with a smaller amount of luxuries." Schacht said this after the failure of the World Economic Conference in London on July 31 in a speech over the wireless to America. He added that many people in Germany were already working voluntarily at a low salary for the good of the community, and he demanded also that work should be provided for the poorer classes by higher taxation of the wealthier. The demand for social justice contained in the last words should not be belittled, but it is permissible to note that it has unfortunately been raised at a time of general want, in which nothing but the exceeding kindliness and goodwill of the proletarianized masses prevents a ghastly social revolution. Schacht's words also show that he had less confidence in private initiative on July 31 than Hitler had on March 23. He says nothing about nursing capital by saving it from taxation and encouraging investment. The fact is that between the two dates the idea of capital initiative had lost the Battle of London. Meanwhile Hitler had indeed spoken strongly against simplicity and frugality to the General Committee of German Industry. But if his words are carefully examined and such expressions as "jealous nature" are found, his meaning is at once plain: he is less anxious for a higher general level of requirement than for higher individual requirements and satiation points. What he really wants is a difference between rich and poor, because that spurs men to action. For the average man, however, self-denial and small wages remain the ideals of National Socialism. Its State of the future rests upon general poverty relieved by enthusiasm and maintained by terrorization. It is the mighty State of economic slovenliness.

LABOUR SERVICE

A singular organization in the great sham fight against unemployment is the Labour Service. Even before Hitler's advent attempts had been made to give work to young unemployed men on road-building and land-improvement schemes. The National Socialists have always demanded that this voluntary labour service shall be made compulsory; hitherto this has not been done.[1] It is nevertheless true that the compulsion that is exercised on certain of the youthful unemployed is an effective substitute for statutory compulsion.

The conduct of the Labour Service is at present in the hands of Colonel Konstantin Hierl, a Nazi Reichstag deputy. A "decree for

[1] This has now been made compulsory (Tr.).

preparation for compulsory labour service," published on May 3, ordered that skeleton corps of unemployed should be set up for the Labour Service. Sixty per cent. of the men in them were to be National Socialists or members of the Stahlhelm, and must have belonged to these associations before January 30, 1933. Only Nazis or Stahlhelm men might hold commissions, i.e. become leaders of the Labour corps. Since July 25, when the Stahlhelm lost its independence in this sphere as in others, there has only been the National Socialist "Reich Association of German Labour Service Unions." Hierl announced several times that compulsory labour service would begin on January 1, 1934, and that all whose nineteenth birthday came during the year 1934 would be liable. The whole year's numbers would not be called up all at once, but would be divided into two half-year lots, so that there would always be 270,000 men in the service. No German was to come into the enjoyment of full civic rights until he had done his labour service. The whole project was to be "a happy mixture of soldierliness, work, and youth." Of the skeleton corps now set up, each is to be subdivided into six corps on December 1, 1934, three of which are to be "leaders" corps and three volunteers, i.e. men. These are, then, to be divided up among the various depots, and will form the nucleus of the compulsory labour service. By December 1 there are to be 620 such corps.

It has often been asked what work these labour corps are actually to do. Before January 30, 1933, the members of the labour corps really did work very hard. The so-called field exercises and other military sports which were practised in their spare time did not play an important part. Nowadays they are probably practised more assiduously in many of the camps. Nevertheless the cost is too great to allow of their general use. A man like Colonel Hierl certainly looks upon the labour service as a preparation for military training. He has said so quite openly. But labour service is not yet actual military training.

The whole problem of the labour service is a question of money. Whence the means are to be found to carry it on is certainly a problem of no small difficulty. Even the funds of the Republic were sometimes barely visible; those of the Third Reich are even less so.

CHAPTER XV

CROSS AGAINST SWASTIKA

THE CO-ORDINATION OF PROTESTANTISM

THE NATIONAL SOCIALIST REVOLUTION has won a victory in the domain of the Church that is as decisive externally as it is doubtful internally. In his Reichstag speech on March 23 Hitler pointed out to the Churches how the political and moral purification of public life by National Socialism would at the same time ensure the need of religious life. "The National Government," he said, "regards the two Christian Confessions as important factors in the preservation of our nationality. It will respect the treaties made between them and the States. But it hopes and expects that its work for the moral and ethical renewal of the German nation will be equally respected by the Churches. The right of the Churches to co-operate in education will be assured and guaranteed." Furthermore, he said that the Government attached the greatest possible value to a continuation and development of friendly relations with the Holy See.

If the Bishops and Superintendents took hope from such statements and trusted that National Socialism would not interfere in the life of the Church, they had not realized Hitler's unique moral capacity whereby the Chancellor might make promises that the Party Leader need not keep. The Government might indeed define its policy; but the National Socialist Revolution coming from below interfered with its execution. The Chancellor negotiated with the Churches; but the fact that the Revolution led by the Party Leader forced its way into the Churches and reorganized them peaceably or with violence was no concern of the Chancellor's. In the Totalitarian State nothing matters except the will of the Leader. But the State has a variety of forms and depends not only upon the authority from above but also upon the pressure from below. Hence the Leader's will must also be polymorphous and must, according as necessity demands, make this authority felt or again yield gracefully to the pressure from below. And he must always preserve the appearance of a uniformity which does not really exist. The real mistake is made by the credulous people who expect so contradictory a personage as a constitutional revolutionary to keep his promises. A Totalitarian State cannot take permanent form because it changes as quickly as life itself changes. This distinguishes it from the Constitutional State, which at least in principle does not break its own laws. In any case an attentive ear must have heard that Hitler only valued the Churches in a very limited sense — as assistants in the preservation of nationality; looked at from a clerical point of view, that is, in a purely subsidiary matter.

The National Socialist Revolution was carried into the Protestant Church in Germany by the so-called religious movement of the " German Christians " which began in June 1932. At the head of it was the radical pastor Hossenfelder, who is the champion of " German " Lutheranism as opposed to " foreign " Calvinism. It cannot be denied that a radical Church movement was needed, for the Protestant Churches in Germany had to a great extent become a bureaucracy of ecclesiastical officials and theologians, and the churches were often empty. On the other hand, it could not possibly be for the spiritual benefit of the people that this condition should be externally and possibly only temporarily overcome by the " co-ordination " demanded by the German Christians. There was enough and to spare of the National Socialist spirit outside the Church. If the Church wanted to keep any significance it must remain evangelical, which is in the profoundest sense something very different.

On the whole the men who have hitherto been leaders of the Protestant Church could and can rely on being supported by the majority of religious people. And the German Christians assert that they and they alone can bring back those who are not religious — and they are the important ones — into the Church.

The power of resistance of the Protestant conscience to Hossenfelder was sufficiently great among German theologians to induce National Socialism to give way. Hitler removed Hossenfelder from office and appointed Ludwig Müller, a chaplain in the Reichswehr and a personal friend of his from East Prussia, as supreme head of the German Christians. At a " religious discussion " which lasted for three days (May 16–19) at the former Friesian monastery of Lokkum, Müller conceded the freedom of the Church from State tutelage. Thereupon the Church authorities in Berlin elected a noted theologian, Friedrich von Bodelschwingh, the bearer of a name famous in Church history, as Reich Bishop on May 26. This showed how much the freedom of the Church was worth. Hitler refused Bodelschwingh, and the Prussian Minister of Public Worship, Rust, at the urgent request of Göring, appointed a " Church Commissar " in the person of a civil servant named Jäger, who deposed the high officials of the Church by the might of the secular arm, and appointed Müller to be leader of the German Evangelical Church Union. Bodelschwingh resigned, and on Sunday, July 2, swastika flags were run up on the Protestant Churches.

Jäger had gone too far. The harassed Church found an advocate in the President, who received Hitler on his East Prussian estate of Neudeck on June 29, and remonstrated with him seriously not only regarding Church affairs. He went so far as to record his displeasure in writing in an open letter containing the first reprimand that the President ever gave his National Socialist Chancellor. He referred to his " anxiety for the inner freedom of the Church "; " the most serious harm must come to people and Fatherland, and national freedom must suffer " if the present state of affairs continued or was even possibly intensified. He demanded that these high-handed proceedings should cease and that peace should be re-established in the Protestant Church by negotiation. At least secretly, Hitler probably disapproved of Göring's and Jäger's arbitrary actions. He obeyed Hindenburg's command and put the conduct of the negotiations into Frick's gentler hands. The most truculent party to the quarrel, Pastor Hossenfelder, had already resigned the leadership of the German Christians in favour of Müller; and was now removed from the post of clerical vice-president of the Supreme Consistorial Council which he had only occupied for a few days. This was a concession to those who had hitherto been leaders of the Church. A second was the rescinding of Müller's autocratic announcement that new " co-ordinated " Church assemblies were to be appointed by the authorities. Even the Aryan clause was dropped in so far as the Church membership of the individual was concerned; but it still holds, nevertheless, for the clergy. The independence of the various local State Churches in creed and worship was maintained, but to the Lutherans was conceded that a Lutheran Reich Bishop should be at the head of all the Churches. The spirit of the existing Church was preserved in the formula that it would act " in accordance with the Bible and the Reformed Faith." The German Christians, however, made their influence felt in the formulation of the aim to be followed: " Its particular care will be devoted to the development of German nationalism." On July 13 Hitler announced to the President that the work of conciliation was complete. On July 14 the Commissar Jäger and his sub-commissars retired, a number of dismissals were revoked, and on July 23 the elections for the Church assemblies took place.

These elections served to quieten the conscience of the old President, who, however dictatorial his actions may be, is determined to be sure in his own mind that he has not broken his oath to the Constitution. Actually these elections were even less free than those for the Reichstag on March 5. It was impossible to canvass publicly for the election platform " Church and Gospel " which was set up by those who advocated the freedom of the Church as against the German Christians. The wireless was at the exclusive disposal of the German Christians. Although a Catholic, Hitler himself spoke in their favour, and in many districts the supporters of the existing Church dared not officially appear against the Party which had the SA on its side. In Frankfurt-am-Main a number of pastors were brave enough to declare openly that it was impossible to carry on the electorial campaign with complete freedom and objectivity. In many cases joint lists were set up by the parties on which the German Christian candidates had an overwhelming majority from the very beginning. In places where they were known to be the weaker party they nevertheless had 51 per cent. of the names on the joint lists — in Hamburg and Württemburg, for example. None the less, the victory of the German Christians, which was numerically indisputable, was not so complete as Hossenfelder's furious propaganda had led people to expect. They did not get their two-thirds majority everywhere.

The reorganization of the Protestant Church was once again interrupted. In the Old Prussian State Church, which is the largest ecclesiastical body in Protestant Germany, the German Christians carried all before them. On August 5 they had Müller elected president of the Supreme Consistorial Council by the Church Senate with the title of " State Bishop," and Hossenfelder was again appointed clerical Vice-President. A month later the general synod of this Church adopted the Aryan clause for the clergy. The General Superintendents, who are the highest ecclesiastical authorities in the country, ventured on gentle protests, and the " Church and Gospel " group issued such a sharp counter-declaration through their pastor, Dr. Koch, that the German Christians shouted them down and threatened physical reprisals. The minority, which had actually spoken of an " offence to their confession of faith," were obliged to flee from the room.

Outwardly the struggle was at an end. On September 27 the National Synod at Wittenberg unanimously elected Müller as Reich Bishop. In his speech after the election he said: " We have no intention of tearing asunder the supertemporal unity of the Church of Christ, the community of work and sacrament, even with those who belong to other races. But equality before God does not exclude inequality among men, which, after all, is caused by the will of God."

There is still bitter opposition to this anti-Protestant casuistry in the Church. It was expressed in a magnificent declaration by the Marburg theologians, in a memorial signed by two thousand pastors, and finally in a pamphlet entitled "*I say no*" by the Bonn theologian, Karl Barth, which aroused much interest. It is the " no " of a clergyman who has a higher regard for his conscience than for politics, and who " fears God more than men."

ROME EVADES THE ISSUE

National Socialism as a fighting creed had once been dogmatically outlawed by the Catholic bishops. The Catholic Chancellor, Hitler, had, in common with Goebbels, taken his revenge at the great ceremony in Potsdam on March 21, by ostentatiously not attending the Catholic service, and, instead, laying a wreath upon the graves in the Luisenstadt cemetery in Berlin of SA men who had been killed. Among the German Christians it was even rumoured that Hitler was about to become a Protestant. That was coldly and abruptly denied.

The Church at least hastened to remove its ban on National Socialism. The Bishops' Conference at Fulda published a pronouncement on March 28 in which acknowledgement was made of the fact that the Chancellor and authoritative Leader of the National Socialist movement had made satisfactory statements in the Reichstag. Without revoking their earlier condemnation of particular religious and moral heresies, " the episcopacy therefore believes itself to be justified in regarding the aforesaid general prohibitions and warnings as no longer necessary." Further, the people were exhorted to be loyal to the lawful authorities; but at the same time they were requested to avoid political demonstrations in the churches out of reverence for their sanctity — a request directed against the SA's consecration of their banners.

In spite of this retraction the Catholic Church did not cease to protest against the excesses of the SA and against the cruelty displayed during the first months of the new régime. On June 10 the Bishops published a joint pastoral letter in which they declared " that national unity is brought into being, not only by identity of blood but also by identity of disposition, and that when it is a question of membership of a nation exclusive recognition of race and blood must lead to injustice."

National Socialism soon showed that it would not tolerate opposition even from the Church. One of the two great Catholic Workers' Unions, the Catholic Journeymen's Association, arranged a meeting in Munich on June 11 and 12. While Herr von Papen was exhorting them in his speech to banish the idea of class-warfare and to re-establish social order, the brown shirts attacked the Journeymen in the streets and beat them, because, among other reasons, the Journeymen were wearing orange shirts. The SA also lay in wait at the exits of the hall where the meetings were held, and tore the shirts off the members as they came out. Cardinal Faulhaber thereupon cancelled the pontifical Mass which was to have been celebrated, and the meeting came to an untimely end. The road to the railway station became a road of suffering for many of those who had attended the meetings.

A fortnight later further blows fell that were this time aimed more directly at the Church itself. The Centre Party and the Bavarian People's Party were dissolved under pressure from the National Socialists, and the Palatine District Leader, Bürckel, even had Catholic priests arrested. The Church, however, had no more intention of being a suffering and persecuted Church, as, for instance, Brüning recommended, in Nazi Germany than in Fascist Italy. It is true that she owes many of the greatest victories in her history to persecution; but she probably felt that this time it would hardly beseem her to be united in suffering with Bolshevism. Papen used this argument — whether true or false — in Rome, where he had been negotiating for a concordat with the Vatican since the end of June. What had been denied to the Catholic Baron as Chancellor a year earlier by the Centre Party leaders, he now obtained from the Cardinals in Rome — namely, toleration.

On July 8 a treaty was signed. It was the first treaty concluded between the Catholic Church and the German Reich. At the signing of the Concordat on July 20 in the Vatican Chancellery the figure of Dr. Kaas also emerged from the background into which he had for some time retired. He had been working in Rome as son and servant of his Church beyond the reach of the Nazi authorities. He played no small part in the drafting of the Concordat.

The best idea of the tenor of the Concordat will perhaps be given by stating that a violent quarrel as to its interpretation at once arose between the German Government and the Holy See. The treaty between the Vatican and Fascist Italy had also been interpreted by each side as it wished, but the Church's interpretation remained a protest and the State's became fact.

The Church obtained in the Concordat nothing that she did not already possess. In fact, she sacrificed important points which had previously been hers undisputedly. Freedom of creed and of public religious worship were guaranteed, the right of clerical legislation within general legislation was admitted, the secrecy of the confessional conceded even in a court of law, the free organization of church management granted as well as the exemption of priests from certain civic duties. On the other hand, by Article 32 the Church bound herself to forbid priests and monks to take any part in politics. Before the appointment of Bishops or Archbishops the District Governor must be asked whether there are any objections to the proposed nominee from a general political standpoint, and the Bishop must swear loyalty to the German Reich as well as to the particular State, and promise to respect the authority of the Government. In the matter of Catholic faculties, of religious instruction, &c., the regulations remain much as before; and also the existing concordats with the different States, which in some cases are more conciliatory to the Church on these points.

Clerical diplomacy believed itself to have achieved a signal victory, since Article 33 of the Concordat expressly relegated to the domain of canon law everything relating to religious affairs that had not been allowed for in the treaty. The far-reaching significance of this regulation was disputed from the German side. It was a concession on the part of the German Government that a final protocol promised that non-Catholic, that is to say Protestant, clerics would also be prohibited from political activity in Germany. It remains to be seen whether National Socialist Germany is capable of fulfilling this promise. The Church was also granted the freedom of numerous Catholic associations; but the difficulties arising out of this provision can be seen, for example, in Dr. Ley's demand that the Catholic Workers Unions shall submit to his leadership. Hence it was only after much hesitation that the Vatican decided finally to ratify the Concordat.

In effect, the Catholic Church has given way step by step, and at times only under the pressure of physical force before the National Socialist spirit. To give one example among many: the archiepiscopal diocesan court in Freiburg instructed its clergy at the end of August to greet their pupils with the Hitler salute. The pupils say with their arms raised: " Blessed be Jesus Christ," and the catechist answers: " for ever and ever, Amen."

JEWS

In his great Reichstag speech on March 23, Hitler said a very curious thing. Among his deferential remarks about the two Christian confessions, he said: " The Government will behave to all confessions with an objective justice. But it cannot permit membership of a particular confession or race to constitute a dispensation from obedience to the common law or a charter for toleration."

Among " other confessions " were first of all to be understood the Jews. What did " objective justice " mean in reference to them? According to the programme of National Socialism and according to Hitler's former speeches and writings, it must mean that the Jews were to be excluded entirely from public life and to a very great extent from professional life as a retaliation for the evil that they had done to the German people. It is undeniable that National Socialism had not hitherto in this respect even suggested objective justice, but had demanded that German nationality should be assured without regard to traditional ideas of justice. Among German Jews there was a widespread belief that the influential leaders of the National Socialist Party no longer really took anti-Semitism seriously; or that at all events they would not seek to realize the anti-Semitic demands in their programme.

This was one of the numerous mistakes which foreign critics of National Socialism made. With the growth of National Socialism during the last few years an anti-Semitism that was dormant in the broad masses of the German people, and that manifested itself very often in a not unfriendly reserve, revived again to strong and aggressive life. As early as the summer of 1932, the life of the Jews in the country and in the smaller towns had in certain districts become unpleasant. Systematic boycotting, social outlawry, and even physical ill-treatment were frequent, especially in eastern Germany and in northern Bavaria. Even in the streets of Berlin Jewish passers-by were continually being attacked. From this temper a systematic persecution of the Jews arose a few weeks after Hitler's taking office.

The signal was given by the burning of the Reichstag. Most of those who were arrested after February 27 were not Jews, but already the search was beginning for the "Jewish wire-pullers." Between March 5 and March 20 the anti-Semitic excesses reached their highest point. They now showed signs of what was practically a class-warfare. They were directed mainly against Jewish department stores and against Jews altogether in their capacity as traders. The "visits" of SA men to Jewish homes, the arrest and maltreatment of Jewish persons were often obviously due to personal and economic motives.

The victims of the terror, of whom more will be said later, were very much more numerous among the mainly non-Jewish officials and members of the three Socialist Parties than among the mainly bourgeois members of the Jewish faith. Nevertheless, the excesses against the Jews found a much greater echo in foreign countries because people could still see some sense in the persecution of "Marxists," and in bourgeois circles at least it was sometimes not even regarded as a matter for regret. An attack on a set of people simply because of their race was not compatible with foreign ideas of political opposition, and was regarded as the oppression of an innocent minority. A strong agitation in Jewish circles, especially in the Anglo-Saxon countries, possibly strengthened this feeling, but it certainly did not arouse it to begin with. This indignation found its classic expression in the famous debate on Maunday Thursday in the British House of Commons on April 13, when the former Foreign Secretary, Sir Austen Chamberlain, summarized the popular and official views of Great Britain by saying that events in Germany made it uncommonly inopportune to talk any more about a revision of the Treaty of Versailles. He said that the North German national spirit was the worst kind of Prussian imperialism with an increased brutality, a racial arrogance, and an exclusiveness that could not concede to those of its fellow-citizens who were not of purely Nordic descent equal justice and civic rights within the nation to which they belonged. Sir Austen pointed out that after what had happened it would be impossible to give back to Germany any place in which there was a population of non-German descent; and as the Polish Corridor was inhabited by

Poles, could they let it come under the heel of the German Government again?

The National Socialists soon realized the danger to their foreign policy arising from these feelings abroad. Some of the leaders thought that they could suppress the Jews and thereby also foreign opinion by increased oppression. Goebbels was the spokesman of this view. On March 27 he visited Hitler at his country house at Berchtesgaden, and suggested that the Party was to be allowed to carry on persecution on a mass scale. All Jewish wage-earners in Germany, whether they were engaged in trade or industry or in independent work, were to be boycotted by terrorist measures on a vast scale, all Jewish officials and employees to be dismissed from their posts. The boycott was to last indefinitely; it was obvious that within a few weeks it must bring the German Jews to a state of utter collapse.

To please his followers, Hitler was weak enough to agree to this senseless suggestion, which if it had been carried out in the proposed form would not only have brought the Jews but the whole of German industry to a collapse. The sudden destruction of the economic sector that was in Jewish hands would have left a sort of vacuum into which considerable parts of the rest of industry would have fallen. Bank failures on the largest scale could not have been avoided. Nor do the results for foreign policy of such a boycott seem to have been clear to the Leader at that time.

A violent opposition to the plan arose among those who saw farther. One of the spokesmen was Dr. Schacht, the President of the Reichsbank, who asked a question in the Cabinet. The ambassadors of the Great Powers said a warning word, and under this pressure Hitler decided to abandon the scheme.

Nevertheless, in order to placate the masses of his supporters, a trial boycott proceeded for one day under the direction of the Nüremberg Reichstag deputy, Streicher. On Saturday, April 1, SA men were stationed outside Jewish shops, offices, and private houses to request visitors not to enter them. In cases where the suggestion was not complied with they actually prevented them by force. Placards were pasted up on the windows, saying, "Don't buy from the Jews," or others with disgusting insults like "Swine of a Jew," or "Look out!

Danger to Life! Get out, Judas! " and " Pack up your traps, Ikey, and get back to Jerusalem! "

In order to keep up appearances, the boycott was after the first day " adjourned " until April 5. If the " atrocity propaganda " was stopped by then it was not to be taken up again. And, in fact, it was not taken up again officially. Streicher indicated in a speech that they had unfortunately capitulated before " World Jewry." He said that he himself had never realized until the time of the boycott how strongly the international Jews were welded together. In practice, however, the after-effects of the boycott, as regards department stores, for example, have not ceased.

It must be admitted, generally speaking, that the boycott of April 1 is not altogether in keeping with the rest of Hitler's ideas. He had previously declared himself to be ready to allow the Jews to carry on trade and industry freely, so long as they did not claim State citizenship with its right to serve as State officials, or to practise a recognized profession. At the same time they must not occupy positions of great economic power. After the boycott had been stopped, National Socialism logically concentrated on removing the Jews from the academic world. Hitler had for a long time been very sparing of anti-Semitic utterances. He now indicated the lines along which this exclusion was to proceed in a speech which he made to a deputation from the " co-ordinated " medical societies on April 6. He explained " that by a rapid elimination of the surplus Jewish intellectuals from the educational and scientific life of Germany they must do justice to the natural desire of Germans to have their own native intellectual leaders. The admission of persons who were to a great extent of alien race to the rest of the people might be regarded as an admission of the intellectual superiority of other races, which must most decidedly be denied. Even America had not been ready to open her doors to Jews ' fleeing ' from Germany, not a hair of whose heads had in reality been harmed in Germany."

The machine of National Socialist legislation worked according to this programme, speedily, thoroughly, and ruthlessly. It did so by means of four great laws: the " law for the restoration of a professional civil service," on April 7; the " law concerning admission to the legal profession," on April 10; the "law against the admission of too great a proportion of foreigners into the schools and universities," on April 26; and a regulation of the Labour Minister's "concerning the appointment of panel doctors."

The Civil Service law goes far beyond the Jewish problem in its systematic and practical significance, and more will be said about it later. The important regulation concerning Jewish officials comes in paragraph three, which runs:

"Officials not of Aryan descent are to be placed on the retired list; in so far as they are honorary officials they shall be deprived of their official duties."

"The first part of this paragraph does not apply to officials who have been officials since before August 1, 1914, or to those who fought during the World War for Germany or her allies, or whose sons or fathers fell in the World War. Other exceptional cases may be admitted by the Minister of the Interior in agreement with the particular Minister concerned, or by the supreme authority for officials engaged in foreign service."

The last sentence provided for exceptions being made for the diplomatic service in which a number of officials would come under the exceedingly wide conception of non-Aryanism. This shows the exceptional position of the Foreign Office, which has up to the present time been maintained in the National Socialist State under the presidency of Hindenburg. A definite proof of the importance of the law, which was drafted by Frick himself, was the first regulation defining the manner of its execution, which was issued on April 12. It defined the concept "non-Aryan" in a manner that those who knew National Socialist ideology had expected, and which for that very reason considerably surprised most of the public. The second section of this regulation ran:

"1. Non-Aryans are those who are descended from non-Aryans, especially from Jewish parents or grandparents. It is sufficient for one parent or grandparent to have been Jewish.

"2. Any official who had not been appointed by August 1, 1914, must prove that he is of Aryan descent, that he is the son or father of a man who fell in the World War, or that he was himself a combatant during the World War. Proof is to be given by producing documents (certificate of birth, certificate of parents' marriage, military papers).

"3. If Aryan descent is doubtful, a certificate must be procured from the expert for ethnology at the Ministry of the Interior."

There is no space here to enter upon a criticism of these regulations, which are of a hitherto unprecedented nature. What was politically unexpected and socially disturbing in the new legislation was not so much the outlawry of the Jewish population, which had had to be reckoned with, but the going back in the matter of ancestry to the grandparents meant the inclusion of people within the scope of this law who had long since ceased to count themselves Jewish, who often knew hardly anything of their descent, and who, possibly on account of the mixture of races, were among the most active and influential members of society. Even aristocratic families with great names were amongst them.

Furthermore, the regulations issued by the Minister of the Interior on June 30 determined that every one who was to be appointed to an official position must prove the Aryan descent of his wife, and so must every official already in office who wishes to marry. The States, municipalities, and other public legal bodies are subject to these regulations, which also apply to non-official employees in public works. They have not yet been officially applied to private enterprises. But the Unions in the German Labour Front admit no Jewish members, and since there will certainly be some attempt made to make employment in any undertaking dependent upon membership of the Labour Front, pressure will by this means be exercised upon the Jews in private concerns. For the present, it is true, these efforts have had to give place to some extent to the more urgent needs of the day and of the provision of work. Nevertheless, the decisions of labour tribunals have admitted as valid the dismissal of employees on account of non-Aryan descent.

The admission of Jewish lawyers was regulated in much the same way as that of the Civil Servants by the law of April 7. According to a statement of the Prussian Ministry of Justice on May 12, of 11,814 lawyers admitted in Prussia 3513 had been non-Aryan. Of these 2158 were readmitted. The Jewish doctors have been legislated for on somewhat different lines from the Civil Servants and lawyers. The chief source of income of most doctors nowadays is derived from their panel patients. Hence the regulation of the Minister for Labour has affirmed as a matter of principle that doctors of non-Aryan descent or who have worked for the Communist Party shall not be allowed to keep or to take on a panel. The same exceptions are made in this case as in that of the Government officials. The associations of panel doctors are to declare the work of the doctors in question to be at an end from July 1. Here, however, an important exception may be made in cases where there is danger that the insured persons will not have any medical attention. According to an official estimate there are in Germany about fifty thousand doctors of whom seven thousand are Jewish. The number of panel doctors is forty thousand, of whom six thousand are Jews.

All these regulations with their ameliorations and exceptions are for the present to be no more than a transitional condition. For the category of those who are still at present admitted cannot in future be filled in the manner prescribed by the law. Moreover, the Aryan clause has been given a foundation in the domain of education upon which a pyramid of the German learned professions will in future be erected that will be wholly free from Jewish components. The law of April 26 regarding the number of aliens admissible to the universities and schools decrees in paragraph 4: " When new students or pupils are admitted, care must be taken to see that the number of Germans within the meaning of the law for the restoration of the professional Civil Service that are of non-Aryan descent does not in the total of students and pupils at any school or faculty exceed the proportion of non-Aryans in the German population. The proportion is uniformly fixed for the whole country (1.5 per cent.). Schools or faculties that are too full may have their numbers reduced, and the number of Jewish pupils already admitted may be reduced by 5 per cent. Here, too, the regulations do not apply in cases where the father was on active service during the War; nor where only one of the parents is non-Aryan and the marriage was concluded before the law came into force.

The material damage to the Jews, of course, goes far beyond the legal provisions. A not inconsiderable part of the population carries on a secret boycott, and others avoid any business or social intercourse because they are afraid. On the other hand, some efforts are perceptible to alleviate the extra-legal pressure on Jewish businesses, lawyers, &c., out of regard for the labour market. At best, this means that the older generation is to be spared. In thirty years at most, if the situation remains unchanged, there will be no Jewish class in German society to be compared with the present one.

What will be a decisive factor in the fate of the German Jews in the long-run will be the social discrimination, which is already putting German Jewry into the mood in which it would rather live in a ghetto. Many Jews nowadays, except for going to work or making necessary purchases, do not dare to leave their houses for fear of molestation.

The degree of this social ill-treatment varies according to place and State. In many places Jews have been prohibited from going to the public baths. One of the most disgusting manifestations is the ferreting out of erotic relations between Jews and non-Jews, and the publication of them in the newspapers. In this matter the worst offender has been Streicher's " yellow " newspapers, the *Stürmer* and the *Hakenkreuzbanner* in Mannheim. The reports in these newspapers, which discussed publicly the most intimate things and deliberately destroyed the reputation of young girls, were not even always true. The Jewish party to such a relationship was accused of bastarding the race, and the Aryan of treason to his race. In various towns such couples were led in procession through the streets wearing placards with such inscriptions as " I have polluted a German girl," or " I have given myself to a Jew." In one case the girl's mother was made to accompany her.

Such excesses will probably grow fewer if only because German Jews will retire to an ever greater extent from social intercourse with non-Jews. They will probably remain restricted to certain callings as in the days before the emancipation. The National Socialist legislation of the year 1933 will force back the Jews into the narrow conditions of life which were once the cause of the very qualities for which they are now blamed; above all, their fanatical love for trade. The National Socialist State is doing its best to create in Germany a class of illiterate Jews that shall have no part in the culture of the nation. This class would depress the general level of the international Jewish community as has happened in the case of the Eastern Jews not only materially but also by intercourse and mixing. No prohibitions on the part of Western Jews, as has been clearly shown in the case of the measures adopted in Germany against the Eastern Jews, would be of any use; the only safeguard is in efforts to keep up the German level that must of necessity result in a greater internationalization of the German Jews, most of whom at present are very much attached to Germany. The German Jews can only prevent themselves from degeneration by voluntarily separating themselves from the German community — since entry into new and revolutionary associations will always remain the refuge of the minority.

It would be hopeless to count on an improvement of the position of the Jews in Germany as long as National Socialism is the ruling power. In the first place, many of the anti-Semitic regulations, such as those concerning lawyers and doctors, must be regarded as due to professional jealousy which is the natural result of an overstocked labour market. This professional jealousy shelters under the theory of the preservation of racial purity. Thus it becomes a philosophical problem that is regarded with great seriousness by nearly all the responsible people in the new State. In the spring a distinguished foreign diplomatist sought out Hitler and found him quite reasonable on many questions upon which the rest of the world disagrees with Germany. Upon the Jewish question, however, he found him absolutely immovable. When the foreigner inquired whether Herr Hitler had ever known a Jew personally, the Chancellor replied that he himself had hardly ever come across Jews; but that in his youth he had had a very bad experience with a Jew in the motor trade who lived in the same house as himself. Then he turned the conversation to other matters, and thus indicated that he regarded any discussion of the Jewish question as useless.

CHAPTER XVI

AN ANTICIPATION OF THE FUTURE

THE PERSECUTION of the Jews appeared in Nazi eyes to form only a part of the much greater task of creating a racial entity that should be governed by the most representative and ideal type of the race. The Germans were not, indeed, to be cleansed of foreign blood and restored to Nordic purity. The degenerate or less valuable elements in the German race were gradually to be eliminated and at the same time a governing class was to be brought into existence as quickly as possible that would display all the most valuable racial characteristics. The attempt was based upon the results of the researches carried out by the Augustinian monk Mendel in Brünn, and the founder of the science of eugenics, Sir Francis Galton, and differed from all other experiments in racial hygiene in that it proceeded from a fundamental, undemonstrable, arbitrary, and even philosophical assumption that the most valuable characteristics — and those which are to be restored in their purity in the future race — are those displayed by the so-called Nordic type. If this very questionable assumption be accepted, it is at least indisputable that this ideal type is to-day mixed with innumerable other " lower " types. Hence National Socialism combines eugenics with a racial theory which originated with the Jewish sociologist Gumplowicz in Graz: the theory that nations are brought into existence by the domination of a higher over a lower race. This theory was given popular expression in Hitler's great valedictory address to the Party Congress in Nüremberg on September 3.

Many of the Party organizations and departments set up their own racial bureaux. The Reich Leadership of the SS under Himmler looked upon their troops as the true source of racial regeneration, the pick of the ruling class, and the concentrated essence of the three million fighters who as a result of Hitler's speech in Nüremberg had organized themselves as the responsible political leaders of the nation. The SS established its own racial bureau. It is romantically and nobly housed away from the maddening crowd in the castle of Schwalenberg, in Lippe. According to Himmler its task is to construct the roads leading to a " period of historical time that will extend over twenty or thirty thousand years." If the creation of a new race is really the objective, then this period will certainly be none too long in which to attain it. Meanwhile the SS has rented the castle of Schwalenberg on a ninety-nine years' lease.

In order to avoid dissension Frick appointed one of the Party leaders, Dr. Achim Gercke, as expert adviser to the Reich Ministry of the Interior on all racial questions and at the same time gave him a number of Nazi politicians, including a few scientists, as assistants. A sufficient indication of the nature of Gercke's position is afforded by the mere statement that he alone can issue the racial certificates that are required by the provisions of the laws regulating the Civil Service and the legal profession. The racial bureaux throughout the country give advice on marriage and on whether or not the proposed marriage in each case can be commended from the standpoint of racial hygiene. The betrothed couple are advised to make their own inquiries into the names and professions of their ancestors, the ages they attained, causes of death, physical characteristics, state of health inclusive of all illness suffered in the course of their lives, and, finally, remarkable characteristics and accomplishments. These researches are to be begun with their four grandparents and are to extend to all their descendants, including themselves. In order to ascertain with greater certainty whether any foreign blood is present in their veins, these happy couples are recommended by the Thuringian Racial Bureau to investigate the antecedents of their forefathers up to and including their great-great-grandparents.

The most important achievement of this new racial policy is the " Law for the Prevention of the Transmission of Hereditary Disease," which was drafted by Frick and published on July 17. The first paragraph is the most important, and runs:

" Whoever is the bearer of an hereditary disease can be sterilized by a surgical operation if the experience of medical science goes to prove that there is great likelihood that his descendants will suffer from serious physical or mental hereditary disease." Hereditary diseases are defined as imbecility, schizophrensy, *folie circulaire,* hereditary epilepsy, hereditary St. Vitus's Dance, hereditary blindness or deafness or physical deformity. Severe alcoholism is also a ground for sterilization. The decision to sterilize a person must be taken by a Court for Hereditary Health (*Erbgesundheitsgericht*) after an inquiry held *in camera.* It is of importance to note that sterilization can be carried out against the will of the person in question.

THE IDOL OF JUSTICE

The Nazi Government quickly and thoroughly altered German law and its practice. The Law for the reconstruction of a professional Civil Service published on April 7 abolished the irremovability of the judges. Nevertheless the Reich Ministry of Justice has at times acted as a brake upon Nazi zeal for reform. Neither the Minister Gürtner nor the Secretary of State Schlegelberger are Nazis. Their opposition was surmounted by the appointment on April 26 by Hitler of his own lawyer, the Reichstag deputy Dr. Frank, to be Reich Commissar for the Co-ordination of Justice in the various States and for the reform of legal administration. President Hindenburg only reluctantly consented to sign his appointment. Frank was also Minister for Justice in Bavaria. In Prussia, a legal official of minor importance, the deputy Kerrl, was appointed Minister for Justice on March 27. But the real head of the Prussian Ministry for Justice was the Nazi Secretary of State, Dr. Roland Freisler.

In the sphere of organization Freisler's creation of a central legal authority — the *Zentralstaatsanwaltschaft* — deserves mention. This is a " flying " corps of public prosecutors who are directly responsible to the Minister and whose duty is to carry out political prosecutions. This " flying " corps has power to interfere in every legal process and to deal directly with the local prosecutors and courts without regard to the ordinary processes of law. According to Freisler this corps is " an efficient body of defence troops who are free from all influences or prejudices lying outside the factual content of the matter in hand." This organization is an extension of an institution which Göring had already founded: the Secret Police (*Geheime Staatspolizeiamt*). According to a circular decree issued by the Prussian Ministry of the Interior on May 3 this body of secret police is entrusted with the duty of carrying out all inquiries into the activities of private individuals in every government district which the police are entitled to make in accordance with the Emergency Decree for the Defence of the Nation and State, of February 28. It can make these inquiries by means of its own executive officials and with the assistance of the so-called State police in each district. All police officials throughout the country are placed at its disposal. The Secret Police exercise in Prussia an omnipotent rule which only a reckless Minister like Göring could place in their hands. They are the Cheka of the Third Reich and the *Zentralstaatsanwaltschaft* is merely an extension of their power into the realm of justice.

An order issued in July by Kerrl effected a complete change in legal education by altering the conditions under which the examinations for entry into the State legal service had hitherto been held. "The National Socialist State," wrote the Minister in his Decree of July 3, "must above all be assured that those in whose hands as judges or public prosecutors it places the responsibility for carrying-out the highest duties of State sovereignty are possessed of character, are German in thought and feeling." Hence the candidates are now required after completing the two chief written examinations to enter a "Common Camp for Aspirant Barristers" (*Gemeinschaftslager der Referendare*) in which they spend the six weeks that must elapse before their oral examination in labour service, sport, military training, &c., under the supervision of legal officials. It is forbidden them to undertake duty on behalf of others and to prepare themselves in any way for their forthcoming examination. No legal text-book is permitted within the camp.

A remarkable form of rivalry sprang up between Kerrl and Frank in the work of co-ordinating the legal associations. Frank enlarged his Union of National Socialist Lawyers to become a "German Legal Front" which was provided as a matter of course with a

" Staff " and a Chief of Staff in the person of a Government Councillor named Schraut. This Legal Front was joined by well-known and respected legal bodies such as the Prussian Association of Judges (*Richterverein*) and the German Lawyers' Association. The Association of German Judges at first contented itself with proclaiming its " enthusiastic " approval of Frank's programme. At the same time the associations of the lesser legal officials united to form a new organization which should constitute a group of experts within the Union of German Civil Servants (*Beamtenbund*). As a former Chief Collector of Taxes under the District High Court in Celle, Kerrl wished to assume the chairmanship of this group of experts. Although avoiding all mention of each others' names, Kerrl and Frank carried on a polemical warfare in which each sought to prove that the Leader had entrusted him — and him alone — with the organization of legal officials.

National Socialism also manifested itself in a political sense in the legal sphere by the Law of April 7, which excluded from legal practice not only Jews but also all " persons who have been employed in Communist activities," and further made no mention in this case of the exceptions otherwise permitted in the case of Jews. Practice showed that innocent persons could come under the suspicion of Communist sympathies, and that a complete refutation of such suspicions was not always of use in establishing their innocence.

The spirit animating National Socialist justice was expressed by Hitler in words which deserve to be recalled here. In his speech in the Reichstag on March 23 Hitler said: " Equality before the Law will be conceded to all who assist the national cause and do not refuse to support the Government." This sentence lifts for a moment the veil thrown over the truth by other sentences such as " The nation and not the individual is the first concern of the Law." Kerrl gave expression in a more verbose fashion to the same conception of Justice in an interview which he gave on assuming office: " It is obvious that the judicial system of a nation which is fighting for its existence cannot be inspired by a lifeless objectivity." And Frank was still more candid in a speech to a Congress of Referendaries in Berlin on May 21: " Justice can never be anything that is contrary to the interest of the nation." In former days German judges had seen their foremost duty in the defence of the weak. Now Frank contemptuously told an audience of students in Cologne on July 21 that all that the Law had done hitherto was "to protect the weak and to build up a moral code of slaves."

On March 21 the Reich Government issued an amnesty for those who had committed legal offences in the past "in the belief that they were acting for the good of the Reich." The five Potempa murderers were accordingly set at liberty. But the most extraordinary of these amnesties was that which was carried out in Prussia on Göring's personal initiative. Towards the end of July the Prussian Prime Minister wrote to Kerrl that in former days in industrial circles actions had been committed which indeed "constituted breaches of the criminal law without the perpetrators having been animated by selfish motives. The Bolshevist taxation of the then Government compelled in many instances the adoption of methods that were not legal in order to prevent a collapse of industry. These methods are to be understood in the then existing circumstances, and it must be remembered that the strict economic attitude of National Socialism had not then become the common property of the nation. A blind prosecution of such crimes would result in injury to persons who are inspired by the spirit of the National Socialist Revolution and are now prepared to assist in the reconstruction of economic life." Whilst in other respects National Socialist legal reform had at least been inspired by idealistic motives, and even in instances where it was actuated by the desire to give preferential advantages to Nazis had still borne a political character, Göring's letter reveals an undoubted misuse of power. He was simply rescuing those guilty of fraud in the payment of taxes from the legal consequences of their crimes. There is well-founded reason to believe that Göring issued this amnesty as a sop to certain industrialists to whom either he or the Party were under financial obligations. Another instance in which private motives can still more clearly be seen at work was provided by the Reich Commissar for Justice and Bavarian Minister for Justice, Dr. Frank. His father had formerly been convicted in his capacity as solicitor of embezzlement, and had been sentenced to a term of imprisonment. His name was also struck off the roll of solicitors. In recent years he had been employed as a book-keeper in his son's office. After Dr. Frank, Junior, became Minister for Justice he contrived to have his father's name restored to the roll. Dr. Frank, Senior, is once more practising as a solicitor.

What had the judges to say to all this? The Presiding Committee of the Union of German Judges drew up a resolution on March 19 which said: "The German Judge was from time immemorial conscious of his responsibility and inspired by national feelings. He has invariably delivered judgement in accordance with the law and the dictates of his conscience. That must continue!" A resolution passed by the Supreme Court was expressed more carefully. It was handed to the Chancellor on March 31 and was in answer to his speech in the Reichstag. It ran: The Supreme Court (*Reichsgericht*) desires to express its gratitude to the Reich Chancellor for having recognized in the Government's declaration of March 23, 1933, that the irremovability of the Judges is the basis of the legal system. Only the consciousness of his independence gives to a judge that inner freedom which he needs in the exercise of his high office. In the enjoyment of such freedom, and subject only to the Law, the true task of the Judge is to assist in his judgements to maintain the existence of the nation. . . ." The Supreme Court was in error in thinking that Hitler had recognized the irremovability of Judges. The Civil Service Law subsequently abolished it. Nevertheless it is possible in reading between the lines to see that the Supreme Court argued as follows: If only the consciousness of independence can give to a Judge the inner freedom necessary for formulating his judgements, and if he loses this feeling of independence through legislative enactments, then a German Judge can no longer maintain that he is independent and free to deliver an impartial judgement.

The legal spirit which was, in Frank's words, to cause such vast changes "that the legal development of past decades will be as nothing in comparison to it" has already accomplished much that is important. A Law of April 4 greatly increased the number of cases in which the penalty of death could be enforced and a Law of March 29 had already introduced the gallows. The infliction of punishment was more rigorously controlled, and in Prussia the death penalty was no longer to be inflicted by the guillotine, which was, in Freisler's eyes, "absolutely foreign to the German people," but by the axe. "This is the most certain method of inflicting death and one that has never given rise to any objections."

After months of opposition on the part of the Reich Ministry of Justice, Göring was finally successful on October 4 in securing the promulgation of a Reich Law "for securing the peace of the Reich." This law afforded greater protection to all officials such as Judges, public prosecutors, policemen, as well as magistrates and juries, and all officials of the Nazi Party, together with all members of the SA and Stahlhelm by imposing the death penalty for conspiracy to kill. Moreover, the death penalty or penal servitude for life awaited those who wrote or published treasonable articles in foreign countries or sought to smuggle them into Germany. If these articles or other writings are only "dangerous to the State" (*staatsgefährlich*) a penalty of anything up to five years' penal servitude can be imposed.

Another addition to these new laws was the "Law concerning the Cancellation of Citizenship and the withdrawal of German Nationality," published on July 14, by which foreign nationals who had adopted German citizenship could be deprived of the citizenship without any explanation — a clause aimed at the Eastern Jews. Moreover, these persons who had shown themselves forgetful of their "duty of loyalty to the nation and the Reich" could be deprived of their German nationality. Among other ways in which this forgetfulness could be manifested were "speaking contemptuously of the National Government and more especially conducting propaganda against Germany." The first to suffer under this Law on August 25 were a number of German politicians and writers who had fled the country.

A new Constitution for the Reich was also announced to be in preparation that was to substitute a "Reich Civil Right" for the existing State citizenship. This was only to be granted after the attainment of a certain age and after proof had been furnished of fitness to receive it. Doubtless it is intended to be granted at the conclusion of military or labour service. Among other Nazi legislative plans that are shortly to be realized are a new criminal code and copyright law, and a reform of the existing company law together with civil and criminal procedure. An " Academy of German Law " established by Frank has been entrusted with the preparation of a scheme for a reform of legal studies. All the " Jewish-Roman " portions of the civil law that are incompatible with German common law are to be removed from the statute book. Frank explained this as follows: What was meant was Roman Law in the degraded and archaic form in which it was introduced to the German people, and not the Italian treasure of Roman Law which would always be an object of admiration.

At the Congress of German Lawyers in Leipzig on October 2–4, 1933, Frank in his speech of welcome revived an old saying of Hitler's: " Justice is what serves the interests of the German nation." Hitler himself voiced a remarkable statement in the course of an involved speech: the Totalitarian State would not recognize any distinction between Justice and Morals. In saying this he flung down a challenge to the philosophy of more than two thousand years. Nevertheless his statement might be capable of being regarded as imposing a noble obligation if the Leader had only gone on to explain what code of morals he had in mind. For in so far as the new Justice is to be modelled on the moral code practised by the Nazis in political warfare it is only possible to regard it as a poor form of Justice.

CIVIL SERVANTS

It has already been shown that the new legislation also effected far-reaching changes in the German Civil Service. The Aryan clauses only formed a part of the immensely important Law of April 7. This Law declares in its first paragraph that Civil Servants can be dismissed " even in cases in which there is no legal justification " for their dismissal. With a stroke of the pen the so-called " well-earned rights " of the Civil Servants were eliminated which had hitherto formed the foundation upon which was built up their conception of duty. In consequence of this provision the second paragraph goes on to declare that those Civil Servants who entered the Civil Service since November 9, 1918, without possessing the prescribed or customary education or other qualification, can be dismissed. The only compensation given to them is three months' salary. According to paragraph 4 those Civil Servants can also be dismissed under these conditions " whose previous political activity does not afford a sufficient guarantee that they will on all occasions ruthlessly devote themselves to the service of the National State." According to paragraph 5 every Civil Servant must be prepared to acquiesce in his transference to another post, even when it is of lesser importance. He nevertheless retains his former rank and his former salary. According to paragraph 6 Civil Servants can be placed on the retired list without any definite reason merely for the purpose of " simplifying the administration."

Although this Law inflicted grave damage upon the existing juridical rights of the Civil Service, a part of the Civil Servants reconciled themselves to it because it rid their Service of the political intruder and consequently made his place free. Innumerable posts, especially in the Police Service and the municipalities, were nevertheless filled up again with outsiders.

THE INTELLECTUAL GAINS

If mention is made of the achievements of National Socialism for or against culture, it is certainly impossible to deny that it has displayed a powerful desire to renew and to criticize, and that it does not want for new definitions. The answer to be returned to the question whether it possesses a great wealth of ideas or not, will vary with what the questioner means by the word " idea." It would be unjust to judge the cultural standards of National Socialism by the wretched commonplaces delivered by one of the intellectual pundits of the system, Reich Commissar Hinkel of the Fighting Union for German Culture, in entering upon his office. And it would be premature to identify Martin Heidegger's finely thought-out inaugural address on becoming Rector of Freiburg University, with its demand that " the three Services " — Labour, Defence, Education — should unite to form an " impressive force," with the spirit of National Socialist culture. The Nazis in their work of permeating the nation with a Nazi culture may fairly claim that the time is not yet ripe for criticism. Nevertheless it will not be easy for them in the meanwhile to justify in the eyes of impartial critics the destruction which they have wrought. The common characteristic of the new cultural standard is indicated sufficiently in saying that the highest intellectual conception known to it is the nation as a whole. Any knowledge that questions this national unity or any desires which lead away from it are in a sense unfit to survive — ghosts lacking flesh and blood. There is no such thing known to National Socialism as independent " eternal " intellectual values. Knowledge " serves." Never again must there exist hypotheses which could cause nationality to be regarded as of secondary value.

Certain events have indelibly impressed themselves upon the memory of the world. At the end of April the German Students Association threw overboard in a public declaration " liberal intellectuality " in every form and proclaimed its allegiance to the " spirit of the SA." Students in brown shirts entered libraries and bookshops, and demanded with threats of violence that books should be handed over to them which they regarded as being " un-German." They burst into scientific institutes and tore the books from the shelves. The works of Karl Marx and Lassalle, Remarque and Rathenau, Arthur Schnitzler and Siegmund Freud, were piled up on public squares and burnt. At the bonfire on the square in front of the Opera in Berlin at midnight on May 10–11, Dr. Goebbels told the students that they were acting wisely in burning this filth. The intellectual foundation of the November Republic was here being reduced to ashes, out of which would arise victoriously and phœnix-like the new spirit " to which we will give its characteristic stamp."

From simple assistants to men of world-wide renown professors of all kinds were expelled from their posts. It was sufficient that they should be of Jewish descent or unreliable from the standpoint of the national movement. Albert Einstein resigned his chair as well as his membership of the Prussian Academy of Science. He also abandoned his Prussian nationality. " I cannot live in a State," he said, " in which the individual is not accorded equality before the law in addition to liberty of speech and of teaching." The Göttingen professor of physics and holder of the Nobel Prize, Professor James Franck, who had volunteered for service on the outbreak of the War and been in the trenches until the Armistice, and who held the Iron Cross, First Class, was not, indeed, expelled from his chair. He resigned voluntarily and gave as his reason for doing so: "We Germans of Jewish descent are treated as foreigners and as the enemies of the Fatherland." A few of his colleagues in Göttingen looked upon this form of resignation as an act of sabotage against the Government in its work of domestic reconstruction. They demanded that disciplinary action should be taken against Franck for his conduct.

The artistic life of Germany was similarly menaced by the forcible proceedings of the National Socialist Government against distinguished artists and musicians. The celebrated conductor Wilhelm Furtwängler addressed a letter to Goebbels at the beginning of April in which he said he only knew one line of demarcation: "the difference between good and bad artists. . . . When, however, the attack (on the Jews) is also directed against real artists, then it becomes detrimental to artistic life. For this reason it must clearly and emphatically be stated that men like Walter, Klemperer, Reinhardt, &c., must be given scope to exercise their art in Germany in the future." Goebbels answered this courageous letter with a verbose reply, in which he declared that "to complain that here and there men like Walter, Klemperer, Reinhardt, &c., had been obliged to cancel concerts seems to me at this moment to be all the less justified in view of the fact that true German artists have been often condemned to complete silence in the past fourteen years." But when he added "that every true artist will be given unrestricted liberty by us to pursue his art," it becomes necessary to ask what the Minister understood by a "true artist"? Furtwängler said that there was only a good or a bad artist. Oh, no! Goebbels retorts in a pedagogic manner. Furtwängler surely cannot be politically indifferent to the movement in Germany? He himself feels as a man with an artistic temperament that it is his task "to form out of the raw material of the masses the clear and stately figure of the nation." And "only an art that takes the nation for its material can in the result be good. Art in the absolute sense known to liberal democracy must not exist."

The problem was regarded from a far more humanitarian standpoint by the Prussian Minister for Public Worship and Education in a speech which he delivered in the University of Berlin at the beginning of May. " I myself am deeply affected by the tragedy of men," said Herr Rust, " who in themselves wish to be numbered among the German nation and who have contributed to its growth. Nothing is more painful for me than to have to place my signature to an order for the discharge of men who, as individuals, have often not given me any ground to dispense with their services." He concluded by advising the non-Aryans to submit themselves to the Aryans as their leaders in order to bring the struggle to an end.

The control of the German cultural institutions has up till now been fought for between the National Socialist rulers, each of whom is desirous of placing as many as possible of them under his personal supervision. At first Göring fought with Rosenberg — the President of the Fighting Union for German Culture — and his deputy, Hinkel, for the control of the theatres. As a great lover of the drama, Göring wanted personally to supervise all the State and municipal theatres in Prussia, and the Minister for Public Worship and Education, under whose jurisdiction they came, was forced to leave the final decisions to him. In the end, however, it was Goebbels who won the day. A Reich Law published on September 22 established no less than seven " Chambers of Culture " (*Kulturkammern*) for literature, Press, broadcasting, theatre, music, plastic or graphic art, and the film under the control of the Reich Minister for Propaganda and National Enlightenment. Goebbels thus became a sort of Reich Minister for Public Worship and Education. These " chambers " mark a step on the road to the unification of the Reich.

The Prussian Minister for Public Worship and Education came off worst in this struggle between Göring, Goebbels, Rosenberg, Frick, and himself to obtain control of these politico-cultural activities. He had by virtue of his official powers co-ordinated the universities. The refractory Universities Association, i.e. conference of rectors, had made its submission and elected a new committee that would be obedient to his wishes. A new Students Law created a " Students Union " (*Studentenschaft*) under Nazi leadership. Nevertheless the jealousies between the rival student associations continually broke forth and resulted in student riots. The old students corps did not allow themselves to be co-ordinated before they had put up a struggle for their existence; the Nazi Students Union was not satisfied with the range of its influence; and the Leader of the Reich Youth Movement, Baldur von Schirach, who had been appointed by Hitler and enjoyed his entire confidence, was disposed to find Rust's policy towards the universities too tolerant. As the result of recriminations Hitler himself—actually von Schirach—ordered that the newly published Students Law should be withdrawn and replaced by a new law to be drawn up and issued by Frick.

It can thus be clearly seen in the cultural sphere in what way the struggle for power between the Nazi rulers prevents the accomplishment of constructive work. It remains to be seen in the future whether the removal of this distraction will improve the situation in this particular respect. Up to the present much has been pulled down and practically nothing constructive put in its place. It is an open secret that both among professors and students intellectual interests have once more revived in the universities. There have been rumours that the Nazis are planning the establishment of Reich universities on the model of Oxford and Cambridge for the education of an intellectual élite.

An essay written by the Hamburg historian, Adolf Rein, declares that there exists to-day in Germany the " political university " instead of the theological universities of the fourteenth to seventeenth centuries and the humanistic universities of the eighteenth and nineteenth centuries. What is meant by " political " ? It is not possible to discuss the problem here in any detail. An illustration may perhaps serve to indicate its meaning. In the name of the Prussian Chamber of Commerce and Industry Dr. Siemond declared at a congress at the end of July that it was necessary " to bring the results and researches of the science of nutrition into line with domestic possibilities of production. It would be intolerable if the theory of nutrition were to take on a form which paid no regard to the domestic possibilities of production. The science of nutrition must be shaped according to politico-economic necessities."

THE RAPE OF YOUTH

National Socialism was looked upon as a youth movement. Its victory appeared to be that of oncoming generations. This is a half-truth — and therefore partly false. German youth — whether proletarian or among the intellectual classes — is far from the intellectual uniformity demanded by National Socialism. Here as elsewhere it was only a minority who were in revolt. Nevertheless it is unquestionable that the generation which saw itself in the middle of the German economic crisis growing up to a life that promised no material future evinced an exceeding readiness to try anything new, no matter whence it came.

Since National Socialism has come to power the German youth, in common with all other generations, no longer possesses freedom of choice. " If there are still to be found in our generation individuals who feel incapable of adapting themselves to the changed conditions, we will take their children from them and educate them to be serviceable to the German nation " — thus Hitler on June 18 at a meeting in Erfurt. His State is carrying out his words in bitter earnestness. Youth must to-day be Nazi. Against this categorical imperative there can be no opposition on the part of those formerly looked upon in law as the proper educators of the children — their parents. There have been many tragedies where children of parents inimical to National Socialism have been literally severed from them in the schools and the Hitler Youth.

Youth organization and the schools are the two methods used to achieve this aim. The so-called Hitler Youth is an organization that has only become important within the Party in very recent years after its founder and leader for many years, Kurt Gruber, was superseded in 1930 by Hitler's youthful friend, Baldur von Schirach, who was born in 1907, and who with the deputy Party Leader Hess is numbered among Hitler's most intimate friends. He is blindly devoted to Hitler, and writes verses to him that contain compliments which might turn the head of a much colder man. For example:

> " Wir sind das letzte Aufgebot
> und tragen Fahnen blutig rot
> für Deutschlands grössten Sohn."

At first Schirach was leader of the Nazi Students and only subsequently brought the Hitler Youth under his command. He led them with enthusiasm and ability in the years of struggle. After January 30, 1933, Schirach continued his successes by occupying on April 5, in conjunction with the SA, the offices of the Reich Committee of the German Youth Associations. Two and a half months later, on June 17, he occupied in similar manner the offices of a Youth Organization of the middle-class Right Wing — the Pan-German Union — and the twenty-six-year-old Youth Leader summarily ejected the President of this Union, Admiral von Trotha, who was one of the most celebrated German naval commanders in the World War and a brilliant naval strategist. Everything had been prepared beforehand. On the same day Hitler appointed his friend to be "Youth Leader of the German Reich," and thereby entrusted him with what is tantamount to a Reich Ministry.

Schirach was determined to bring under his personal control all Youth organizations in Germany. For this purpose he established a "Reich Council of Leaders" of the Youth organizations which was composed of representatives of various associations — confessional, sport, federative, and vocational. In this Council are representatives of those Youth groups which are also members of other organizations such as, for example, the vocational Youth groups composing the Labour Front, the confessional groups belonging to the several Churches, i.e. German Christians and the Sport Youth under the Reich Leader for Sport, von Tschammer-Osten. For months Schirach has been waging war with these various organizations and the victory still hangs in the balance. At the same time it must be admitted that the Youth Movement has created for itself a magnificent organization that affords much employment. This organization has published an account of itself that deserves reproduction here. "At the head of the German Youth is the Reich Chancellor Adolf Hitler, and under him as his personal representative is the Youth Leader of the German Reich, Baldur von Schirach. This latter has a personal aide-de-camp, Ensign (*Bannführer*) Horst Krutschinna, and a private secretary, Ensign Heinrich Lür. The deputy for the Reich Youth Leader and Chief of his Staff is Walter Kaul. The Reich Youth Leadership is divided into thirteen divisions, which are again subdivided into sections. . . ." It is hardly astonishing that even the *Völkischer Beobachter* on August 4 uttered a gentle complaint: "A year ago the Reich Youth Leadership occupied two moderate-sized rooms in the Brown House in Munich. To-day it requires a four-storied house; and even that is already too small for an organization that grows and grows. . . ." It must be added that in previous years all this magnificence had to be paid for either by the Hitler Youth or else out of the Party funds. Who pays for it to-day? Perhaps the Reich Audit Office will find that out at some future time.

In spite of certain tactical mistakes and the exaggerated growth of its organization, the Nazi Youth Movement exercises a powerful intellectual influence. This is specially noticeable in the case of the schools, in which the activities of the Hitler Youth are given every support by the educational authorities. It is true that the vast reform of education planned by National Socialism has not yet been carried out: the fact that the existing training colleges for elementary school-teachers have been renamed "Teachers Universities" (*Hochschulen für Lehrerbildung*), in fulfilment of a long-standing desire on the part of the teachers themselves, cannot be regarded as an achievement. It is of greater interest to note that the Prussian Ministry for Public Worship and Education is striving to increase the number of these "Universities" in the country districts for the purpose of impregnating them with peasant thought and culture in opposition to the decivilizing influences of the great cities. As the Minister stated in the programme which he published in June, the Nazi Movement is to a very large extent a peasant revolution. These Peasant Universities are intended to preserve and intensify peasant customs, racial feeling, communal spirit, and readiness to assist in national defence. Moreover, it is hoped through intensifying the colonizatory instincts of the peasantry to combat the emigration to the towns. On June 24, in his speech at the opening of a Teachers' University in the Pomeranian frontier town of Lauenburg the Minister stressed the necessity to inspire the German youth with an "unexampled spirit of comradeship." "We must train up a race of Spartans," he said, "and those who are not willing to enter voluntarily into this Spartan community must be prepared to renounce any hope of becoming citizens in the future."

A few instances will serve to reveal in what manner the youth of Germany are to be educated in the future. In July, Frick, who as Reich Minister for the Interior controls the entire educational system of Germany, issued directions to the several States for the reform of the teaching of history in which he demanded *inter alia* that the teachers should in future combat the low opinion hitherto held of the cultural *niveau* of the early Germans; the importance of race must be properly emphasized; nationalism rather than internationalism must be stressed in their teaching; and, finally, the idea of racial nationalism demanded that the teaching of German history should not be confined to Germany itself, but should also take into account the destiny of those branches of the Germanic race who lived beyond the frontiers of the Reich and who composed a good third of the entire German race. The teaching of history must be inspired throughout by the heroic ideal as well as the modern principle of leadership. The history of the most recent times must receive special attention in the elementary schools.

A memorandum issued by Frick at the beginning of August attacked the " desire for importance and the artificially nourished love of advancement " which had resulted in diminishing the importance of the elementary school. The new corporative State knew no advancement or degradation in the sense of the former class State inasmuch as its citizens were not classified according to a vertical scale of rank. The nation only had need of a very limited number of persons possessed of a university education. If Nature were to produce a large number of persons fitted to receive such an education, the State could only choose the very best from among them to fill the required number and without any regard for their social or vocational origin.

Teachers will not be wanting who are prepared to teach in this spirit. In a decree issued at the beginning of November the Prussian Minister of Public Worship and Education demanded that elementary school teachers should in their student days have been members of a fighting organization (which meant the SA above all others); that they should appear whenever possible in their uniforms at the university; that they should live in community houses; and that they should show proof of their fitness for field sports (*Geländesport*) at the time of passing their final examination. Such teachers would indeed be able to realize in practice what Hitler promised in a speech at Weimar on November 1: " If to-day in Germany there are still to be found people to say ' We will not join your company, but we will remain in the future as we are to-day,' then I reply: ' You will disappear. But after you there will come a generation which knows nothing else! ' "

In saying this, Hitler touched upon the decisive aspect of the question and at the same time returned to it an answer that did not lack conviction. It is nevertheless probable that his confidence will not be so easily justified in the event. The youth of Germany will unquestionably be educated to-day with little or no opposition in the spirit of National Socialism. And for as long as this generation remains youthful this spirit will continue to inspire it. The attainment of maturity by the individual may probably be delayed as the result of pressure and uniformity. Nevertheless, youth passes and with it comes the ever-growing tendency to criticism. After attaining a certain age these " youths " will ask themselves the question whether or not the achievements of the leadership are reconcilable with its teachings. What is the spirit animating this teaching? Baldur von Schirach wrote in the *Völkischer Beobachter* on June 22, that: " *Socialist* and anti-capitalist behaviour and feeling is the most prominent characteristic of young nationalist Germany."

It is not difficult to give ideals to these youths. The problem will be to give them a world to live in consonant with these ideals.

EXCESSES

In the speeches of the Nazi leaders the statement continually recurs that there has never in history been so disciplined and bloodless a revolution as the "national rising" of 1933 in Germany. The assiduity with which it is repeated serves to prove what little belief these assurances find. A saying of Hitler's that " not the hair of a Jew has been touched " has become notorious. In an interview he spoke of the twenty deaths caused by the Revolution. But the most shameless statement of all was that made by Rosenberg, in an interview published by the French journalist Sauerwein on September 25, in which he is reported to have said that hitherto a social revolution had always been imagined as accompanied by the wildest excesses. The world — he added — was astonished that this had not occurred in Germany. Herr Rosenberg forgot to explain the reasons why the boycott of April 1 was imposed at a time when the world was astonished at the peaceful nature of the National Revolution. In those days it was rumoured that the boycott was rendered imperative because the world was flooded with stories of atrocities in Germany.

These atrocities cannot be described in detail here. Nevertheless, the number of those killed deserves to be recorded if only to refute Hitler's story of the twenty dead. The murders of political opponents or Jews by SS or SA which have been reported by German newspapers or telegraph agencies have alone been counted, and the two chief newspapers used for this purpose have been the *Völkischer Beobachter* and the *Frankfurter Zeitung*. Other newspapers from which instances have been taken at random are the *Münchner Neueste Nachrichten*, *Berliner Tageblatt*, *Vossische Zeitung*, and certain provincial papers. In compiling the figures, those instances in which a prisoner was reported to have been shot "in attempting to escape," to have "hung himself," or to have "thrown himself from a window in an unobserved moment" have been counted as political murders. According to these statistics, 196 opponents of National Socialism (Reichsbanner, Social Democrats, Communists, and Jews) and 24 National Socialists were murdered in the period from January 31 to August 23, 1933. Up to March 5 alone 51 anti-Nazis and 18 Nazis had been murdered. During the period March 5 to August 23, 145 anti-Nazis were murdered as compared with 6 Nazis. These figures do not tell the whole story. A glance at random through the columns of the provincial Press, including Nazi newspapers, reveals that many cases of murder never reached the Press Bureaux from whence they are passed on to the great newspapers. It is only possible to guess at the total of these murders, and probably the total of those which have never found any mention at all is still greater. Reliable statistics of such cases are available from relatives, as, for example, at the time of the great SA round-up in Berlin-Köpenick on June 21, when at least nine people were killed. Only four were officially reported as dead, and of these two were SA men. The appalling murder of the Social Democrat Reichstag deputy Stelling, whose body was tied up in a sack and flung into water, was never reported in the German newspapers. Murders in Brunswick and in the concentration camp at Dachau, near Munich, were similarly hushed up. The figure of 196 dead most certainly only represents a part of the murders committed during this period.

The newspapers in their reports of these murders sometimes unintentionally reveal the truth. One type of story may be illustrated from a report from Berlin published in the *Frankfurter Zeitung:* " A Communist distributor of pamphlets was brought to an SA House under temporary arrest. At a moment when he was unobserved he succeeded in throwing himself from the window of the lavatory. He was killed on the spot. The man in question — it is said — was a notorious Communist agitator who has for long been known to the political police." The concluding sentence unintentionally reveals that its object is to excuse a case of murder. A notorious agitator known to the political police was synonymous with a peculiarly hated opponent of the SA. Even if the many reports of suicides were to be assumed to contain the truth, these suicides could only be explained by inhuman treatment of prisoners. Hitler and Röhm have often been in prison during their political careers. Neither of them has ever made even an attempt to throw himself from the window. Occasionally murder was admitted to be murder. On July 17 a police report from Frankfurt-am-Main stated that the former Nazi member of the Diet Schäfer had been found murdered on a railway embankment. Schäfer was suspected of treason by the Nazis and had been arrested on June 10 — five weeks previously — by the Hessian police. It is easy to understand where the murderer of a man already in police custody is to be found. Nevertheless, the police report added: " No trace has yet been found of the murderers."

The German concentration camps have become notorious throughout the world. Nobody knows how many people are imprisoned in them. On July 11 the figure for the entire Reich was officially given as about 18,000. This figure was even then difficult to believe, and to-day it is certainly false. Towards the end of October the number of prisoners must have been approximately 80,000 to 100,000. The police had the power to arrest any one without producing him before a magistrate. The prisoner was brought to a concentration camp which had often been established in a disused factory. A laid-up ship was used for this purpose in Bremen. The reports as to the treatment meted out to prisoners in these concentration camps are contradictory. All that is certain is that murders and torture did take place. It is more difficult to determine whether these were only individual and isolated instances. It is officially admitted that severe discipline is maintained and that much is demanded of the prisoners. Each prisoner naturally reacts differently to this treatment. If the threat uttered by the Prussian Secretary of State for Justice, Friesler, that criminals would again have reason to tremble before the doors of the prison be recalled, it is improbable that a concentration camp is the home of rest which the authorities seek to represent it to be. Gymnastics and exercises are capable of being used as a means of torture by prison governors who are disposed to cruelty. There are, indeed, some among these camps which have a fairly " good " name. Others, such as Dachau, near Munich, Oranienburg, near Berlin, or Dürrgoy, near Breslau, must certainly at least at times have been scenes of brutality. It is said on reliable authority that twenty to thirty prisoners were murdered in Dachau alone.

Has the treatment meted out to the prisoners in the concentration camps improved with the passage of time? Although it would seem likely that this has been the case, the facts appear to prove the contrary; and at least in Dachau there has been no improvement up to the time of writing. The worst brutalities have occurred during the more or less arbitrary arrests among the SA themselves. The *Deutsche Allgemeine Zeitung* that for years pleaded that Hitler should be made Chancellor reported cautiously on March 10 that " as a matter of fact events have occurred since Monday in Berlin and throughout the Reich which cannot be permitted by the Government in any circumstances. The intentions and motives of those who have committed this large number of terrorist actions can only be ascertained with difficulty. The worst feature of these terrorist actions is the fact that they have frequently been committed by bands of eighteen to twenty-year-old youths, of whom many are still at school." There have also been almost pathological cases of Sadism, like the action of certain SA men in Nuremberg in June in forcing Jewish prisoners to pull up grass with their teeth. The police did indeed make an end to these excesses, whose authors, nevertheless, went unpunished. Friends and relatives of wanted political opponents have officially been imprisoned as hostages in concentration camps where they are punished for illegal political actions of their comrades by being placed on a starvation diet. These " reprisals " are published in the newspapers.

On August 26 an official of the supreme SA leadership published in the *Völkischer Beobachter* an " appeal " in which he complained of numerous useless complaints. He said: " Individual comrades (*Volksgenossen*) make frequent complaint of alleged excesses on the part of SA men. It remains to be proved whether these complaints are justified or not. In this case the neighbouring SA depot is the first instance. If the supreme SA leadership was to investigate each individual complaint, the Staff must be multiplied tenfold and the Brown House transformed into a skyscraper." The incidents which have given rise to these complaints are at times — doubtless unintentionally — revealed in the official announcements. A report dated April 6 runs: " The Police Press Bureau in Bochum issues the following notice: A wanted Communist was discovered and handed over to the police. As he was incapable of being cross-examined, he was brought to hospital, where his body was found to be covered with wounds inflicted by blows. At times he became unconscious, and his pulse was very weak. His condition is critical. It has hitherto been impossible to discover in what circumstances the injuries came to be inflicted inasmuch as he is still incapable of answering questions." And so on.

A minor incident that cost nobody their lives or injuries serves to increase confidence in the truth of reports of more serious cases, resulting in severe bodily injuries or loss of life. The truth of the episode can be vouched for. Towards the end of July the inhabitants of a settlement in Berlin were arrested and brought before the examining magistrate. The magistrate first asked each individual the customary questions. Then he asked: " Were you a Communist? " If the answer was in the affirmative, the magistrate rose from his seat and gave the person in front of him a blow on the ear. Among the arrested persons were many women, including one who was sixty-one years of age. The examining magistrate also boxed the ear of the woman of sixty-one.

GERMANY AND THE POWERS

The ideas on foreign policy of National Socialism in its early days have already been described, and the actual foreign policy of the Nazi Government will only be analysed here in its broad outlines.

It was to be expected that Hitler would encounter distrust in foreign countries in view of the fact that what he had hitherto preached — notwithstanding that he denied it — was *revanche.* It is customary that the great step from agitation to responsible government acts like a dash of cold water. The policy of France, which was represented in Berlin by the French Ambassador, François-Poncet, held out before German nationalism the possibility of at least a *modus vivendi,* if not a sincere alliance. The German protagonist of this policy was Herr von Papen, who was now Vice-Chancellor in Hitler's Cabinet. A conservative European policy could only welcome a collaborator in the Chancellor who was engaged on the destruction of Communism.

This possibility of achieving an understanding was destroyed by the Jewish boycott of April 1. The Nazis have sought to make it appear as if " world Jewry," out of sheer hatred, has roused the world against Germany by means of its mighty influence. The truth is far simpler. The boycott appeared to the world at large to be a proof that the now ruling National Socialism had not abandoned even the most indefensible of its youthful theories. A Hitler who, despite an appearance of statesmanlike prudence, did not hesitate to carry out his anti-Semitic programme in this relentless manner would one day seek to realize his *revanche* plans: nor was it of any great importance in either case whether he did so of his own volition or as the result of pressure from his supporters. To say nothing of humanitarian considerations, National Socialism naturally would not admit that such considerations could originate anywhere except in egotistic calculations.

National Socialism would only have temporarily suffered from the dislike which made itself apparent in England, and in the debates in the House of Commons, if it had not destroyed a new international combination that was only just coming into existence. On March 18 in Rome Mussolini laid before the British Prime Minister, and Sir John Simon, the draft of a Four-Power Pact between England, France, Italy, and Germany for the purpose of promoting a Franco-German understanding and simultaneously securing recognition as an aim of European policy for Mussolini's dearest wish for a revision of the Treaty of Versailles. This would have been of enormous advantage to Germany. National Socialism could have welcomed the Pact as justifying its Italophil policy, and Mussolini would have become a sort of arbiter of Europe's destinies. The inimical feeling against Germany prevailing in England and France nevertheless threatened to destroy all these hopes. Hence Hitler sent two special agents from among his most intimate advisers to Italy and to England in order to report on the state of opinion in those countries and to endeavour to allay their mistrust. Göring flew to Rome on many occasions. On his second visit, in the middle of April, Göring was followed after a brief interval by Papen, who nevertheless held himself aloof from him and watched him jealously and suspiciously. It was Papen who achieved most in a diplomatic sense. The honours heaped upon Göring did not avail to conceal entirely Italian resentment at the clumsiness of a German policy that had disturbed the negotiations for the Four Power Pact by its Jewish boycott — an action that in any case met with little sympathy from the Italians. In order to calm public opinion in England, Rosenberg left on May 10 for London where he had formerly awakened sympathy in many quarters for the Nazis in their struggle against Bolshevism. On this occasion Rosenberg was received with an enmity which showed itself in various incidents and even in discourteous interpellations in the House of Commons on the subject of his visit. The visit proved a disastrous failure for Germany in general and for Rosenberg in particular. On March 31 he had created for himself within the Party a " Bureau for Foreign Policy " that was intended to put the official Foreign Office in the shade in the course of the general undermining of State institutions by the Nazi Party. If his visit to London was intended to serve as a justification for the existence of his Bureau, it was certainly a miserable failure; and in any case Rosenberg himself has not yet become Secretary of State for Foreign Affairs nor are his chances of becoming Foreign Minister any too good.

The most useful achievement of National Socialism in combating the inimical feeling prevalent in foreign countries was the speech delivered by Hitler on May 17 in the Reichstag. When the situation had already become such that France openly talked of sanctions, the Reichstag was summoned to meet, and Hitler delivered a speech which deserves commendation for its wisdom. Two points were specially successful in making an impression abroad: Firstly, Hitler declared himself " in agreement in principle with a transition period of five years for the establishment of our national security in the expectation that after the expiration of this period Germany would be placed on a footing of real equality with the other powers." Secondly, Hitler proposed the conclusion of an international convention for the abandonment by all States of offensive armaments, and declared himself prepared to place the SA under international control — if the other Powers were willing to submit their armed forces to a similar control. These were his most important proposals in the sphere of foreign policy. He then went on to seek to convince the world that National Socialism did not cherish any notions of *revanche.*

" In speaking at this moment as a National Socialist I wish to announce in the name of the National Government and the entire National Revolution that in this young Germany we in particular are possessed by a deep understanding of, and sympathy for, similar feelings and sentiments in other peoples, as well as for their just claims. This young Germany has only up to the present known want and misery in its own nation, and has suffered too much from folly to entertain any notion of bringing others into a similar state of misery. Our National Socialism is a principle which imposes upon us an international outlook. It is because we feel a boundless love for, and loyalty to, our own nation that we respect the national rights of other peoples, and desire from the depths of our hearts to live with them in peace and amity. Hence we are also free from any notions of Germanization. The intellectual attitude of recent centuries that thought it possible to make Germans out of Poles and Frenchmen is as unquestionably foreign to us as it is certain that we would passionately defend ourselves against any similar attempt. We look upon the European nations surrounding us as given facts. Frenchmen, Poles, &c., are our neighbours. We know that no conceivable historical event can alter this truth."

An internationalism based upon nationalism was thus put forward by Hitler as the political ideal of the future. He was certainly sincere in what he said in this speech. Was he any less sincere in demanding in his book that there should one day be a " forcible settlement with France in order that Germany may achieve great aims "? The two attitudes are not incompatible. Indeed, Hitler's belief may thus be summarized: he is opposed to imperialism and deems war to be necessary. An imperialist war ends, or should end, in conquests. A war conducted by the new nationalism ends in the establishment of a domination which has no longer any need of formal annexations. Japan does not annex Manchuria. She " liberates " it and erects it into an " independent " State. As compared with the old and brutal imperialism this procedure is what the modern international credit system is to the rough-and-ready restrictions upon gold employed by the mercantilism of the seventeenth and eighteenth centuries. Neither method excludes war or deception.

The pacific speech delivered by Hitler in the Reichstag on May 17 failed to prevent the Four Power Pact — finally signed on July 15 — from becoming the exact opposite of what it had originally been intended to be. In agreement with Article 19 of the Covenant of the League of Nations the Four Power Pact now made any revision of the Treaty of Versailles contingent upon the agreement of each of the signatory Powers. Thus the existing state of affairs remained unchanged in its most important aspect. In this form the Pact was little more than a personal triumph for Mussolini, and did not bring any real gain to Germany. The German Government nevertheless signed the Pact out of regard for — it might almost be said out of submissiveness to — the Roman dictator.

Hitler's speech on May 17 laid down the lines more or less consistently followed by German foreign policy since that date. The German Government has shown itself conciliatory in matters lying outside the sphere of German racial interests. In this respect it has done more than any of the previous German Governments that were subject to Nazi criticism dared to do. On June 20 a National Socialist Government came into power in the Free City of Danzig, and on July 3 the President of the Senate, Dr. Rauschning, paid a State visit to Warsaw, where he delivered a speech lauding the Treaty of Versailles as the " Magna Charta of Danzig's rights and liberties." One result of this speech was the conclusion on August 8 of a treaty between Danzig and Poland regulating the traffic passing through the two ports of Danzig and Gdynia at the cost of considerable concessions on the part of the former. Moreover, it is long since the world heard so little as in the past few months of the " Corridor."

National Socialism showed itself more resolute in its insistence upon its rights to interfere in Austrian affairs on the ground that this was a domestic concern of the German nation. After a long period of stagnation the Nazi movement revived in Austria and outvied in popularity the local Fascist *Heimwehr* movement led by Prince Starhemberg. Nevertheless, the results so far obtained by Hitler's Austrian policy cannot be regarded as satisfactory for Germany. Up till now France has taken the lead in defending Austrian independence. Italy has remained silent and would only have shown her hand at the decisive moment. But recent German policy towards Austria has compelled Italy to an activity which she would probably have preferred to have postponed to a later date. It is clear that in event of any revision of the Treaty of Versailles the decision must be taken as to which Power is to sway the destiny of Central Europe — Mussolini's Italy or Hitler's German. Mussolini is making his preparations for the day when this decision can no longer be postponed. He has stretched his hand out towards Vienna. After a meeting with Mussolini at Riccione on August 20, Dollfuss announced the creation of a corporative State after the Italian pattern. Although previously not unwilling to negotiate with National Socialism on easy terms, Dollfuss has lately shown himself under Mussolini's protection to be unwilling to accept conditions proffered to him. If the Nazis come into power in Austria in any shape or form (a possibility that must be taken into account), their Government will nevertheless be at least as much subject to Italian as to German influence; and since Germany cannot afford out of regard for her Italian policy to risk Italy's grave displeasure, it follows that while the German influence may be more open, that of Italy will be the more powerful. As in Danzig so in Austria, the world will be told that the Treaty of St. Germain is sacrosanct and that the Brenner frontier cannot be subject to any revision.

As a whole, German foreign policy is unquestionably inspired by pacific desires — until the day comes for peace to cease. It will certainly not deliberately work to hasten the coming of that day. Nevertheless, Germany prepares for it because she believes it to be inevitable. It is clear that Germany desires above all else to avoid a collision on her Western frontier. For with the exception of the restoration of the Saar and the abolition of the demilitarized zone in the Rhineland — neither of them objects worth fighting for — Germany has nothing in the West to win and everything to lose. Nazi Germany thinks as little of waging war for Alsace-Lorraine as for German South Tyrol. For here its intellectual influence is powerless against the impenetrable wall of Latin civilization. In the East, however, Germany sees new worlds to conquer. An opportunity for such conquests might be given one day by vast revolutionary changes in the Soviet Union. In this connexion Hitler's and Rosenberg's plans regarding the Ukraine are well known. The occurrence of great revolutions in the Near and Far East are what German foreign policy is waiting for in the hope that Germany will then find herself able to intervene decisively. Her desire is to intervene rather than to attack. If the Soviet Union collapses, and Hitler is convinced that it must collapse, then Germany, with the submissive assistance of Poland, will bring order out of chaos and become arbiter of the destiny of Eastern Europe. In that case Germany will also be ruler of Central Europe. The Soviet Union has sought to counter this dangerous policy by the conclusion of a far-reaching system of conventions directed against Germany, by entering into friendly relations with France, and by feverishly negotiating with England for a commercial treaty and with America for official recognition.

It is to all appearances clear that German foreign policy has achieved little, and is only to be understood in the light of the confidence which it reposes in its attainment of vast and distant aims. It is based upon the assumption that the existing balance of power must shortly be upset, and that Germany will profit by the change inasmuch as she has nothing to lose. Is this really true? In the first place, Germany can still lose her independent existence as a State. She seeks indeed to convince the world that her existence is its defence against chaos. In doing so she forgets that the world may not find the prospect of a German ordering of Society after the Nazi pattern any more attractive than the, possible, chaos. In truth German policy is founded not upon a desire for order but upon a desire for revolution. It is undeniable that Nazi Germany believes herself called upon by reason of her constructive ability and force to make an end to this revolutionary situation after its occurrence and to set before the world new aims. She therefore needs revolution in order to be able to translate her thoughts into deeds. This is in truth a " Bolshevist " spirit in comparison with which the Soviet Union to-day belongs to the Conservative Powers struggling for the retention of the *status quo.*

Germany consciously takes great risks for the sake of the future. Nevertheless, Göring's achievements in the sphere of aviation must not be looked upon as merely forming part of a vast general plan. The opinions held by German experts on the subject of Germany's military strength are very contradictory, and especially in the Reichswehr Ministry there are to be found many who are sceptical. The leader of each department within the Nazi organization — Sport, Youth, Labour, Service, &c. — may regard himself as more or less the Scharnhorst of to-day, and it is an open secret that the youth of Germany is being made more and more fit for war. It is quite another question whether responsible men believe that Germany can be placed in the immediate future in such a state of military preparedness that she can take upon herself the risk of war in order to achieve her aims. It is also an open secret that Germany speculates upon the possibility of this armed conflict being postponed for years to come owing to the want of determination and the diplomatic divisions in the opposing forces. German policy may very well be compared to a skier who travels at full speed over a slope rendered dangerous by the possibility of avalanches, in the hope that at least he will have got safely across before the avalanche comes down.

In any case Germany found herself in the danger zone as a result of her own policy. The formula which Schleicher's Government had been conceded by England, France, Italy, and America in Geneva on December 11, 1932, was: German equality within the limits of security. After the events of 1933, however, it was claimed that international security had been still more endangered by the German Revolution. Many of the arguments brought forward in this connexion must be regarded impartially as propagandist weapons or objects for diplomatic barter to secure the success of the Disarmament Conference. Nevertheless, the fact remains that Hitler's Government are responsible for an accompanying loss of confidence. Stresemann achieved the evacuation of the Rhineland; Brüning secured the abolition of reparations; and Papen and Schleicher together placed Germany on a footing of equality with the other Powers. Hitler immediately threw away Papen's and Schleicher's gains, if the position remains unchanged — one of the worst defeats sustained by German foreign policy since the War, since it is obvious that the German view that the Simon Plan of October 14 involves a discrimination against Germany is right: a probationary period of eight years before the favoured position accorded to the Allied Powers in the Treaty of Versailles ceases is the very opposite of equality of rights. The German Government is perfectly justified in protesting against this discrimination. Nevertheless, it is at the same time its duty to ask itself what failure on its part has brought this fateful constellation into existence. It is stupid in politics to seek to change the inimical disposition of an opponent. It is wise to correct one's own failures.

It is obvious that the German Government was conscious of its international isolation before October 14, 1933, and that it already knew that it had lost the support formerly accorded it by English public opinion. Now it saw Italy following in England's path. Thereupon the German Government resolved to draw the logical conclusion. Germany withdrew from the Disarmament Conference and from the League of Nations. Her position was already so bad that her action could not make it any worse. In accordance with the principle on which it has always acted hitherto, National Socialism now seized the most powerful weapon in its armoury — propaganda. If regarded from this standpoint Germany's action in leaving the League of Nations must be looked upon as a deliberately planned explosion of feeling calculated to arouse the self-criticism that is always dormant in English public opinion. An appeal was made to the English spirit of fairness. At the same time Hitler, in his wireless speech on October 14, sought to awaken England to anxiety for her own interests by inviting France to come to a direct understanding with Germany, and by repeating the renunciation of Alsace-Lorraine already made by Stresemann in the Locarno Pact. Moreover, Hitler turned Germany's loss in foreign policy into a personal gain in domestic policy by holding new elections for the Reichstag as well as a referendum that gave him a vote of confidence which was influenced by terror and one-sided propaganda, but nevertheless expressed the real state of opinion among the majority of the nation.

An examination of German foreign policy in those days reveals the existence of a logical connexion between the Nazi methods in foreign as in domestic policy. The National Socialist German Workers Party attained to power in Germany by threatening the upper classes with the advent of Bolshevism in event of a collapse of National Socialism. To-day the Nazi Government is playing this same game in foreign policy by threatening Germany's neighbours with the prospect that Hitler's downfall would mean the extension of Bolshevism to the Rhine and beyond. Behind this warning there lies concealed an urgent plea: Germany's neighbours should decide in principle between Bolshevism and Fascism. Germany cannot force them to take this decision. Nevertheless, Germany counts upon a collapse of the political systems existent in the Western democratic Powers that will bring with it the necessity for such a decision. Nor does she doubt that in that event the decision will be for Fascism. During the transition period that must elapse before the stabilization of Fascism, Hitler, like Mussolini, is endeavouring to associate Fascism with the idea of pacifism, on the principle that force should be employed at home and conciliation abroad.

An attempt is being made to influence the public opinion of the Anglo-Saxon and Latin countries by a direct propaganda waged against their Governments. On the day following Germany's withdrawal from the League of Nations, the *Völkischer Beobachter* began to propagate the idea that Hitler was a " good European " who was inspired by better intentions towards the European peoples than were their own Governments. Another line of attack is the attempt to sow dissension among the several European Governments — an attempt that certainly holds out greater prospects of success than does that of trying to bring them into disfavour with their own peoples. The National Socialist German Workers Party was a minority in comparison with the total number of its opponents in the domestic political struggle. Nevertheless it was stronger than its opponents, who could not come to an agreement among themselves. In similar fashion the Nazi Government makes its calculations in the field of foreign policy. If Germany's opponents cannot agree among themselves in decisive issues, then Germany must prove stronger in its unity than they are in their dissensions. This calculation is based upon the assumption that France is condemned for years to come to internal weakness and to the rank of a second-class Power; that it is already incapable from a psychological standpoint of contemplating a war with Germany; and, finally, that Germany can therefore permit herself almost any violation of treaty obligations without any risk of encountering more than a verbal protest.

A glance at this policy in the clearer light that obtains outside Germany serves to show that Hitler has returned to the same policy that brought William II and Bülow to disaster. Moreover, the methods employed by the Nazis in Germany itself cannot be used in their foreign policy for the simple reason that their opponents in this field are not Germans. These opponents are superior to the Germans in political wisdom and caution rather than imagination. The class in Germany which was most mature in a political sense — the organized working class — has been excluded from politics to the injury of the nation. The Nazi leaders, and especially Hitler himself, are men who have travelled little. Although as good psychologists they have a keen apprehension of certain feelings that in the present situation of the world can seize upon all peoples, they have too little knowledge of the national characteristics of these peoples to realize in what manner they react to these feelings. National Socialism believes in the diversity of races and does not put its belief into practice. It is because it treats foreign nations as if they were Germans that it will meet with disaster.

CHAPTER XVII

FORWARD INTO LEGEND

WHAT is the purpose of it all?

It is certain that all Hitler's followers attach some meaning to the movement and that this meaning differs with each individual. But is there any unanimity of aim among the leaders?

Yes, there is. It is not, indeed, contained in the programme and its twenty-five points; there it may at most be said to germinate, barely suspected by the authors, between the lines. Meanwhile it has been grasped by Hitler, taught to others, and in the teaching has been further moulded. It can, moreover, be seen from all the announcements how the National Socialist leadership is growing to be more and more master of it.

The aim is to make of the Germans a nation fit for heroes. Let it be clearly understood, not a nation *of* heroes but *for* heroes. Thus it is not an attempt based upon a long passed stage of political development, but one that must be taken very seriously — an endeavour to breed a new and purer racial type, and to allot to it the higher rights but also the higher duties of a new aristocracy of achievement. The National Socialist trainers of humanity are seeking to approach their goal in many different ways. A practical spirit of enterprise and mystical dilettantism run side by side, and Hitler is waiting to see the result before deciding which method is the most successful. As a whole, the seriousness of the attempt, and the part that is noteworthy in its success or otherwise for the rest of the world, is the effort to make a people of strongly individual traits fit into a uniform mould of rulers. Material which does not evolve creatively but suffers itself to be moulded — that is the secret of German nationalism.

The German masses are undoubtedly filled with a feeling of unity such as has seldom been found in Germany. The consciousness of being one, of a unity that goes deeper than any clash of interests, knits together the East Prussian agricultural labourer and the wine-grower of the Rhineland and the chemical worker from central Germany. This occurs at a level of general culture and intellectual awareness that the German people only reached under the Weimar Republic. The feeling of unity in its present intensity was given the German people by the World War. The intellectual means of raising it to a concept came through the Republic. And National Socialism has made use of these means and this freedom with supreme success.

Meanwhile, mere existence cannot be the highest task of a nation. The idea of nationality is extraordinarily powerful in Germany, but there is something morbid about its force. For a national character which the German people is now striving to develop can in its very essence not be the content and purpose of national action and life, but only its form and means of expression. It is not what the nation does but the way it does it that makes it German. Fichte once expressed it proudly: to be German means to do a thing for its own sake. There is no doubt that present-day National Socialism is very far removed from this form of Teutonism, and is inclined, on the contrary, to do everything for the sake of the German; and especially to excuse everything as Teutonism, every folly, every barbarity.

And so to-day National Socialism is hard put to it to find a task for this nation which it has gathered together that will go beyond its mere process of emergence from the crucible. For the life-force of a nation can only be kindled afresh by great achievements. This task, it has been said, consists in giving to the world a non-Marxist German Socialism.

But what is Socialism? Let us consider for a moment how the hostility of National Socialism to capital began. It arose from the complaint of the small capitalist against the banking system of the large capitalists, whose money was at the disposal of the small man only at impossibly high rates of interest. Since, however, material property only keeps its value in the process of production by the continual presence of working capital, the idea of property was depreciated by the enhancing of the value of capital, and in time came also to be profaned in the eyes of its previous adorers. The arrogance of the great managing directors toward the small shareholders whose dividends they withheld also finally decreased the pride of the latter in their property. Thus the small propertied man who continually found less source of pride in his useless property was left with only that form of pride which the unpropertied worker knows — the pride of skill, of his power of work. When the worker realized that this pride of competence did not better his material situation so long as man-power remained a cheap and superabundant article, he organized self-help and entered upon class-warfare. When the property-owner realized the depreciation of his property he demanded State help and became a National Socialist. As is well known, this was the path upon which Lassalle also wanted to lead the proletariat, but the self-consciousness of the class that was coming into being preferred the independence that Marxism offered. This was true also in places where the Labour movement was not externally associated with Marxism. Not help from, but mastery of, the State was the aim of the Labour movement. The State they were envisaging, however, was the State of the future. The existing State was as useless for their purpose as wafers to hungry Jacobins.

History is made by classes that are coming into being, not by those who already exist; by movement, not by stability. The working class came into existence in the second half of the nineteenth century, and its historical period lasted until about 1918. By then it had attained nearly all that it could have in peaceful conditions and began to settle down. Meanwhile, however, a new class had begun to emerge. The middle class, or lower bourgeoisie, were spoken of — old-fashioned expressions for something that no longer exists. The new class is composed both of men of independent means and of employees (mostly in fairly high positions). This union is possible because the "profane" property no longer has the separating power that it had in former times. This new class — I should like to call it the SA class — does not want to rule the State, but yearns to be obedient; or, more accurately, for hierarchies, rank, authoritative rules of behaviour, sure leadership, and a guaranteed existence. The alleged Liberalism that was in former times attributed to this class was never anything but a fantasy. It never wanted anything but authority and an assured existence. Freedom to earn was, indeed, a matter of course; but equally a matter of course was State help in case of bankruptcy; and an assured job on the strength of "well-earned rights" was always its ideal. Hence this class always clung closely to the State, and never assumed the revolutionary character that is natural to the really dependent labourer who does not exert authority over any one below him. Thus this class's political Party — National Socialism in Germany — has always, even at times of the most violent agitation, stood well with the really influential State authority (which was not always the same as the formal), beginning with the Prime Minister von Kahr up to President Hindenburg.

The political aim of this class is State assistance. People have spoken of the politico-social welfare State of the workers. But the idea of politico-social aid for the workers in the narrower sense has always aimed at the insurance principle, that is to say, has taken on the character of self-government, while the subsidies and vast schemes for assistance have always been based upon taxation. The working class at the time of its greatest self-consciousness put forward claims to the State; the SA class makes claims on the State. Ideologically there is a certain approximation between the two claims in the feeling that fundamentally the State is a productive power. In Germany this feeling took on a particular national tinge, in which Germany appeared as a productive nation over against the capitalist, grabbing, Western Powers. The more small capitalists were destroyed under the pressure of the crisis during the last few years, the more attractive did a National Socialist State appear to many who had hitherto had small private means. For they visualized the Nazi State as provided with a vast bureaucracy (which, in fact, is so provided), in which they might occupy a safe official position. A Party of bankrupts? It is certain that many who belong to the SA class have meant by National Socialism that popular hope of an official post which has been described as "loyal, German, and entitled to a pension."

The revolution of those who are not yet subsidized certainly has at present a better outlook than ever did the revolution of the badly paid, i.e. the working classes. When the working class came into existence and began to agitate, the middle class was still too well-off and therefore did not join in with it. To-day, when the SA class is coming into existence and agitating, the working class is seriously weakened in its greatest power, its power of striking, has been split into two hostile groups — those who have work and those who have not — its self-confidence is wavering, and it is therefore ready for its part to join the rest. It has also lost its leaders, and its attitude to the State is growing more like that of the SA class.

The danger threatening the régime from this side is clearly discernible. Hitherto it has derived an advantage from the reorganization of the classes. Whatever the classes of the future are likely to be, at all events the conditions of life and the political ideals of classes whose conditions of life have hitherto been dissimilar have come to approximate much more closely; except that the lower-middle classes have not, as the Marxists expected, adopted the ideals of the proletariat, but the proletariat has at least to some extent adopted the ideals of the bourgeoisie. The fate of the régime will depend upon whether it is able to detach the conditions of existence of a sufficiently large class from those of the SA class again. The attempt will certainly be made, and we shall probably see certain proletarian sections of the SA, which are to-day still locally influential, being officially denounced in the name of law and order as rowdies. Nevertheless, the smaller is the class that is capable of removing the régime from the onward rush of general impoverishment, the more quickly will the myth be destroyed, the sooner will the end come.

The myth that is here to be destroyed is the myth of Order. National Socialism has used it to soothe the inferiority complex of the German bourgeoisie. It has been said that the disorderly condition of the State and industry infuriated the bourgeoisie and drove it into National Socialism. If the former conditions were really ill-regulated, those at present — as probably even the upholders of the system would admit — are materially no better. National Socialism, however, came as a counterbalance to the feelings of disintegration and lack of direction in the bourgeoisie. It has driven its brown columns through the disorganized masses of this class like a firm scaffolding, and by means of them has produced a tremendous suggestion of consolidation. The readiness with which the German bourgeoisie yielded to the National Socialist suggestion can only be understood from its tremendous need for new self-confidence, and a self-confidence that was acquired by service and by division into corporations (*Stände*) of varying importance. Some even of the Jews were obliged in this instance to obey their bourgeois natures in contradiction to the interests of their peculiar racial position. And the present mental attitude of the German people can only be understood as the result of a most powerful suggestion adapted to the unconscious desires of the middle class. Only a national spirit that had been vitiated by the crisis and which was obviously in a pathological condition could have fallen victim to the suggestion.

National Socialism, however, cannot only accommodate itself to the demand for gradations of rank, it must also deal with the fact of material levelling. Hence it announces the abolition of class distinctions, which has, in fact, taken place between the proletariat and the lower-middle class as a result of the depreciation of small property. Thus it is giving ideological unity to the opponents who will one day overthrow it. In vain does it try to dissolve the union transversely by ordering Society into a hierarchy of grades of authority, in which each has responsibility to those above and power over those below. For a form of Society the ideals of which are autarchy, economic contraction, and heroic poverty must sooner or later arrive at the point at which its members are no longer capable of fulfilling the demands made of them. From this moment onwards the division of authority into hierarchic grades becomes unworkable, because the lower grades are forced with increasing want to make common cause with the lowest — even if it only came in the form of passive resistance. This is the historical punishment for Fascism's raising to an ideal under the name of autarchy the present disintegration of world economy and the traditional division of the world into heavily armed States.

The régime seeks to postpone the day when interests will once again be victorious over symbols by a cult of blind obedience (" Authority downwards, responsibility upwards "). This obedience is favoured by the emergence of a class which was formerly known only as a generation, but which seems now to be acquiring something like a sociological character of permanence — the youth. When grey-bearded SA men are observed, for example, zealously guarding newly planted Hitler oaks, one has the feeling that this is youth that would like to perpetuate itself. There is some inward resistance against coming to maturity, a desire to remain under the protection of a prolonged youthfulness, saved from the torment of independence. It is because it has personally no desire to mature that this youth is also against social advancement.

If this youth is asked to state its ideals, it will certainly first of all name Socialism. Once again, what does that imply? Hitler means by it a social ideal that might have been called solidarity in earlier days. It begins with the recognition of private property, and goes on with the demand that everything private, both property and life, shall serve the community. To all appearances the old Liberalism which was founded upon the idea of harmony taught much the same thing. Nevertheless, a difference exists. The idea of Liberalism was that the individual was serving the community by pursuing his own interests productively. The new doctrine is not clearly so optimistic. It fears that the community may be harmed by the unlimited pursuit of private interests, which can only be averted by the individual's giving up certain advantages out of solidarity with the community. Nor is it assumed that the individual will always be induced by kindness to assent to the renunciation demanded by the nation. The individual is to live as an individual and to own property, but he will be forced to serve the community with it. Who will force him to do so? The State. What is the State? Not by any means the majority, but the best men in the nation. And who are the best men? So long as no divine voice indicates them, unfortunately it will probably — since there is no majority decision — be the most successful, the most forceful, the most ruthless; men, therefore, who possess many anti-social qualities.

It must be admitted that this form of Socialism offers the individual less than he hitherto had, and perhaps also less than he could have wished for himself. It limits a man's control over his property; but demands, nevertheless, that he shall have initiative and a sense of responsibility, that he shall shoulder the worry and the risk. The Third Reich has undoubtedly in practice fulfilled many of the desires for maintenance of its functionaries, but Hitler has not fulfilled the demands that the SA has made as a class. He has thereby shown that he possesses a power without which no revolutionary who has come to the top can stay there — the power of creative ingratitude.

Thus during the next months and years it will always be his aim to be in control of circumstances, not always mastering them but always borne up by them. He has realized one thing that his opponents and those who prophesy an evil ending to his attempt have not, and that is an element in all sovereign policy — that much more can be expected of men than they themselves realize. A master like Hitler can assuredly accomplish much with this soft and plastic material. And why should he not succeed in making at least some of them enthusiastic for hunger at times? The Soviets also managed to do it now and then.

Thus the National Socialists will pass their days with victories carefully spaced out from one period to the next, and with even more celebrations of victory; reverses will be disguised and kept secret as far as possible; and in the midst of this dangerous gamble they will pin their hopes to a revival of world trade. They will attempt as far as possible to take the great decisions out of the material domain — wherein, of course, there is a lack of popular ideals that can be used for propaganda — into the sphere of the struggle for power. For naturally the internal tensions in Germany, which are kept under with an iron hand by National Socialism, have not slackened. At the moment of writing Hitler quite indubitably disposes of the tacit power of more than half the electors; but this critical, expectant power that reserves its right to withdraw itself again is something very different from the ardent enthusiasm of the closer ring of adherents and fellow-workers who try to animate the lukewarmness all about them with their own zeal. It is never easy to get a clear idea of the real temper of the people in any country, and unexpected election results cause the expert judges to make fools of themselves from time to time. Of Germany it may be said with a certain reserve that Hitler has probably won over a good many adherents since March 5, who are prepared to give him a quiet run for his money and who are ready to enjoy the fruits of his success. On the other hand, many of the most fanatical of the Old Guard are disappointed — a change of adherents which would not necessarily be disadvantageous for a period of quiet and detailed work, if the struggle were really over. Social Democrat and Communist workers, depressed by the capitulation of their leaders, are setting their Socialist and Trades Union hopes upon Hitler. Nevertheless, in spite of all changes of opinion and adherence, there will always remain a strong minority that is at heart utterly in opposition; a minority that, it is true, is powerless, without leadership or spokesman, that can only speak its mind under danger, and that can for the time being not turn its opposition into political activity. Beyond this there is assuredly not a small section of the majority whose assent to National Socialism means something quite different. It will be a matter of life or death for the Hitler régime whether the various currents will be able to be directed into legal channels within the system, lest they seek dangerous ways outside it.

Up to now National Socialism has only succeeded in reducing the multifarious forms of expression of a free internal political life in Germany to pure, homogeneous, submissive ashes. If the fiery way of National Socialism was to be made intelligble, especially to foreigners, it was necessary to emphasize the militant force and the ardent will to victory as signs differentiating it from other Parties — although people may ask whether Germans can regard politics only as clawing at the enemy's throat, stabbing him in the vitals, and cutting a way through enemy lines to victory. In truth, that does seem the only idea nowadays. During the last few years students in Germany have favoured the political theories of Professor Carl Schmitt, who defined politics as a relationship between friends and enemies. That politics might also be concerned with calculation and with productiveness is quite alien to this doctrine. Any one who wishes to be successful in German politics must be destructive.

What about the rest of the world? The possibility must be reckoned with that Europe will reply to the intellectual union between Italian Fascism and German National Socialism by stiffening up its own internal political life. In other words — an internal political competition among the nations, in the course of which many hitherto highly valued democratic principles would be sacrificed.

It may be objected that the old classic democratic tradition in the Anglo-Saxon countries, for example, or even in France, was too strong to allow of such a thing happening. But France has several times shown itself very susceptible to Bonapartism and Boulangism. Indeed it is the real parent, as of so many other political forms of life, of the modern — that is to say, not traditional but plebiscite — form of dictatorship. And England in its time endured not only Cromwell for a few years but the Stuarts for close on a century, and it does not look as if parliamentarianism in its present form was very popular any more — at all events, not among the younger generation.

Nevertheless, there is within the wide framework of this general tendency to political rigidity plenty of room for counteraction. The propagandist emanations of National Socialism are certain to be dimmed by the shadows cast by its first internal political crisis. Such a crisis is inevitable after the triumphal progress of the summer, and clever governance can do no more than keep it as quiet and as secret as possible. The unhealthy ambiguous division of power between revolution and reaction; the strained relationships among the National Socialist leaders; the material unsoundness of trade and society, and the approaching reaction to the hazardous attempts at healing that have been made; and, finally, foreign policy — all this is bound to lead the régime into its first crisis. It will not die of it. But its influence upon the minds of men will wane. Will the Socialist Parties outside Germany make the most of this opportunity? That the masses expect it is shown by the electoral victories all over Europe with which the Labour Parties have replied to German Fascism. These Parties, however, can change the perpending psychological crisis of Fascism into victory only if they get over the crisis that lies in themselves, and which is expressed by open divisions or quarrels on points of theory and hence in lack of purpose. The parties whose aim it is to have the State run to plan have still to learn that they must also conduct their political campaign on large plans.

The crisis, however, is a mortal one for all countries alike. The national idiosyncrasy of every country will cause each to defend itself after its own manner. Nevertheless, in each country as it begins to defend itself there will be an abandonment of the existing demoralization of middle-class life in the course of which the spirit might become productive in its whole manifoldness. The age of toleration, when all intellectual production was approved on principle, even if it included the most violent antitheses, and possibly even involved the whole community in contradictions — the epoch of toleration has probably for the time being come to an end, and not only in Germany. We believe that the dimming of this brightest intellectual day in History is only a passing darkness, and are convinced that German National Socialism, being a rank weed of decadence, will not itself long outlive it — but it must be remembered that a generation is a very short space of time when History is turning over a page. The fall of Fascism will not mean the end of the revolutionary period in which we are living.

National Socialism is asserting that it is not the creation but the conqueror of the crisis; that it is setting authority against decay, and an unhesitating red-blooded will against sickly intellect. This authority permits no more than did the knight Lohengrin that its origin should be inquired into. Authority simply exists. It has put an end to the sovereignty of the intellect by forbidding inquiries after the why and the wherefore, and insisting by means of rubber truncheons, revolvers, and concentration camps upon a submission that is not otherwise justified. Nevertheless, authority too will see its last dawn when young minds begin again to inquire and to demand to be given reasons for their obedience. Then the intellectual mob will suddenly realize that the snobbery against reason and logic, against argument and classification, that is so popular to-day, was at bottom nothing more than humbug on the part of an overbearing authority that was making life easy for itself by training people to be proud of their ignorance.

Whence comes, after all, this enthusiasm on the part of living beings to allow themselves to be rammed into a mould, to a monotony of black and brown shirts? Whence this pleasure at being turned from human beings into soldier-like and burden-carrying ants? This effacement of personality is the expression of a time that finds its delight in intellectual exhaustion. National Socialism which welds individuals into the body of the nation thereby does exactly the same thing in politics that the new methods are doing in science. According to these, instead of induction, logical building-up from individual observations, a general view is taken, things are looked at and thought of as collective units. Theoretical physics are beginning to substitute for the classic chain of causes, consisting of thousands of isolated facts, the more imposing but less reliable conception of the statistical series. In the domain of politics as of service, the collective unit is taking precedence of the individual, will the precedence of cause, and intuition the precedence of proof. This complete change-over of all methods of thought may be temporarily justified as adaptation to an emergency condition; a mental turning of oneself into a chrysalis and shutting oneself up before the superabundance of tasks and impressions that has arisen out of the vast growth of the intellectual world during the nineteenth century. This state of chrysalization into which Fascism and morphology are leading us is in its essence defensive, unheroic, and a surrender; it has nothing in it of the vikingesque that Fascism deludes us into believing in by its attitude. Is this contradiction? Is this the lie?

Hitler has accustomed us to thousands of contradictions. Has not he — a Conservative — been seen making a revolution that is utterly alien to his innermost being, a revolution for the preservation of what exists? The fact is, as he puts it so beautifully, it is no longer conditions that are revolutionized, but thought. This logical, eternally critical, eternally restless thought will now be kept quiet, and will be adapted to circumstances, be they never so unreasonable and unpleasant.

We have seen the man who always spoke of the sword come into power by diplomatic juggling. And, above all, we have seen this man canvassing the masses whom he despises passionately, and always concentrating the whole force of his agitation, the spirit of his Party, upon the last, the worst voter. We have seen how he brought the unpolitical to the polling-booths, how he made those who were uninterested in politics interested in them, and how he used them to outvote those who understood politics — and we have heard how he extolled this inert mass as the élite of the nation. We have seen how he gathered the discontented about him, gave dignities to those who had come off badly, made leaders of those who had failed in ordinary bourgeois life, and then expected the silent, hard-working part of the nation to recognize these men as the elect of the people and as exemplars. For the mass crisis that tore even the most capable from their normal sphere, and made them susceptible to Hitler's blandishments, has only been in operation for a few years and has only filled the outer ring of the Party with adherents. The kernel of the Party, on the other hand, the Old Guard that is so touchingly extolled, consists very largely of inexperienced people, failures, who had for years not done anything in life, men who were wholly or partly pathological cases. It was a definite selection of the second-rate. The leadership principle — as is proved by the personnel of the National Socialist Party — leads to selection not only according to actual capability but also according to personal devotion to the leader. National Socialism as an agitatorial force reduced democracy *ad absurdum* by making its greatest source of danger — demagogy — overflow automatically. National Socialism as a regnant force will destroy the leadership principle by its own source of error — administration by tools.

It is only necessary to glance at Lieutenant Heines. This is a man whose authority is equalled by few men in Germany. He was appointed Chief of Police in Breslau and Supreme Group Leader in Eastern Germany by Hitler himself — and is a condemned murderer. Heines is the primitive type of man who seeks to lay about him with a club. Hitler himself expelled him from the Party only a few years ago. It is only necessary to take a look at General Göring, whose pathological state of continuous excitement has aroused anxiety even in a man like Röhm; at Rust, the Prussian Minister for Public Worship and Education, whose undoubted ability is not sufficient compensation for his abnormal nervousness; at Karl Kaufmann, Governor of Hamburg, against whom his own fellow-members in the Party, including the Governor of East Prussia, Koch, brought unanswered charges of fraud and forgery; at Julius Streicher, who was appointed by Hitler to conduct the anti-Jewish boycott; at Hermann Esser; at

. . . Enough. The endless list of these unworthy officials of the Third Reich cannot be covered by the names of men like General von Epp, Frick, Siebert, &c., who are at least personally above reproach. In the Party organization and in positions of authority are far too many men of doubtful character. And at the head of them all stands the Leader himself. As a whole, Hitler's supporters are probably the men most inclined to render obedience in the whole nation. But they are not the men most fitted to co-operate in the work of building up a new communal life, and certainly the least fitted for individual and independent work. The " Saintly Company " is composed for the most part of stupid saints.

The fact that the "rowdy" rules to-day in Germany is not a temporary phenomenon nor the accompaniment of the " birth-pangs " of a Revolution. The official ideology speaks of " political soldiers." In fact, it is the armed man of action who is abroad in Germany to-day. It is the officer in the wrong place. The officer in his proper place has no desire beyond that of being a soldier. Indeed he regards politics with contempt. The best representatives of this soldierly type of mind are to be found in the Reichswehr, which is not nearly so much interested in politics as certain of its members — notably Schleicher — sought to have believed. For this very reason the Reichswehr is not a danger to a clever politician like Hitler, but rather an instrument to be used skilfully — until the day comes when Fate gives it a statesman among its generals. The business of the officer is the conduct of war against foreign enemies, and that of the " political soldier " the conduct of war against domestic enemies. It was for such men that the theory was invented of the preponderance of politics over economics that implies the right of the amateur to destroy economic life. For an harmonious relationship between political and economic life can only exist either in the case in which each avoids all interference with the other, is entirely independent of the other, or in the case in which the two become united to form a single entity. The first is Liberalism and the second is Socialism. In practice there exists a third and intermediary form in which politics and economics are intermingled — dilettantism. That in Germany to-day this third form is in existence is revealed by the system of personal government.

It has already been shown in what manner Hitler filled administrative posts with incapable, if often well-meaning, men for whom those officials of the former Weimar Republic who retained their posts were forced to draft proposals and speeches. Germany saw all this also, and would have had a silent sympathy for the difficulties attendant upon such a constructive task, if it had not been that these new officials in an orgy of self-glorification that became intolerable had not repeatedly declared that an end must be made of slow routine and the corruption of parliamentary government. A mob of brown-shirted berserkers seized all paid posts and all those which entitled their holders to " expenses allowances," and ejected their middle-class occupants. It was said that this struggle was waged in the name of objectivity, cleanliness, and honesty. Honesty! And then on January 30 came the news of the oath of fidelity taken by the allies forming this Government — the oaths of fealty sworn to the Field-Marshal — followed by charges of corruption brought against the intimate collaborators of the Reich President and Field-Marshal for the purpose of destroying the old man's authority and prestige. The Government of National Concentration is in truth a system of perjury from which each individual hopes to profit by being a better liar and more disloyal than his fellow.

The contradictions in the Nazi doctrine were reproduced in the Nazi practice of governance. This doctrine claimed to teach heroism. In reality it lauded cowardice. The Nazi doctrine is inspired by the fear of progress, responsibility, and action. It seeks to escape individual responsibility by laying emphasis upon the necessity for obedience and dutiful acceptance of orders. It is inspired by a fear of fresh storms and unknown stars. It is a protest on the part of the human body in need of repose against the restlessness of the intellect. The exaggerated value which the present age sets upon emotion and its deliberate depreciation of reason only serve to prove that it is feminine in character. It is, indeed, significant that among the intellectual ancestors of the nationalist ideal is to be found that slave of women and idol of his mother, Bachofen, the great authority on family law. The fashionable decrying of progress and reason is in its essential nature prudish and infantile. A cause for its present popularity is probably to be found in the fact that the finest sons of all nations are lying buried on the battlefields of the World War. The survivors, who were in any case not Homeric heroes but the modern nervous type of humanity, were only intensified in their need of quiet and order. The readiness with which the German nation threw off its burden of democratic responsibility and entrusted its political destiny to a dictator is perhaps to be explained by the horrors of the four years of war and the fourteen years of suffering that succeeded to it. The burden of responsibility was too heavy to be borne by a martyred nation.

It is nevertheless undeniable that National Socialism daily set in motion mighty physical and mental forces. But these forces were turned inwards upon themselves and not directed against externals. They destroyed the nation in their passage and drove nothing along with them. The deeds of this Nationalism whose admiring gaze is always turned upon itself only affect its own inner nature. It employs the best energies in the nation in self-complacency and self-imprisonment. Its precedent is to be found in the great anti-Semitic movement in Central Europe in the fourteenth century — the Flagellants. A pathological love of self-sacrifice inspires all the speeches about devotedness and the pledges that are daily delivered to the SA that have long since exceeded the limits of decency. These orators talk of sacrifice in a vulgar matter-of-fact tone as if it were a gymnastic exercise.

For fourteen years National Socialism armed itself against an imaginary superior force and collected round it a mountain of weapons that now presses its fatal weight upon a diminutive enemy. Political mythology occupies the German stage to-day. Göring covers his walls with the swords of old-time German headsmen and receives his visitors at the Ministry in a dark room illuminated only by candle-light. His worth as a politician may be open to question. As a symbolic figure, however, Göring superbly represents his age, his cause, and — perhaps — even his nation. As the ice giants and Midgard snakes loomed terrifyingly forth from the Nordic mists, so to-day the French machine-guns and English Navy stand forth in Nazi imagination from the gas-clouds thickened with propaganda of the

World War as the clutching tentacles of the Jewish octopus. The Allied propaganda was Hitler's greatest intellectual experience and inspiration, and from it sprang the idea of Nazi agitation. In order to hack off the tentacles of the octopus, National Socialism constructed a scythed-wheel — a want of imagination caused it to be called a swastika (*Hakenkreuz*) — and organized the SA as a military force with which to continue the World War on the home front. It was here that the sleep-walking German genius first discovered the battlefield on which the demons were awaiting him unmasked and no longer clad in Allied uniforms. His prejudices were now given full play. Party comrades became heroes and their enemies traitors. Here he continued the fight which he had broken off in 1918 externally, but not in his inner man. The spirit of the World War rose again in this ghostly battle — for the World War has become for ever a part of the German mind. It is not looked upon as an accident or a blood-stained misreading of history, but as the battle of the nations from which Germany can only emerge victorious or annihilated. This contest of the slain with the survivors has lasted for fourteen years in Germany. On January 30, 1933, the dead defeated the living — for the moment.

The German spirit seeks to take refuge from the hard daylight of a cruel fate in the pleasant shades of a heroic legend. A play was recently produced in many German theatres that had for its subject the strategical incidents of the Battle of the Marne. German General Staff officers were to be seen studying maps dotted over with little flags. Their conversation — an invention of the dramatist — gave the audience to understand that the German Army had really won the Battle of the Marne and the World War if a few unfortunate officers had not lost their nerve at the critical moment. German military experts protested against this falsification of history. Of what use was it? A vast public only too willingly allowed itself to be convinced by the dramatist that the Battle of the Marne was "really" a German victory. A dramatic critic wrote in a Western German newspaper that with all due respect for military history it was the business of a dramatist to create a legend.

A legend. . . .

And who tells the nation the truth?

Truth and Justice and Freedom are not popular in Germany to-day. It is possible that they may even be put to the test in other countries. Sincerity in political belief is to-day being subject to an acid test. In the opinion of the present writer that is only a matter for rejoicing. If the horrors of the present age are great its possibilities are no less great. Once more mankind has reached a stage at which a new world can be won and only fetters can be thrown off.

An aspect of the problem arises here that must never be lost sight of, and must be emphasized at every possible opportunity. Many of those who have been the victims of National Socialism are to-day at war with their own nation. Men and women whose Teutonism is not to be disputed, even in the light of present racial theories, have been foremost in criticizing their own nation and not only its present rulers. Their reproaches are levelled at their fellow-countrymen for tolerating and supporting the existing Nazi rule. This is to commit a fundamental error. A nation possesses no definite character; it is a conglomerate of tendencies. If the German nation to-day shows itself in an unfavourable light, and draws a veil across its possession of those characteristics for which it has been admired, the fault is entirely that of all members of the German race.

Fate does not confer its character upon a nation. It is the result of education and, indeed — to use the word in its highest sense — political training. Each successive generation, which is after all only the child of the nation, has in its turn the task of imprinting upon the nation its own individual stamp. The nation becomes, as it were, the child of its own children. And whoever stands in this relationship to his nation cannot blame the child for the mistakes made by the children. It is because we continue to love Germany that we carry on the struggle for her. If we did not do so, we should not have the feeling of sincere love for our country.

Others hate the present rulers of Germany and yet refrain from fighting against them in the belief that such an action is in reality a fight against Germany itself. They say to themselves that the overthrow of this Government would mean chaos and the downfall of Germany. For reasons that have partly been advanced here it is clear that no sacrifice of conscientious scruples and no act of desperation will prevent the fall of the present Nazi rule. Nevertheless, when the day comes for their downfall, men must be waiting who have prepared themselves for such an eventuality, who have deliberately desired it and are therefore not surprised by its occurrence. A movement must already be in existence that will be capable of filling the horrible gap left by the overthrow of National Socialism. In that event — only in that event — will the downfall of National Socialism not entail chaos and a concomitant destruction of Germany.

Fascism has in the long-run only the choice between poverty and war. Both will prove its destruction. It is to be hoped that this will come through the former. Nevertheless, it is necessary to be prepared for the latter. Every one who loves liberty contributes to making the end of Fascism the beginning of a new Europe. In the day of its birth this new Europe must already be alive in the hearts and minds of the peoples. Until that day comes it is our task and our duty so to demean ourselves that future generations will say of us: "Your life was indeed noble. For you were privileged to fight for the freedom that we can only enjoy."

A HISTORY OF NATIONAL SOCIALISM

FINAL CHAPTER

THE REICHSTAG TRIAL

NATIONAL SOCIALISM was at the height of its success between November 12, 1933, and March 21, 1934. Then began the descent — how far it will go cannot yet be said.

After Germany had left the League of Nations on October 14, 1933, Hitler held a plebiscite to ascertain whether the nation agreed with the policy followed at Geneva and to elect a new Reichstag — for which there was only a single list of candidates — the governmental — although a few non-Nazi names, including Dr. Hugenberg's, stood on the list. An overwhelming majority undoubtedly approved of Germany's withdrawal from the League — many with enthusiasm. Hitler made the most of the popular mood to bring into being a Reichstag that should be perfectly submissive to his will. In the parliament that had just been dissolved less than half the deputies had belonged to the National Socialist Party. They had assured themselves of a majority by the simple expedient of shutting up most of those in the Opposition in concentration camps.

The nation was worked upon for weeks by an incredibly intensive propaganda. Moreover, it was widely believed that the ballot would not be secret, and that there was no point in uselessly risking what might be very unpleasant consequences by not voting in the required sense, since — so most people were also convinced — the authorities would in any case falsify the results to suit themselves. It was in fact afterwards proved that the ballot was not secret, because certain persons were openly persecuted for having voted against Hitler. In several cases it became known that results had been faked, though these cases were punished. At all events, it may be said that the results did not express the true opinion of the nation; but what percentage of error there was is, of course, impossible to state. It should be added that anyone who abstained from voting was branded officially as a traitor to the country and the Leader.

According to official figures, of 43,460,000 electors 42,120,000 voted. On the question of Germany's withdrawal from the League of Nations, 40,610,000 answered in the affirmative, 2,050,000 in the negative, and 790,000 were void — probably mostly also noes with some remark derogatory to the Government added. To the Reichstag list, 39,650,000 gave their assent, and 3,350,000 votes were void.

Despite the fact that it was somewhat unreliable, this result gave the impression in other countries that the régime had come to stay.

The political impression was temporarily strengthened by a moral one when the Supreme Court pronounced sentence in the Reichstag case. The Bulgarians — Dmitroff, Popoff, Taneff — and even the Communist Torgler, were acquitted. Van der Lubbe's execution could be formally justified by his confession. The suspicion cannot, nevertheless, be avoided that he was in some way influenced — possibly by being drugged — in making the "confession," and that his death removed one who knew too much. If this be thought improbable, it must be remembered that officially "Whatever is profitable to the German Nation is right."

Van der Lubbe's execution and the treatment of the acquitted men did much to spoil the favourable impression held abroad of the impartiality of the Supreme Court. Dmitroff's bearing throughout the case roused the admiration of the whole world and even that of many Nazis. The suspicion that the National Socialist Party was itself responsible for the burning of the Reichstag grew almost to a certainty as the case proceeded, although, of course, no proof was ever found. It was discovered that the accused were fettered, which is contrary to the usual custom with political prisoners; and the attitude of the leading German statesmen to the judicial powers is shown by one scene in particular. Göring was in the witness box answering Dmitroff's acute questions with increasing excitement. When Göring lost his temper completely, Dmitroff asked: " Are you afraid of my questions? " Göring shouted: " Wait till you come out! You'll live to be afraid of me! " This showed that Göring intended taking Dmitroff into " protective custody," and probably to have him mishandled. The whole world was shocked by the episode; nor did the impression wear off when it was found that the men were not set free after being acquitted, until the Soviet Union made them Russian citizens and demanded their release, after which they were sent out of the country by aeroplane. Torgler, however, up to the time of writing (September 1934) remains in custody.

NAZI FOREIGN POLICY

National Socialist foreign policy has been determined purely by propagandist necessity. Hitler's dream is to find " room in the East " — that is, in Russia — for Germany, and hence to have his hands free in other respects. He planned to do this by the military overthrow of France, and by cultivating the friendship of England and Italy. In practice, Hitler did the exact opposite. He made an offer of alliance to France, though this was not taken very seriously by anyone, least of all by the French themselves. Instead of coming to an understanding with England and Italy, he is on bad terms with both. The one political success he has to show is the pact of friendship and non-aggression with Poland. Poland's friendship with France has cooled somewhat and Poland looks upon Germany as affording surer protection against Soviet Russia. Poland feels safer so long as Germany and Russia are not united— for then she is free of the ever-present spectre of being re-partioned. Germany's hope is that she might obtain help from Poland in event of war with Russia, which is the very thing that Poland most wishes to avoid — for the overthrow of Russia would end in Poland's becoming the vassal of Germany and having to resign the Corridor and Upper Silesia. Thus the real achievement of the Pact is the surprise occasioned by Hitler's making friends with the " traditional enemy " in the East, and thus temporarily renouncing the hope of regaining the lost provinces.

As regards the remainder of his foreign policy, Hitler's schemes for aerial defence have alienated England, which had for a long time been very ready to be friendly and had brought pressure to bear on France to come to terms over disarmament. He gambled away his friendship with Italy by the terrorist campaign in Austria which was designed to bring that country under German domination. His interview with Mussolini at Strà, though extolled in the German newspapers as a pact of friendship the consequences of which would be world-wide, had in reality no result at all — because, unkind people have said, Mussolini could not get in a word edgeways!

Nazi activities in Austria were carried on with bombs and wireless speeches from the Reich until on July 25, 1934, the Austrian Chancellor was assassinated in the course of an attempted *coup d'état.* The act aroused especial horror all over the world as Dollfuss was left for hours bleeding to death, and was afforded neither physical nor spiritual ministrations. Germany's share in the abominable murder is not yet clear, but it is a fact that the German wireless service immediately announced the *coup* with rejoicing as the uprising of the German people in Austria.

Mussolini at once concentrated troops on the Austrian frontier. It was clear that Italy would cross that frontier in case of a Nazi triumph. Hitler realized the complications that would ensue and forbore to follow up the "victory."

Germany's isolation in international politics is evidenced by three fundamental facts — the Franco-Russian alliance and Russia's entry into the League of Nations; the initiation of a Franco-Italian understanding; and the complete swing round of public opinion — and with it of foreign policy — in England. Mr. Baldwin stated in the House of Commons that England's frontier now is the Rhine, and on September 7, 1934, Mussolini pointed out insultingly at Bari that Italy had produced Caesar, Virgil, and Augustus at a time when to the north of the Alps the art of writing had not yet been discovered.

Owing to a common hatred of Russia, Germany's sole possible ally remains Japan.

During the second half of 1934 German policy has been concentrated on the Saar. This small strip of land on the French frontier, containing some 800,000 inhabitants, is rich in coal-mines. By the

Treaty of Versailles, France was given the use of the territory for fifteen years in compensation for the damage done to her own mines during the War. At the end of that time the district is to vote as to its own future. The people are preponderantly German, and up to 1933 there was no doubt that a 95% vote would have been cast for return to Germany. Now, although the existence of the Hitler régime as such would not necessarily alter its wish to become German once more, the feeling seems to be that it would be better to wait until a fresh form of government is introduced into Germany — one that does not interfere so much with life and liberty, and especially with the Church. By denouncing his opponents on the Saar as traitors and criminals, Hitler has made the struggle an unequal one from the very outset..Realizing that the 95% vote that he had expected would not now be forthcoming, Hitler has tried to induce France to return the district without holding a plebiscite. The matter, however, does not lie in France's hands, but in those of the League of Nations. The date for the plebiscite has been fixed by the Council of the League for January 13, 1935. In case of a strong minority voting against immediate return to Germany, the League will be faced with the necessity of protecting this minority, which will be a difficult matter in Germany under present conditions. According to the Treaties, the League might arrange in case of such a minority that the territory should be divided and part only returned to Germany. But Hitler has indicated that he would regard this as a *casus belli.* While he is not in a position to wage a real war, he could introduce the same reign of terror as was done in Austria. Then if France were to move her troops into the Saar district to maintain order, Hitler would be provided with the opportunity to rouse nationalist feelings to fever heat, which would always be a considerable gain to him. Hence, if the Nazis are convinced that they will suffer a defeat (even if only a moral one) in this district, a *coup* is to be anticipated there, if only in order to postpone the holding of a decisive plebiscite.

These examples show to what straits Nazi foreign policy is reduced — it has achieved the isolation of Germany within six months.

The "controlled" Press of Germany is careful not to allow the people to ascribe this isolation to any incapacity on the part of the

Government, but puts it all down to the malevolence of other countries. On the other hand, it cannot prevent the nation from realizing the economic crisis which has been brought about by Hitler's lack of understanding of economic principles.

In order to put millions of men back to work an immense amount of capital of all kinds has been used up without any corresponding increase in production. The necessary consequence is that the standard of living throughout the nation must be lowered. This has been further intensified by the difficulties of foreign trade. Increased production at home necessitated increased imports of raw materials from abroad, and these could no longer be paid for by exports, which were falling off. Thus it is partly due to the artificial creation of work for the unemployed that Germany under Hitler is no longer paying her foreign debts.

The reasons for the fall in the German export trade are various. It is primarily due to the prohibition of the import of certain goods, which led to measures of reprisal being taken by the countries affected. Secondly, the German re-armament policy as well as the persistent refusal of Germany to pay her debts has caused foreign countries to boycott German merchandise. Thirdly, Germany, in common with other countries, has suffered from the competition of cheap Japanese goods. Further, Germany increased her import of certain raw materials that could be used in the manufacture of armaments, and hence the imports often exceeded the exports, so that Germany was through lack of currency no longer able to pay her way.

It has been doubted whether Germany's inability to pay is as great as she says. This is not the place in which to discuss the problem. It is at all events true that Germany has got into serious economic difficulties in the course of the year 1934, and to a great extent owing to her own policy. According to the reports of the Reichsbank, there were 922 million Marks in its vaults in gold and securities when Hitler came to power. By August 1934, there were only seventy-seven millions. The Mark was covered only up to two per cent.

The Government took two measures to deal with the situation. It refused to pay its foreign debts, including those contracted by private persons, and restricted imports to a dangerous degree.

Various attempts to make an arrangement regarding the payment of the debts failed; and on June 14, 1934, Germany declared that she would no longer repay even Government guaranteed loans. Most foreign countries retorted by non-payment of debts to Germany (clearing). But by the autumn, Germany was approaching the declaration of a general moratorium for a number of years.

The gravity of the economic situation was revealed even more clearly by the restrictions on imports. Commissars were established everywhere to oversee imports, which were considerably restricted on things like textiles, non-ferrous metals, rubber, leather, etc., and totally prohibited on others, such as wool. Extraordinary measures — resembling those adopted during the War — were taken to counteract these restrictions. Housewives were asked not to throw away rags, paper, or scraps of wool; and rubbish dumps were carefully searched for anything that might be used as raw material. Production was restricted to some extent during the summer. The textile industry went on to a thirty-six-hour week, and the wages of 1,200,000 workers were correspondingly reduced. German economic policy began to resemble a sort of war-time Communism.

Obviously, if hours were shortened and wages cut, the general power of consumption was lowered. Thus, though many more men were employed, there was no real rise in prosperity. Employers sometimes took on more men than they needed, but a general lowering of wages was the inevitable result. Others, again, took on more workers, but dismissed them after a short period. It is interesting — though of course not of practical value for objective proof — that even among the supporters of the régime in Germany there are many who do not regard the figures of the decrease in unemployment as reliable.

According to the official figures, unemployment sank from 6,110,000 at the end of January 1933, to 2,400,000 at the end of August 1934. The numbers of workers in employment rose from 12,600,000 in April 1933, to 15,500,000 in June 1934. During the same period the yield of the Income Tax (ten per cent. of the wages) rose from 182 to 197 millions of Marks. Thus while the number of employed persons rose by twenty-three per cent., the wages only rose by about eight per cent. This means that there was an average drop in wages of about twelve per cent.

It must be noted here that a new spirit is considered to have been infused into labour in Germany. On May 1, 1934, a " Law to regulate National Labour " was promulgated. The employer is to be the " leader," the workpeople his " followers." Work is to be done " for the benefit of people and State." Private property, however, is still to exist.

At one time German exporters demanded the devaluation of the Mark. But Dr. Schacht, the President of the Reichsbank, refused to allow it. If only on psychological grounds, the German nation could not stand another crash like that of the Mark in 1922–3, even on a modified scale. Schacht was created Economic Dictator, and seems to be making determined efforts to render Germany at least partially independent of foreign raw materials. The best-known example of this policy in action is the manufacture of artificial cotton, called " Vistra "—which has, however, up to the present proved to be more expensive than cotton itself.

Disastrous economic conditions caused troubles and produced a state of tension that was still further increased by the rivalries within the Nazi governmental apparatus. On January 30, 1934, the Reichstag unanimously voted the abolition of individual State frontiers within Germany. In practice, of course, they persist. Thus neither President von Hindenburg nor Göring would agree to Prussia's losing its individuality. In the end Göring relinquished his post as Minister of the Interior in Prussia, but remained chief of the Prussian police, the real instrument of power.

These real or apparent advances in high politics did not interest the masses particularly. While confidence in Hitler remained practically unabated, conditions in the country were severely criticized. This criticism was stimulated by subterranean Communist and Social Democrat propaganda, which by now is once again well-organized, despite the ferocity with which it is suppressed by the authorities. Up to the present more than fifty persons have been pole-axed for their political opinions, and long years of imprisonment have been meted out to others.

Resistance to the régime was also manifested by the Churches. Although the so-called "State Evangelical Church" with its Reich Bishop Müller has been in existence for a full year, many of the clergy are still in opposition. The Reich Bishop was not formally inducted into his office before the year had expired and the last independent Churches in Bavaria and Württemberg had been suppressed.

Equally violent and perhaps still more dangerous has been the Government's struggle with the Roman Catholic Church. A concordat was signed in 1933 which, while curtailing the Church's rights to some extent, appeared to guarantee the remainder. Nevertheless, the agreement has not been kept on the Nazi side, and Catholic organizations have been relentlessly persecuted. In June 1934, negotiations for a final settlement were instituted in Berlin between representatives of the Nazi Government on the one hand and three Catholic Bishops on the other. The Curia, however, did not immediately accept the draft agreement, and the matter still remains in abeyance (September 1934).

A further centre of unrest, and possibly the most serious, was the SA. Upon the Party's first coming into power in 1933, Röhm had enormously increased the numbers of the SA. It then contained 600,000 men. Eventually the membership rose to three millions. A good many of these were workmen who had found other Parties disappointing, and who hoped that Hitler would realize their aspirations. Others joined the SA with the intention of remaining Socialists or Communists and converting their fellows. In the end numbers of SA troops were really Socialist or Communist in spirit and organization. Humorists called them "beefsteaks" — brown outside and red inside.

As the spokesman who voiced SA desires, Röhm often — perhaps unconsciously — gave expression to these tendencies. His own early life as the son of a minor government official had predisposed him to such views. Moreover, many who joined the SA in the hope of social advancement found their hopes unfulfilled and were embittered. Unfortunately Röhm and his fellow-officers were too fond of good living themselves. The possession of magnificent cars and luxurious quarters was only a part of their sins. Personal enrichment, seizing the property of political opponents, and the appropriation of more or less ownerless parcels of shares were others.

THE STAHLHELM

A last attempt to overcome these difficulties was made in the autumn of 1933. President von Hindenburg was obliged to withdraw his objections; Röhm was admitted to the Cabinet as Minister without Portfolio, and the local SA leaders were attached to the police. They were allowed to take part in political actions and even to intervene on their own initiative. Peace seemed to be assured, and towards the end of January 1934 Hitler wrote a cordial letter to Röhm, which ran:

"My dear Chief of Staff Röhm, The struggle of the National Socialist movement and the National Socialist revolution were only made possible by the well-timed suppression of the Marxist terror by the SA. Hence at the completion of the first year of the National Socialist revolution, my dear Ernst Röhm, I feel the urge to thank you for the imperishable services you have rendered the National Socialist movement and the German nation, and to express my thankfulness that Destiny should have permitted me to number such men as yourself among my friends and comrades-in-arms.

In cordial friendship and grateful appreciation,

Your

Adolf Hitler."

Röhm, however, had not the political gifts necessary to enable him to make the most of his immense potential power. The enormous increase of the SA made it appear as though he were only concerned to increase his own personal influence, and not to form a homogeneous whole with the rest of the movement.

Röhm proceeded somewhat too vigorously in two directions. Firstly, he continually harassed the Stahlhelm. True, the Stahlhelm under General Reinhardt was officially subordinate to him as first Reserve, and junior organizations of the Stahlhelm had been incorporated in the SA. But the Stahlhelm remained as a solid phalanx of dissatisfied Conservatives, and comprised Junkers as well as members of the middle classes. The last independent action of the SA under Röhm was to demand that the remainder of the Stahlhelm should be disbanded.

Röhm's persistence had brought him thus far. Matters only became really dangerous for him when he entered upon a conflict with the Reichswehr.

RÖHM VERSUS BLOMBERG

As is well known, Germany is working to obtain an army of 300,000 men. To be exact, this is a "programme" only as far as foreign countries are concerned. Actually, it may be taken as a fact that these 300,000 men are already under arms.

In the Nazi State it is obvious that additions to the Reichswehr strength should come from the SA. The Reichswehr, however, in many instances gave insulting preference to Stahlhelm or even Reichsbanner men. Nevertheless, the SA remained the chief source of Reichswehr reserves.

Röhm wished SA companies to be taken over complete with their leaders into the Reichswehr. That would have meant that SA leaders of all ranks and origins — former car-drivers, railwaymen, postmen, labourers — would have become officers in the Reichswehr. Napoleon achieved such transformations. But Hitler could not; or, rather, to be accurate, he would not. The Reichswehr refused to allow SA men to enter its ranks except as ordinary individual recruits who were required to cease to belong to the SA on enlistment. At the end of April, Hitler went over to Blomberg's side. A quarrel between Blomberg and Röhm on this occasion appears to have been the ultimate cause of Röhm's being suddenly sent on furlough. Things were, however, working up to a head — if only because the SA was causing international difficulties. On May 17, 1933, Hitler made a speech offering as earnest of his desire for peace to allow foreign supervision of the SA if it were made reciprocal. It was only a diplomatic gesture. But how if the other side had translated it into actual fact — as well it might, having nothing to conceal? Röhm and his militarily drilled SA would have been sacrificed to Hitler's diplomacy.

Foreign governments, moreover, knew very well that Röhm was not satisfied with the 300,000 men programme. His aim was to have at least a million men under arms, and thus to raise an army equal to that of pre-War Germany and greater than that of any other present-day State.

The realization of this plan was impossible in Germany's present international situation. Moreover it would have meant the admission of non-Nazi — and therefore unreliable — men into the SA. It was already clear to Hitler that the SA could not continue to exist at its present size. While on furlough in July 1934, the SA was to be purged of its undesirable elements and decreased in numbers.

Matters came to a climax early in June, when Röhm and Hitler had a long discussion on the subject. Röhm protested violently against the "abolition" of the SA; Hitler replied that only a reduction in size was intended. No satisfactory solution was arrived at.

RÖHM GOES INTO MUFTI

Having fallen out with Hitler and Blomberg, Röhm retired for a time into private life. On June 7 he announced that his doctors had ordered him to take a long rest. In his last Order to the SA he referred to the leave that they were all to take in July, and in so many words enjoined resistance to any reduction in their numbers. It is, however, unlikely that he had formulated any definite plans as to what form resistance should take.

Röhm's holiday began with a scandal. He went to Heidelberg, where his behaviour and that of his friends were such as to cause a threat to be conveyed to him that unless they left at once, they would be forcibly turned out by the students of the University. They went. They did not know that they had been under the constant supervision of an emissary of the Baden Minister of the Interior, who was staying in the same hotel.

Reports of further happenings are unreliable. But two definite tendencies made themselves felt from now onwards. On the one side were the Conservatives who wanted a reconstitution of the Government and the removal of extremists, but who wished Hitler to remain as Chancellor. This group suddenly became vocal in Papen's speech on June 17, at Marburg. Amid great applause from all present, he said that the predominance of the Nazi Party and the exaggerated personal cult must cease, that free criticism must be allowed, that "despairing patriots" must no longer be branded as public enemies, and that doctrinaire fanatics must be silenced. The speech created a great sensation, for the initiated knew what lay behind it — the removal from the Cabinet of "doctrinaire fanatics," such as the Reich Minister for Agriculture, Darré.

The group favouring these plans was not really very influential, for though most influential persons would have sympathized in a greater or less degree, very few had the courage to come out into the open. In complete contrast to these plans were those of Röhm and the SA leaders. They wanted, if anything, to make the Government still more extremist.

During the first days of his leave Röhm wrote to a number of his friends among the SA leaders, regretting that Hitler was so "badly advised." He counselled them all to keep in touch during their month's leave, so that the SA might reassemble in full strength at the end of the time. Thus it was evident that the "revolutionary" SA leaders as well as the Conservative Party intended to keep Hitler for his publicity value. So long as the two groups balanced each other, Hitler was in no danger. But he must have been alarmed when the rumour reached him that the two groups were coming to terms with each other — in other words, that Röhm and Schleicher were conspiring against him.

It is conceivable that Röhm may have intended to lead another revolution and to misuse Hitler's name for his own purposes. But what of the alleged plot to murder Hitler? No definite proof, documentary or otherwise, has ever been found to justify the shooting of seventy-seven men (the official number, though Hitler admitted that a further, unstated, number had been killed).

These alleged revolutionary plots that come to nothing are always a trifle suspicious. The burning of the Reichstag on February 27, 1933, was said to be such a one — crushed by Göring. Then on June 30, 1934, it was said that the SA was about to rebel. Actually Hitler ordered a mass-murder.

These two occasions have furnished Hitler and Göring with excellent pretexts for arresting and doing away with their enemies.

The public was not altogether unprepared for the second "revolution." It had been spoken of — but, curiously enough, only by its opponents. Papen had referred to it at Marburg on June 17. On

June 20, Göring said before the Prussian Cabinet: " It is not for us to say whether a second revolution is necessary. If the Leader wishes for a second revolution we will, if he so desires, go out and fight for him again tomorrow. If he does not wish it, then we will suppress anyone who tries to make it against his will."

A similar and even clearer warning was given by Hitler's deputy, Hess, on June 25 over the wireless from Cologne: " Revolutions in complicated modern States cannot be carried out after the pattern of the eighteenth century, nor on the model of those that occur perennially in little exotic republics."

This was an unmistakable allusion to Röhm, late Lieutenant-Colonel in the Bolivian army. In the same speech Hess defended the very men who were afterwards declared to be a moral plague-spot in the nation: " Anyone who has the honour to be in the Leader's company for any length of time learns to be generous towards the human failings and foibles of other Leaders of National Socialism, so long as they go hand in hand with great deeds. . . . I am far from having a standard of perfection for all National Socialists."

Thus five days before the mass-murders of June 30, Hitler's closest adviser was prepared to forgive all — and all would have been forgiven had not Hitler suddenly grown to be personally afraid of these men.

Once again the question arises: What was the connexion between Röhm and the Conservatives?

The draft of a so-called Cabinet List was circulated by persons who were wholly unassociated with Herr von Papen. Some of those whose names appear in it certainly knew nothing of it. Indeed, it is not improbable that it was not the work of any of those whose names figured in it, but was put together by the men who needed some excuse for the mass-murders that were to be committed.

The vital question was always: What would happen when Hindenburg died? Should Hitler become President or someone more neutral — say, a Hohenzollern Prince, to prepare the way for a restoration of the monarchy (though this would certainly have been contrary to Hitler's wishes)?

The so-called Cabinet List contained the name of Prince August

Wilhelm, one of the sons of the ex-Kaiser, as President. He had for many years been a member of the National Socialist Party, as has already been told, and was said to have expressed himself as happy to work under Hitler despite his rank. Group Leader Karl Ernst of the Berlin SA was one of his close friends.

According to this List, Hitler was to remain Chancellor; but General von Schleicher was to be Vice-Chancellor instead of Papen; Röhm, Reichswehr Minister; and Gregor Strasser, who had seceded from Hitler in 1932, was to be Minister for Labour. It was hoped through him to win back the Social Democrats and the Trades Unions, which, though they no longer existed officially, still had a considerable influence among the working classes.

It is questionable whether anyone in authority took this List seriously. But it gives some semblance of truth to the rumour of an agreement between Röhm and Schleicher.

HEYDRICH'S INFORMATION

From Hitler's speech in the Reichstag on July 13, it is clear that neither he nor Göring nor Himmler had any definite information prior to June 30 regarding the intentions of their opponents. Göring was in possession of the usual police information concerning all the doings of the SA. In addition, numbers of persons unconnected with the SA were watched, and connexions proved or merely suspected. Further reports came from spies within the SA itself — among whom were Lutze, now Chief of Staff, and Himmler, the Reich Leader of the SS, as well as Himmler's Second-in-Command, Lieutenant Heydrich, a man said to possess exceptional detective gifts. Lutze is a personal friend of Hitler and Goebbels. Himmler, who was formerly a friend of Strasser's and Röhm's, had been Chief of the Prussian secret police and thus one of Göring's subordinates.

These three men — Lutze, Himmler, and Heydrich — are jointly responsible for the information from which the picture of the SA revolution was pieced together. The underlying idea of this revolt was said to be that the minds of the nation were to be prepared for a "second revolution," in order to "liberate Hitler" — which is impossible to prove. The ringleaders were, of course, said to be Röhm, his Second-in-Command, Captain von Krauser, and Group Leader Wilhelm Schmid, chief of the SA Press Bureau, all of whom were shot.

On June 29 Hitler was in the Rhineland, first in Essen and then at Godesberg. Here he finally took the decision, as he says, owing to the receipt of very alarming news. There is also an undisputed story that he was shot at by a " workman " in Essen. Himmler's car was also said to have been riddled with bullets on June 20 at Schorfheide, and Himmler himself wounded, on the occasion of the transfer of the body of Göring's wife to the vault " Carinshall." Hitler was present at this ceremony, and it was alleged that the shots — if they were really fired — were intended for him. It is a well-known fact that it is the hardest possible thing for an assassin to find the right opportunity to attack, especially in the case of a man like Hitler whose plans are never known beforehand. These shots could only have come from the hand of one who knew the day's programme — and there are reasons for thinking that they may have been fired by one of those who wished to bring things to a head and force Hitler to make up his mind to act. If it was really believed that this marked the beginning of the SA revolt, then it is strange that no mention of it should have been made after June 30. If the riddle of these shots were solved, it might also explain much of what happened on June 30. On June 26 the rule that no flowers must be thrown to the Chancellor was made more strict — an obvious precaution against assassination.

On June 25 Hitler was in Bavaria inspecting the new Alpine road that was in course of construction. On the 29th he was in a Westphalian Labour Camp. Towards midnight on June 29/30, he was given a torchlight procession in the form of a giant swastika. An hour later, so he says, the alarming news came in, and he decided to act. At 2 a.m. he left by 'plane from the aerodrome at Hangelaar near Bonn. With him were Goebbels, Lutze, Dietrich (the Reich Press Chief), and his adjutants Brückner, Schaub, and Schreck. At the same time a number of District Leaders went to Munich, summoned by telegram. At 4 a.m. Hitler landed at the Munich aerodrome. Here it was evident that all was quiet. It is open to doubt whether anything was otherwise anywhere. The first official notice stated that the SA had been called out. Hitler himself said in the Reichstag that they were only standing to arms in their barracks. One (or both) of these statements must be false. The Munich Senior Group Leader, Schneidhuber, as well as the SA Press Chief, Wilhelm Schmid, had already been arrested by Adolf Wagner, the Minister of the Interior, which does not look as if Schneidhuber had warned his men for active resistance. Hitler himself, so says report, tore off the shoulder-straps from Schneidhuber and Schmid. Then he went with his SS body-guard to Wiessee to find Röhm. It was no mere handful of men that set out, but a long train — six private cars and three lorries containing his body-guard; there was also an armoured car full of police. All told, at least a hundred men.

In Hitler's company were some curious figures. Among them Christian Weber and Emil Maurice, two of the oldest fighters in the movement. Maurice may be called the spiritual father of the movement's tactics. He was the first to resort to direct action, in the sense that he roved through the streets at night seeking opponents — especially Jews — that he might beat them up. Weber was of the same type. Once he was haled before the courts for attacking an elderly and invalid Jewish merchant, and he said that when he met a Jew he saw red and was no longer responsible for his actions. Here were two bravos eminently suited to the work that Hitler was about to require of them.

Wiessee is a small watering-place not far from the Austrian frontier, where Röhm had a house. On the other side of the lake lived a friend of Hitler's, one Adolf Müller, with whom the Chancellor often stayed. It is permissible to wonder whether this was not an observation post.

Röhm had summoned a number of the higher SA Leaders to Wiessee on that June 30 which was now dawning. At 7 a.m. Hitler and his men forced their way into the house. It was unguarded and undefended. Everyone was in bed. Röhm was fetched out of bed and taken into custody. Report says that Heines was found in bed with a boy. Hitler commanded that Heines should be dispatched at once. This was Emil Maurice's moment. He had an old score to pay off, dating from 1922, when Heines and his friends from the Rossbach Free

Corps had taken the place of the old Munich SA men. Maurice had borne him a grudge ever since. Heines was taken out clad only in a shirt and trousers, and a few shots did the rest. The " clean-up " had claimed its first victim. Röhm was taken to the prison in Munich where he had lain in 1923 as a companion of Hitler's. It was looked upon as an act of grace that he was given a revolver to enable him to commit suicide " as an officer and a gentleman." But Röhm refused to do so, declaring that he was innocent. " If I am guilty, let Adolf come and shoot me himself." He was allowed ten minutes. Then the executionary squad came in and did it for him. Much the same story was told of Schneidhuber. Later one of his sons laid a wreath on his grave; it was removed by the police.

Röhm's staff when they appeared gave no trouble, and Hitler returned to Munich. Here he made a long speech to those SA Leaders and others who had been convened, appointed Lutze to be Röhm's successor, pronounced death sentences, dictated his twelve points concerning the reconstitution of the SA, flew back to Berlin, and arrived there at ten o'clock that night.

These twelve points form an unforgettable document. They have inflicted a possible irreparable injury upon German credit by revealing the conditions prevailing in the ruling clique.

Hitler wrote to Lutze:

" In making you Chief of Staff of the SA, I expect you to set before yourself the following precepts:

" *1.* I demand blind obedience and unquestioning discipline from SA Leaders as from SA men.

" *2.* I demand that every SA Leader, like every political Leader, shall realize that he must in his behaviour and conduct set an example to his men, and indeed to our whole following.

" *3.* I demand that SA Leaders, like political Leaders, whose conduct is in any respect open to criticism shall be inexorably removed from the SA and from the Party.

" *4.* I demand especially that the SA Leader shall be a model of simplicity and not of extravagance. I do not wish SA Leaders to give expensive dinners nor to accept invitations to such. In the old days we were not invited to them, nor is there any reason why we should indulge in them now. Millions of our countrymen are suffering the lack of even the barest necessaries. They are not envious of those whom fortune has blessed.

"But it is unworthy of a National Socialist to emphasize the immense disparity that exists between poverty and riches.

"I forbid in particular that the funds of the Party or of the SA or any other public money shall be used for banquets or similar purposes. It is inexcusable that money which comes in part from the pence of our poorest fellow-citizens should be squandered in revelry. The luxurious Staff quarters in Berlin, where, as has been shown, anything up to 30,000 Marks were spent in revelry every month, are to be closed down at once.

"Hence I prohibit the provision of so-called gala dinners or banquets for any Party occasion out of public moneys of any description, and I forbid all Party and SA Leaders to attend any such functions. The sole permissible exceptions are those called for by the exigencies of State, for which the President and the Foreign Minister are primarily responsible. I forbid all SA Leaders and all Party Leaders in general to give so-called diplomatic dinners. There is no reason for any SA Leader to practise representation; it is no part of his duty.

"*5.* I do not wish SA Leaders to undertake official journeys in expensive limousines or cabriolets, or to spend public money in procuring them. The same holds good for Leaders of political organizations.

"*6.* SA Leaders or political Leaders who allow themselves to be overcome by drink in public are unworthy to be the leaders of their people. The prohibition of nagging criticism implies the duty of model behaviour. Mistakes can always be forgiven, but not misconduct. Hence SA Leaders who behave in an unseemly fashion in public, who create disturbances or indulge in debauchery, must immediately and unhesitatingly be expelled from the SA. The higher ranks are responsible for seeing that this rule is enforced. I expect the State authorities to mete out a more severe punishment in such cases than they would to men who are not members of the National Socialist Party. National Socialist Leaders and especially SA Leaders are to hold high rank in the nation. This also implies higher responsibilities.

"*7.* I expect all SA Leaders to help to establish and to keep the SA as a clean and pure institution. I particularly wish every mother to feel that she may give her son to the SA, to the Party, or to the Hitler Youth without any fear that he may be morally or spiritually corrupted. Hence I wish all SA Leaders to be most carefully on the watch for infringements of paragraph 175, and to punish any such infringement with instant dismissal from the SA and from the Party. I want to see *men* as Leaders of the SA and not perverted jackanapes.

"*8.* I demand of all SA Leaders that they shall requite my loyalty with their own and support it by their own. And I demand especially that they shall attend to their own affairs and not seek to interfere in those of others. I demand above all that every SA Leader shall conduct himself with perfect probity, loyalty, and respect towards the military forces of the Reich.

"*9.* I demand of SA Leaders that they shall not require more courage and self-sacrifice of their subordinates than they are prepared themselves to show. Hence I demand that in their conduct and treatment of that part of the national inheritance which I have confided to their care, SA Leaders shall prove themselves to be true leaders, friends, and comrades. I further expect them to reckon quality higher than quantity in their units.

"*10.* And I expect you as Chief of Staff to ensure that old and tried members of the Party, men who have fought in the SA for years, shall not be forgotten. I do not wish the Service to be inflated by numerous unnecessary and costly staffs; and in the matter of promotion I desire that not so much abstract intellectual achievement shall be regarded as inborn capacity for leadership, long and faithful service, and self-sacrifice. There is in my SA a tremendous force of most true and trusty men. It is they who have fought for Germany and not clever time-servers who joined in 1933 or later.

"*11.* I desire that the SA man shall be mentally and physically trained to be the best among National Socialists. The complete identification of the individual's outlook on life with that of the Party constitutes the unique strength of this organization.

"*12.* I wish obedience, loyalty, and comradeship to be the ruling principles in the Party; and just as every Leader demands obedience of his men, so I demand of every SA Leader respect for the Law and obedience to my command.

(Signed) Adolf Hitler."

RÖHM'S PRIVATE LIFE

Hitler justified the death of Röhm by saying that he must clear out of the Party a cesspool full of the most abominable corruption. On the other hand, if Hitler was the all-powerful Leader and if he had been sufficiently strong, he should have been able to put a stop to the excesses of Röhm and his friends without resorting to extremes. However, he had evidently reposed too much confidence in men like Röhm and Heines, and when the scandal grew to too great proportions, he was obliged to put them out of the way rather than run the risk of their talking — they knew too much.

The central authorities of the National Socialist Party had for a long time known of Röhm's propensities, but Hitler, upon being approached by some of the soberer members of the Party on the subject, refused to take any action. In March 1932, a journal called *Die Welt am Montag* (The World on Mondays) published the story of Röhm's private life, which had been compiled largely from material gathered in 1923 by Dr. Helmuth Klotz, a former National Socialist who had taken part in the Hitler *Putsch* of 1923. Röhm at first proposed to take legal proceedings, but afterwards changed his mind. Hitler made the defence of Röhm a personal matter, and insisted upon his remaining a member of the Party. If it had been only Röhm, the situation would not have been so serious, but he surrounded himself with men of like tendencies — Heines, Reiner, Ernst, Count Helldorf, Count Spreti, Count du Moulin-Eckhardt, jr. And at the same time he passed a rule in 1931 forbidding the admission to the SA of anyone who was sexually abnormal.

So long as Röhm was blindly obedient to Hitler, no notice was taken of his mode of life. Nevertheless, Hitler knew that Röhm and his friends were causing untold misery among the boys and youths in their companies by forcing them to their will.

Heines had an equally bad reputation. He had been expelled from the Party in 1927, but reinstated three years later, when he became National Socialist deputy to the Reichstag and SA Leader in Breslau. This was simply due to the fact that Heines knew too much and Hitler was afraid of what he might say if it were not made more profitable for him to keep his mouth shut. He might, for instance, have told that the future Minister Hess, and the future Minister of Justice, Dr. Frank, were open to the same suspicion.

Nevertheless, Heines was obliged to leave Bavaria, where he had grown too notorious. With the help of his friend Röhm, he rose to be Chief of the Police in Breslau. And Hitler said: " Nothing happens in the Party except by my express will." In the spring of 1933 there was so much scandal about Heines and the youths in the upper forms of the schools at Breslau that an attempt was made to transfer him to Stettin under pretext of promotion. But Heines simply refused to go. The twenty-two-year-old SA Leader Schmidt continued to play pandar to Heines. The stories of this young man's sexual and other excesses roused as much indignation in Breslau as did those of Heines. On one occasion when he was drunk he shot at and killed a waiter in a restaurant, and merely observed: " You'd better put the waiter on the bill."

THE EXECUTIONS AT LICHTERFELDE

Meanwhile Göring and Himmler had been at work in other parts of the Reich.

The Reichswehr and SS had been on the alert ever since June 25; a fact that naturally came to the knowledge of those personally concerned. Karl Ernst, the Leader of the Berlin SA and a friend of Röhm's, telephoned to General von Blomberg and Göring and enquired whether anything was the matter. The answer was: " No."

General von Schleicher's experience was the same. He tried a second time on June 29 to get Blomberg on the telephone, but failed. A few hours later he was dead. Ernst insisted to the last that he was innocent, and is said to have died with the words: " *Heil Hitler!* " on his lips.

Of the executions at Munich little is known. Major Buch was in charge in his capacity as President of the Supreme Court of the Party. He is said to have ordered the SS men to fire blindly into a room full of the accused men. Hitler is reported to have wept at the sight of the bodies, but then to have comforted himself by saying: " They were traitors." Whereupon he shook hands individually with each of the SS men who had taken part in the massacre.

In Berlin the executions took place in the former cadet school at Lichterfelde. The firing parties consisted of eight men, four of whom had rifles loaded with blanks so that none should know who had fired the fatal shots. The command to fire was: " The Leader wishes it. *Heil Hitler!* Fire! "

GÖRING AND A PRINCE

Prince August Wilhelm narrowly missed being among the victims of June 30. He was sent for by Göring in order to explain his movements. Here he watched long lines of accused men being led before the Minister, who, after interrogating them, sent them out by one of two doors — one meant life, the other death. Göring then turned his attention to the Prince and said:

" You have got the silliest face I have ever seen."

The Prince said nothing. Thereupon Göring confronted him with the Cabinet List referred to above, upon which the name of the Prince stood as President, and asked: " You were a friend of Ernst's? " — " Yes." — " When did you last speak to him? " — " At such and such a time." — " How and where? " — " On the telephone." — " What did you talk about? " — The Prince told him; it was nothing of any importance; Ernst had only wanted to say good-bye before starting off for a holiday. To which Göring replied: " It's lucky for you that you spoke the truth . . ." and put a record onto a gramophone. The Prince heard his own conversation with Ernst over the telephone, which the secret police had taken down from a tapped wire.

Göring continued: " You are of course intending to spend some time in Switzerland now? " The Prince answered that as a matter of fact he had not thought of doing so. Göring interrupted him:

" But I've already told you that you have the silliest face I have ever seen. So — of course you are intending to spend some time in Switzerland now? "

The Prince took the hint, and caught the night train to Switzerland.

CONTRADICTIONS

It was said by Hitler that the SA had planned a revolution for June 30. Nevertheless, the various statements are so contradictory that they are worth considering in detail.

1. If a revolution was due on June 30, why were all the SA Leaders summoned to meet Röhm at a small out-of-the-way spot on that date? The revolution could not be carried out in Berlin, Munich, etc., without leaders. It has been suggested — and this is the most plausible argument on Hitler's side — that they were summoned by telegrams forged by the Government's men (Heydrich, Lutze) with the joint objects of collecting them all in one place and preventing the outbreak of the alleged rebellion.

2. According to official accounts, the watchword of the revolution in Munich was: "The Leader is against us. Fight." And, according to Hitler's speech in the Reichstag, in Berlin it was: "We must save the Leader! We are fighting for Hitler!" It seems odd that a revolution should be started with two opposing aims.

3. Röhm is said to have summoned his Leaders to Wiessee in order to begin the revolution. Ernst, on the contrary — according to Hitler — remained in Berlin for the same purpose.

4. Ernst was said to have been arrested just as he was boarding a ship in Bremen to take a trip to Madeira with his young wife. If he had really been trying to escape, he would hardly have chosen to do so on a German liner, which is still German territory.

It is not improbable that the SA was planning some political action. But since the statements of the other side are so contradictory, it is fair to question whether the alleged violence against Hitler was really intended.

It seems probable that the SA would have laid their desires before Hitler, and that they would very likely have brought pressure to bear on him to get the form of government changed. This happens frequently in well-ordered States; and nobody need lose his life over it. The events of June 30 have shown once again what safeguards are provided by the much-abused institution of parliament. If the matter had been discussed publicly, all those men might still be alive and Hitler would not have been branded as the murderer of his comrades.

THE ALLEGED COMPLICITY OF SCHLEICHER

The " revolution " grows even more improbable when it gets beyond the SA.

There is the alleged plot between Röhm and Schleicher to make Röhm Reichswehr Minister and Schleicher Vice-Chancellor. Röhm's ambition had been known and counteracted by the Reichswehr authorities some weeks earlier by his expulsion from the Officers' Corps.

As regards Schleicher, it is well known that the General felt nothing but contempt for Hitler's Government, and that he expressed himself in this sense with considerable freedom among his friends. But no evidence is forthcoming as to the precise details of the supposed plot. He had been " in communication " with Röhm, said Hitler; Gregor Strasser was " involved "; a " correspondence with a foreign country " had been mentioned by one of the Group Leaders, von Detten, " presumably explained on false pretexts," as Hitler expressed it; etc., etc.

The intermediary between Röhm and Schleicher was said to be a certain Herr von Alvensleben (not to be confused with the President of the *Herrenklub*). Hitler calls him a confidence trickster. Nevertheless, he himself used Alvensleben as a political emissary in 1932. And in the night of January 29/30, 1933, this man, by bringing news of Schleicher's intended *coup d'état,* set the negotiations between Hitler, Hugenberg, and Papen in motion again. Hence he is in some sort the father of the Hitler Government.

Thus Röhm, Schleicher, Strasser, General von Bredow, von Detten, and Alvensleben are alleged to have been a particularly dangerous gang of conspirators. But exactly in what way they conspired has never been stated, nor whether they really knew anything of each other's actual plans. Only in one matter has there been a definite accusation — a " foreign power " was named as being involved in the conspiracy. Obviously France was meant. It was said that several of the " conspirators " had been in conference with a " foreign statesman " — presumably the French Ambassador — behind locked doors, and that they had sworn all the servants to secrecy. Hitler said: " If three traitors arrange a meeting with a foreign statesman, taking the greatest precautions to keep the matter secret from me, then I shall have those three men shot, even if it turns out that they were only discussing the weather and old coins."

On this principle, Hitler, Göring, Rosenberg, and Prince Philip of Hesse should all have been shot by Brüning, for they were equally traitors in this sense. They also met foreign statesmen, representatives of England, Italy, and Hungary, and said nothing about it.

THE TRUE REASON

Hitler's speech in the Reichstag contains one remarkable admission — that the death of Schleicher was intentional. At the time, it was said that he and his wife were killed " in self-defence," because Schleicher fired at the men who entered his house. The foreign Pressmen were given to understand that " the deaths of Röhm and Schleicher were certainly connected in time " — but not causally, therefore. One or other story must be a lie. Once again the enquirer is driven to wonder whether there was not a real connexion — a political one. Simply that Röhm and Schleicher were shot because they knew too much.

Various arguments speak in favour of this theory. Schleicher and Röhm had been working together in 1932, long before Hitler's seizure of power. Röhm was occupied with his favourite scheme for training the SA as a " secret Reichswehr." Hitler refused to co-operate unless he were made Chancellor. Neither Hindenburg nor Schleicher wanted this. Nevertheless, Röhm and Schleicher worked together to find some way out of the *impasse* for Hitler that would enable him to pursue his self-appointed career as a national leader. The result of their efforts was the fall of Brüning.

In the course of these negotiations Röhm did something for which Hitler never forgave him — he gave Schleicher documentary information about Hitler. At all events, Schleicher told various people that he held Hitler in the hollow of his hand. Nevertheless, he did not use his power, nobody quite knows why, though he should have known that it was imperative to do so for his own sake. He also possessed information about Hugenberg and Hindenburg. Schleicher thus had the power to explode a mine at almost any moment. If this be remembered, it explains much of what occurred.

GÖRING'S PERSECUTION OF PAPEN

The suspicion that the deaths of Röhm and Schleicher were due to their knowing too much gains in probability when the third group of murders is considered. The crime in this case was called " well-poisoning," and the victims were all friends of Papen's — Dr. Erich Klausener, Gustav von Kahr, Dr. Edgar Jung, Dr. Walther Schotte, Franz Beck, Dr. Morsbach, and von Bose, Papen's assistant. Göring in his statement to the Berlin Press said that he had " extended " the task entrusted to him by Hitler to strike a blow at reaction.

Since then Göring has persecuted Papen in every possible way. He has ousted him from his posts, has had his house searched on more than one occasion, and by watching his secretary found that certain of Papen's private papers were concealed in the house of one of the secretary's friends. These papers included a diary containing among other things, it is said, all that Papen knows or thinks about the burning of the Reichstag.

On June 30, Göring appears to have made an attempt to clear Papen out of the way for good and all. He had him arrested, though Papen was permitted to remain in his own home. It is said that SS men knocked out one of his teeth in a scuffle. Hindenburg interceded for him and prevented his death. But he has not taken part in any of the Cabinet meetings since then. After the murder of Dollfuss he was sent to Vienna in the rôle of " Peace-maker."

THE DEATH OF EDGAR JUNG

Jung was the author of Papen's speech at Marburg — by far the most important speech that has been made in Germany since March 5. His family came from the Palatinate. He was himself a lawyer in Munich and had written some politico-philosophical books, which reveal him as sharing more or less in Alfred Rosenberg's political opinions. Nevertheless, Jung had greater depth of mind and knowledge. He was one of the men who took part in the shooting of Heinz-Orbis, the Separatist, in December 1923. Heinz-Orbis had at one time boasted that he was in communication with Hitler. Hitler denied this. But possibly Jung knew something about it. — He was arrested several days before he was shot. So he could not possibly be supposed to be connected with the SA plot.

KLAUSENER'S DEATH

The murder of Dr. Erich Klausener, as well as the still unexplained murder of Alfred Probst, the leader of the "German Youth Force," was in the highest degree significant politically. Both murders were a challenge to the Catholic Church, since both men were ardent Catholics. And — if only for the sake of the Saar — Hitler should be coming to terms with the Catholic Church.

Klausener had for many years been head of the Catholic Action — a society founded by Pope Pius XI — and under the Socialist Minister Severing had been head of the police department in the Prussian Ministry of the Interior. Under Papen he became Secretary of State. Göring turned him out of the Ministry, but he remained an official in the Reich Ministry of Transport. Thus he could not be called an opponent of the Third Reich. But his crime appears to have been that he was too observant a man.

In the course of the Reichstag trial Göring was sarcastic at the expense of the Information Department of the Prussian Ministry of the Interior. Either he was bluffing or else he really did not know that Klausener had had charge of all the documents referring to the National Socialist Party. The present writer has seen a part of them. The stories concerning Göring, his illness, his morphinism, as also his business transactions with aeroplane factories, were well known. Even at that date Klausener's knowledge might have come to the ears of the President, and could have been supported with documentary proof.

In other words, Klausener, like Röhm and Schleicher, was in possession of information that was uncomfortable for Göring and Hitler. And they knew that he had it. If Papen had made up his mind to act — and the Marburg speech must be regarded as an indication of some such decision — then Klausener would be one of his most useful suppliers of munitions.

The shooting of Klausener was carried out as a real murder. Some unknown men entered his office at the Ministry of Transport and shot him through the head from behind. His clerks came in later and found him lying dead on the floor, face downwards. His body was burnt and the ashes subsequently sent to his family. The fact of the cremation, which is contrary to Catholic practice, roused great indignation in the Church.

At the Ministry of the Interior in Berlin paper bags containing the ashes of shot men stood about on the desks for days until the addresses of the dead men's relatives could be ascertained. It is said that the widow of one of them received her husband's ashes by post at breakfast one morning. It is at all events a fact that the relations were informed of the executions in the most brutal manner possible.

THE DEATH OF GREGOR STRASSER

The death of Gregor Strasser must also be set down to Göring's particular account. Both Göring and Goebbels were old friends of Strasser's. Some weeks before June 30, a meeting had taken place between Strasser and Hitler, and Hitler was said to have offered him a ministerial post, which, however, was refused unless Göring and Goebbels should previously resign.

On June 30 Strasser was fetched from his home on the pretext that his presence was desired whilst his office was searched. When he got outside, he was put in a car, bound, and taken to the Grunewald. Some hours later the men returned to the house, and one of them told Frau Strasser in answer to a question that " nobody could say where her husband was now, and nobody would recognize him." Evidently he had been horribly disfigured. When the unhappy woman tried to see Daluege at the Ministry of Police, she was told to " Shut up, or she'd go the same way." A week later she received an urn containing the ashes of her husband.

Hitler is the godfather of Strasser's twin sons. After his father's death, one of the boys was asked by a neighbour, a Frenchwoman, what he, a member of the Hitler Youth, thought of Hitler now. The boy replied with a set face: " He is our Leader in spite of everything."

WILLI SCHMIDT

One more victim must be particularly mentioned. This was the musical critic of the *Münchener Neueste Nachrichten,* who died only because his name was Willi Schmidt. He had been confused with Group Leader Wilhelm Schmid. And since the Leader had ordered swift death, Willi Schmidt lost his life. The *Münchener Neueste Nachrichten* made some reference to an "accident" having befallen this member of its staff. And no doubt some one of the perpetrators apologized to the murdered man's widow.

HOW MANY WERE KILLED?

Up to the present the number of deaths is not known. The *Manchester Guardian* claims to know of 282. Hitler declared that seventy-seven guilty persons had been slain, and that in addition a certain number of acts of violence had been committed that would be duly and suitably punished. Up to the present nothing more has been heard either of the number of acts of violence or of their punishment. At all events uncertainty exists as to the fate of a number of people who up to a short time ago were well-known figures. Neither the number nor the names of the dead have been published, nor in his famous apologia in the Reichstag did Hitler bring real proof or justification for a single one of the executions. In other words, he stated the existence of a plot, but brought no evidence of any kind to support his assertions.

The fact that innocent persons were killed was admitted by Hitler in this speech on July 13: "Divisions who mutiny," he said, "have from time immemorial been reduced to order by decimation." His deputy, Hess, explained the meaning of decimation in a speech which he made at Königsberg on July 8. It means that "every tenth man is shot without question of his guilt or innocence." He said in the same speech that "one man was guilty rather than another only because of the tragic concatenation of circumstances" — in other words, that many were innocent. Group Leader von Detten was one such unfortunate. Hess himself appeared at his grave and expressed his own sympathy and that of Hitler to the widow.

Since the events of June 30 could be justified by no known law, human or divine, it was necessary to legalize them artificially, and the Cabinet absolved its Chancellor by saying that the measures taken against traitors had been dictated by necessities of State. Hitler himself spoke the words in the Reichstag that have since become famous:

"If anyone should ask why we did not have these men tried in the usual manner by the Courts of Justice, I can only say that in that hour I was responsible for the fate of the German nation, and thus *I myself embodied the supreme legal authority*."

To sum up, what were the cause and effect of the acts of June 30, 1934?

A momentary glimpse is given of the underlying reason in Hitler's words: ". . . from time immemorial. . . ." It was his need to furnish a historic example. A dictator must inspire fear. Cruelty is an essential part of dictatorship. The throne of dictators has always stood upon a fundament of skulls.

That is the metaphysical explanation of the events of June 30. The motives suggested by the actual situation are of purely secondary importance. They explain the fact of something's happening on that particular day. But only the nature of dictatorship explains the abominable form that the event took.

The natural psychic state of all dictators — fear — caused the murders. Fear of attacks on his own life; fear of the revelation of uncomfortable secrets by old confidants. Röhm knew all Hitler's past; Herr von Kahr knew the connexions that once existed between Hitler's Party and France; Herr von Papen, who only narrowly escaped death, knows the secret of the burning of the Reichstag, as did his murdered colleagues, Jung, von Bose, Schotte, and possibly Klausener.

It is a mistake to suppose that the SA was destroyed on June 30. On the contrary, it has become a much more useful and better weapon in the hands of the dictator. It has grown smaller, but the unreliable portions have been cut away, and it has therefore gained in reliability what it has lost in weight. It remains a powerful political factor. It is no longer the propulsive force of the movement. The Nazi Party no longer needs such a force. It has become instead a Prætorian guard, of which it stands in need.

It is, further, an error to say that Hitler is the "prisoner" of the Reichswehr. The Reichswehr does not interfere in politics, but it is none the less a political factor. And its tendency is all in Hitler's favour — no more experiments, no more construction, no more revolution. A dictatorship requires stability. Permanent revolution would swallow up even the strongest dictator. Hence the Conservative course was not forced upon Hitler. It is bound in the nature of things to be his course.

It was therefore not surprising but only logical that after Hindenburg's death he should have become his successor by an act of usurpation and with the full support of the Reichswehr. It was logical that he should unite the two offices of President and Chancellor in his own person. It was a logical elevation of his own position and its consolidation for life that has led him to call himself not President but Leader and Chancellor of the Reich.

Only one shadow dims the new glory. In order to prove to other countries and also to the Reichswehr that he still drew a great part of his power from demagogy, Hitler held a plebiscite immediately after his usurpation. Naturally he still had the majority with him, if only because there was no opposition candidate. Naturally he again manœuvred the machinery of the voting in his own favour, as has been proved in numerous cases. None the less, he met with something of a disappointment. In the Rhineland there were places that dared to vote up to 48 per cent. against him, and where, in view of the temper of the people, the results could not be tampered with. On the other hand, eastern Germany remained overwhelmingly in his favour. The total results were: 38,360,000 for Hitler, 4,290,000 against him, and 872,000 votes void — that is to say, also against him. One million nine hundred and fifty thousand persons did not vote at all. In view of the fact that much pressure was brought to bear to make the electors record their votes, this amounted in itself to an anti-Hitler demonstration. The number of opponents officially admitted had doubled since November 12, 1933.

If Hitler were to give the German nation a fortnight's freedom of the Press and then a really free election with opposition candidates, he and all the world would soon see where the real sympathies of the German people lie.

BIBLIOGRAPHY

Völkischer Beobachter. München, 1919–1930.
Grossdeutsche Zeitung. München, 1924.
Völkischer Kurier. München, 1924.
Deutsche Presse. München, 1924.
Münchner Post. München, 1919–1923.
Berliner Arbeiterzeitung. Berlin, 1926–1930.
Der Angriff. Berlin, 1927–1930.
Nationalsozialistisches Jahrbuch. München, 1927–1931.

BILLUNG, R.: *N S D A P Die Geschichte einer Bewegung*. München, 1931.
CZECH-JOCHBERG, ERICH: *Hitler, eine deutsche Bewegung*. Oldenburg, 1930.
DINTER, ARTUR: *Ursprung Ziel und Weg der deutsch-volkischen Freiheitsbewegung*. Weimar, 1924.
DREXLER, ANTON: *Mein politisches Erwachen*. München, 1923.
ECKART, DIETRICH: *Der Bolschewismus von Moses bis Lenin. Zwiegespräch zwischen Adolf Hitler und mir*. München, 1924.
FEDER, GOTTFRIED: *Das Programm der N S D A P und seine weltanschaulichen Grundlagen*. München, 1932.
GEISMAIER, MICHAEL: *Gregor Strasser*. Leipzig, 1932.
GOEBBELS, JOSEPH: *Wege ins Dritte Reich*. München, 1927.
HITLER, ADOLF: *Mein Kampf*. München, 1932. [English translation, *My Struggle*. 1933.]
HITLER and KAHR (*Aus dem Untersuchungsausschuss des bayrischen Landtags*) *: Hsrg. vom Landesausschuss der S P D in Bayern*. München, 1928.
Hitler-Prozess, Der (*Verhandlungsbericht der Münchener Neuesten Nachrichten*. 2 Bände). München, 1924.
JUNG, RUDOLF: *Der nationale Sozialismus*. Troppau und München, 1922.
JUNIUS ALTER: *Nationalisten*. Leipzig, 1930.
KLOTZ, HELMUT: *Ehren-Rangliste der N S D A P*. Berlin-Tempelhof, 1932.

MILTENBERG, WEIGAND VON: *Adolf Hitler, Wilhelm III.* Berlin, 1930.

LEERS, JOHANN VON: *Hitler.* Leipzig, 1932.

RÖHM, ERNST: *Die Geschichte eines Hochverräters.* München, 1928.

ROSENBERG, ALFRED: *Wesen, Grundsätze und Ziele der N S D A P.* München, 1923 and 1932.

ROSENBERG, ALFRED: *H. St. Chamberlain als Verkünder und Begründer einer deutschen Zukunft.* München, 1927.

SCHAPKE, RICHARD: *Die schwarze Front.* Leipzig, 1932.

SCHOTT, GEORG: *Das Volksbuch vom Hitler.* München, 1924.

SCHWEYER, FRANZ: *Politische Geheimverbände.* Freiburg i. B., 1925.

STRASSER, OTTO: *Ministersessel oder Revolution?* Berlin, 1930.

The literature of National Socialism is immense. Only those books have been included in this Bibliography which afford first-hand information about the history of the movement, its ideology, and its leaders.

INDEX